APICS Dictionary

FOURTEENTH EDITION

Editor

John H. Blackstone Jr., PhD, CFPIM, Jonah's Jonah
Department of Management
Terry College of Business
University of Georgia

APICS Dictionary

Fourteenth edition—2013
Thirteenth edition—2010
Twelfth edition—2008
Eleventh edition—2005
Tenth edition—2002
Ninth edition—1998
Eighth edition—1995
Seventh edition—1992
Sixth edition—1987
Fifth edition—1982
Fourth edition—1980
Third edition—1970
Second edition—1966
First edition—1963

Copyright 2013 by APICS

International Standard Book Number: 978-0-9882146-1-3

APICS
8430 West Bryn Mawr Avenue
Suite 1000
Chicago, IL 60631-3439
1-800-444-2742 or +1-773-867-1777
apics.org

Acknowledgements

Thank you to the following volunteers for their careful review of the *APICS Dictionary,* 14th edition.

Louise Beauchamp, CFPIM; Stephen N. Chapman, PhD, CFPIM; Rick Donahoue, CPIM, CSCP; Ann K. Gatewood, CFPIM, CIRM, CSCP; Rebecca B. Hallock, CPIM; Mark C. Hardison, CFPIM, CSCP; William R. Leedale, CFPIM, CIRM, CSCP; Frank L. Montabon, PhD, CPIM, CIRM, CSCP; Murray R. Olsen, CFPIM, CIRM; Anthony L. Patti, PhD, CFPIM; Andrea M. Prud'homme, PhD, CPIM, CIRM, CSCP; and Fran Scher.

The Institute of Industrial Engineers provided permission to include several definitions reprinted from the text *Industrial Engineering Terminology*, revised edition, Copyright 1991, Institute of Industrial Engineers, 3577 Parkway Lane, Suite 200, Norcross, Georgia 30092.

The American Society of Quality provided permission to include several terms from Karen Bemowski's "The Quality Glossary," published in the February 1992 issue of *Quality Progress*.

The Theory of Constraints International Certification Organization provided permission to include several terms from the *TOCICO Dictionary*.

The Spectrum Publishing Company provided permission to use terms from the book, *Synchronous Management*, by Michael Umble, CFPIM, and M.L. Srikanth.

The Association for Manufacturing Excellence provided the definition for kaizen blitz, which is trademarked.

The Supply Chain Council provided the definition for Supply Chain Operations Reference model (SCOR), which is trademarked. For the latest information about SCOR, visit the Supply Chain Council's website, supply-chain.org.

A

abandonment—Giving up a route by a carrier. For example, a railroad.

ABB—Abbreviation for activity-based budgeting.

ABC—Abbreviation for activity-based cost accounting.

ABC analysis—Syn: ABC classification.

ABC classification—The classification of a group of items in decreasing order of annual dollar volume (price multiplied by projected volume) or other criteria. This array is then split into three classes, called A, B, and C. The A group usually represents 10 percent to 20 percent by number of items and 50 percent to 70 percent by projected dollar volume. The next grouping, B, usually represents about 20 percent of the items and about 20 percent of the dollar volume. The C class contains 60 percent to 70 percent of the items and represents about 10 percent to 30 percent of the dollar volume. The ABC principle states that effort and money can be saved through applying looser controls to the low-dollar-volume class items than will be applied to high-dollar-volume class items. The ABC principle is applicable to inventories, purchasing, sales, and so on. Syn: ABC analysis, distribution by value. See: 80-20, Pareto analysis, Pareto's law.

ABC frequency of access—A warehouse location that is determined by both a product's ABC classification and by the frequency with which it is removed or replaced.

ABC inventory control—An inventory control approach based on the ABC classification.

ABM—Abbreviation for activity-based management.

abnormal demand—Demand in any period that is outside the limits established by management policy. This demand may come from a new customer or from existing customers whose own demand is increasing or decreasing. Care must be taken in evaluating the nature of the demand: is it a volume change; is it a change in product mix; or is it related to the timing of the order? See: outlier.

ABP—Abbreviation for activity-based planning.

absentee policy—The policy that discusses allowed job absences and the penalties from too many absences.

absentee rate—A ratio comparing the number of employee-days lost with the total number of available employee-days of employment during some base period, usually one month.

absorption costing—An approach to inventory valuation in which variable costs and a portion of fixed costs are assigned to each unit of production. The fixed costs are usually allocated to units of output on the basis of direct labor hours, machine hours, or material costs. Syn: allocation costing. See: activity-based costing.

accelerated depreciation—A depreciation method involving high write-offs in the early years of an asset's life and lower write-offs later. This method lowers the value of an asset faster than straight-line depreciation.

accept—The receipt of an item as being complete and sound.

acceptable outgoing quality level (AOQL)—A demarcation between the level of defects in a lot at which the lot will be accepted or rejected.

acceptable quality level (AQL)—When a continuing series of lots is considered, a quality level that, for the purposes of sampling inspection, is the limit of a satisfactory process average.

acceptable sampling plan—A specific plan that indicates the sampling sizes and the associated acceptance or nonacceptance criteria to be used.

acceptance criteria—Those performance requirements and conditions that must be reached before projects or products are accepted.

acceptance number—1) A number used in acceptance sampling as a cutoff at which the lot will be accepted or rejected. For example, if x or more units are bad within the sample, the lot will be rejected. 2) The value of the test statistic that divides all possible values into acceptance and rejection regions.

acceptance plan—How an organization determines which product lots to accept or reject based on samples. See: acceptance sampling.

acceptance sampling—1) The process of sampling a portion of goods for inspection rather than examining the entire lot. The entire lot may be accepted or rejected based on the sample even though the specific units in the lot are better or worse than the sample. There are two types: attributes sampling and variables sampling. In attributes sampling, the presence or absence of a characteristic is noted in each of the units inspected. In variables sampling, the numerical magnitude of a characteristic is measured and recorded for each inspected unit; this type of sampling involves reference to a continuous scale of some kind. 2) A method of measuring random samples of lots or batches of products against predetermined standards.

accessibility—1) In transportation, the facility with which a carrier provides service from one point to another. 2) In warehousing, the ability to get to and within the point of storage easily.

accessorial charges—A bill for services, such as inside deliveries, which are made in addition to transportation charges.

accessory—A choice or feature added to the good or service offered to the customer for customizing the end product. An accessory enhances the capabilities of the product but is not necessary for the basic function of the product. In many companies, an accessory means that the choice does not have to be specified before shipment but can be added at a later date. In other companies, this choice must be made before shipment. See: feature.

accidental death and disability (AD&D)—Insurance that often is part of an employee benefit package, providing payment for either accidental death or disability.

accident prevention—The application of basic scientific and technical principles—including education and training—for the detection, analysis, and minimization of hazards, with the objective of avoiding accidents.

acclimatization—The physiological, emotional, and behavioral adjustment to changes in the environment. Proper performance depends on adequate acclimatization to the workplace, including significant mechanical features such as seat height and lighting. Heat, cold, humidity, and light are important physiologically.

accountability—Being answerable for, but not necessarily personally charged with, doing the work. Accountability cannot be delegated, but it can be shared.

accounting—The function of maintaining, analyzing, and explaining the financial records and status of an organization.

account manager—A manager who has direct responsibility for a customer's interest.

accounts payable—The value of goods and services acquired for which payment has not yet been made.

accounts receivable—The value of goods shipped or services rendered to a customer on which payment has not yet been received. Usually includes an allowance for bad debts.

accreditation—Certification by a recognized body of the facilities, capability, objectivity, competence, and integrity of an agency, service, operational group, or individual to provide the specific service or operation needed. For

example, the Registrar Accreditation Board accredits those organizations that register companies to the ISO 9000 Series Standards.

accumulation bin—A place, usually a physical location, used to accumulate all components that go into an assembly before the assembly is sent out to the assembly floor. Syn: assembly bin.

accuracy—The degree of freedom from error or the degree of conformity to a standard. Accuracy is different from precision. For example, four-significant-digit numbers are less precise than six-significant-digit numbers; however, a properly computed four-significant-digit number might be more accurate than an improperly computed six-significant-digit number.

acid test—Syn: quick asset ratio.

acid test ratio—Syn: quick asset ratio.

acknowledgment—A communication by a supplier to advise a purchaser that a purchase order has been received. It usually implies acceptance of the order by the supplier.

acquisition cost—The cost required to obtain one or more units of an item. It is order quantity times unit cost. See: ordering cost.

action message—An output of a system that identifies the need for, and the type of action to be taken to correct, a current or potential problem. Examples of action messages in an MRP system include release order, reschedule in, reschedule out, and cancel. Syn: exception message, action report.

action plan—A process to obtain results identified by one or more objectives.

action report—Syn: action message.

activation—Putting a resource to work.

active data gathering—Data gathered when a company initiates conversation with the customer.

active inventory—The raw materials, work in process, and finished goods that will be used or sold within a given period.

active load—Work scheduled that may not be on hand.

active tag—A radio frequency identification tag that broadcasts information and contains its own power source. See: radio frequency identification (RFID).

activity—1) In activity-based cost accounting, a task or activity, performed by or at a resource, required in producing the organization's output of goods and services. A resource may be a person, machine, or facility.

Activities are grouped into pools by type of activity and allocated to products. 2) In project management, an element of work on a project. It usually has an anticipated duration, anticipated cost, and expected resource requirements. Sometimes "major activity" is used for larger bodies of work.

activity analysis—In project management, the identification and description of activities within an organization for the purpose of activity-based costing.

activity attributes—Multiple features associated with each activity to be performed. These include predecessor activities, successor activities, and resource requirements.

activity-based budgeting (ABB)—In activity-based cost accounting, a budgeting process employing knowledge of activities and driver relationships to predict workload and resource requirements in developing a business plan. Budgets show the predicted consumption and cost of resources using forecast workload as a basis. The company can use performance to budget in evaluating success in setting and pursuing strategic goals; this activity is part of the activity-based planning process.

activity-based cost accounting—A cost accounting system that accumulates costs based on activities performed and then uses cost drivers to allocate these costs to products or other bases, such as customers, markets, or projects. It is an attempt to allocate overhead costs on a more realistic basis than direct labor or machine hours. Syn: activity-based costing, activity-based cost accounting. See: absorption costing.

activity-based costing (ABC)—In activity-based cost accounting, a model, by time period, of resource costs created because of activities related to products or services or other items causing the activity to be carried out. Syn: activity-based cost accounting, activity-based costing model.

activity-based costing system—A set of activity-based cost accounting models that collectively define data on an organization's resources, activities, drivers, objects, and measurements.

activity-based management (ABM)—The use of activity-based costing information about cost pools and drivers, activity analysis, and business processes to identify business strategies; improve product design, manufacturing, and distribution; and remove waste from operations. See: activity-based cost accounting.

activity-based planning (ABP)—In activity-based cost accounting, a continuing definition of activity and resource requirements (for both financial and operational systems) based on future demand for products or services by specific customer needs. Demand for resources is related to resource availability; capacity overages and shortfalls are corrected. Activity-based budgeting derives from the outputs of ABP.

activity code—In project management, a value that allows filtering or ordering of activities in reports.

activity definition—The specific work to be performed that defines a project deliverable.

activity dictionary—In activity-based cost accounting, a set of standard definitions of activities including descriptions, business process, function source, cost drivers, and other data important to activity-based planning.

activity driver—In activity-based cost accounting, a yardstick of demands placed on an activity by given cost objects. Its purpose is to assign activity costs to cost objects.

activity duration—The planned difference between the start and finish dates of a project activity.

activity identifier—A unique alphanumeric code that differentiates one project activity from other activities.

activity level—A description of how reactive one activity is to changes in the level of another activity or cost object.

activity list—A record of planned activities in a project, including an activity description and an activity identifier.

activity network diagram—One of the seven new tools of quality. A drawing including nodes that represent operations to be performed and arrows representing precedence relationships. This drawing represents all of the activities to be finished to complete a project. Also known as a critical path diagram or PERT chart.

activity-on-arc network—Syn: activity-on-arrow network.

activity-on-arrow network (AOA)—A project management network in which the passage of time, via activities, takes place on the arrows. The start of an activity is represented by the tail of the arrow, while the completion of the activity is represented by the tip of the arrow. The sequence of the arrows represents the sequence of activities. Arrows are connected by nodes, which are usually circles. Syn: activity-on-arc network, arrow diagram method, event-on-arrow network.

activity-on-node network (AON)—A project management network in which the passage of time, via activities, takes place on circles called nodes. Each node contains a number representing the estimated duration of the activity it represents. Nodes are connected by arrows that give precedence relationships. Syn: event-on-node network, precedence diagram method.

activity ratio—A financial ratio to determine how an organization's resources perform relative to the revenue the resources produce. Activity ratios include inventory turnover, receivables conversion period, fixed-asset turnover, and return on assets.

activity resource estimating—Estimating the types and amounts of resources that will be needed for various project activities.

activity sequencing—The process of defining and documenting dependencies among project activities.

actual cost of work performed—The direct costs actually incurred in, and the indirect costs applied to, accomplishing work performed within a given time period. These costs should reconcile with the contractor's incurred-cost ledgers, which are regularly audited by the client.

actual costs—The labor, material, and associated overhead costs that are charged against a job as it moves through the production process.

actual cost system—A cost system that collects costs historically as they are applied to production and allocates indirect costs to products based on the specific costs and achieved volume of the products.

actual demand—Actual demand is composed of customer orders (and often allocations of items, ingredients, or raw materials to production or distribution). Actual demand nets against or "consumes" the forecast, depending upon the rules chosen over a time horizon. For example, actual demand will totally replace forecast inside the sold-out customer order backlog horizon (often called the demand time fence) but will net against the forecast outside this horizon based on the chosen forecast consumption rule.

actual duration—The difference between the actual start date of a project activity and the current date (if the activity is still in progress) or the difference between the actual start date of a project activity and the actual completion date (if the activity is completed).

actual finish date—In project management, the date on which an activity in a project was actually completed.

actual start date—In project management, the date on which an activity in a project was actually started.

actual volume—Actual output expressed as a volume of capacity. It is used in the calculation of variances when compared with demonstrated capacity (practical capacity) or budgeted capacity.

AD&D—Abbreviation for accidental death and disability.

adaptable website—In e-commerce, a site that a visitor can change to customize.

adaptive control—1) The ability of a control system to change its own parameters in response to a measured change in operating conditions. 2) Machine control units in which feeds and/or speeds are not fixed. The control unit, working from feedback sensors, is able to optimize favorable situations by automatically increasing or decreasing the machining parameters. This process ensures optimum tool life or surface finish and/or machining costs or production rates.

adaptive smoothing—A form of exponential smoothing in which the smoothing constant is automatically adjusted as a function of forecast error measurement.

adaptive website—In e-commerce, a site that records a visitor's behavior, uses artificial intelligence software to "learn" this behavior, and chooses what to present to the visitor based on this learning.

additive manufacturing—Syn: 3D printing.

additives—A special class of ingredients characterized either by being used in minimal quantities or by being introduced into the processing cycle after the initial stage.

adjudicate—To hear and decide an issue under legal dispute.

adjustable capacity—Capacity, such as labor or tools, that can be changed in the short term.

administrative contracting officer—A government employee who ensures compliance with the terms and conditions of contracts.

advanced planning and scheduling (APS)—Techniques that deal with analysis and planning of logistics and manufacturing during short, intermediate, and long-term time periods. APS describes any computer program that uses advanced mathematical algorithms or logic to perform optimization or simulation on finite capacity scheduling, sourcing, capital planning, resource planning, forecasting, demand management, and others. These techniques simultaneously consider a range of constraints and business rules to provide real-time planning and scheduling, decision support, available-to-promise, and capable-to-promise capabilities. APS often generates and evaluates multiple scenarios. Management then selects one scenario to use as the "official plan." The five main components of APS systems are (1) demand planning, (2) production planning, (3) production scheduling, (4) distribution planning, and (5) transportation planning.

advanced planning system (APS)—Syn: advanced planning and scheduling.

advanced production system (APS)—Syn: advanced planning and scheduling.

advance material request—Ordering materials before the release of the formal product design. This early release is required because of long lead times.

advance ship notice (ASN)—An electronic data interchange (EDI) notification of shipment of product.

advertising—Sponsored promotions that are nonpersonal in nature.

aesthetics—A dimension of product quality that intends to appeal to the senses.

affidavit—A sworn written statement.

affinity diagram—A total quality management tool whereby employees working in silence generate ideas and later categorize these ideas.

affirmative action—A hiring policy that requires employers to analyze the workforce for underrepresentation of protected classes. It involves recruiting minorities and members of protected classes, changing management attitudes or prejudices toward them, removing discriminatory employment practices, and giving preferential treatment to protected classes.

aftermarket—A secondary market for parts and accessories used to repair or enhance an item.

after-sale service—Syn: field service.

agency tariff—Rates for a variety of carriers published in a single document.

agent—One who acts on behalf of another (the principal) in dealing with a third party. Examples include a sales agent and a purchasing agent.

agglomeration—Having a common location with a variety of other companies.

aggregate demand—Demand that is grouped (e.g., all sedans) for making forecasts or plans. See: aggregate forecast.

aggregate forecast—An estimate of sales, often time-phased, for a grouping of products or product families produced by a facility or firm. Stated in terms of units, dollars, or both, the aggregate forecast is used for sales and production planning (or for sales and operations planning) purposes. See: product group forecast.

aggregate inventory—The inventory for any grouping of items or products involving multiple stockkeeping units. See: base inventory level.

aggregate inventory management—Establishing the overall level (dollar value) of inventory desired and implementing controls to achieve this goal.

aggregate lead time—Syn: cumulative lead time.

aggregate plan—A plan that includes budgeted levels of finished goods, inventory, production backlogs, and changes in the workforce to support the production strategy. Aggregated information (e.g., product line, family) rather than product information is used, hence the name aggregate plan.

aggregate planning—A process to develop tactical plans to support the organization's business plan. Aggregate planning usually includes the development, analysis, and maintenance of plans for total sales, total production, targeted inventory, and targeted customer backlog for families of products. The production plan is the result of the aggregate planning process. Two approaches to aggregate planning exist: (1) production planning and (2) sales and operations planning. See: production planning, sales and operations planning, sales plan.

aggregate production plan (APP)—A long-range plan that is used to determine timing and quantity of total future production for a family of products. Syn: long-term production plan.

aggregate reporting—1) Reporting of process hours in general, allowing the system to assign the actual hours to specific products run during the period based on standards. 2) Also known as gang reporting, the reporting of total labor hours.

aggregate unit of capacity—Combined capacity unit of measure when a variety of outputs exist.

aggregation—The concept that pooling random variables reduces the relative variance of the resulting aggregated variable. For example, the relative variance in sales of all models of automobiles sold by a firm is less than that for a single model.

agile manufacturing—The ability to respond quickly to unpredictable changes in customer needs by reconfiguring operations.

agility—The ability to successfully manufacture and market a broad range of low-cost, high-quality products and services with short lead times and varying volumes that provide enhanced value to customers through customization. Agility merges the four distinctive competencies of cost, quality, dependability, and flexibility.

AGVS—Abbreviation for automated guided vehicle system.

AI—Abbreviation for artificial intelligence.

AIDC—Abbreviation for automatic identification and data capture.

AIS—Abbreviation for automated information system.

algorithm—A prescribed set of well-defined rules or processes for solving a problem in a finite number of steps (e.g., the full statement of the arithmetic procedure for calculating the reorder point).

alliance development—Strengthening the capabilities of a key supplier.

allocated item—In an MRP system, an item for which a picking order has been released to the stockroom but not yet sent from the stockroom.

allocated material—Syn: reserved material.

allocation—1) The classification of quantities of items that have been assigned to specific orders but have not yet been released from the stockroom to production. It is an "uncashed" stockroom requisition. 2) A process used to distribute material in short supply. Syn: assignment. See: reservation.

allocation costing—Syn: absorption costing.

allocative efficiency—The use of resources to produce those goods and services most wanted by consumers.

allowable cost—A reasonable cost specifically permitted under Federal Acquisition Regulation (FAR) requirements.

allowance—1) In work measurement, a time value or percentage of time by which the normal time is increased, or the amount of nonproductive time applied, to compensate for justifiable causes or policy requirements that necessitate performance time not directly measured for each element or task. Usually includes irregular elements, incentive opportunity on machine-controlled time, minor unavoidable delays, rest time to overcome fatigue, and time for personal needs. 2) In assembly, the minimum clearance or maximum interference distance between two adjacent objects.

allowed time—A normal time value increased by appropriate allowances.

alpha factor—Syn: smoothing constant.

alpha release—An extremely early version of a product released to obtain feedback about its suitability.

alternate feedstock—A backup supply of an item that either acts as a substitute or is used with alternate equipment.

alternate operation—Replacement for a normal step in the manufacturing process. Ant: primary operation.

alternate part—When a buyer can purchase similar products from different suppliers. This increases the buyer's power as the buyer does not have to rely on just one supplier.

alternate routing—A routing that is usually less preferred than the primary routing but results in an identical item. Alternate routings may be maintained in the computer or off-line via manual methods, but the computer software must be able to accept alternate routings for specific jobs.

alternate work center—The work center where an operation is not normally performed but can be performed. Ant: primary work center.

American customer satisfaction index—A metric cosponsored by the University of Michigan and the American Society for Quality that measures the satisfaction of U.S. customers with the goods and services available to them from both domestic and foreign origins.

American National Standards Institute (ANSI)—The parent organization of the interindustry electronic interchange of the business transaction standard. This group is the clearinghouse on U.S. electronic data interchange standards.

American Society for Quality (ASQ)—Founded in 1946, a not-for-profit educational organization with more than 100,000 individual and organizational members who are interested in quality improvement.

American Standard Code for Information Interchange (ASCII)—Standard seven-bit character code used by computer manufacturers to represent 128 characters for information interchange among data processing systems, communications systems, and other information system equipment. An eighth bit is added as a parity bit to check a string of ASCII characters for correct transmission.

amortization—The process of recovering (via expensing) a capital investment over a period of time. See: capital recovery.

analog—As applied to an electrical or computer system, the capability of representing data in continuously varying physical phenomena (as in a voltmeter) and converting them into numbers.

analysis of variance (ANOVA)—A statistical analysis system that estimates what portion of variation in a dependent variable is caused by variation in one or more independent variables. It also produces a number used to infer whether any or all of the independent-dependent variable relationships have statistical significance (i.e., have not been caused by randomness in the data).

analytic workplace design—A design based on established biomechanical and behavioral concepts, including the known operating characteristics of people. Produces a workplace situation well within the range of human capacity and does not generally require modification, improvement, or preliminary experimental "mock-up."

analyze phase—One of the six sigma phases of quality. It consists of the following steps: (a) define performance objective, (b) identify independent variables, and (c) analyze sources of variability. See: design-measure-analyze-improve-control process.

andon—A sign board with signal lights used to make workers and management aware of a quality, quality, or process problem.

annual inventory count—Syn: physical inventory.

annualized contract—A negotiated agreement with a supplier for one year that sets pricing, helps ensure a continuous supply of material, and provides the supplier with estimated future requirements.

annual percentage rate—In finance, the rate of interest paid for a loan after compounding is considered. Syn: effective interest rate.

annual physical inventory—Syn: physical inventory.

annuity—A stream of fixed payments for a stipulated time, yearly or at other intervals.

ANOVA—Acronym for analysis of variance.

ANSI—Acronym for American National Standards Institute.

anticipated delay report—A report, normally issued by both manufacturing and purchasing to the material planning function, regarding jobs or purchase orders that will not be completed on time. This report explains why the jobs or purchases are delayed and when they will be completed. This report is an essential ingredient of the closed-loop MRP system. It is normally a handwritten report. Syn: delay report.

anticipation inventories—Additional inventory above basic pipeline stock to cover projected trends of increasing sales, planned sales promotion programs, seasonal fluctuations, plant shutdowns, and vacations.

anticipation order—An order placed before an item has been made available for delivery.

anti-dumping duty—An imposed responsibility in which a company sells imported goods at prices below what is charged in their domestic market.

any-quantity rate—A situation in which no quantity discount is available for large shipments.

AOA—Abbreviation for activity-on-arrow network.

AON—Abbreviation for activity-on-node network.

AOQ—Abbreviation for average outgoing quality.

AOQL—1) Abbreviation for average outgoing quality limit. 2) Abbreviation for acceptable outgoing quality level.

APICS—Founded in 1957 as the American Production and Inventory Control Society, APICS The Association for Operations Management builds operations management excellence in individuals and enterprises through superior education and training, internationally recognized certifications, comprehensive resources, and a worldwide network of accomplished industry professionals.

APP—Abbreviation for aggregate production plan.

apparent authority—Authority perceived by a third party to flow from a principal to an ostensible agent when in fact no agency relationship exists.

appellant—One who appeals a court decision to higher authority.

application package—A computer program or set of programs designed for a specific application (e.g., inventory control, MRP).

application service provider (ASP)—A firm that produces outsourced services for clients.

applications software—A computer program or set of programs designed to assist in the performance of a specific task, such as word processing, accounting, or inventory management. See: application system.

application system—A set of programs of specific instructions for processing activities needed to compute specific tasks for computer users, as opposed to operating systems that control the computer's internal operations. Examples are payroll, spreadsheets, and word processing programs. See: application software.

application-to-application—The exchange of data between computers without reentry of data.

appraisal—1) An evaluation of employee performance. 2) In total quality management, the formal evaluation and audit of quality.

appraisal costs—Those costs associated with the formal evaluation and audit of quality in the firm. Typical costs include inspection, quality audits, testing, calibration, and checking time.

appreciation of a currency—An increase in the buying power of a country's currency in terms of other countries' goods and services.

approved vendor list (AVL)—A list of parties that have been approved by a company as its suppliers. This list usually is based on product quality and financial stability of the firm.

APR—Abbreviation for annual percentage rate.

APS—1) Abbreviation for advanced planning and scheduling. 2) Abbreviation for advanced planning system.

AQL—Abbreviation for acceptable quality level.

arbitrage—Risk-free buying of an asset in one market and simultaneous selling of an identical asset at a profit in another market.

arbitration—The process by which an independent third party is brought in to settle a dispute or to preserve the interest of two conflicting parties.

arithmetic mean—Syn: mean.

arrival—In queuing theory, a unit that arrives for service, such as a person or part.

arrival date—The date purchased material is due to arrive at the receiving site. The arrival date can be input, it can be equal to the current due date, or it can be calculated from the ship date plus transit time. See: due date.

arrival rate—In queuing theory, the value or distribution describing how often a person or thing arrives for service.

arrow—1) In activity-on-arrow networks, the graphic presentation of an activity. The tail of the arrow represents the start of the activity. The head of the arrow represents the finish. Unless a timescale is used, the length of the arrow stem has no relation to the duration of the activity. Length and direction of the arrow are usually a matter of convenience and clarity. 2) In activity-on-node networks, an arrow represents a precedence requirement.

arrow diagram—A technique to determine the relationships and precedence of different activities and the time estimate for project completion. The technique is useful in identifying potential problems and improvement opportunities.

arrow diagram method—Syn: activity-on-arrow network.

artificial intelligence (AI)—1) Computer programs that can learn and reason in a manner similar to humans. The problem is defined in terms of states and operators to generate a search space that is examined for the best solution. In contrast, conventional programming collects and processes data by algorithm or fixed step-by-step procedures. 2) An area in computer science that attempts to develop AI computer programs.

ASC—Abbreviation for accredited standards committee.

ASCII—Acronym for American Standard Code for Information Interchange.

ASN—Abbreviation for advance ship notice.

ASP—Abbreviation for application service provider.

ASQ—Abbreviation for American Society for Quality.

ASQC—Abbreviation for American Society for Quality Control, now simply American Society for Quality (ASQ).

AS/RS—Abbreviation for automated storage/retrieval system.

assays—Tests of the physical and chemical properties of a sample.

assemble-to-order—A production environment where a good or service can be assembled after receipt of a customer's order. The key components (bulk, semi-finished, intermediate, subassembly, fabricated, purchased, packing, and so on) used in the assembly or finishing process are planned and usually stocked in anticipation of a customer order. Receipt of an order initiates assembly of the customized product. This strategy is useful where a large number of end products (based on the selection of options and accessories) can be assembled from common components. Syn: finish-to-order. See: make-to-order, make-to-stock.

assembly—A group of subassemblies and/or parts that are put together and that constitute a major subdivision for the final product. An assembly may be an end item or a component of a higher level assembly.

assembly bin—Syn: accumulation bin.

assembly chart—Overview of a product containing assembly and subassembly operations, materials, and components.

assembly lead time—The time that normally elapses between the issuance of a work order to the assembly floor and work completion.

assembly line—An assembly process in which equipment and work centers are laid out to follow the sequence in which raw materials and parts are assembled. See: line, production line.

assembly order—A manufacturing order to an assembly department authorizing it to put components together into an assembly. See: blend order.

assembly parts list—As used in the manufacturing process, a list of all parts (and subassemblies) that make up a particular assembly. See: batch card, manufacturing order.

assets—An accounting/financial term (balance sheet classification of accounts) representing the resources owned by a company, whether tangible (cash, inventories) or intangible (patent, goodwill). Assets may have a short-term time horizon—such as cash, accounts receivable, and inventory—or a long-term value (such as equipment, land, and buildings). See: balance sheet, liabilities, owner's equity.

asset value—The adjusted purchase price of the asset plus any costs necessary to prepare the asset for use.

assignable cause—A source of variation in a process that can be isolated, especially when it's significantly larger magnitude or different origin readily distinguishes it from random causes of variation. Syn: special cause. See: common causes, assignable variation.

assignable variation—Variation made by one or more causes that can be identified and removed. See: assignable cause, common causes.

assigned material—Syn: reserved material.

assignee—One who receives a transfer of contract rights from a party to the contract.

assignment—Syn: allocation.

assignor—One who sells contract rights to a third person.

associative forecasting—Uses one or more variables that are believed to affect demand in order to forecast future demand.

assortment warehousing—A warehousing technique that stores the goods close to the customer to ensure short customer lead times.

assumed receipt—A receiving technique based on the assumption that a shipment is as expected. Receiving personnel do not verify the delivery quantity. This technique is used to eliminate invoices.

assurance—One of the dimensions of service quality. The ability of employees to inspire trust and confidence.

assured source of supply—A guaranteed supply source generally created by a contract.

asynchronous process—A condition with two related processes run to finish independently of each other.

A3 method—A means of compactly describing a business process.

ATP—Abbreviation for available-to-promise.

attachment—An accessory that has to be physically attached to the product. See: feature.

attractability efficiency—In e-commerce, a measure of how well an organization persuades people who are aware of its website to actually use the site. See: conversion efficiency.

attractor—In information systems, a website that, over time, continues to attract a large number of visitors.

attribute—1) Quality control value that is either a yes/no value or is counted rather than being measured on a continuous scale. See: variable, attribute data. 2) A description of an item or service that specifies either a presence or an absence, such as "on-time" versus "late."

attribute data—Go/no-go information. The control charts based on attribute data include percent chart, number of affected units chart, count chart, count-per-unit chart, quality score chart, and demerit chart. See: attribute, attribute inspection.

attribute inspection—Inspection for a go/no-go decision or yes/no decision or to count the number of defects on a unit. See: attribute, attribute data.

attrition factor—The budget fraction apportioned for replacement personnel training because of projected personnel losses (retirements, promotions, and terminations).

audit—An objective comparison of actions to policies and plans.

audit trail—Tracing the transactions affecting the contents or origin of a record.

authentication—In information systems, the act of identifying a person or confirming the source of a message.

authentication key—In information systems, a key that ensures that data in an electronic business transaction are not changed. It can also be used as a form of digital signature.

authorized deviation—Permission for a supplier or the plant to manufacture an item that is not in conformance with the applicable drawings or specifications.

autodiscrimination—The ability of a bar code reader to read several different types of symbols consecutively.

automated assembly system—A system that produces completed products or assemblies without the contribution of direct labor.

automated clearinghouse—A U.S. nationwide system for electronic payments preferred by a myriad of banks, consumers, and corporations. This system can carry payment information in a standardized, computer accessible format.

automated flow line—A production line that has machines linked by automated parts transfer and handling machines.

automated guided vehicle system (AGVS)—A transportation network that automatically routes one or more material handling devices, such as carts or pallet trucks, and positions them at predetermined destinations without operator intervention.

automated information system (AIS)—Computer hardware and software configured to automate calculating, computing, sequencing, storing, retrieving, displaying, communicating, or otherwise manipulating data and textual material to provide information.

automated process controls system—A system that can measure the performance of a process, compare the result to predetermined standards, and then make adjustments to the process.

automated quality control inspection system—A system that employs machines to help inspect products for quality control.

automated storage/retrieval system (AS/RS)—A high-density, rack inventory storage system with vehicles automatically loading and unloading the racks.

automatic identification and data capture (AIDC)—A set of technologies that collect data about objects and then send these data to a computer without human intervention. Examples include radio frequency wireless devices and terminals, bar code scanners, and smart cards.

automatic identification system (AIS)—A system that can use various means, including bar code scanning and radio frequencies, to sense and load data in a computer.

automatic relief—A set of inventory bookkeeping methods that automatically adjusts computerized inventory records based on a production transaction. Examples of automatic relief methods are backflushing, direct-deduct, and pre-deduct processing.

automatic rescheduling—Rescheduling done by the computer to automatically change due dates on scheduled receipts when it detects that due dates and need dates are out of phase. Ant: manual rescheduling.

automation—The substitution of machine work for human physical and mental work, or the use of machines for work not otherwise able to be accomplished, entailing a less continuous interaction with humans than previous equipment used for similar tasks.

autonomation—Automated shutdown of a line, process, or machine upon detection of an abnormality or defect.

autonomous work group—A production team that operates a highly focused segment of the production process to an externally imposed schedule but with little external reporting, supervision, interference, or help.

auxiliary item—An item required to support the operation of another item.

availability—The percentage of time that a worker or machine is capable of working. The formula is

$$\text{availability} = \frac{(S - B)}{S} \times 100\%$$

where S is the scheduled time and B is the downtime.

available capacity—Syn: capacity available.

available inventory—The on-hand inventory balance minus allocations, reservations, backorders, and (usually) quantities held for quality problems. Often called beginning available balance. Syn: beginning available balance, net inventory.

available time—The number of hours a work center can be used, based on management decisions regarding shift structure, extra shifts, regular overtime, observance of weekends and public holidays, shutdowns, and the like. See: capacity available, utilization.

available-to-promise (ATP)—The uncommitted portion of a company's inventory and planned production maintained in the master schedule to support customer-order promising. The ATP quantity is the uncommitted inventory balance in the first period and is normally calculated for each period in which an MPS receipt is scheduled. In the first period, ATP includes on-hand inventory less customer orders that are due and overdue. Three methods of calculation are used: discrete ATP, cumulative ATP with look-ahead, and cumulative ATP without look-ahead. See: discrete available-to-promise, cumulative available-to-promise.

available work—Work that is actually in a department ready to be worked on as opposed to scheduled work that may not yet be physically on hand. Syn: live load.

average chart—A control chart in which the subgroup average, X-bar, is used to evaluate the stability of the process level. Syn: X-bar chart.

average collection period—Syn: receivables conversion period.

average cost per unit—The estimated total cost, including allocated overhead, to produce a batch of goods divided by the total number of units produced.

average cost system—In cost accounting, a method of inventory valuation for accounting purposes. A weighted average (based on quantity) of item cost is used to determine the cost of goods sold (income statement) and inventory valuation (balance sheet). Average cost provides a valuation between last-in, first-out and first-in, first-out methods. See: first in, first out; last in, first out.

average fixed cost—The total fixed cost divided by units produced. This value declines as output increases.

average forecast error—1) The arithmetic mean of the forecast errors. 2) The exponentially smoothed forecast error. See: bias, forecast error.

average inventory—One-half the average lot size plus the safety stock, when demand and lot sizes are expected to be relatively uniform over time. The average can be calculated as an average of several inventory observations taken over several historical time periods; for example, 12-month ending inventories may be averaged. When demand and lot sizes are not uniform, the stock level versus time can be graphed to determine the average.

average outgoing quality (AOQ)—The expected average quality level of outgoing product for a given value of incoming product quality.

average outgoing quality limit (AOQL)—The maximum average outgoing quality over all possible levels of incoming quality for a given acceptance sampling plan and disposal specification.

average payment period—The average time between receipt of materials and payment for those materials.

average total cost—The ratio of total costs (the sum of total fixed costs and total variable costs) over units produced.

average variable cost—The ratio of total variable costs over units produced.

AVL—Abbreviation for approved vendor list.

avoidable cost—A cost associated with an activity that would not be incurred if the activity was not performed (e.g., telephone cost associated with vendor support).

avoidable delay—The delay controlled by a worker and therefore not allowed in the job standard.

award audits—Site visits associated with award programs such as the Malcolm Baldrige National Quality Award or similar state-sponsored award programs.

awareness efficiency—In e-commerce, a measurement of how well an organization informs people who have access to the web that the organization's website exists.

B

BAC—Acronym for budget at completion.

backflush—A method of inventory bookkeeping where the book (computer) inventory of components is automatically reduced by the computer after completion of activity on the component's upper-level parent item based on what should have been used as specified on the bill of material and allocation records. This approach has the disadvantage of a built-in differential between the book record and what is physically in stock. Syn: explode-to-deduct, post-deduct inventory transaction processing. See: pre-deduct inventory transaction processing.

backflush costing—The application of costs based on the output of a process. Backflush costing is usually associated with repetitive manufacturing environments.

backhauling—The process of a transportation vehicle returning from the original destination point to the point of origin. The 1980 Motor Carrier Act deregulated interstate commercial trucking and thereby allowed carriers to contract for the return trip. The backhaul can be with a full, partial, or empty load. An empty backhaul is called deadheading. See: deadhead.

backlog—All the customer orders received but not yet shipped. Sometimes referred to as open orders or the order board. See: order backlog, past due order.

backorder—An unfilled customer order or commitment. A backorder is an immediate (or past due) demand against an item whose inventory is insufficient to satisfy the demand. See: stockout.

back room—In service operations, the part of the operation that is completed without direct customer contact. Many service operations contain both back room and front room operations. See: front room.

backroom costs—Indirect costs for operations that do not add direct value to a product and may or may not be necessary to support its production.

back scheduling—A technique for calculating operation start dates and due dates. The schedule is computed starting with the due date for the order and working backward to determine the required start date and/or due dates for each operation. Syn: backward scheduling. Ant: forward scheduling.

backsourcing—Company processes that, previously handled externally, have been reassigned internally.

backup/restore—The procedure of making backup copies of computer files or disks and, in case of loss of or damage to the original, using the backups to restore the files or disks. In such a case, the only work lost is that done since the backup was made.

backup support—An alternate location or maintainer that can provide the same service response or support as the primary location or maintainer.

backward integration—The process of buying or owning elements of the production cycle and channel of distribution back toward raw material suppliers. See: vertical integration.

backward pass—In the critical path method of project planning, working from the finish node backward through the network logic to the start node to determine the various late start dates and late finish dates. See: critical path method, forward pass.

backward scheduling—Syn: back scheduling.

bad-debt loan ratio—In financial management, the fraction of accounts receivable that is never recovered.

balance—1) The act of evenly distributing the work elements between the two hands performing an operation. 2) The state of having approximately equal working times among the various operations in a process, or the stations on an assembly line. See: balance delay.

balance delay—1) The idle time of one hand in an operation caused by uneven workload balancing. 2) The idle time of one or more operations in a series caused by uneven workload balancing. See: balance, lost time factor.

balanced scorecard—A list of financial and operational measurements used to evaluate organizational or supply chain performance. The dimensions of the ba-

lanced scorecard might include customer perspective, business process perspective, financial perspective, and innovation and learning perspectives. It formally connects overall objectives, strategies, and measurements. Each dimension has goals and measurements.

balance-of-stores record—A double-entry record system that shows the balance of inventory items on hand and the balances of items on order and available for future orders. Where a reserve system of materials control is used, the balance of material on reserve is also shown.

balance of trade—A plus or minus amount found by comparing a country's exports of merchandise to its imports.

balance sheet—A financial statement showing the resources owned, the debts owed, and the owner's share of a company at a given point in time. See: funds flow statement, income statement.

balancing operations—In repetitive just-in-time production, matching actual output cycle times of all operations to the demand or use for parts as required by final assembly and, eventually, as required by the market.

balancing the line—In repetitive manufacturing, regulating the assignments given to each workstation in order to ensure that all tasks at each workstation on the line are done in as close to the same time as possible.

Baldrige Award—Syn: Malcolm Baldrige National Quality Award.

Baldrige lite—A state or company quality award program modeled after the Malcolm Baldrige National Quality Award but with a simplified application process.

Baldrige-qualified—A designation claimed by companies that have been granted a site visit by the Malcolm Baldrige National Quality Award examiners.

balking—When customers will not join a queue when they learn how long it is. See: reneging.

bandwidth—In telecommunications, a measurement of how much data can be moved along a communications channel per unit of time, usually measured in bits per second.

banner—In e-commerce, a portion of a web page that contains advertising or the name of a website. The banner usually contains a hypertext connection to a web page of the company doing the advertising.

bar code—A series of alternating bars and spaces printed or stamped on parts, containers, labels, or other media, representing encoded information that can be read by electronic readers. A bar code is used to facilitate timely and accurate input of data to a computer system.

bar coding—A method of encoding data using bar code for fast and accurate readability.

bar graph—A graphical method of displaying data by grouping observations into specific clusters.

barrier to entry—Factors that prevent companies from entering into a particular market, such as high initial investment in equipment.

baseband coax—A coaxial cable offering a single channel for text, voice, or video transmission.

base demand—The percentage of a company's demand that derives from continuing contracts and/or existing customers. Because this demand is well known and recurring, it becomes the basis of management's plans. Syn: baseload demand.

base index—Syn: base series.

base inventory level—The inventory level made up of aggregate lot-size inventory plus the aggregate safety stock inventory. It does not take into account the anticipation inventory that will result from the production plan. The base inventory level should be known before the production plan is made. Syn: basic stock. See: aggregate inventory.

baseline—In project management, the approved time-phased plan for the schedule or cost of a piece of work, including approved changes.

baseline measures—A set of measurements (or metrics) that seeks to establish the current or starting level of performance of a process, function, product, firm, and so on. Baseline measures are usually established before implementing improvement activities and programs.

baseload demand—Syn: base demand.

base point pricing—A type of geographic pricing policy where customers order from designated shipping points without freight charges if they are located within a specified distance from the base point. Customers outside area boundaries pay base price plus transportation costs from the nearest base point.

base series—A standard succession of values of demand-over-time data used in forecasting seasonal items. This series of factors is usually based on the relative level of demand during the corresponding period of previous years. The average value of the base series over a seasonal cycle will be 1.0. A figure higher than 1.0 indicates that the demand for that period is more than the average; a figure less than 1.0 indicates less than the average. For forecasting purposes, the base series is superimposed upon the average demand and trend in demand for the item in question. Syn: base index. See: seasonal index, seasonality.

base stock system—A method of inventory control that includes, as special cases, most of the systems in practice. In this system, when an order is received for any item, it is used as a picking ticket, and duplicate copies, called replenishment orders, are sent back to all stages of production to initiate replenishment of stocks. Positive or negative orders, called base stock orders, are also used from time to time to adjust the level of the base stock of each item. In actual practice, replenishment orders are usually accumulated when they are issued and are released at regular intervals.

basic producer—A manufacturer that uses natural resources to produce materials for other manufacturing. A typical example is a steel company that processes iron ore and produces steel ingots; other examples are companies that make wood pulp, glass, and rubber.

basic seven tools of quality (B7)—Tools that help organizations understand their processes to improve them. The tools are the cause-and-effect diagram (also known as the fishbone diagram or the Ishikawa diagram), check sheet, flowchart, histogram, Pareto chart, control chart, and scatter diagram. Syn: seven tools of quality. See: seven new tools of quality.

basic stock—Syn: base inventory level.

batch—1) A quantity scheduled to be produced or in production. See: process batch, transfer batch. 2) For discrete products, the batch is planned to be the standard batch quantity, but during production, the standard batch quantity may be broken into smaller lots. See: lot. 3) In nondiscrete products, the batch is a quantity that is planned to be produced in a given time period based on a formula or recipe that often is developed to produce a given number of end items. 4) A type of manufacturing process used to produce items with similar designs and that may cover a wide range of order volumes. Typically, items ordered are of a repeat nature, and production may be for a specific customer order or for stock replenishment. See: project manufacturing.

batch bill of materials—A recipe or formula in which the statement of quantity per is based on the standard batch quantity of the parent. Syn: batch formula.

batch card—A document used in the process industries to authorize and control the production of a quantity of material. Batch cards usually contain quantities and lot

B

numbers of ingredients to be used, processing variables, pack-out instructions, and product disposition. See: assembly parts list, batch sheet, blend formula, fabrication order, manufacturing order, mix ticket.

batch formula—Syn: batch bill of materials.

batch manufacturing—A type of manufacturing process in which sets of items are moved through the different manufacturing steps in a group or batch.

batch number—Syn: lot number.

batch picking—A method of picking orders in which order requirements are aggregated by product across orders to reduce movement to and from product locations. The aggregated quantities of each product are then transported to a common area where the individual orders are constructed. See: discrete order picking, order picking, zone picking.

batch processing—1) A manufacturing technique in which parts are accumulated and processed together in a lot. 2) A computer technique in which transactions are accumulated and processed together or in a lot. Syn: batch production.

batch production—Syn: batch processing.

batch sensitivity factor—A multiplier that is used for the rounding rules in determining the number of batches required to produce a given amount of product.

batch sheet—In many process industries, a document that combines product and process definition. See: batch card.

baud—The number of bits transmitted per second.

Bayesian analysis—Statistical analysis where uncertainty is incorporated, using all available information to choose among a number of alternative decisions.

beginning available balance—Syn: available inventory.

beginning inventory—A statement of the inventory count at the end of last period, usually from a perpetual inventory record.

benchmarking—Comparing a company's costs, products, and services to that of a company thought to have superior performance. The benchmark target is often a competitor but is not always a firm in the same industry. Seven types of benchmarking have been cited: (1) competitive benchmarking, (2) financial benchmarking, (3) functional benchmarking, (4) performance benchmarking, (5) process benchmarking, (6) product benchmarking, and (7) strategic benchmarking. See: competitive benchmarking, financial benchmarking, functional benchmarking, performance benchmarking, process benchmarking, product benchmarking, strategic benchmarking.

benchmark measures—A set of measurements (or metrics) that is used to establish goals for improvements in processes, functions, products, and so on. Benchmark measures are often derived from other firms that display best-in-class achievement.

bench stocks—Syn: floor stocks.

bespoke—A custom-made product or service. The term originally was applied to clothing, but now applies to software as well.

best-in-class—An organization, often from another industry, recognized for excellence in a specific process area. See: process benchmarking.

best practices—In benchmarking, the measurement or performance standard by which similar items are evaluated. Defining a best practice identifies opportunities to improve effectiveness. The process of comparing an actual result to a best practice may be applied to resources, activities, or cost objects.

beta distribution—A type of probability distribution often used to model activity times.

beta release—A version of a product sent to certain customers prior to general release in order to receive feedback on product performance.

beta test—A term used to describe the pilot evaluation of a good or service (i.e., "the second evaluation").

bias—A consistent deviation from the mean in one direction (high or low). A normal property of a good forecast is that it is not biased. See: average forecast error.

bid—A quotation specifically given to a prospective purchaser upon request, usually in competition with other vendors. See: quotation.

bid evaluation—A comparison of supplier quotes for a product based on price, quality, lead time, delivery performance, and other criteria and, based on that comparison, selecting a supplier.

bid pricing—Offering a specific price for each job rather than setting a standard price that applies for all customers.

bid proposal—The response to the written request from a potential customer asking for the submission of a quotation or proposal to provide goods or services. The bid proposal is in response to a request for proposal (RFP) or request for quote (RFQ).

big data—A collection of data and technology that accesses, integrates, and reports all available data by filtering, correlating, and reporting insights not attainable with past data technologies. It describes data processing beyond the human scale. In the past, databases tended to be limited—they only had to meet the demands of human users entering and retrieving data. With the emergence of e-commerce and internet search engines, database technology is evolving to manage humans and computers. Today, with the amount of data growing by 50 percent each year, it is information technology that is capable of managing, processing, and finding value.

big Q, little q—A term used to contrast the difference between managing for quality in all business processes and products (big Q) and managing for quality in a limited capacity—traditionally in only factory products and processes (little q).

bilateral contract—An agreement wherein each party makes a promise to the other party.

bill-back—A penalty given to the supplier because a late delivery or poor quality resulted in extra costs.

billing and collection costs—In transportation, the costs related to issuing invoices or bills. These amounts can be reduced by combining shipments in an order to limit transportation frequency.

bill of activities—In activity-based cost accounting, a summary of activities needed by a product or other cost object. The bill of activities includes volume and cost of each activity.

bill of batches—A method of tracking the specific multi-level batch composition of a manufactured item. The bill of batches provides the necessary where-used and where-from relationships required for lot traceability.

bill of capacity—Syn: bill of resources.

bill of distribution—Syn: distribution network structure.

bill of labor—A structured listing of all labor requirements for the fabrication, assembly, and testing of a parent item. See: bill of resources, capacity bill procedure, routing.

bill of lading (uniform)—A carrier's contract and receipt for goods the carrier agrees to transport from one place to another and to deliver to a designated person. In case of loss, damage, or delay, the bill of lading is the basis for filing freight claims.

bill of material (BOM)—1) A listing of all the subassemblies, intermediates, parts, and raw materials that go into a parent assembly showing the quantity of each required to make an assembly. It is used in conjunction with the master production schedule to determine the items for which purchase requisitions and production orders must be released. A variety of display formats exist for bills of material, including the single-level bill of material, indented bill of material, modular (planning) bill of material, transient bill of material, matrix bill of material, and costed bill of material. 2) A list of all the materials needed to make one production run of a product, by a contract manufacturer, of piece parts/components for its customers. The bill of material may also be called the formula, recipe, or ingredients list in certain process industries.

bill-of-material accuracy—The degree to which a list of specified items conforms to administrative specifications and with correct quantities.

bill-of-material explosion—The process of determining component identities, quantities per assembly, and other parent/component relationship data for a parent item. Explosion may be single level, indented, or summarized.

bill-of-material processor—A computer program for maintaining and retrieving bill-of-material information.

bill-of-material structuring—The process of organizing bills of material to perform specific functions.

bill of operations—Syn: routing.

bill of resources—A listing of the required capacity and key resources needed to manufacture one unit of a selected item or family. Rough-cut capacity planning uses these bills to calculate the approximate capacity requirements of the master production schedule. Resource planning may use a form of this bill. Syn: bill of capacity. See: bill of labor, capacity planning using overall factors, product load profile, resource profile, rough-cut capacity planning, routing.

bin—1) A storage device designed to hold small discrete parts. 2) A shelving unit with physical dividers separating the storage locations.

bin location file—A file that specifically identifies the location where each item in inventory is stored.

bin reserve system—Syn: two-bin inventory system.

bin tag—1) A type of perpetual inventory record, designed for storekeeping purposes, maintained at the storage area for each inventory item. 2) An identifying marking on a storage location.

bin transfer—An inventory transaction to move a quantity from one valid location (bin) to another valid location (bin).

bin trips—Usually, the number of transactions per stockkeeping unit per unit of time.

bit—Acronym for binary digit. It can have only the values 0 or 1.

black belt—In six sigma, team leader for process improvement. Responsibilities include defining, measuring, and controlling the improvement process.

black box design—When suppliers or company functions are given general design guidelines and are requested to complete the technical details.

blank check purchase order—An order with a signed blank check attached that is usually only good up to a specific amount.

blanket order—Syn: blanket purchase order.

blanket order release—A message that is used to release a quantity from a blanket order.

blanket purchase order—A long-term commitment to a supplier for material against which short-term releases will be generated to satisfy requirements. Often blanket orders cover only one item with predetermined delivery dates. Syn: blanket order, standing order.

blanket rate—A rate that does not depend on the distance cargo is transported.

blanket release—The authorization to ship and/or produce against a blanket agreement or contract.

blanket routing—A routing that lists groups of operations needed to produce a family of items. The items may have small differences in size, but they use the same sequence of operations. Specific times or tools for each individual item can be included.

bleeding edge—An innovative process that may be unusual enough to pose a risk to the customer or client.

blemish—An imperfection that is severe enough to be noticed but should not cause any real impairment with respect to intended normal or reasonably foreseeable use. See: defect, imperfection, nonconformity.

blend formula—An ingredient list for a product in process industries. See: batch card, manufacturing order, mix ticket.

blending—The process of physically mixing two or more lots or types of material to produce a homogeneous lot. Blends normally receive new identification and require testing.

blending department—In process industries, the name of the department where the ingredients are mixed. See: final assembly department.

blend off—In process industries, the rework of material by introducing a small percentage into another run of the same product.

blend order—A manufacturing order to a blending department authorizing it to mix the ingredients of a product. See: assembly order.

blockage—See: blocking.

block control—Control of the production process in groups, or "blocks," of shop orders for products undergoing the same basic processes.

block diagram—A diagram that shows the operations, interrelationships, and interdependencies of components in a system. Boxes, or blocks (hence the name), represent the components; connecting lines between the blocks represent interfaces. There are two types of block diagrams: (1) functional block diagrams, which show a system's subsystems and lower level products, their interrelationships, and interfaces with other systems and (2) reliability block diagrams, which are similar to functional block diagrams except they are modified to emphasize those aspects influencing reliability. See: flowchart.

blocked operation—An upstream work center that is not permitted to produce because of a full queue at a downstream work center or because no kanban authorizes production.

blocked operations—A group of operations identified separately for instructions and documentation but reported as one.

blocking—The condition requiring a work center that has parts to process to remain idle as long as the queue to which the parts would be sent is full or kanbans authorizing production are not present.

blocking bug—A defect that prevents a thorough investigation as to the cause, or that prevents shipment of a product.

block scheduling—An operation scheduling technique where each operation is allowed a "block" of time, such as a day or a week.

block stacking—A storage method in which pallets, cases, or cartons are stacked upwards from the floor to whatever practical height is available without the use of shelves.

block system—A system for selecting items to be cycle counted by a group or block of numbers.

blowthrough—Syn: phantom bill of material.

blueprint—In engineering, a line drawing showing the physical characteristics of a part.

blue sky—Goodwill associated with the acquisition of a company asset.

body of knowledge—The knowledge in a given area that a person is expected to understand to be certified as a practitioner.

boilerplate—The standard terms and conditions on a purchase order or other document.

BOM—Abbreviation for bill of material.

bona fide—Latin for "in good faith."

bond—A long-term debt of a firm.

bond (performance)—A guarantee of satisfactory work completion that is executed in connection with a contract and that secures the performance and fulfillment of all the undertakings, covenants, terms, conditions, and agreements contained in the contract.

bonded warehouse—Buildings or parts of buildings designated by the U.S. Secretary of the Treasury for storing imported merchandise, operated under U.S. Customs supervision.

booked orders—Demand that has been confirmed. See: customer order, demand, order penetration point.

bookings—The value of all sales after discounts and rebates have been applied.

book inventory—An accounting definition of inventory units or value obtained from perpetual inventory records rather than by actual count.

book value—The accounting value of an asset.

Boolean algebra—A form of algebra that, like ordinary algebra, represents relationships and properties with symbols. However, Boolean algebra also has classes, propositions, on-off circuit elements, and operators (and, or, not, except, if, then). Boolean algebra is useful in defining the logic of a complex system.

bottleneck—A facility, function, department, or resource whose capacity is less than the demand placed upon it. For example, a bottleneck machine or work center exists where jobs are processed at a slower rate than they are demanded. Syn: bottleneck operation.

bottleneck operation—Syn: bottleneck.

bottom-up estimating—A method of estimation that involves disaggregating a piece of work into components, estimating each component requirement, and adding the resulting times and/or costs to arrive at the estimate for the whole.

bottom-up planning—Planning for resource requirements by starting at the bottom of the bill of material or services, estimating the resources required to produce each product or service, and then adding the resources up.

bottom-up replanning—In MRP, the process of using pegging data to solve material availability or other problems. This process is accomplished by the planner (not the computer system), who evaluates the effects of possible solutions. Potential solutions include compressing lead time, cutting order quantity, substituting material, and changing the master schedule.

bounded—The adjustment of a shop order quantity of a parent to use the remaining units of a component, raw material, or lot.

Box-Jenkins model—A forecasting method based on regression and moving average models. The model is based not on regression of independent variables, but on past observations of the item to be forecast at varying time lags and on previous error values from forecasting. See: forecast.

BPM—Abbreviation for business process management.

BPR—Abbreviation for business process reengineering.

bracketed recall—Recall from customers of suspect lot numbers plus a specified number of lots produced before and after the suspect ones.

brainstorming—A technique that teams use to generate ideas on a particular subject. Each person on the team is asked to think creatively and write down as many ideas as possible. The ideas are not discussed or reviewed until after the brainstorming session.

branch and bound—Operations research models for determining optimal solutions based on the enumeration of subsets of possible solutions, which implicitly enumerate all possible solutions.

branch warehouse—Syn: distribution center.

branch warehouse demand—Syn: warehouse demand.

branding—The use of a name, term, symbol, or design, or a combination of these, to identify a product.

brand loyalty—The tendency of some consumers to stay with a preferred product in spite of a competitor's advantages.

brand manager—The person in charge of the marketing program for a given brand. Syn: product manager.

brand name—A word or combination of words used to identify a product and differentiate it from other products; the verbal part of a trademark, in contrast to the pictorial mark; a trademark word.

brand plan—Syn: market plan.

brand recognition—The degree to which customers recognize a particular brand identity and associate it with a particular product line relative to other available brands.

breadman—In kanban, an arrangement in which the customer does not specify the quantity to be delivered on a specific basis, but instead gives the supplier a set of guidelines. The delivery person determines the quantity according to these rules.

break-bulk—Dividing truckloads of homogeneous items into smaller, more appropriate quantities for use.

break-bulk warehousing—A form of cross-docking in which the incoming shipments are from a single source or manufacturer.

breakdown maintenance—Remedial maintenance that occurs when equipment fails and must be repaired on an emergency or priority basis. Syn: irregular maintenance, reactive maintenance.

break-even analysis—A study of the number of units, or amount of time, required to recoup an investment.

break-even chart—A graphical tool showing the total variable cost and fixed cost curve along with the total revenue curve. The point of intersection is defined as the break-even point (i.e., the point at which total revenues exactly equal total costs). See: total cost curve.

break-even point—The level of production or the volume of sales at which operations are neither profitable nor unprofitable. The break-even point is the intersection of the total revenue and total cost curves. See: total cost curve.

break-even time—The total elapsed time of a technology transfer beginning with a scientific investigation and ending when the profits from a new product offset the cost of its development.

breeder bill of material—A bill of material that recognizes and plans for the availability and usage of by-products in the manufacturing process. The breeder bill allows for complete by-product MRP and product/by-product costing.

bricks and mortar—A company that sells through a physical location. Ant: clicks and mortar (selling over the internet).

broadband—A coaxial cable offering several channels for text, voice, and/or video transmission.

broadcast system—A sequence of specific units to be assembled and completed at a given rate. This sequence is communicated to supply and assembly activities to perform operations and position material so that it merges with the correct assembled unit.

browser—Software used on the web to retrieve and display documents on-screen, connect to other sites using hypertext links, display images, and play audio files.

B7—Abbreviation for the basic seven tools of quality.

B2B—Abbreviation for business-to-business commerce.

B2C—Abbreviation for business-to-consumer sales.

bubble chart—A diagram that attempts to display the interrelationships of systems, functions, or data in a sequential flow. It derives its name from the circular symbols used to enclose the statements on the chart.

bucket—A time period, usually a week.

bucketed system—An MRP, DRP, or other time-phased system in which all time-phased data are accumulated into time periods called buckets. If the period of accumulation is one week, then the system is said to have weekly buckets.

bucketless system—An MRP, DRP, or other time-phased system in which all time-phased data are processed, stored, and usually displayed using dated records rather than defined time periods (buckets).

budget—A plan that includes an estimate of future costs and revenues related to expected activities. The budget serves as a pattern for and a control over future operations.

budget at completion (BAC)—The total planned budget for a project.

budgeted capacity—The volume/mix of throughput on which financial budgets were set and overhead/burden absorption rates established.

budgeted cost of work performed—In project management, this term has been replaced with the term earned value.

budgeted cost of work scheduled—In project management, this term has been replaced with the term planned value.

buffer—1) A quantity of materials awaiting further processing. It can refer to raw materials, semifinished stores or hold points, or a work backlog that is purposely maintained behind a work center. 2) In the theory of constraints, buffers can be time or material and support throughput and/or due date performance.

Buffers can be maintained at the constraint, convergent points (with a constraint part), divergent points, and shipping points.

buffer management—In the theory of constraints, a process in which all expediting in a shop is driven by what is scheduled to be in the buffers (constraint, shipping, and assembly buffers). By expediting this material into the buffers, the system helps avoid idleness at the constraint and missed customer due dates. In addition, the causes of items missing from the buffer are identified, and the frequency of occurrence is used to prioritize improvement activities.

buffer stock—Syn: safety stock.

build cycle—The time period between a major setup and a cleanup. It recognizes cyclical scheduling of similar products with minor changes from one product/model to another.

build-up forecasts—A qualitative forecasting technique in which individuals who are familiar with specific market segments estimate the demand within these segments. The overall forecast then is obtained by calculating the sum of the forecasts for these segments.

bulk issue—Parts issued from stores to work-in-process inventory, but not based on a job order. They are issued in quantities estimated to cover requirements of individual work centers and production lines. The issue may be used to cover a period of time or to fill a fixed-size container.

bulk packing—Placing several small packages in a larger container to prevent damage or theft.

bulk storage—Large-scale storage for raw materials, intermediates, or finished products. Each vessel normally contains a mixture of lots and materials that may be replenished and withdrawn for use or pack-out simultaneously.

bullwhip effect—An extreme change in the supply position upstream in a supply chain generated by a small change in demand downstream in the supply chain. Inventory can quickly move from being backordered to being excess. This is caused by the serial nature of communicating orders up the chain with the inherent transportation delays of moving product down the chain. The bullwhip effect can be eliminated by synchronizing the supply chain.

bundle—One or more unassembled items shipped together as a set of items.

bundling—Combining two or more products or services into a single transaction.

burden—Syn: overhead.

burden rate—A cost, usually in dollars per hour, that is normally added to the cost of every standard production hour to cover overhead expenses.

burn rate—The rate at which a company consumes cash. It can be used to determine when more cash must be raised.

business clusters—When businesses locate in close proximity for competition purposes.

business cycle—A period of time marked by long-term fluctuations in the total level of economic activity. Measures of business cycle activity include the rate of unemployment and the level of gross domestic product.

business environment—Syn: operating environment.

business intelligence—Information collected by an organization on customers, competitors, products or services, and processes. Business intelligence provides organizational data in such a way that the organizational knowledge filters can easily associate with this data and turn it into information for the organization. Persons involved in business intelligence processes may use application software and other technologies to gather, store, analyze, and provide access to data, and present that data in a simple, useful manner. The software aids in business performance management and aims to help consumers make better business decisions by offering them accurate, current, and relevant information. Some businesses use data warehouses because they are a logical collection of information gathered from various operational databases for the purpose of creating business intelligence.

business judgment rule—Under common law, an absence of liability for corporate directors and officers if they have used rational business judgment and have no conflict of interest.

business market—Syn: industrial market.

business plan—1) A statement of long-range strategy and revenue, cost, and profit objectives usually accompanied by budgets, a projected balance sheet, and a cash flow (source and application of funds) statement. A business plan is usually stated in terms of dollars and grouped by product family. The business plan is then translated into synchronized tactical functional plans through the production planning process (or the sales and operations planning process). Although frequently stated in different terms (dollars versus units), these tactical plans should agree with each other and with the business plan. See: long-term planning, strategic plan. 2) A document consisting of the business details (organization, strategy, and financing tactics) prepared by an entrepreneur to plan for a new business.

business planning—The process of constructing the business plan. See: business plan.

business process—A set of logically related tasks or activities performed to achieve a defined business outcome.

business process management (BPM)—A business discipline or function that uses business practices, techniques, and methods to create and improve business processes. BPM is a holistic approach to the use of appropriate process-related business disciplines to gain business performance improvements across the enterprise or supply chain. It promotes business effectiveness and efficiency while striving for innovation, flexibility, and integration with technology. Most process improvement disciplines or activities can be considered as BPM.

business process outsourcing—Contracting with third parties to perform non-core activities within a business. Functions often outsourced include human resources, accounts receivable, accounts payable, and payroll.

business process reengineering (BPR)—A procedure that involves the fundamental rethinking and radical redesign of business processes to achieve dramatic organizational improvements in such critical measures of performance as cost, quality, service, and speed. Any BPR activity is distinguished by its emphasis on (1) process rather than functions and products and (2) the customers for the process.

business service—The software aspect of electronic commerce. It performs activities, such as encryption, that are required to support business transactions.

business strategy—A plan for choosing how to compete. Three generic business strategies are (1) least cost, (2) differentiation, and (3) focus.

business-to-business commerce (B2B)—Business conducted over the internet between businesses. The implication is that this connectivity will cause businesses to transform themselves via supply chain management to become virtual organizations—reducing costs, improving quality, reducing delivery lead time, and improving due-date performance.

business-to-consumer sales (B2C)—Business being conducted between businesses and final consumers largely over the internet. It includes traditional brick and mortar businesses that also offer products online and businesses that trade exclusively electronically.

business unit—A division or segment of an organization generally treated as a separate profit-and-loss center.

buyer—An individual whose functions may include supplier selection, negotiation, order placement, supplier follow-up, measurement and control of supplier performance, value analysis, and evaluation of new materials and processes. In some companies, the functions of order placement and supplier follow-up are handled by the supplier scheduler.

buyer behavior—The way individuals or organizations behave in a purchasing situation. The customer-oriented concept finds out the wants, needs, and desires of customers and adapts resources of the organization to deliver need-satisfying goods and services.

buyer code—A code used to identify the purchasing person responsible for a given item or purchase order.

buyer cycle—The purchasing sequence that generally follows the buyer's product and budget cycles.

buyer/planner—A buyer who also does material planning. This term should not be confused with planner/ buyer, which is a synonym for supplier scheduler.

buyer's market—A market in which goods can easily be secured and in which the economic forces of business tend to cause goods to be priced at the purchaser's estimate of value.

buying capacity—Syn: capacity buying.

buying down—Given a product that historically experienced price swings, attempting to buy when the price is low or down. See: hedging, speculative buying.

by-product—A material of value produced as a residual of or incidental to the production process. The ratio of by-product to primary product is usually predictable. By-products may be recycled, sold as-is, or used for other purposes. See: co-product.

byte—A string of 8 bits used to represent a single character in a computer code.

C

cache—A high-speed device used within a computer to store frequently retrieved data.

CAD—Acronym for computer-aided design.

CAD/CAM—The integration of computer-aided design and computer-aided manufacturing to achieve automation from design through manufacturing.

CAE—Abbreviation for computer-aided engineering.

cage—A secure area used to store valuable items.

CAIT—Abbreviation for computer-aided inspection and test.

calculated capacity—Syn: rated capacity.

calculated usage—The determination of usage of components or ingredients in a manufacturing process by multiplying the receipt quantity of a parent by the quantity per of each component or ingredient in the bill or recipe, accommodating standard yields.

calendar time—The passage of days or weeks as in the definition of lead time or scheduling rules, in contrast with running time.

calendar unit—The smallest unit of time in a project plan.

calibration—The comparison of a measurement instrument or system of unverified accuracy with a measurement instrument or system of a known accuracy to detect any variation from the required performance specification.

calibration frequency—The interval in days between tooling calibrations.

call center—A facility housing personnel who respond to customer phone queries. These personnel may provide customer service or technical support. Call center services may be in-house or outsourced.

CAM—Acronym for computer-aided manufacturing.

campaign—A series of batches of the same product run together (back to back).

cancellation charge—A fee charged by a seller to cover its costs associated with a customer's cancellation of an order. If the seller has started engineering work, purchased raw materials, or started manufacturing operations, these charges could also be included in the cancellation charge.

can-order point—An ordering system used when multiple items are ordered from one vendor. The can-order point is a point higher than the original order point. When any one of the items triggers an order by reaching the must-order point, all items below their can-order point are also ordered. The can-order point is set by considering the additional holding cost that would be incurred should the item be ordered early.

capability study—Syn: process capability analysis.

capable-to-promise (CTP)—The process of committing orders against available capacity as well as inventory. This process may involve multiple manufacturing or distribution sites. Capable-to-promise is used to determine when a new or unscheduled customer order can be delivered. Capable-to-promise employs a finite-scheduling model of the manufacturing system to determine when an item can be delivered. It includes any constraints that might restrict the production, such as availability of resources, lead times for raw materials or purchased parts, and requirements for lower-level components or subassemblies. The resulting delivery date takes into consideration production capacity, the current manufacturing environment, and future order commitments. The objective is to reduce the time spent by production planners in expediting orders and adjusting plans because of inaccurate delivery-date promises.

capacity—1) The capability of a system to perform its expected function. 2) The capability of a worker, machine, work center, plant, or organization to produce output per time period. Capacity required represents the system capability needed to make a given product mix (assuming technology, product specification, etc.). As a planning function, both capacity available and capacity required can be measured in the short term (capacity requirements plan), intermediate term (rough-cut capacity plan), and long term (resource requirements plan). Capacity control is the execution through the I/O control report of the short-term plan. Capacity can be classified as budgeted, dedicated, demonstrated, productive, protective, rated, safety, standing, or theoretical. See: capacity available, capacity required. 3) Required mental ability to enter into a contract.

capacity available—The capability of a system or resource to produce a quantity of output in a particular time period. Syn: available capacity. See: capacity, available time.

capacity bill procedure—A rough-cut capacity planning method that takes into account any shifts in product mix. Bill of material and routing information are required with direct labor-hour or machine-hour data available for each operation. See: bill of labor.

capacity buying—A purchasing practice whereby a company commits to a supplier for a given amount of its capacity per unit of time. Subsequently, schedules for individual items are given to the supplier in quantities to match the committed level of capacity. Syn: buying capacity.

capacity-constrained resource (CCR)—A resource that is not a constraint but will become a constraint unless scheduled carefully. Any resource that, if its capacity is not carefully managed, is likely to compromise the throughput of the organization. (Also called capacity constraint resource.)

capacity control—The process of measuring production output and comparing it with the capacity plan, determining if the variance exceeds pre-established limits, and taking corrective action to get back on plan if the limits are exceeded. See: input/output control.

capacity cushion—Extra capacity that is added to a system after capacity for expected demand is calculated. Syn: safety capacity. See: protective capacity.

capacity management—The function of establishing, measuring, monitoring, and adjusting limits or levels of capacity in order to execute all manufacturing schedules (i.e., the production plan, master production schedule, material requirements plan, and dispatch list). Capacity management is executed at four levels: resource requirements planning, rough-cut capacity planning, capacity requirements planning, and input/output control.

capacity pegging—Displaying the specific sources of capacity requirements. This is analogous to pegging in MRP, which displays the source of material requirements.

capacity planning—The process of determining the amount of capacity required to produce in the future. This process may be performed at an aggregate or product-line level (resource requirements planning), at the master-scheduling level (rough-cut capacity planning), and at the material requirements planning level (capacity requirements planning). See: capacity requirements planning, resource planning, rough-cut capacity planning.

capacity planning using overall factors (CPOF)—A rough-cut capacity planning technique. The master schedule items and quantities are multiplied by the total time required to build each item to provide the total number of hours to produce the schedule. Historical work center percentages are then applied to the total number of hours to provide an estimate of the hours per work center to support the master schedule. This technique eliminates the need for engineered time standards. Syn: overall factors. See: bill of resources, capacity planning, resource profile, rough-cut capacity planning.

capacity-related costs—Costs generally related to increasing (or decreasing) capacity in the medium-to-long-range time horizon. Personnel costs include hiring and training of direct laborers, supervisors, and support personnel in the areas related to the capacity increase. Equipment purchases to increase capacity are also considered. In contrast, costs related to decreasing capacity include layoffs, the fixed overhead spread over fewer units, the impact of low morale, and the inefficiencies of lower production levels.

capacity required—The capacity of a system or resource needed to produce a desired output in a particular time period. Syn: required capacity. See: capacity.

capacity requirements—The resources needed to produce the projected level of work required from a facility over a time horizon. Capacity requirements are usually expressed in terms of hours of work or, when units consume similar resources at the same rate, units of production.

capacity requirements plan—A time-phased display of present and future load (capacity required) on all resources based on the planned and released supply authorizations (i.e., orders) and the planned capacity (capacity available) of these resources over a span of time. See: load profile.

capacity requirements planning (CRP)—The function of establishing, measuring, and adjusting limits or levels of capacity. The term capacity requirements planning in this context refers to the process of determining in detail the amount of labor and machine resources required to accomplish the tasks of production. Open shop orders and planned orders in the MRP system are input to CRP, which through the use of parts routings and time standards translates these orders into hours of work by work center by time period. Even though rough-cut capacity planning may indicate that sufficient capacity exists to execute the MPS, CRP may show that capacity is insufficient during specific time periods. See: capacity planning.

capacity simulation—The ability to do rough-cut capacity planning using a simulated master production schedule or material plan rather than live data.

capacity smoothing—Syn: load leveling.

capacity strategy—One of the strategic choices that a firm must make as part of its manufacturing strategy. There are three commonly recognized capacity strategies: lead, lag, and tracking. A lead capacity strategy adds capacity in anticipation of increasing demand. A lag strategy does not add capacity until the firm is operating at or beyond full capacity. A tracking strategy adds capacity in small amounts to attempt to respond to changing demand in the marketplace.

capacity utilization—Goods produced, or customers served, divided by total output capacity.

capital—Money or resources used to invest in assets that produce products.

capital asset—A physical object that is held by an organization for its production potential and that costs more than some threshold value.

capital budgeting—Actions relating to the planning and financing of capital outlays for such purposes as the purchase of new equipment, the introduction of new product lines, and the modernization of plant facilities.

capital expenditure—Money invested in a long-term asset, one that is expected to last longer than one year. The investment is expected to generate a stream of future benefits.

capital-intensive—A situation in which the largest expenditure in an operation is capital as opposed to labor. See: labor-intensive.

capital rationing—In financial management, the process of apportioning capital expenditures among prospective projects to conserve limited investment funds.

capital recovery—1) Charging periodically to operations amounts that will ultimately equal the amount of capital expenditure. See: amortization, depletion, depreciation. 2) The replacement of the original cost of an asset plus interest. 3) The process of regaining the net investment in a project by means of revenue in excess of the cost from the project. (Usually implies amortization of principal plus interest on the diminishing unrecovered balance.)

capital structure—The combination of permanent short-term debt, long-term debt, preferred stock, and common equity used to finance a firm.

CAPP—Acronym for computer-aided process planning.

carcass—A nonserviceable item obtained from a customer which is intended for use in remanufacturing.

cargo—A product shipped in an aircraft, railroad car, ship, barge, or truck.

cargo container capacity—The inside usable cubic volume of a container.

carbon footprint—A measure of carbon emissions from a person, organization, building, or operation.

carload lot—A shipment that qualifies for a reduced freight rate because it is greater than a specified mini-

mum weight. Since carload rates usually include minimum rates per unit of volume, the higher LCL (less than carload) rate may be less expensive for a heavy but relatively small shipment.

carrier—A company that provides air, sea, or land transportation services.

carrying cost—The cost of holding inventory, usually defined as a percentage of the dollar value of inventory per unit of time (generally one year). Carrying cost depends mainly on the cost of capital invested as well as such costs of maintaining the inventory as taxes and insurance, obsolescence, spoilage, and space occupied. Such costs vary from 10 percent to 35 percent annually, depending on type of industry. Carrying cost is ultimately a policy variable reflecting the opportunity cost of alternative uses for funds invested in inventory. Syn: holding costs.

cartel—A group of companies that agree to cooperate, rather than compete, in producing a product or service, thus limiting or regulating competition.

cascaded systems—Multistage operations. The input to each stage is the output of a preceding stage, thereby causing interdependencies among the stages.

cascading yield loss—The condition where yield loss happens in multiple operations or tasks, resulting in a compounded yield loss. Syn: cumulative yield. See: composite yield.

CASE—Acronym for computer-assisted software engineering.

cash budget—A budget based on planned cash receipts and disbursements of a plant, division, or firm.

cash conversion cycle—1) In retailing, the length of time between the sale of products and the cash payments for a company's resources. 2) In manufacturing, the length of time from the purchase of raw materials to the collection of accounts receivable from customers for the sale of products or services.

cash cow—A highly profitable product in a low-growth market. See: growth-share matrix.

cash discount—A price break offered for the early payment of an invoice.

cash flow—The net flow of dollars into or out of the proposed project. The algebraic sum, in any time period, of all cash receipts, expenses, and investments. Also called cash proceeds or cash generated.

cash flow management—Syn: funds flow management.

cash flow statement—Syn: funds flow statement.

C

cash spin or free cash spin—The advantage of reducing inventory in the supply chain and reallocating the saved capital in a more profitable direction.

cash-to-cash cycle time—An indicator of how efficiently a company manages its assets to improve cash flow. Inventory days + accounts receivable days – accounts payable days = cash-to-cash cycle time. See: cash conversion cycle.

catalog channel—A facility that receives orders based on a published book of offerings and ships from its warehouse to the customer.

catchball—A business process of floating ideas and comments around in an iterative manner, much like tossing a ball back and forth.

categorical plan—A method of selecting and evaluating suppliers that considers input from many departments and functions within the buyer's organization and systematically categorizes that input. Engineering, production, quality assurance, and other functional areas evaluate all suppliers for critical factors within their respective scopes of responsibility. For example, engineering would develop a category evaluating suppliers' design flexibility. Rankings are developed across categories, performance ratings are obtained, and supplier selections are made. See: weighted-point plan.

category management—In marketing, an organizational structure giving managers responsibility for planning and implementing marketing systems for certain product lines.

causal forecast—A type of forecasting that uses cause-and-effect associations to predict and explain relationships between the independent and dependent variables. An example of a causal model is an econometric model used to explain the demand for housing starts based on consumer base, interest rates, personal incomes, and land availability.

cause-and-effect diagram—A tool for analyzing process dispersion. It is also referred to as the Ishikawa diagram (because Kaoru Ishikawa developed it) and the fishbone diagram (because the complete diagram resembles a fish skeleton). The diagram illustrates the main causes and subcauses leading to an effect (symptom). The cause-and-effect diagram is one of the seven tools of quality. Syn: fishbone chart, Ishikawa diagram.

caveat emptor—A Latin phrase meaning "Let the buyer beware." (i.e., the purchase is at the buyer's risk.)

c chart—A control chart for evaluating the stability of a process in terms of the count of events of a given classification occurring in a sample. Syn: count chart, number defective chart.

CCR—Abbreviation for capacity-constrained resource.

cell—A manufacturing or service unit consisting of a number of workstations and the materials transport mechanisms and storage buffers that interconnect them.

cellular layout—An equipment configuration to support cellular manufacturing.

cellular manufacturing—A manufacturing process that produces families of parts within a single line or cell of machines controlled by operators who work only within the line or cell.

center—In statistics, values near the middle of results from a process.

center-of-gravity approach—A methodology for locating distribution centers at approximately the location representing the minimum transportation costs between the plants, the distribution centers, and the markets.

center-of-gravity models—Syn: gravity models.

centralized authority—Limiting the ability to make decisions to a few managers.

centralized computer network—A network in which there is one computer (or possibly more) linked to all others in a given enterprise.

centralized dispatching—The organization of the dispatching function into one central location. This structure often involves the use of data collection devices for communication between the centralized dispatching function, which usually reports to the production control department, and the shop manufacturing departments.

centralized inventory control—Inventory decision making for all stockkeeping units exercised from one office or department for an entire company.

centralized marketing system—An organizational structure in which a central marketing group manages functionally divided areas, such as advertising, sales, and marketing research.

centralized purchasing—A system in which all purchasing decisions are made from a corporate purchasing office.

central limit theorem—A theorem that states that a distribution consisting of sample means can be assumed to be normally distributed, even if the population from which the samples are drawn is not normally distributed.

central point scheduling—A variant of scheduling that employs both forward and backward scheduling, starting from the scheduled start date of a particular operation.

central processing unit (CPU)—The electronic processing unit of a computer, where mathematical calculations are performed.

central storage—Using a central location for storing all inventory items in order to obtain more control of inventory and to improve inventory record accuracy.

CEP—Abbreviation for cost equalization point.

certificated carrier—A regulated for-hire air carrier that provides service under an operating certificate.

certificate of analysis—A certification of conformance to quality standards or specifications for products or materials. It may include a list or reference of analysis results and process information. It is often required for transfer of the custody of materials.

certificate of compliance—A supplier's certification that the supplies or services in question meet specified requirements.

certificate of origin—A document attesting to a shipment's country of origin.

certificate of public convenience and necessity—A certificate that grants authority to a particular carrier, enabling that carrier to act as a common carrier in serving and transporting commodities to a specific area.

certification—Documentation of competency by a supplier or by an organization, such as ISO 9000 certification. See: supplier certification, ISO 9000.

certification audits—Audits occurring within registration processes (e.g., for ISO 9000:2000).

Certified Fellow in Production and Inventory Management (CFPIM)—The APICS designation that is a recognition of superior knowledge and performance in contributing to the profession.

certified fixtures—The inspection models that conform to known specifications.

Certified in Integrated Resource Management (CIRM)—The APICS designation that is a recognition of a high level of professional knowledge in enterprise-wide processes and activities.

Certified in Production and Inventory Management (CPIM)—The APICS designation that is a recognition of a

high level of professional knowledge in production and inventory management.

Certified Purchasing Manager—1) Certification from The Institute for Supply Management (ISM), formerly NAPM. This is no longer being tested (C.P.M.). 2) Certification from the American Purchasing Society (CPM).

certified supplier—A status awarded to a supplier who consistently meets predetermined quality, cost, delivery, financial, and count objectives. Incoming inspection may not be required.

Certified Supply Chain Professional—The APICS designation that recognizes a high level of professional knowledge in supply chain management.

ceteris paribus—Latin for all other things being the same.

CFPIM—Abbreviation for Certified Fellow in Production and Inventory Management.

chain of customers—The sequence of customers who in turn consume the output of each other, forming a chain. For example, individuals are customers of a department store, which in turn is the customer of a producer, who is the customer of a material supplier.

chain reaction—A chain of events proposed by W. Edwards Deming: improve quality, and costs will go down because of less scrap and rework, while revenues will go up because the company will be able to sell more product at higher prices. Thus, better quality means more profitability.

champion—(1) In quality control, sponsor of a six sigma implementation project. (2) In general, sponsor of an improvement effort.

chance variation—Variation in process results occurring because of numerous small factors such as workers, equipment, raw material, work methods, and environmental differences.

change agent—A person who facilitates change within an organization. This person may or may not be within the organization and may or may not be the initiator of the change.

change control—The process of determining, approving, or rejecting changes to a plan baseline.

change management—The business process that coordinates and monitors all changes to the business processes and applications operated by the business as well as to their internal equipment, resources, operating systems, and procedures. The change management discipline is carried out in a way that minimizes the risk of problems that will affect the operating environment and service delivery to the users.

change order—A formal notification that a purchase order or shop order must be modified in some way. This change can result from modifications such as a revised quantity, date, or customer specification; an engineering change; or a change in inventory requirement date.

changeover—Syn: setup.

changeover costs—Syn: setup costs.

changeover flexibility—Syn: setup flexibility.

change request—An application to change scopes of work, budgets, and/or schedules.

channel—1) In queuing theory, a line for waiting. 2) In distribution, a route from raw materials through consumption. See: distribution channel, marketing channel.

channel conflict—Two or more agencies of one business competing for the same customer. For example, retail, catalog, or web sales.

channel equity—Important affiliations between suppliers and purchasers that improve value for everyone.

channel integration—Strengthening relationships up and down the supply chain from suppliers' suppliers to customers' customers.

channel partners—Suppliers, manufacturers, distributors, and retailers who form a supply chain to make and distribute a set of products.

channels of distribution—Any series of firms or individuals that participates in the flow of goods and services from the raw material supplier and producer to the final user or consumer. See: distribution channel.

charge—The initial loading of ingredients or raw materials into a processor, such as a reactor, to begin the manufacturing process.

chargeback provisions—Contractual terms specifying how a company may charge a supplier for failure to perform.

charge ticket—A document used for receiving goods and charging those goods to an operating cost center.

chart of accounts—In accounting, a list of general ledger accounts used to track costs, revenues, assets, liabilities, and so on by category.

chase-demand strategy—Syn: chase production method.

chase production method—A production planning method that maintains a stable inventory level while vary-

ing production to meet demand. Companies may combine chase and level production schedule methods. Syn: chase strategy, chase-demand strategy.

chase strategy—Syn: chase production method.

check digit—A digit added to each number in a coding system that allows for detection of errors in the recording of the code numbers. Through the use of the check digit and a predetermined mathematical formula, recording errors such as digit reversal or omission can be discovered.

checking—Verifying and documenting the order selection in terms of both product number and quantity.

checklist—A tool used to ensure that important steps or actions in an operation have been taken. Checklists contain items that are important or relevant to an issue or situation.

check sheet—A simple data-recording device. The check sheet is designed by the user to facilitate the user's interpretation of the results. The check sheet is one of the seven tools of quality. Check sheets are often confused with data sheets and checklists

churn—The process of customers changing their buying preferences because they find better and/or cheaper products and services elsewhere. The internet makes it easy for customers to shop electronically in search of a better deal.

churn reduction—Not losing as many customers to the competition.

CIF—Abbreviation for cost, insurance, freight.

CIM—Acronym for computer-integrated manufacturing.

CIRM—Acronym for Certified in Integrated Resource Management.

CISG—Abbreviation for contracts for the international sale of goods.

city driver—A delivery person who drives a local route, as opposed to long-haul route.

claim—A charge made against a company because of loss or damage.

classification—The designation of the job function that an employee is assigned to and is proficient in—for example, assembler, machinist, or welder.

classification of defects—The delineation of possible defects on a unit, classified by seriousness: critical (A), major (B), minor (C), or incidental (D).

clean technology—A technical measure taken to reduce or eliminate at the source the production of any nuisance, pollution, or waste and to help save raw materials, natural resources, and energy.

cleanup—The neutralizing of the effects of production just completed. It may involve cleaning residues, sanitation, equipment refixturing, and so on.

clearinghouse—An entity restricted to providing services such as settling accounts.

clerical/administration—Several related activities necessary for the organization's operation, generally including but not limited to the following: updating records and files based on receipts, shipments, and adjustments; maintaining labor and equipment records; and performing locating, order consolidation, correspondence preparation, and similar activities.

clicks and mortar—Refers to a brick and mortar company that also has succeeded in making online sales. Ant: bricks and mortar.

clickstream—The way a customer moves through a website.

client—In information systems, a software program that is used to contact and obtain data from a server program on another computer. Each client program is designed to work with one or more specific kinds of server programs, and each server requires a specific kind of client. A browser is one type of client.

client/server system—A distributed computing system in which work is assigned to the computer best able to perform it from among a network of computers.

CLIN—Abbreviation for contract line items number.

clock card—Syn: time card.

closed-loop feedback system—A planning and control system that monitors system progress toward the plan and has an internal control and replanning capability.

closed-loop MRP—A system built around material requirements planning that includes the additional planning processes of production planning (sales and operations planning), master production scheduling, and capacity requirements planning. Once this planning phase is complete and the plans have been accepted as realistic and attainable, the execution processes come into play. These processes include the manufacturing control processes of input-output (capacity) measurement, detailed scheduling and dispatching, as well as anticipated delay reports from both the plant and suppliers, supplier scheduling, and so on. The term closed loop implies not only that each of these processes is included in the overall system, but also

that feedback is provided by the execution processes so that the planning can be kept valid at all times.

closed period—The accounting time period for which the adjusting and closing entries have been posted. Ant: open period.

closely held—A description of an organization owned by a small number of people.

closeness ratings—In layout analysis, to begin yielding. In layout analysis, measures of how beneficial it would be for one department to be located near another.

cloud computing—An emerging way of computing where data is stored in massive data centers which can be accessed from any connected computers over the internet.

CMI—Abbreviation for co-managed inventory.

CNC—Abbreviation for computer numerical control.

co-design—Syn: participative design/engineering.

co-destiny—The evolution of a supply chain from intra-organizational management to interorganizational management.

coefficient of correlation—A value used to express the relationship between two variables, whether there is a strong or weak correlation. The coefficient of correlation varies from 0 to 1 with values close to 0 indicating no relationship, or a weak relationship, and values close to 1 indicating a strong relationship. The existence of a relationship does not prove causality.

coefficient of determination—Used to measure the expected accuracy of a forecast; measures the variation in one variable due to a different variable.

coefficient of variation—In statistics, the ratio of the standard deviation to the mean for a particular process.

COFC—Abbreviation for container on a railroad flatcar.

cold chain—A term referring to the storage, transfer, and supply chain of temperature-controlled products. Industries in the cold chain include food and agriculture, pharmaceuticals, and chemicals.

collaboration—Joint work among people to achieve common business objectives.

collaborative forecasting—The process for collecting and reconciling information from within and outside the organization to come up with a single projection of demand.

collaborative planning—Syn: collaborative planning, forecasting, and replenishment.

collaborative planning, forecasting, and replenishment (CPFR)—1) A collaboration process whereby supply chain trading partners can jointly plan key supply chain activities from production and delivery of raw materials to production and delivery of final products to end customers. Collaboration encompasses business planning, sales forecasting, and all operations required to replenish raw materials and finished goods. 2) A process philosophy for facilitating collaborative communications. CPFR is considered a standard, endorsed by the Voluntary Interindustry Commerce Standards. Syn: collaborative planning.

collaborative supply relationship—Syn: supplier partnership.

collaborative transportation management—A method of sharing information among suppliers, buyers, and transporters to add value to the service.

collective bargaining—A highly regulated system established to control conflict between labor and management. It defines and specifies the rules and procedures of initiating, negotiating, maintaining, changing, and terminating the labor-management relationship.

co-location—Placing project team members in physical proximity to facilitate communication and working relationships.

co-managed inventory (CMI)—Continuous replenishment where the manufacture is responsible for managing the inventory of standard merchandise and the retailer manages promotional items.

combined lead time—Syn: cumulative lead time.

commercial invoice—An official document indicating the names of the seller and buyer, the product being shipped, and its value. The document is provided by the seller.

commercial-off-the-shelf (COTS)—A term describing computer software made available for sale by commercial developers.

commercial speech—Communication that is primarily for a business purpose. Such speech is protected under the First Amendment to the U.S. Constitution but less so than is noncommercial speech.

committed capability—The portion of the production capability that is currently in use or is scheduled for use.

commodity—An item that is traded in commerce. The term usually implies an undifferentiated product competing primarily on price and availability.

commodity buying—Grouping like parts or materials under one buyer's control for the procurement of all requirements to support production.

commodity procurement strategy—The purchasing plan for a family of items. This would include the plan to manage the supplier base and solve problems.

commonality—A condition where given raw materials or ingredients are used in multiple parents.

common carrier—Transportation available to the public that does not provide special treatment to any one party and is regulated as to the rates charged, the liability assumed, and the service provided. A common carrier must obtain a certificate of public convenience and necessity from the Federal Trade Commission for interstate traffic. Ant: private carrier.

common carrier duties—The requirements of common carriers to offer reasonable services and rates and to avoid discrimination.

common causes—Causes of variation that are inherent in a process over time. They affect every outcome of the process and everyone working in the process. Syn: random cause. See: assignable cause, assignable variation, common cause variability.

common cause variability—The variability in product quality that results from numerous uncontrollable everyday factors, such as temperature, humidity, and tool wear. Syn: common variation. See: common causes.

common cost—A cost that is incurred by the business as a whole.

common law—Law flowing from judicial decisions over the years rather than from legislative action.

common material—Readily available items used in industry that require no special handling.

common parts bill—Syn: common parts bill of material.

common parts bill of material—A type of planning bill that groups common components for a product or family of products into one bill of material, structured to a pseudoparent item number. Syn: common parts bill.

common-size income statement—In accounting, an income statement having values expressed as a percentage of sales rather than dollar values.

common variation—Syn: common cause variability.

communication management plan—A document that describes the communications needs and expectations within a project, including format, dates, locations, and responsibilities.

company culture—A system of values, beliefs, and behaviors inherent in a company. To optimize business performance, top management must define and create the necessary culture.

compensation—The pay and benefits given for services rendered to an organization.

compensation laws—Laws designed to pay employees for injuries sustained on the job.

competitive advantage—The advantage a company has over its rivals in attracting customers and defending against competitors. Sources of the advantage include characteristics that a competitor cannot duplicate without substantial cost and risk, such as a manufacturing technique, brand name, or human skill set. Syn: competitive edge.

competitive analysis—An analysis of a competitor that includes its strategies, capabilities, prices, and costs.

competitive benchmarking—Benchmarking a product or service against competitors. Syn: performance benchmarking. See: benchmarking.

competitive bid—A price offering by one company that a buyer will consider along with price offerings from other companies.

competitive differentiator—A characteristic that makes a company or product unique within a marketplace.

competitive edge—Syn: competitive advantage.

competitive intelligence—The information required to conduct a competitive analysis about external events and trends that can affect a company's plans.

complete and on-time delivery (COTD)—A metric defining customer service. To be considered as complete and on time, all items in the order—in the correct quantity and with the correct line items—must arrive on time.

component—The raw material, part, or subassembly that goes into a higher level assembly, compound, or other item. This term may also include packaging materials for finished items. See: ingredient, intermediate part.

component availability—The availability of component inventory for the manufacture of a specific parent order or group of orders or schedules.

component lead-time offset—Syn: lead-time offset.

composite lead time—Syn: cumulative lead time.

composite manufacturing lead time—Syn: cumulative manufacturing lead time.

composite part—A part that represents operations common to a family or group of parts controlled by group technology. Tools, jigs, and dies are used for the composite part; therefore, any parts of that family can be processed with the same operations and tooling. The goal here is to reduce setup costs.

composite yield—A condition where loss occurs along several operations resulting in a decreased yield for the end item. Syn: cumulative yield.

composition—The makeup of an item, typically expressing chemical properties rather than physical properties.

compound interest—1) The type of interest that is periodically added to the amount of investment (or loan) so that subsequent interest is based on the cumulative amount. 2) The interest charges under the condition that interest is charged on any previous interest earned in any time period, as well as on the principal.

compound yield—The cumulative effect of yield loss at multiple operations within the manufacturing cycle.

comptroller—Syn: controller.

computer-aided design (CAD)—The use of computers in interactive engineering drawing and storage of designs. Programs complete the layout, geometric transformations, projections, rotations, magnifications, and interval (cross-section) views of a part and its relationship with other parts.

computer-aided engineering (CAE)—The process of generating and testing engineering specifications on a computer workstation.

computer-aided inspection and test (CAIT)—The use of computer technology in the inspection and testing of manufactured products.

computer-aided manufacturing (CAM)—The use of computers to program, direct, and control production equipment in the fabrication of manufactured items.

computer-aided process planning (CAPP)—A method of process planning in which a computer system assists in the development of manufacturing process plans (defining operation sequences, machine and tooling requirements, cut parameters, part tolerances, inspection criteria, and other items). Artificial intelligence and classification and coding systems may be used in the generation of the process plan.

computer-assisted software engineering (CASE)—The use of computerized tools to assist in the process of designing, developing, and maintaining software products and systems.

computer-integrated manufacturing (CIM)—The integration of the total manufacturing organization through the use of computer systems and managerial philosophies that improve the organization's effectiveness; the application of a computer to bridge various computerized systems and connect them into a coherent, integrated whole. For example, budgets, CAD/CAM, process controls, group technology systems, MRP II, and financial reporting systems are linked and interfaced.

computer numerical control (CNC)—A technique in which a machine tool controller uses a computer or microprocessor to store and execute numerical instructions.

concentration—The percentage of an active ingredient within the whole. For example, a 40 percent solution of hydrochloric acid.

concept phase—In project management, the first phase in which a project is defined and the scope is planned.

concurrency—Syn: resource contention.

concurrent design—Syn: participative design/ engineering.

concurrent engineering—Syn: participative design/ engineering.

conference room pilot—Simulation of all business processes from end-to-end within the new information system in a controlled environment.

confidence interval—The range on either side of an estimated value from a sample that is likely to contain the true value for the whole population.

confidence level—The probability that a particular value lies between an upper and a lower bound—the confidence limits.

confidence limit—The bounds of an interval. A probability can be given for the likelihood that the true value will lie between the confidence limits.

configuration—The arrangement of components as specified to produce an assembly.

configuration audit—A review of the product against the engineering specifications to determine whether the engineering documentation is accurate, up-to-date, and representative of the components, subsystems, or systems being produced.

configuration control—The function of ensuring that the product being built and shipped corresponds to the product that was designed and ordered. This means that the correct features, customer options, and engi-

neering changes have been incorporated and documented.

configuration management system—Formal procedures to identify and document the physical characteristics of a product or project, control changes, and support an audit to verify conformance.

configuration system—Syn: customer order servicing system.

configurator—Software system that creates, uses, and maintains product models that allow complete definition of all possible product options and variations with a minimum of data entries.

confirming order—A purchase order issued to a supplier, listing the goods or services and terms of an order placed orally or otherwise before the usual purchase document.

confiscation—The taking of property without adequate compensation for it.

conflict of interest—Any business activity, personal or company-related, that interferes with a company's goals or that entails unethical or illegal actions.

conformance—An affirmative indication or judgment that a product or service has met the requirements of a relevant specification, contract, or regulation.

conformance perspective—A measure of how closely a product or service performs to its intended quality.

connectivity—The ability to communicate effectively with supply chain partners to facilitate interorganization synchronization.

consideration—In contract law, an obligation that is to the detriment of one party (promisee) or to the benefit of the other party (promisor).

consigned stocks—Inventories, generally of finished goods, that are in the possession of customers, dealers, agents, and so on, but remain the property of the manufacturer by agreement with those in possession. Syn: consignment inventory, vendor-owned inventory. See: consignment.

consignee—The receiver of a shipment of freight.

consignment—1) A shipment that is handled by a common carrier. 2) The process of a supplier placing goods at a customer location without receiving payment until after the goods are used or sold. See: consigned stocks.

consignment inventory—Syn: consigned stocks. See: consignment.

consignor—The originator of a shipment of freight.

consolidation—Packages and lots that move from suppliers to a carrier terminal and are sorted and then combined with similar shipments from another supplier's container load or truckload for travel to a final destination. See: milk run.

consolidation warehouses—Collection points that receive less-than-truckload (LTL) shipments from regional sources and then ships in cargo load or truckload quantities to a manufacturing facility.

consolidator—A company that groups together various shipments or orders to facilitate movement.

consortia trade exchanges (CTX)—An online marketplace, usually owned by a third party, that allows members to trade with each other. This site lowers members search costs and enables lower prices for the buyer.

consortium—A group of companies that work together to jointly produce a product, service, or project.

constant—A quantity that has a fixed value. Ant: variable.

constrained optimization—Achieving the best possible solution to a problem in terms of a specified objective function and a given set of constraints.

constraint—1) Any element or factor that prevents a system from achieving a higher level of performance with respect to its goal. Constraints can be physical, such as a machine center or lack of material, but they can also be managerial, such as a policy or procedure. 2) One of a set of equations that cannot be violated in an optimization procedure.

constraint accounting—Syn: theory of constraints accounting.

constraint-oriented finite loading—A finite loading technique that plans orders around bottleneck work centers. The objective is to maximize total production throughput. Orders in small lot sizes aggregate into large lot sizes at the constraint and then load forward. Prior operations are then backward-scheduled, and downstream operations are forward-scheduled. See: drum-buffer-rope, order-oriented finite loading.

constraints management—The practice of managing resources and organizations in accordance with the theory of constraints (TOC) principles. See: theory of constraints.

constraint theory—Syn: theory of constraints.

consumables—Supplies or materials (such as paint, cleaning materials, or fuel) that are consumed or exhausted in the production or sale of a good or service. Syn: consumable tooling, supplies; expendables.

consumable tooling, supplies—Syn: consumables.

consumer—A person who purchases a good or service for his or her own use (not for resale). See: customer.

consumer durable goods—A division of durable goods for items intended for consumer use, such as refrigerators, as opposed to industrial goods, such as fork lifts. See: durable goods.

consumer market—A market composed of individuals and families who buy products and services for consumption. See: government market, industrial market, institutional market.

consumer price index—A measure of the overall level of prices. It attempts to relate the cost of buying a specific set of goods and services with the cost of buying the same set of goods and services during an earlier time period.

consumer's risk (ß)—For a given sampling plan, the probability of acceptance of a lot, the quality of which has designated numerical value representing a level that is worse than some threshold value. See: type II error.

consumer surplus—The difference between the highest price a consumer is willing to pay for a good or service and the price actually paid.

consuming the forecast—The process of reducing the forecast by customer orders or other types of actual demands as they are received. The adjustments yield the value of the remaining forecast for each period. Syn: forecast consumption.

consumption—The amount of each bill-of-material component used in the production process to make the parent.

contact efficiency—A measure of how well an organization transforms website hits into visits.

contactless—Using radio frequency identification or similar technologies to record data about an item electronically without physical contact with the item.

container—A large box in which commodities to be shipped are placed.

container design—The characteristics of the product that make it transportable with ease of handling and stowability. Container concepts include packaging, monetary density, and physical density.

containerization—A shipment method in which commodities are placed in containers, and after initial loading, the commodities per se are not rehandled in shipment until they are unloaded at the destination.

container on a flatcar (COFC)—A specialized form of containerization in which rail, motor, and sea transport coordinate.

content management applications—Supports the evolutionary life cycle of digital-based information and makes information dynamically updatable online; includes the ability to publish content to a repository and support access to digital-based content.

contestable market—A market having low entry costs.

contingency planning—A process for creating a document that specifies alternative plans to facilitate project success if certain risk events occur.

contingency reserve—A budget of money or time allowed over an initial estimate to reduce the likelihood of overruns.

contingent project—A project that can be accepted only if one or more other projects are accepted first. See: independent project, mutually exclusive project.

continuous flow distribution—A pull system diverting products in response to customer requirements while keeping distribution costs low.

continuous flow (production)—Syn: continuous production.

continuous improvement—The act of making incremental, regular improvements and upgrades to a process or product in the search for excellence.

continuous manufacturing—A type of manufacturing process that is dedicated to the production of a very narrow range of standard products. The rate of product change and new product information is very low. Significant investment in highly specialized equipment allows for a high volume of production at the lowest manufacturing cost. Thus, unit sales volumes are very large, and price is almost always a key order-winning criterion. Examples of items produced by a continuous process include gasoline, steel, fertilizer, glass, and paper. Syn: continuous production.

continuous process—Syn: continuous production.

continuous process control—The use of transducers (sensors) to monitor a process and make automatic changes in operations through the design of appropriate feedback control loops. Although such devices have historically been mechanical or electromechanical, there is now widespread use of microcomputers and centralized control.

continuous process improvement (CPI)—A never-ending effort to expose and eliminate root causes of problems: small-step improvement as opposed to big-step improvement. Syn: continuous improvement. See: kaizen.

continuous production—A production system in which the productive equipment is organized and sequenced according to the steps involved to produce the product. This term denotes that material flow is continuous during the production process. The routing of the jobs is fixed and setups are seldom changed. Syn: continuous flow (production), continuous process, continuous manufacturing. See: mass production, project manufacturing.

continuous replenishment—A process by which a supplier is notified daily of actual sales or warehouse shipments and commits to replenishing these sales (by size, color, and so on) without stockouts and without receiving replenishment orders. The result is a lowering of associated costs and an improvement in inventory turnover. See: rapid replenishment, vendor-managed inventory.

continuous review system—The inventory level on-hand and on-order for this system is checked whenever a change in inventory level occurs and when the reorder point is reached a restocking order is released. See: fixed reorder cycle inventory model.

continuous variable—A variable, such as height, temperature, or weight, that can be measured along a continuous scale. See: discrete variable.

contract—An agreement between two or more competent persons or companies to perform or not to perform specific acts or services or to deliver merchandise. A contract may be oral or written. A purchase order, when accepted by a supplier, becomes a contract. Acceptance may be in writing or by performance, unless the purchase order requires acceptance in writing.

contract accounting—The function of collecting costs incurred on a given job or contract, usually in a progress payment situation. Certain U.S. government contracting procedures require contract accounting.

contract administration—Managing all aspects of a contract to guarantee that the contractor fulfills his obligations.

contract carrier—A carrier that does not serve the general public, but provides transportation for hire for one or a limited number of shippers under a specific contract.

contract date—The date when a contract is accepted by all parties.

contract labor—Self-employed individuals or firms contracted by an organization to perform specific services on an intermittent or short-term basis.

contract line items number (CLIN)—Specific items that are priced separately on a contract.

contract manufacturing—A situation in which a third party makes products that are packaged under another company's label.

contract pegging—Syn: full pegging.

contract reporting—Reporting of and the accumulation of finished production against commitments to a customer.

contracts for the international sale of goods (CISG)—Govern the sale of goods in the international environment. They enable exporters to avoid choice-of-law issues.

contract target cost—The estimated cost negotiated in a contract.

contribution—The difference between sales price and variable costs. Contribution is used to cover fixed costs and profits.

contribution margin—An amount equal to the difference between sales revenue and variable costs.

contribution margin pricing—A method of setting prices based on the contribution margin. It provides a ceiling and a floor between which the price setter operates. The ceiling is the target selling price—what the seller would like to get—and the floor is the total variable costs of the product using traditional accounting.

contribution relativities—An investment by one stakeholder may benefit others in the supply chain.

contributory negligence—A rule under which a defendant may escape liability if it can be shown that the plaintiff was negligent to some extent.

control—Comparing actual to planned performance and taking corrective action, as needed, to align performance with plan.

control board—A visual means of showing machine loading or project planning, usually a variation of the basic Gantt chart. Syn: dispatch(ing) board, planning board, schedule board. See: schedule chart.

control center—In a centralized dispatching operation, the place at which the dispatching is done.

control chart—A graphic comparison of process performance data with predetermined computed control limits. The process performance data usually consist of groups of measurements selected in regular sequence of production that preserve the order. The primary use of control charts is to detect assignable causes of variation in the process as opposed to random variations. The control chart is one of the seven tools of quality. Syn: process control chart.

control decision—A decision about the planning or controlling of daily operations.

controllable cost—A cost that is under the direct control of a given level of management.

controlled access—Fenced or walled areas within a warehouse or yard usually monitored by security cameras. These areas are used to store high-value items.

controlled issue—Syn: planned issue.

controller—The person responsible for financial and managerial accounting within a company. Syn: comptroller.

control limit—A statistically determined line on a control chart (upper control limit or lower control limit). If a value occurs outside of this limit, the process is deemed to be out of control.

control number—Typically, the manufacturing order or schedule number used to identify a specific instance or period of production.

control phase—One of the six sigma phases of quality. Process performance is observed, often with control charts, for steady results.

control points—In the theory of constraints, strategic locations in the logical product structure for a product or family that simplify the planning, scheduling, and control functions. Control points include gating operations, convergent points, divergent points, constraints, and shipping points. Detailed scheduling instructions are planned, implemented, and monitored at these locations. Other work centers are instructed to "work if they have work; otherwise, be prepared for work." In this manner, materials flow rapidly through the facility without detailed work center scheduling and control.

control system—A system that has as its primary function the collection and analysis of feedback from a given set of functions for the purpose of controlling the functions. Control may be implemented by monitoring or systematically modifying parameters or policies used in those functions, or by preparing control reports that initiate useful action with respect to significant deviations and exceptions.

convergent point—An operation in a production process where multiple materials/parts/components are combined into a single component. An assembly operation is an example of a convergent point.

conversion efficiency—In e-commerce, a measure of how well an organization transforms visits to its website into customer orders. See: attractability efficiency.

convertible security—An asset (stock or bond) that may be changed for another asset at the owner's request.

conveyor—A device following a fixed route that has the capability of moving material between points in a facility. This device commonly is used when there is a high volume of flow along the route.

cooperative training—An educational process in which students alternate formal studies with actual on-the-job experience. Successful completion of the off-campus experience may be a prerequisite for graduation from the program of study.

co-product—A product that is usually manufactured together or sequentially because of product or process similarities. See: by-product.

core competencies—Bundles of skills or knowledge sets that enable a firm to provide the greatest level of value to its customers in a way that is difficult for competitors to emulate and that provides for future growth. Core competencies are embodied in the skills of the workers and in the organization. They are developed through collective learning, communication, and commitment to work across levels and functions in the organization and with the customers and suppliers. For example, a core competency could be the capability of a firm to coordinate and harmonize diverse production skills and multiple technologies. To illustrate, advanced casting processes for making steel require the integration of machine design with sophisticated sensors to track temperature and speed, and the sensors require mathematical modeling of heat transfer. For rapid and effective development of such a process, materials scientists must work closely with machine designers, software engineers, process specialists, and operating personnel. Core competencies are not directly related to the product or market.

core process—That unique capability that is central to a company's competitive strategy.

core team—A cross-functional team of specialists formed to manage new product introduction. See: cross-functional team.

corporate culture—The set of important assumptions that members of the company share. It is a system of shared values about what is important and beliefs about how the company works. These common assumptions influence the ways the company operates.

corporate purchasing cards—Syn: procurement credit card.

corrective action—The implementation of solutions resulting in the reduction or elimination of an identified problem.

corrective maintenance—The maintenance required to restore an item to a satisfactory condition.

correlated demands—Demands that consistently vary in the same direction because of the relationship between the items demanded.

correlation—The relationship between two sets of data such that when one changes, the other is likely to make a corresponding change. If the changes are in the same direction, there is positive correlation. When changes tend to occur in opposite directions, there is negative correlation. When there is little correspondence or random changes, there is no correlation.

correlation coefficient—A measure of the degree of correlation between two values, which has a range from -1 to 1.

cost accounting—The branch of accounting that is concerned with recording and reporting business operating costs. It includes the reporting of costs by departments, activities, and products.

cost allocation—The assignment of costs that cannot be directly related to production activities via more measurable means (e.g., assigning corporate expenses to different products via direct labor costs or hours).

cost analysis—A review and an evaluation of actual or anticipated cost data.

cost-based contract—A type of purchasing contract where the price of goods or services is tied to the cost of key inputs or other economic factors, such as interest rates.

cost-benefit ratio—A ratio of total measurable benefits to the initial capital cost. This might be used in deciding which projects to pursue in a continuous improvement effort.

cost-budgeting—In project management, accumulating the estimated costs of individual activities to arrive at a cost baseline.

cost center—The smallest segment of an organization for which costs are collected and formally reported, typically a department. The criteria in defining cost centers are that the cost be significant and that the area of responsibility be clearly defined. A cost center is not necessarily identical to a work center; normally, a cost center encompasses more than one work center, but this may not always be the case.

cost control—Applying procedures that monitor the progress of operations against authorized budgets, and taking action to achieve minimal costs.

cost driver—Syn: driver (first definition).

cost driver analysis—In activity-based cost accounting, the examination of the impact of cost drivers. The results of this analysis are useful in the continuous improvement of cost, quality, and delivery times.

costed bill of material—A form of bill of material that extends the quantity per of every component in the bill by the cost of the components.

cost element—In activity-based cost accounting, the lowest subdivision of a resource, activity, or cost object.

cost engineer—An engineer whose judgment and experience are used in the application of scientific principles and techniques to problems of cost estimation and cost control in business planning, profitability analysis, project management and production planning, scheduling, and control.

cost estimation—(1) Specification of the relationship between cost and the underlying cost drivers. (2) In project management, creating an approximation of the resources and associated costs needed to complete a project.

cost equalization point (CEP)—A point or quantity at which the cost curves of two manufacturing methods have an equal value.

cost, insurance, freight (CIF)—A freight term indicating that the seller is responsible for cost, the marine insurance, and the freight charges on an ocean shipment of goods.

cost management—Control of activities to eliminate waste, improve cost drivers, and plan operations. This process should affect the organization's setting of strategy. Factors such as product pricing, introduction of new products, and distribution of existing products are examples of strategic decisions that are affected by cost management.

cost object—In activity-based cost accounting, anything for which a separate cost measurement is desirable. This may include a product, a customer, a project, or other work unit.

cost object driver—In activity-based cost accounting, a numerical measure of the demand placed on one cost object by other cost objects.

cost of capital—The cost of maintaining a dollar of capital invested for a certain period, normally one year. This cost is normally expressed as a percentage and may be based on factors such as the average expected return on alternative investments and current bank interest rate for borrowing.

cost of goods sold—An accounting classification useful for determining the amount of direct materials, direct labor, and allocated overhead associated with the products sold during a given period of time. See: cost of sales.

cost of lost sales—Profit that is foregone because of a stock-out situation.

cost of poor quality—The cost associated with providing poor quality products or services. There are four categories of costs: (1) internal failure costs (costs associated with defects found before the customer receives the product or service); (2) external failure costs (costs associated with defects found after the customer receives the product or service); (3) appraisal costs (costs incurred to determine the degree of conformance to quality requirements); and (4) prevention costs (costs incurred to keep failure and appraisal costs to a minimum). Syn: cost of quality.

cost of quality—Syn: cost of poor quality.

cost of sales—The total cost attached (allocated) to units of finished product delivered to customers during the period. See: cost of goods sold.

cost performance index (CPI)—A measure of project efficiency. Earned value over actual costs.

cost-plus contract—A pricing method where the buyer agrees to pay the seller all the acceptable costs of the product or service up to a maximum cost plus a fixed fee. Syn: cost-type contract.

cost-plus-fixed-fee contract—A contract in which the seller is paid for costs specified as allowable in the contract plus a stipulated fixed fee.

cost-plus-incentive-fee contract—A contract in which the seller is paid for costs specified as allowable in the contract plus a profit provided certain provisions are met.

C

C

cost pool—In activity-based cost accounting, an aggregation of resources assigned to activities or activities assigned to cost objects. Items may be aggregated or disaggregated depending on how the data are to be used.

cost-ratio plan—A variation of the weighted-point plan of supplier evaluation and selection. The cost ratio is obtained by dividing the bid price by the weighted scores determined by the weighted-point plan. This procedure determines the true costs by taking into account compensating factors. Suppliers are selected and/or evaluated based on the lowest cost ratio.

cost reduction—The act of lowering the cost of goods or services by securing a lower price, reducing labor costs, and so forth. In cost reduction, the item usually is not changed, but the circumstances around which the item is secured are changed—as opposed to value analysis, in which the item itself is actually changed to produce a lower cost.

cost tradeoff—Considering the advantages and disadvantages of one method to another, such as different avenues of distribution or providing customer service.

cost-type contract—Syn: cost-plus contract.

cost variance—In cost accounting, the difference between what has been budgeted for an activity and what it actually costs.

cost-volume-profit analysis—The study of how profits change with various levels of output and selling price.

COTD—Abbreviation for complete and on-time delivery.

COTS—Abbreviation for commercial-off-the-shelf.

Council of Supply Chain Management Professionals (CSCMP)—A not-for-profit worldwide organization of logistics and supply chain managers. It provides educational opportunities through a variety of activities.

counseling—The providing of basic, technical, and sometimes professional human assistance to employees to help them with personal and work-related problems.

count chart—Syn: c chart.

counterpurchase—When an exporter buys unrelated goods or services from an importer.

countertrade—Any transaction in which partial or full payment is made with goods instead of money. This often applies in international trade.

count frequency—The number of times an item in inventory is counted during a period of time. Generally, high-value inventories are counted more frequently than low-value items, although properties other than value can influence the frequency.

count-per-unit chart—Syn: U chart.

count point—A point in a flow of material or sequence of operations at which parts, subassemblies, or assemblies are counted as being complete. Count points may be designated at the ends of lines or upon removal from a work center, but most often they are designated as the points at which material transfers from one department to another. Syn: pay point.

coupon—A promotional device offering special savings when a product is purchased.

C_p—A widely used process capability index. It is calculated by dividing the difference between the upper specification limit (USL) and the lower specification limit (LSL) by 6 times the standard deviation (s) or

$$C_p = \frac{\text{upper specification limit (USL)} - \text{lower specification limit (LSL)}}{6s}$$

CPFR—Abbreviation for collaborative planning, forecasting, and replenishment.

CPI—1) Abbreviation for continuous process improvement. 2) Abbreviation for cost performance index.

CPIM—Abbreviation for Certified in Production and Inventory Management.

C_{pk}—An index method of the variability of a process. A widely used process capability index. It is expressed as:

$$C_{pk} = \frac{m - \text{nearer specification unit}}{3s}$$

where m is the mean and s is the standard deviation.

CPM—Abbreviation for critical path method.

C.P.M.—Abbreviation for Certified Purchasing Manager.

CPOF—Abbreviation for capacity planning using overall factors.

CPU—Abbreviation for central processing unit.

cranes and hoists—Equipment capable of moving items up and down or side to side.

crashing—In project management, adding resources to critical path or near-critical path activities on a project to shorten project duration after analyzing the project to identify the most cost-effective course of action.

credit period—The time allowed a customer to pay an invoice in full.

crew size—The number of people required to perform an operation. The associated standard time should represent the total time for all crew members to perform the operation, not the net start to finish time for the crew.

crew-size standard—A labor estimate of the number of workers necessary to complete the required output for a given shift.

critical activity—Any activity on the critical path of a project; an activity with no slack time (i.e., any delay in the activity will delay project completion). See: critical path, critical path method.

critical chain—The longest sequence of dependent events through a project network, considering both technical and resource dependencies in completing the project. The critical chain is the constraint of a project.

critical chain method—In the theory of constraints, a network planning technique for the analysis of a project's completion time, used for planning and controlling project activities. The critical chain, which determines project duration, is based on technological and resource constraints. Strategic buffering of paths and resources is used to increase project completion success. See: critical chain, critical path method.

critical characteristics—The attributes of a product that must function properly to avoid the failure of the product. Syn: functional requirements.

critical failure—The malfunction of those parts that are essential for continual operation or the safety of the user.

critical mass—Individuals who add value to the product or service. These individuals include personnel working directly on the product, personnel providing a service to the customer, and personnel who provide support for the product or service (e.g., after-sale service).

critical path—The longest sequence of activities through a network. The critical path defines the planned project duration. See: critical activity, critical path method.

critical path activity—In project management, any activity on a network's critical path as determined by the critical path method.

critical path lead time—Syn: cumulative lead time.

critical path method (CPM)—A network planning technique for the analysis of a project's completion time used for planning and controlling the activities in a project. By showing each of these activities and their associated times, the critical path, which identifies those elements that actually constrain the total time for the project, can be determined. See: critical chain method, network analysis, critical activity, critical path.

critical point backflush—Backflush performed at a specific point in the manufacturing process, at a critical op-

eration, or at an operation where key components are consumed.

critical processes—Processes that have large potential for loss—either money, property, or human life.

critical process parameters—A variable or a set of variables that dominates the other variables. Focusing on these variables will yield the greatest return in investment in quality control and improvement.

critical ratio—A dispatching rule that calculates a priority index number by dividing the time to due date remaining by the expected elapsed time to finish the job. For example,

$$\text{critical ratio} = \frac{\text{time remaining}}{\text{work remaining}} = \frac{30}{40} = .75$$

A ratio less than 1.0 indicates the job is behind schedule, a ratio greater than 1.0 indicates the job is ahead of schedule, and a ratio of 1.0 indicates the job is on schedule.

critical success factor—One of a few organizational objectives whose achievement should be sufficient for organizational success.

critical-to-quality characteristics (CTQs)—Critical-to-quality characteristics (CTQs) are the important and measurable traits of a product or process whose performance targets must be met to satisfy the customer. They adjust improvement efforts to meet consumer requirements. CTQs represent customer expectations for a product.

critical value analysis—A modified ABC analysis where a subjective metric of the criticality of an item is assigned to each item.

CRM—Abbreviation for customer relationship management and customer relations management.

cross-docking—The concept of packing products on the incoming shipments so they can be easily sorted at intermediate warehouses or for outgoing shipments based on final destination. The items are carried from the incoming vehicle docking point to the outgoing vehicle docking point without being stored in inventory at the warehouse. Cross-docking reduces inventory investment and storage space requirements. Syn: direct loading.

cross-functional integration—Thread that weaves the entire organization and manufacturing process into one fabric in which each of the different parts serves and supports the whole. See: integrated enterprise.

cross-functional organization—Organization where groups of directors, executives, and managers with a diversity of skills and backgrounds work on problems outside the bounds of their functional responsibilities. See: integrated enterprise.

cross-functional team—A set of individuals from various departments assigned a specific task such as implementing new computer software. See: core team.

cross plot—Syn: scatter chart.

cross-selling—Occurs when customers buy additional products or services after the initial purchase.

cross-shipment—Material flow activity where materials are shipped to customers from a secondary shipping point rather than from a preferred shipping point.

cross-sourcing—A method of sourcing that uses one supplier in one area of business for a product or service and uses a different supplier in a different area of business for similar products or services. The suppliers can then compete for future business.

cross-subsidy—In activity-based cost accounting, the situation of assigning too much or too little cost to a cost object. This may lead to poor decision making relative to the economic goals of the organization.

cross-training—Providing training or experience in several different areas (e.g., training an employee on several machines). Cross-training provides backup workers in case the primary operator is unavailable.

CRP—Abbreviation for capacity requirements planning.

CRT—Abbreviation for current reality tree.

CSCMP—Abbreviation for Council of Supply Chain Management Professionals.

CSCP—Abbreviation for Certified Supply Chain Professional.

CSR—Abbreviation for customer service representative.

CTP—Abbreviation for capable-to-promise.

CTQs—Abbreviation for critical-to-quality characteristics

cubage—Cubic volume of space being used or available for shipping or storage.

cube utilization—In warehousing, a measurement of the utilization of the total storage capacity of a vehicle or warehouse.

cubic space—In warehousing, a measurement of space available or required in transportation and warehousing.

cultural environment—The sociocultural factors of the organization's external environment. It includes values,

work ethics, education, religion, and consumer and ecological factors.

cumulative available-to-promise—A calculation based on the available-to-promise (ATP) figure in the master schedule. Two methods of computing the cumulative available-to-promise are used, with and without look-ahead calculation. The cumulative with look-ahead ATP equals the ATP from the previous period plus the MPS of the period minus the backlog of the period minus the sum of the differences between the backlogs and MPSs of all future periods until, but not to include, the period where point production exceeds the backlogs. The cumulative without look-ahead procedure equals the ATP in the previous period plus the MPS, minus the backlog in the period being considered. See: available-to-promise.

cumulative lead time—The longest planned length of time to accomplish the activity in question. It is found by reviewing the lead time for each bill of material path below the item; whichever path adds up to the greatest number defines cumulative lead time. Syn: aggregate lead time, combined lead time, composite lead time, critical path lead time, stacked lead time. See: planning horizon, planning time fence.

cumulative manufacturing lead time—The cumulative planned lead time when all purchased items are assumed to be in stock. Syn: composite manufacturing lead time.

cumulative MRP—The planning of parts and subassemblies by exploding a master schedule, as in MRP, except that the master-scheduled items and therefore the exploded requirements are time phased in cumulative form. Usually these cumulative figures cover a planning year.

cumulative receipts—A cumulative number, or running total, as a count of parts received in a series or sequence of shipments. The cumulative receipts provide a number that can be compared with the cumulative figures from a plan developed by cumulative MRP.

cumulative sum—The accumulated total of all forecast errors, both positive and negative. This sum will approach zero if the forecast is unbiased. Syn: sum of deviations.

cumulative sum control chart—A control chart on which the plotted value is the cumulative sum of deviations of successive samples from a target value. The ordinate of each plotted point represents the algebraic sum of the previous ordinate and the most recent deviations from the target.

cumulative system—A method for planning and controlling production that makes use of cumulative MRP, cumulative requirements, and cumulative counts.

cumulative trauma disorder—An occupational injury believed to be caused by repetitive motions such as typing or twisting.

cumulative yield—Syn: cascading yield loss, composite yield.

current assets—An accounting/financial term (balance sheet classification of accounts) representing the short-term resources owned by a company, including cash, accounts receivable, and inventories. See: assets, balance sheet.

current cost—1) The current or replacement cost of labor, material, or overhead. Its computation is based on current performance or measurements, and it is used to address today's costs before production as a revision of annual standard costs. 2) An asset's value based on the cost of an identical asset purchased today.

current finish time—In project management, the present estimate of an activity's finish time.

current liabilities—The debts owed by a company and expected to be paid within 12 months. See: liabilities, balance sheet.

current price—The price currently being paid as opposed to standard cost.

current ratio—Current assets divided by current liabilities.

current reality tree (CRT)—A logic-based tool for using cause-and-effect relationships to determine root problems that cause the observed undesirable effects of the system. See: root cause analysis.

current start date—In project management, the present estimate of an activity's start date.

curve fitting—An approach to forecasting based on a straight line, polynomial, or other curve that describes some historical time series data.

customer—1) A person or organization receiving a good, service, or information. See: external customer, internal customer. 2) In project management, every project has a customer who may be internal or external to the organization and who is responsible for the final project acceptance.

customer acquisition—In marketing, the rate at which new customers are switching to an organization's brand.

customer-as-participant—A service system that contains a high level of customer involvement in part of the service delivery.

customer-as-product—A service system designed to actually perform the service on the customer, such as in health care or hair salons.

customer contact centers—Centers that combine phone centers and web contact services to enable customers to contact the center 24 hours a day via phone, web, or email.

customer convergence—An internet-based marketing concept in which organizations must provide descriptions of the goods and services they offer so that potential customers locate or converge on the appropriate websites.

customer coproduction—The customer is part of the service delivery process. For example, in grocery stores customers often have the option to use the self checkout.

customer defection analysis—Analyzing the customers who have stopped buying to determine why.

customer-defined attributes—The characteristics of a good or service that are viewed as being important in addressing the needs of the customer. See: house of quality.

customer driven—A company's consideration of customer wants and desires in deciding what is produced and its quality.

customer facing—A hardware or software product, technology, or any thing or person that a business's customer deals with directly.

customer order—An order from a customer for a particular product or a number of products. It is often referred to as an actual demand to distinguish it from a forecasted demand. See: booked orders.

customer/order fulfillment process—A series of customers' interactions with an organization through the order filling process, including product/service design, production and delivery, and order status reporting.

customer order promising—Syn: order promising.

customer order servicing system—An automated system for order entry, where orders are keyed into a local terminal and a bill-of-material translator converts the catalog ordering numbers into required manufacturing part numbers and due dates for the MRP system. Advanced systems contain customer information, sales history, forecasting information, and product option compatibility checks to facilitate order processing, "cleaning up" orders before placing a demand on the manufacturing system. Syn: configuration system, sales order - configuration.

customer partner—A customer organization with which a company has formed a customer-supplier partnership. See: outpartnering.

customer partnership—Syn: customer-supplier partnership.

customer profitability—Estimating the profit retained on business with a specific customer.

customer relationship management (CRM)—A marketing philosophy based on putting the customer first. The collection and analysis of information designed for sales and marketing decision support (as contrasted to enterprise resources planning information) to understand and support existing and potential customer needs. It includes account management, catalog and order entry, payment processing, credits and adjustments, and other functions. Syn: customer relations management.

customer relations management (CRM)—Syn: customer relationship management.

customer satisfaction—The results of delivering a good or service that meets customer requirements.

customer segmentation—The practice of dividing a customer base into groups of individuals that are similar in specific ways relevant to marketing. Traditional segmentation focuses on identifying customer groups based on demographics and attributes such as attitude and psychological profiles.

customer service—1) The ability of a company to address the needs, inquiries, and requests from customers. 2) A measure of the delivery of a product to the customer at the time the customer specified.

customer service level—Syn: customer service ratio.

customer service life cycle—In information systems, a model that describes the relationship with a customer as having four phases: requirements, acquisition, ownership, and retirement.

customer service management process—A process that enables a business to offer post-purchase service and information to the customer.

customer service ratio—1) A measure of delivery performance of finished goods, usually expressed as a percentage. In a make-to-stock company, this percentage usually represents the number of items or dollars (on one or more customer orders) that were shipped on schedule for a specific time period, compared with the total that were supposed to be shipped in that time period. Syn: customer service level, fill rate, order-fill ratio, percent of fill. Ant: stockout percentage. 2) In a make-to-order company, it is usually some comparison of the number of jobs or dollars shipped in a given time period (e.g., a week) compared with the number of jobs or dollars that were supposed to be shipped in that time period.

customer service representative (CSR)—Personnel assigned to customer relations who answer customer questions and who provide technical support.

customer share—In marketing, a measurement (usually a percentage) of how many potential customers are attracted to a brand. It is a measurement of the recognition of the brand in the marketplace and the predisposition of the customer to buy the brand when presented with a choice of competing brands.

customer-supplier partnership—A long-term relationship between a buyer and a supplier characterized by teamwork and mutual confidence. The supplier is considered an extension of the buyer's organization. The partnership is based on several commitments. The buyer provides long-term contracts and uses fewer suppliers. The supplier implements quality assurance processes so that incoming inspection can be minimized. The supplier also helps the buyer reduce costs and improve product and process designs. Syn: customer partnership. See: outpartnering.

customer surveys—Devices such as interviews or questionnaires that aim to collect user data and preferences about product or service characteristics.

customer tolerance time—Syn: demand lead time.

custom product—A product that is made to meet the requirements of specific customers.

customs broker—A person who manages the paperwork required for international shipping and tracks and moves the shipments through the proper channels.

custom service—A service that is created to meet the requirements of specific customers.

cut-off control—A procedure for synchronizing cycle counting and transaction processing.

cwt—Abbreviation for hundredweight.

cybercash—The technology that enables online acceptance of credit cards, approving customers for payment before delivery is made.

cybermarketing—Any type of internet-based promotion. Many marketing managers use the term to refer to any type of computer-based marketing.

cybernetics—The study of control processes in mechanical, biological, electrical, and information systems.

cybernetic system—The information flow or information system (electronic, mechanical, logical) that controls an industrial process.

cyberspace—A common name encompassing both the internet and other forms of electronic communication.

cycle—1) The interval of time during which a system or process, such as seasonal demand or a manufacturing operation, periodically returns to similar initial conditions. 2) The interval of time during which an event or set of events is completed.

cycle counter—An individual who is assigned to do cycle counting.

cycle counting—An inventory accuracy audit technique where inventory is counted on a cyclic schedule rather than once a year. A cycle inventory count is usually taken on a regular, defined basis (often more frequently for high-value or fast-moving items and less frequently for low-value or slow-moving items). Most effective cycle counting systems require the counting of a certain number of items every workday with each item counted at a prescribed frequency. The key purpose of cycle counting is to identify items in error, thus triggering research, identification, and elimination of the cause of the errors.

cycle inventory—Syn: cycle stock.

cycle reduction stock—Stock held to reduce delivery time.

cycle service level—The probability of not having a stockout in any one ordering cycle, which begins at the time an order is placed and ends when the goods are placed in stock. Syn: measure of service, service level.

cycle stock—One of the two main conceptual components of any item inventory, the cycle stock is the most active component; the cycle stock depletes gradually as customer orders are received and is replenished cyclically when supplier orders are received. The other conceptual component of the item inventory is the safety stock, which is a cushion of protection against uncertainty in the demand or in the replenishment lead time. Syn: cycle inventory.

cycle time—1) In industrial engineering, the time between completion of two discrete units of production. For example, the cycle time of motors assembled at a rate of 120 per hour would be 30 seconds. 2) In materials management, it refers to the length of time from

when material enters a production facility until it exits. Syn: throughput time.

cyclical component—A component of demand, usually describing the impact of the business cycle on demand. See: decomposition, time series analysis.

cyclical demand—Demand influenced by the increases and decreases in the economy over time.

D

dampeners—User-input parameters to suppress the reporting of insignificant or unimportant action messages.

dark factory—A completely automated production facility with no labor. Syn: lightless plant.

dashboard—An easy-to-read management tool similar to an automobile's dashboard designed to address a wide range of business objectives by combining business intelligence and data integration infrastructure. See: executive dashboard.

data—Any representations, such as alphabetic or numeric characters, to which meaning can be assigned.

data acquisition—Obtaining data from a source, such as a database, and communicating that data to another database or a data warehouse.

database—A data processing file-management approach designed to establish the independence of computer programs from data files. Redundancy is minimized, and data elements can be added to, or deleted from, the file structure without necessitating changes to existing computer programs.

database management system (DBMS)—The software designed for organizing data and providing the mechanism for storing, maintaining, and retrieving that data on a physical medium (i.e., a database). A DBMS separates data from the application programs and people who use the data and permits many different views of the data.

data cleansing—Sifting through a database to find and fix mistakes such as misspelling, missing information, and false data.

data collection—The act of compiling data for recording, analysis, or distribution.

data communications—Transmission of data in computer-readable form using various transmission vehicles and paths.

data date—The date through which a report has provided actual accomplishment. Syn: time-now date.

data dictionary—1) A catalog of requirements and specifications for an information system. 2) A file that stores facts about the files and databases for all systems that are currently being used or for the software involved.

data element—A group of characters that defines an item at a basic level. Syn: data field.

data file—A collection of related data records organized in a specific manner (e.g., one record for each inventory item showing product code, unit of measure, production costs, transactions, selling price, and production lead time).

data integrity—Assurance that data accurately reflects the environment it is representing.

data mining—The process of studying data to search for previously unknown relationships. This knowledge is then applied to achieving specific business goals.

data normalization—A database maintenance term used in the context of relational databases, which helps to minimize the duplication of information or safeguard the database against certain types of logical or structural data anomalies. It is often used when merging data from one or more databases.

data transfer—The movement by electronic means of data from one location to another. The data can take the form of voice, text, image, or others. The movement is accomplished by communication links between computers and a variety of input/output devices.

data warehouse—A repository of data that has been specially prepared to support decision-making applications. Syn: decision-support data. See: information data warehouse.

date code—A label on products with the date of production. In food industries, it is often an integral part of the lot number.

date effectivity—A technique used to identify the effective date of a configuration change. A component change is controlled by effective date within the bill of material for the unchanged parent part number.

days of supply—Inventory-on-hand metric converted from units to how long the units will last. For example, if there are 2,000 units on hand and the company is using 200 per day, than there are 10 days of supply.

days outstanding—A term used to imply the amount of an asset or liability measured in days of sales. For example, accounts payable days are the typical number of days that a firm delays payments of invoices to its suppliers.

DBMS—Abbreviation for database management system.

DBR—Abbreviation for drum-buffer-rope.

D chart—A control chart for evaluating a process in terms of a demerit (or quality score); for example, a weighted sum of counts of various classified nonconformities. Syn: demerit chart.

DDP—Abbreviation for distributed data processing.

deadhead—The return of an empty transportation container to its point of origin. See: backhauling.

debenture—A bond that is backed by the general credit of the issuing firm.

deblend—The further processing of a product to adjust specific physical and chemical properties to within specification ranges.

debt—An amount owed to creditors. It is generally equal to the total assets in a company less the equity. See: liabilities.

debt-to-equity ratio—The amount of bonds and preferred stocks relative to the owners' equity position. The debt to equity ratio is a measurement of the use of borrowed funds to leverage owners' equity.

decentralized authority—The process of dispersing decision-making governance to staff people below the executive level of an organization.

decentralized computer network—A network where there is no central computer or computers linked to all other computers in the group.

decentralized dispatching—The organization of the dispatching function into individual departmental dispatchers.

decentralized inventory control—Inventory decision making exercised at each stocking location for SKUs at that location.

decentralized purchasing—When purchasing decisions are made locally and not at a central location.

decision matrix—A matrix used by teams to evaluate problems or possible solutions. After a matrix is drawn to evaluate possible solutions, for example, the team lists the solutions in the far left vertical column. Next, the team selects criteria to rate the possible solutions, writing them across the top row. Third, each possible solution is rated on a scale of 1 to 5 for each criterion and the rating recorded in the corresponding grid. Finally, the ratings of all the criteria for each possible solution are added to determine its total score. The total score is then used to help decide which solution deserves the most attention.

decision theory—A systematic approach to making decisions, particularly when uncertainty is present.

decisions under certainty—Simple decisions that assume complete information and no uncertainty connected with the analysis of decisions.

decisions under risk—Decision problems in which the analyst elects to consider several possible futures, the probabilities of which can be estimated.

decisions under uncertainty—Decisions for which the analyst elects to consider several possible futures, the probabilities of which cannot be estimated.

decision-support data—Syn: data warehouse.

decision support system (DSS)—A computer system designed to assist managers in selecting and evaluating courses of action by providing a logical, usually quantitative, analysis of the relevant factors.

decision table—A means of displaying logical conditions in an array that graphically illustrates actions associated with stated conditions.

decision tree—A method of analysis that evaluates alternative decisions in a tree-like structure to estimate values and/or probabilities. Decision trees take into account the time value of future earnings by using a rollback concept. Calculations are started at the far right-hand side, then traced back through the branches to identify the appropriate decision.

decision variables—The variables that will be changed to find the optimal solution in an optimization problem.

declared value—The value of goods declared on a bill of lading, used to determine a freight rate or limit the carrier's liability.

decomposition—A method of forecasting where time series data are separated into up to three components: trend, seasonal, and cyclical; where trend includes the general horizontal upward or downward movement over time; seasonal includes a recurring demand pattern such as day of the week, weekly, monthly, or quarterly; and cyclical includes any repeating, nonseasonal pattern. A fourth component is random, that is, data with no pattern. The new forecast is made by projecting the patterns individually determined and then combining them. See: cyclical component, random component, seasonal component, trend component.

decoupling—Creating independence between supply and use of material. Commonly denotes providing inventory between operations so that fluctuations in the production rate of the supplying operation do not constrain production or use rates of the next operation.

decoupling inventory—An amount of inventory kept between entities in a manufacturing or distribution network to create independence between processes or entities. The objective of decoupling inventory is to disconnect the rate of use from the rate of supply of the item. See: buffer.

decoupling points—The locations in the product structure or distribution network where inventory is placed to create independence between processes or entities. Selection of decoupling points is a strategic decision that determines customer lead times and inventory investment. See: control points.

decryption—Transformation of encrypted text into a readable format.

dedicated capacity—A work center that is designated to produce a single item or a limited number of similar items. Equipment that is dedicated may be special equipment or may be grouped general-purpose equipment committed to a composite part.

dedicated contract carrier—A third-party hauler that works exclusively for a single customer.

dedicated equipment—Equipment whose use is restricted to specific operations on a limited set of components.

dedicated line—A production line permanently configured to run well-defined parts, one piece at a time, from station to station.

de-expedite—The reprioritizing of jobs to a lower level of activity. All extraordinary actions involving these jobs stop.

defamation—Injury to another's reputation by a public utterance: print (libel) or oral (slander).

default—The action that will be taken by a computer program when the user does not specify a variable parameter.

defect—A good's or service's nonfulfillment of an intended requirement or reasonable expectation for use, including safety considerations. There are four classes of defects: Class 1, Very Serious, leads directly to severe injury or catastrophic economic loss; Class 2, Serious, leads directly to significant injury or significant economic loss; Class 3, Major, is related to major problems with respect to intended normal or reasonably foreseeable use; and Class 4, Minor, is related to minor problems with respect to intended normal or reasonably foreseeable use. See: blemish, imperfection, nonconformity.

defects per million opportunities—The quantity of defects per one million defect opportunities—a potential problem that is important to the customer.

defects per unit—The average number of blemishes on a particular product (e.g., a television cabinet).

deficiency—Failure to meet quality standards.

define-measure-analyze-design-verify—A six sigma process that outlines the steps needed to create a completely new business process or product at six sigma quality levels.

define-measure-analyze-improve-control (DMAIC)—The sequence of steps for improvement projects within six-sigma quality control.

define, measure, analyze, improve, control (DMAIC) process—A six sigma improvement process comprised of five stages: (1) Determine the nature of the problem, (2) Measure existing performance and commence recording data and facts that offer information about the underlying causes of the problem, (3) Study the information to determine the root causes of the problem, (4) Improve the process by effecting solutions to the problem, and (5) Monitor the process until the solutions become ingrained.

define phase—A step in the six sigma DMAIC process in which project goals and customer deliverables are identified. See: design-measure-analyze-improve-control process.

degrees of freedom—A statistical term indicating the number of variables or data points used for testing a relationship. The greater the degrees of freedom, the greater the confidence that can be placed on the statistical significance of the results.

delay report—Syn: anticipated delay report.

delay reporting—Reporting against an operation status of a manufacturing order on an exception basis, when delays are anticipated.

delinquent order—Syn: past due order.

deliverable—Any unique and verifiable product or result that is needed to complete a process or project.

delivery appointment—The time for goods to arrive at a selected location.

delivery cycle—Syn: delivery lead time.

delivery lead time—The time from the receipt of a customer order to the delivery of the product. Syn: delivery cycle.

delivery policy—The company's goal for the time to ship the product after the receipt of a customer's order. The policy is sometimes stated as "our quoted delivery time."

delivery reliability—A performance criterion that measures how consistently goods and services are delivered on, or before, the promised time.

delivery schedule—The required or agreed time or rate of delivery of goods or services purchased for a future period.

delivery speed—A performance criterion that measures how quickly a product or service can be delivered once the demand is identified.

delivery window—A time frame for when goods or services should be delivered.

Delphi method—A qualitative forecasting technique where the opinions of experts are combined in a series of iterations. The results of each iteration are used to develop the next, so that convergence of the experts' opinions is obtained. See: management estimation, panel consensus.

demand—A need for a particular product or component. The demand could come from any number of sources (e.g., a customer order or forecast, an interplant requirement, a branch warehouse request for a service part or the manufacturing of another product). At the finished goods level, demand data are usually different from sales data because demand does not necessarily result in sales (i.e., if there is no stock, there will be no sale). There are generally up to four components of demand: cyclical component, random component, seasonal component, and trend component. See: booked orders.

demand-based order quantity—An order system using forecast or derived demand for one or more future periods (rather than a fixed quantity as in economic order quantity).

demand chain—1) A demand chain is composed of the enterprises that sell a business's goods or services. 2) Supply chain as seen from the viewpoint of the customer, the entity who chooses among competing products and services and thus controls the demand.

demand chain management—A supply chain inventory management approach that concentrates on demand pull rather than supplier push inventory models.

demand curve—A graphic description of the relationship between price and quantity demanded in a market, assuming that all other factors stay the same. Quantity demanded of a product is measured on the horizontal axis for an array of different prices measured on the vertical axis.

demand deposits—Deposits that can be withdrawn on demand or paid to a third party by check.

demand-driven supply network—A situation where a customer purchase initiates real-time information flows through the supply chain which then causes movement of product through the network.

demand during lead time—The quantity of a product expected to be withdrawn from stock or to be consumed during its replenishment lead time when usage is at the forecasted rate. See: expected demand.

demand filter—A standard that is set to monitor sales data for individual items in forecasting models. It is usually set to be tripped when the demand for a period differs from the forecast by more than some number of mean absolute deviations.

demand forecasting—Forecasting the demand for a particular good, component, or service.

demand forecast updating—Recomputing a forecast after deleting the oldest data and adding data that occurred since the last forecast revision.

demand lead time—The amount of time potential customers are willing to wait for the delivery of a good or a service. Syn: customer tolerance time.

demand management—1) The function of recognizing all demands for goods and services to support the marketplace. It involves prioritizing demand when supply is lacking. Proper demand management facilitates the planning and use of resources for profitable business results. 2) In marketing, the process of planning, executing, controlling, and monitoring the design, pricing, promotion, and distribution of products and services to bring about transactions that meet organizational and individual needs. Syn: marketing management. See: demand planning.

demand management process—A process that weighs both customer demand and a firm's output capabilities, and tries to balance the two. Demand management is made up of planning demand, communicating demand, influencing demand, and prioritizing demand.

demand manager—Person who assists sales and marketing in the development and maintenance of sales forecasts and reconciles volume and mix variations in the forecast.

demand planning—The process of combining statistical forecasting techniques and judgment to construct demand estimates for products or services (both high and low volume; lumpy and continuous) across the supply chain from the suppliers' raw materials to the consumer's needs. Items can be aggregated by product family, geographical location, product life cycle, and so forth, to determine an estimate of consumer demand for finished products, service parts, and services. Numerous forecasting models are tested and combined with judgment from marketing, sales, distributors, warehousing, service parts, and other functions. Actual sales are compared with forecasts provided by various models and judgments to determine the best integration of techniques and judgment to minimize forecast error. See: demand management.

demand pull—The triggering of material movement to a work center only when that work center is ready to begin the next job. In effect, it shortens or eliminates the queue from in front of a work center, but it can cause a queue at the end of a previous work center. Demand pull also can occur within a supply chain, in which case it often is called a demand chain.

demand rate—A statement of requirements in terms of quantity per unit of time (hour, day, week, month, etc.).

demand risk—The risk that declining economic activity substantially reduces the demand for a firm's products or services.

demand segmentation—Categorizing demand types into groups that share similar characteristics (e.g., government, large customers, seasonal products). Similar segments can be treated alike in business or capacity planning.

demand shaping—The practice of using the four Ps (product, pricing, placement, and promotion) and other market variables to influence the demand of a product or service so that the demand better matches the available supply. See: four Ps.

demand-side analysis—Techniques such as market research, surveys, focus groups, and performance/cost modeling used to identify emerging technologies.

demand time fence (DTF)—1) That point in time inside of which the forecast is no longer included in total demand and projected available inventory calculations; inside this point, only customer orders are considered. Beyond this point, total demand is a combination of actual orders and forecasts, depending on the forecast consumption technique chosen. 2) In some contexts, the demand time fence may correspond to that point in the future inside which changes to the master schedule must be approved by an authority higher than the master scheduler. Note, however, that customer orders may still be promised inside the demand time fence without higher authority approval if there are quantities available-to-promise (ATP). Beyond the demand time fence, the master scheduler may change the MPS within the limits of established rescheduling rules, without the approval of higher authority. See: option overplanning, planning time fence, time fence.

demand uncertainty—The uncertainty or variability in demand as measured by the standard deviation, mean absolute deviation (MAD), or variance of forecast errors.

demerit chart—Syn: D chart.

Deming circle—The concept of a continuously rotating wheel of plan-do-check-action (PDCA) used to show the need for interaction among market research, design, production, and sales to improve quality. See: plan-do-check-action.

Deming Prize—An award given annually to organizations that, according to the award guidelines, have successfully applied companywide quality control based on statistical quality control and will keep up with it in the future. Although the award is named in honor of W. Edwards Deming, its criteria are not specifically related to Deming's teachings. There are three separate divisions for the award: the Deming Application Prize, the Deming Prize for Individuals, and the Deming Prize for Overseas Companies. The award process is overseen by the Deming Prize Committee of the Union of Japanese Scientists and Engineers in Tokyo.

Deming's 14 Points—Syn: 14 Points.

demographics—The characteristics of a specific population, such as a set of potential customers.

demographic segmentation—In marketing, dividing potential markets by characteristics of potential customers, such as age, sex, income, and education.

demonstrated capacity—Proven capacity calculated from actual performance data, usually expressed as the average number of items produced multiplied by the standard hours per item. See: maximum demonstrated capacity.

demurrage—The carrier charges and fees applied when rail freight cars and ships are retained beyond a speci-

fied loading or unloading time. See: detention, express.

denied party list—A list of organizations that are unauthorized to submit a bid for an activity.

density—A measure of the weight of an item compared to its volume. Because density can influence the number of units that can be carried by a particular truck, this is a factor in defining transportation charges.

departmental stocks—An informal system of holding some stock in a production department. This action is taken as a protection from stockouts in the stockroom or for convenience; however, it results in increased inventory investment and possible degradation of the accuracy of the inventory records.

department overhead rate—The overhead rate applied to jobs passing through a department.

dependent demand—Demand that is directly related to or derived from the bill of material structure for other items or end products. Such demands are therefore calculated and need not and should not be forecast. A given inventory item may have both dependent and independent demand at any given time. For example, a part may simultaneously be the component of an assembly and sold as a service part. See: independent demand.

depletion—The reduction in the value of a capital asset (usually a natural resource) in the balance sheet and charging this amount as an expense against income for the period. See: capital recovery.

deployment planning and scheduling—Planning how to use existing inventory to meet demand requirements.

deposition—The sworn questioning, outside of court, of a potential witness by the other side's attorney.

depreciation—An allocation of the original value of an asset against current income to represent the declining value of the asset as a cost of that time period. Depreciation does not involve a cash payment. It acts as a tax shield and thereby reduces the tax payment. See: capital recovery, depletion, double-declining-balance depreciation, straight line depreciation, units-of-production depreciation.

depreciation of a currency—A decrease in the buying power of a country's currency in terms of other countries' goods and services.

derived demand—Demand for component products that arises from the demand for final design products. For example, the demand for steel is derived from the demand for automobiles.

description by brand—A method to identify a product or service required; requesting by brand usually means the product or service provides some advantage over other brands.

description by market grade/industry standard—A method to identify a product or service required when there is a high level of understanding between user and supplier.

description by performance characteristics—A method to identify a product or service by specifying the performance required.

description by specification—A method to identify a product or service required by communicating its characteristics in detail.

deseasonalized data—Data from which seasonality has been removed using annual moving averages.

deshi—A Japanese word meaning student.

design—The conversion of a need or innovation into a product, process, or service that meets both the enterprise and customer expectations. The design process consists of translating a set of functional requirements into an operational product, process, or service.

design changeover flexibility—The capability of the existing production system to accommodate and introduce a large variety of major design changes quickly.

design cycle—The interval of time between the start of the design process of one model and the completion of the design process for the model.

design engineering—The discipline consisting of process engineering and product engineering.

design for maintainability—Syn: design for service.

design for manufacturability—Simplification of parts, products, and processes to improve quality and reduce manufacturing costs.

design for manufacture and assembly (DFMA)—A product development approach that involves the manufacturing function in the initial stages of product design to ensure ease of manufacturing and assembly. See: early manufacturing involvement.

design for quality—A product design approach that uses quality measures to capture the extent to which the design meets the needs of the target market (customer attributes), as well as its actual performance, aesthetics, and cost. See: total quality engineering.

design for remanufacture—Products developed in a manner that allows components to be used in other products. This process is associated with green manufacturing.

design for service—Simplification of parts and processes to improve the after-sale service of a product. Syn: design for maintainability.

design for six sigma—An approach to designing products and processes that attempts to ensure the firm can provide products or services that meet six sigma quality levels. These quality levels correspond to approximately 3.4 defects per million opportunities.

design for the environment (DFE)—Considering health, safety, and environmental aspects of a product during the design and development phase of product development.

design for the supply chain—Enhancement of a firm's product design in consideration of the issues that will arise in the supply chain, from raw materials to the final stage of the product's life cycle.

designing in quality vs. inspecting in quality—Syn: prevention vs. detection.

design of experiments (DOE)—1) A process for structuring statistically valid studies in any science. 2) A quality management technique used to evaluate the effect of carefully planned and controlled changes to input process variables on the output variable. The objective is to improve production processes.

design phase—One of the six sigma phases of quality. It involves improvement project identification and selection. See: design-measure-analyze-improve-control process.

design review—A technique for evaluating a proposed design to ensure that the design (1) is supported by adequate materials and materials that are available on a timely basis, (2) will perform successfully during use, (3) can be manufactured at low cost, and (4) is suitable for prompt field maintenance.

design simplification—A process of reducing the number of pieces in a product or machine, eliminating features that are seldom needed, and eliminating steps in the production process.

design-to-order—Syn: engineer-to-order.

destructive testing—Inspection that renders the inspected part inoperable.

detailed planning and control—The planning of a project in the short term, covering the present time up until a few weeks out.

detailed scheduling—Syn: operations scheduling.

D

detail file—A file that contains manufacturing, routing, or specification details. See: master file.

detention—Carrier charges and fees applied when truck trailers are retained beyond a specified loading or unloading time. See: demurrage, express.

deterioration—Product spoilage, damage to the package, and so forth. This is one of the considerations in inventory carrying cost.

deterministic models—Models where no uncertainty is included (e.g., inventory models without safety stock considerations).

deviation—The difference, usually the absolute difference, between a number and the mean of a set of numbers, or between a forecast value and the actual value.

Dewey's reflective thinking—A problem solving technique with a formal sequence of (1) problem definition, (2) problem analysis, (3) brainstorming solutions, (4) development of proposed solutions, and (5) solution testing and validation.

DFMA—Abbreviation for design for manufacture and assembly.

diagnostic journey and remedial journey—A two-phase investigation used by teams to solve chronic quality problems. In the first phase—the diagnostic journey—the team journeys from the symptom of a chronic problem to its cause. In the second phase—the remedial journey—the team journeys from the cause to its remedy.

diagnostic study—A brief investigation or cursory methods study of an operation, process, group, or individual to discover causes of operational difficulties or problems for which more detailed remedial studies may be feasible. An appropriate work measurement technique may be used to evaluate alternatives or to locate major areas requiring improvement.

die—A special form used in general-purpose equipment to make specific parts.

differentiated marketing—Marketing to different market segments with a different marketing strategy for each segment.

differentiated oligopoly—A market in which a few companies produce partially differentiated products or services that are marketed within a given geographical area. Differentiation may be based on quality, features, styling, or services offered along with the product. See: industry structure types.

differentiation strategy—A business strategy that focuses on setting a product or service apart from the competition—focusing on making a product or service unique.

digital cash or money—An electronic currency equivalent of currency or coins.

dimensions of quality—An aspect of quality that is specified to enhance the ability to define quality. The most commonly used list for products was created by David Garvin. His dimensions are aesthetics, conformance, durability, features, perceived quality, performance, reliability, and serviceability. The most commonly used list for service quality was created by Parasuraman, Zeithamel, and Berry. This list is assurance, availability, completeness, empathy, pleasantness, professionalism, responsiveness, service reliability, tangibles, and timeliness.

direct costing—Syn: variable costing.

direct costs—1) In traditional cost accounting, variable costs that can be directly attributed to a particular job or operation. Direct material and direct labor are traditionally considered direct costs. 2) In activity-based cost (ABC) accounting, a cost that can specifically be traced and is economically feasible to track to a particular cost object (e.g., the units produced, a production line, a department, a manufacturing plant). In contrast, if the cost must be allocated across various cost objects, it is an indirect cost. Based on the cost object under consideration, the classification of direct and indirect can change. ABC accounting assumes that more costs traditionally viewed as fixed costs are variable and can be traced to cost objects.

direct-deduct inventory transaction processing—A method of inventory bookkeeping that decreases the book (computer) inventory of an item as material is issued from stock, and increases the book inventory as transactions processed for each item. The key concept here is that the book record is updated coincidentally with the movement of material out of or into stock. As a result, the book record is a representation of what is physically in stock. Syn: discrete issue.

direct delivery—The consignment of goods directly from the supplier to the buyer, frequently used where a third party acts as intermediary between supplier and buyer.

direct labor—Labor that is specifically applied to the good being manufactured or used in the performance of the service. Syn: touch labor.

direct labor cost—The compensation of workers who are involved in converting material into a finished product.

direct loading—Syn: cross-docking.

direct marketing—Communicating directly with consumers in an effort to elicit a response or a transaction.

direct material—Material that becomes a part of the final product in measurable quantities.

direct materials cost—The acquisition cost of all materials used directly in the finished product.

direct materials purchasing—Purchasing from suppliers on a contractual basis for a fixed period of time or amount of product. For job shops, the purchasing contract can be only for one job. For repetitive manufacturing, the materials are usually purchased on contracts that last for a model run or at least a year.

direct numerical control (DNC)—A system in which sets of numerical control machines are connected to a computer, allowing direct control of machines by the computer without use of external storage media.

direct offset—Similar to bartering, trading goods or services for related goods or services or agreeing on co-production.

direct sales—Sales from the manufacturer to the ultimate consumer without going through a distributor or retailer.

direct store delivery (DSD)—A shipment that bypasses the customer's warehouse and goes directly from the manufacturer's plant to the retail store.

direct truck shipment—Shipment made without any additional stops, such as for loading or changing trucks.

disability—A limitation of capability that limits functioning within a plant or a company.

disassembly bill of material—In remanufacturing, a bill of material used as a guide for the inspection in the teardown and inspection process. On the basis of inspection, this bill is modified to a bill of repair defining the actual repair materials and work required. Syn: teardown bill of material. See: repair bill of material.

disbursement—The physical issuance and reporting of the movement of raw material, components, or other items from a stores room or warehouse. Taking a part out of inventory. See: issue.

disbursement list—Syn: picking list.

disciplinary action—An action taken to enforce compliance with organizational rules and policies.

discontinuous demand—A demand pattern that is characterized by large demands interrupted by periods with no demand, as opposed to a continuous or steady (e.g., daily) demand. Syn: lumpy demand.

discount—An allowance or deduction granted by the seller to the buyer, usually when the buyer meets certain stipulated conditions that reduce the price of the products purchased. A quantity discount is an allowance determined by the quantity or value of the purchase. A cash discount is an allowance extended to encourage payment of an invoice on or before a stated date. A trade discount is a deduction from an established price for goods or services made by the seller to those engaged in certain businesses. See: price break.

discounted cash flow—A method of investment analysis in which future cash flows are converted, or discounted, to their value at the present time. The net present value of an item is estimated to be the sum of all discounted future cash flows.

discount period—The time allowed a customer to receive a cash discount for timely payment of an invoice.

discount rate—The rate of interest charged to commercial banks by a central banking authority.

discrete available-to-promise—A calculation based on the available-to-promise figure in the master schedule. For the first period, the ATP is the sum of the beginning inventory plus the MPS quantity minus backlog for all periods until the item is master scheduled again. For all other periods, if a quantity has been scheduled for that time period then the ATP is this quantity minus all customer commitments for this and other periods until another quantity are scheduled in the MPS. For those periods where the quantity scheduled is zero, the ATP is zero (even if deliveries have been promised). The promised customer commitments are accumulated and shown in the period where the item was most recently scheduled. Syn: incremental available-to-promise. See: available-to-promise.

discrete issue—Syn: direct-deduct inventory transaction processing.

discrete manufacturing—The production of distinct items such as automobiles, appliances, or computers.

discrete order picking—A method of picking orders in which the items on one order are picked before the next order is picked. See: batch picking, order picking, zone picking.

discrete order quantity—An order quantity that represents an integer number of periods of demand. Most MRP systems employ discrete order quantities. See: fixed-period requirements, least total cost, least unit cost, lot-for-lot, part period balancing, period order quantity, Wagner-Whitin algorithm.

D

discrete variable—A variable, such as number of defects, that can take on only certain values (such as integers). See: continuous variable.

discussion list—A group of people who have all signed up on a listserver to participate via email in the discussion of a given topic.

diseconomies of scale—Occurs when more outputs are required than the efficient quantity that the facility is designed to produce; this causes an increase in unit cost.

disintermediation—The process of eliminating an intermediate stage or echelon in a supply chain. Total supply chain operating expense is reduced, total supply chain inventory is reduced, total cycle time is reduced, and profits increase among the remaining echelons. See: echelon.

dispatch(ing) board—Syn: control board.

dispatcher—1) A production control person whose primary function is dispatching. 2) A transportation worker who sends out and tracks cars, buses, trucks, railcars, and other vehicles.

dispatching—The selecting and sequencing of available jobs to be run at individual workstations and the assignment of those jobs to workers.

dispatching rule—The logic used to assign priorities to jobs at a work center.

dispatch list—A listing of manufacturing orders in priority sequence. The dispatch list, which is usually communicated to the manufacturing floor via paper or electronic media, contains detailed information on priority, location, quantity, and the capacity requirements of the manufacturing order by operation. Dispatch lists are normally generated daily and oriented by work center. Syn: work center schedule, priority report.

dispersion—The scattering of the observations of a frequency distribution around its average.

dispute resolution—The process of arbitration or mediation to settle arguments without going to court.

distinctive competency—A sustainable advantage that a company has over its competitors. distributed data processing (DDP)—A data processing organizational concept under which computer resources of a company are installed at more than one location with appropriate communication links. Processing is performed at the user's location generally on a smaller computer and under the user's control and scheduling, as opposed to processing for all users being done on a large, centralized computer system.

distressed goods—Products that are damaged or close to their expiration date and cannot be sold at full price.

distributed inventory—Maintaining inventory in a variety of locations to provide better customer service.

distributed numerical control—An approach to automated machining in which each machine tool has its own dedicated microcomputer or computer numerical control (CNC). Each machine tool's CNC is connected via a network with a minicomputer that handles distributed processing between the host mainframe computer and the CNC. This minicomputer handles part program transfers and machine status data collection. This approach is considered more advanced than direct numerical control, in which several machine tools are tied directly to a central computer.

distributed systems—Computer systems in multiple locations throughout an organization, working in a cooperative fashion, with the system at each location primarily serving the needs of that location but also able to receive and supply information from other systems within a network.

distribution—1) The activities associated with the movement of material, usually finished goods or service parts, from the manufacturer to the customer. These activities encompass the functions of transportation, warehousing, inventory control, material handling, order administration, site and location analysis, industrial packaging, data processing, and the communications network necessary for effective management. It includes all activities related to physical distribution, as well as the return of goods to the manufacturer. In many cases, this movement is made through one or more levels of field warehouses. Syn: physical distribution. 2) The systematic division of a whole into discrete parts having distinctive characteristics.

distribution by value—Syn: ABC classification.

distribution center—A location used to store inventory. Decisions driving warehouse management include site selection, number of facilities in the system, layout, and methods of receiving, storing, and retrieving goods.

distribution channel—The distribution route, from raw materials through consumption, along which products travel. See: channels of distribution, marketing channel.

distribution cost—Those items of cost related to the activities associated with the movement and storage of finished products. Distribution costs can include inventory costs, transportation costs, and order processing costs.

distribution curve—A graphic display of numerous data points showing the mean and frequency of occurrences of observations on a chart. See: normal distribution curve.

distribution inventory—Inventory, usually spare parts and finished goods, located in the distribution system (e.g., in warehouses, in-transit between warehouses and the consumer).

distribution network structure—The planned channels of inventory disbursement from one or more sources to field warehouses and ultimately to the customer. There may be one or more levels in the disbursement system. Syn: bill of distribution.

distribution of forecast errors—Tabulation of the forecast errors according to the frequency of occurrence of each error value. The errors in forecasting are, in many cases, normally distributed even when the observed data do not come from a normal distribution.

distribution planner—A person who plans inventories and schedules replenishment shipments for the distribution centers.

distribution planning—The planning activities associated with transportation, warehousing, inventory levels, materials handling, order administration, site and location planning, industrial packaging, data processing, and communications networks to support distribution.

distribution requirements planning (DRP)—1) The function of determining the need to replenish inventory at branch warehouses. A time-phased order point approach is used where the planned orders at the branch warehouse level are "exploded" via MRP logic to become gross requirements on the supplying source. In the case of multilevel distribution networks, this explosion process can continue down through the various levels of regional warehouses (master warehouse, factory warehouse, etc.) and become input to the master production schedule. Demand on the supplying sources is recognized as dependent, and standard MRP logic applies. 2) More generally, replenishment inventory calculations, which may be based on other planning approaches such as period order quantities or "replace exactly what was used," rather than being limited to the time-phased order point approach.

distribution resource planning (DRP II)—The extension of distribution requirements planning into the planning of the key resources contained in a distribution system (warehouse space, workforce, money, trucks, freight cars, etc).

distribution system—A group of interrelated facilities—manufacturing and one or more levels of warehousing—linking the production, storage, and consumption activities for spare parts and finished goods inventory. See: pipeline stock.

distribution warehouse—A facility where goods are received in large-volume uniform lots, stored briefly, and then broken down into smaller orders of different items required by the customer. Emphasis is on expeditious movement and handling.

distributor—A business that does not manufacture its own products, but purchases and resells these products. Such a business usually maintains a finished goods inventory. Syn: wholesaler.

divergent point—An operation in a production process in which a single material/component enters and, after processing, can then be routed to a number of different downstream operations.

diversification strategy—An expansion of the scope of the product line to exploit new markets. A key objective of a diversification strategy is to spread the company's risk over several product lines in case there should be a downturn in any one product's market.

dividend—A payment to stockholders either in cash or stock.

dividend yield—The ratio of dividends per share over stock price.

DMAIC—Acronym for define-measure-analyze-improve-control.

DMAIC process—Acronym for define, measure, analyze, improve, and control process.

DNC—Abbreviation for direct numerical control.

dock receipt—A receipt recorded for a shipment received or delivered at a pier or dock.

dock-to-stock—A program by which specific quality and packaging requirements are met before the product is released. Prequalified product is shipped directly into the customer's inventory. Dock-to-stock eliminates the costly handling of components, specifically in receiving and inspection and enables product to move directly into production.

dock-to-stock inventory—A supplier-customer relationship where specified quality and packaging requirements are met before the product is released. The product is then received directly into the customer's inventories. See: point-of-use inventory, stockless purchasing.

dock-to-stock time—Syn: put-away time.

Dodge-Romig tables—Information about the correct sample size and maximum defective quantity in a sample to satisfy lot acceptance; a quality control measurement.

DOE—Abbreviation for design of experiments.

dog—A slang term used to refer to a low-growth, low-market-share product. See: growth-share matrix.

dojo—A Japanese word meaning hall.

domestic corporation—A company incorporated in a particular state or country.

double-declining-balance depreciation—A type of accelerated depreciation. See: depreciation.

double order point system—A distribution inventory management system that has two order points. The smallest equals the original order point, which covers demand during replenishment lead time. The second order point is the sum of the first order point plus normal usage during manufacturing lead time. It enables warehouses to forewarn manufacturing of future replenishment orders.

double-sampling plan—A way to control quality by taking one sample and making an accept or reject decision, and, if the decision cannot be made, taking a second sample and making the accept or reject decision by combining the results of both samples.

double smoothing—Syn: second-order smoothing.

downgrade—The substitution of a product of lower quality, value, or status for another either in planning or in fact.

download—The process of transferring data or programs from one computer to another (and usually saving to a disk).

downstream—Used as a relative reference within a firm or supply chain to indicate moving in the direction of the end customer.

downstream operation—The tasks subsequent to the task currently being planned or executed.

downtime—Time when a resource is scheduled for operation but is not producing for reasons such as maintenance, repair, or setup.

drawback—A refund of customs duties paid on material imported and later exported.

driver—1) In activity-based cost accounting, an operation that influences the quantity of work required and cost of an activity. Syn: cost driver. 2) In the theory of constraints, an underlying cause that is responsible for several observed effects.

drop-dead date—The last possible date to apply influence to a future activity.

drop ship—To take the title of the product but not actually handle, stock, or deliver it (i.e., to have one supplier ship directly to another or to have a supplier ship directly to the buyer's customer).

DRP—Abbreviation for distribution requirements planning.

DRP II—Abbreviation for distribution resource planning.

drum—In the theory of constraints, the constraint is viewed as a drum, and nonconstraints are like soldiers in an army who march in unison to the drumbeat; the resources in a plant should perform in unison with the drumbeat set by the constraint.

drum-buffer-rope (DBR)—The theory of constraints method for scheduling and managing operations that have an internal constraint or capacity-constrained resource.

drum schedule—The detailed production schedule for a resource that sets the pace for the entire system. The drum schedule must reconcile the customer requirements with the system's constraint(s).

DSD—Abbreviation for direct store delivery.

DSS—Abbreviation for decision support system.

DTF—Abbreviation for demand time fence.

dual-card kanban system—Syn: two-card kanban system.

dual sourcing—A method for sourcing requirements by using a few suppliers for the same products or services. See: multisourcing, multiple sourcing, single sourcing.

due date—The date when purchased material or production material is due to be available for use. Syn: expected receipt date. See: arrival date.

due date rule—A dispatching rule that directs the sequencing of jobs by the earliest due date.

dummy activity—In activity-on-arrow diagramming, an activity with zero duration used to express a precedence relationship that can't otherwise be diagrammed. It is shown graphically with a dashed arrow.

dumping—Selling goods below costs in selected markets.

dunnage—The packing material used to protect a product from damage during transport.

durability—1) A measurement of time or amount of use before a product needs repair or replacement. 2) One of the eight dimensions of quality that refers to the length of a product's economic life.

durable goods—Generally, any goods whose continuous serviceability is likely to exceed three years (e.g., trucks, furniture). See: consumer durable goods.

duration—In project management, the length of time an activity is estimated to require.

duty—A tax levied by a government on the importation, exportation, or use and consumption of goods.

duty-free zone—An area where merchandise is brought into the country for further work to be done. Duty is paid only on the items brought in, normally at a lower rate than finished goods, and paid only at the time of sale.

dynamic congruence—In simulation, the situation where a physical system and a simulation model mimic one another closely.

dynamic kanban—An electronic signal using kanban to create an automatic purchase order to a supplier or a manufacturing order to a shop. Dynamic kanban is one of the elements of a manufacturing execution system that enables just-in-time deliveries to production. See: kanban.

dynamic lot sizing—Any lot-sizing technique that creates an order quantity subject to continuous recomputation. See: least total cost, least unit cost, part period balancing, period order quantity, Wagner-Whitin algorithm.

dynamic programming—A method of sequential decision making in which the result of the decision at each stage affords the best possible means to exploit the expected range of likely (yet unpredictable) outcomes in the following decision-making stages.

E

EAC—Abbreviation for estimate at completion.

EAP—Abbreviation for employee assistance program.

earliest due date (EDD)—A priority rule that sequences the jobs in a queue according to their (operation or job) due dates. See: earliest operation due date.

earliest operation due date (ODD)—A dispatching rule that selects the job having the earliest due date for the impending operation. See: earliest due date.

earliest start date—The earliest date an operation or order can start. It may be restricted by the current date, material availability, or management-specified "maximum advance."

earliness—If a job is finished before its due date, the difference between its completion date and the due date. See: lateness, tardiness.

early finish date (EF)—In the critical path method of project management, the earliest time at which a given activity is estimated to be completed. This date can change as the project is executed.

early manufacturing involvement—The process of involving manufacturing personnel early in the product design activity and drawing on their expertise, insights, and knowledge to generate better designs in less time and to generate designs that are easier to manufacture. Early involvement of manufacturing, field service, suppliers, customers, and so on means drawing on their expertise, knowledge, and insight to improve the design. Benefits include increased functionality, increased quality, ease of manufacture and assembly, ease of testing, better testing procedures, ease of service, decreased cost, and improved aesthetics. See: design for manufacture and assembly, participative design/engineering.

early start date (ES)—In the critical path method of project management, the earliest time at which a given activity is estimated to begin. This date can change as the project is executed.

early supplier involvement (ESI)—The process of involving suppliers early in the product design activity and drawing on their expertise, insights, and knowledge to generate better designs in less time and designs that are easier to manufacture with high quality. See: participative design/engineering.

earmarked material—The reserved material on hand that is physically identified, rather than merely reserved in a balance-of-stores record.

earned hours—A statement reflecting the standard hour assigned for actual production reported during the period. Syn: earned volume.

earned value—In project management, the total value, including overhead, of approved estimates for completed activities or portions thereof.

earned value method—In project management, a comparison of planned activity time and cost to actual activity time and cost to see if a project is on schedule by time and by budget.

earned volume—Syn: earned hours.

earnings before interest and taxes (EBIT)—Syn: net operating income.

earnings before taxes (EBT)—Earnings before interest and taxes minus interest charges.

EBIT—Acronym for earnings before interest and taxes

eBPP—Abbreviation for electronic bill presentment and payment.

EBT—Abbreviation for earnings before taxes.

e-cash—An electronic system that provides for deposits and withdrawals of digital money. It permits a payer using it to remain anonymous.

echelon—A level of supply chain nodes. For example, a supply chain with two independent factory warehouses and nine wholesale warehouses delivering product to 350 retail stores is a supply chain with three echelons between the factory and the end customer. One echelon consists of the two independent factory warehouses, one echelon consists of the nine wholesale warehouses, and one echelon consists of the 350 retail stores. Each echelon adds operating expense, holds inventory, adds to the cycle time, and expects to make a profit. See: disintermediation.

e-commerce—Abbreviation for electronic commerce.

econometric model—A set of equations intended to be used simultaneously to capture the way in which dependent and independent variables are interrelated.

econometric modeling—The process of developing econometric models. See: econometric model.

economic indicator—An index of total business activities at the regional, national, and global levels.

economic infrastructure—A nation's networks for supporting commerce, including transportation, communications, and finance.

economic life—The time until a product is scrapped—not because it is unusable but because repairs are becoming too expensive to justify further use.

economic lot size—Syn: economic order quantity.

economic order quantity (EOQ)—A type of fixed order quantity model that determines the amount of an item to be purchased or manufactured at one time. The intent is to minimize the combined costs of acquiring and carrying inventory. The basic formula is:

$$\text{quantity} = \sqrt{\frac{2AS}{iC}}$$

where A = annual usage in units, S = ordering costs in dollars, i = annual inventory carrying cost rate as a de-

cimal, and C = unit cost. Syn: economic lot size, minimum cost order quantity. See: total cost curve.

economic value added—In managerial accounting, the net operating profit earned above the cost of capital for a profit center.

economy of scale—A phenomenon whereby larger volumes of production reduce unit cost by distributing fixed costs over a larger quantity. See: economy of scope.

economy of scope—Using one versatile plant to produce many different products at a lower cost than making each product in different plants at a higher cost. See: economy of scale.

ECR—Abbreviation for efficient consumer response.

EDD—Abbreviation for earliest due date.

EDI—Abbreviation for electronic data interchange.

EDIFACT—Abbreviation for EDI for administration, commerce, and transport.

EDI for administration, commerce, and transport (EDIFACT)—A set of United Nations rules for electronic data interchange. These are international guidelines and standards for the electronic exchange of data regarding trade.

EDT—An abbreviation for electronic data transfer.

edutainment—Mixing entertainment and education elements to make learning more fun.

EEO—Abbreviation for equal employment opportunity.

EEOC—Abbreviation for Equal Employment Opportunity Commission.

EF—Abbreviation for early finish date.

effective capacity—Syn: rated capacity.

effective date—The date on which a component or an operation is to be added or removed from a bill of material or an assembly process. The effective dates are used in the explosion process to create demands for the correct items. Normally, bills of material and routing systems provide for an effectivity start date and stop date, signifying the start or stop of a particular relationship. Effectivity control also may be by serial number rather than date. Syn: effectivity, effectivity date.

effective interest rate—Syn: annual percentage rate.

effectivity—Syn: effective date.

effectivity date—Syn: effective date.

efficiency—A measurement (usually expressed as a percentage) of the actual output to the standard output expected. Efficiency measures how well something is performing relative to existing standards; in contrast, productivity measures output relative to a specific input (e.g., tons/labor hour). Efficiency is the ratio of (1) actual units produced to the standard rate of production expected in a time period or (2) standard hours produced to actual hours worked (taking longer means less efficiency) or (3) actual dollar volume of output to a standard dollar volume in a time period. Illustrations of these calculations follow. (1) There is a standard of 100 pieces per hour and 780 units are produced in one eight-hour shift; the efficiency is 780/800 converted to a percentage, or 97.5 percent. (2) The work is measured in hours and took 8.21 hours to produce 8 standard hours; the efficiency is 8/8.21 converted to a percentage or 97.5 percent. (3) The work is measured in dollars and produces $780 with a standard of $800; the efficiency is $780/$800 converted to a percentage, or 97.5 percent.

efficiency variance—In cost accounting, the difference between the actual volume of a resource used and the budgeted volume, multiplied by the budgeted or standard price.

efficient consumer response (ECR)—Replenishment through a distribution network based on point-of-sale information.

e-form—Abbreviation for electronic form.

EFT—Abbreviation for electronic funds transfer.

EI—Abbreviation for employee involvement.

80-20—A term referring to the Pareto principle. The principle suggests that most effects come from relatively few causes; that is, 80 percent of the effects (or sales or costs) come from 20 percent of the possible causes (or items). See: ABC classification.

EIPP—Abbreviation for electronic invoice presentment and payment.

elasticity of demand (supply)—The ratio of the percentage change in quantity demanded (supplied) to the percentage change in price.

e-learning—Training or schooling done online.

electronic bill presentment and payment (eBPP)—A system that connects the bill issuer, bill payer, and the payer's bank to facilitate electronic payment. Payment is usually by credit card.

electronic commerce (e-commerce)—The use of computer and telecommunication technologies to conduct business via electronic transfer of data and documents.

electronic commerce application—A computer interface between two organizations that is used to carry out business transactions electronically.

electronic communities—Communities of people who communicate exclusively electronically.

electronic data interchange (EDI)—The paperless (electronic) exchange of trading documents, such as purchase orders, shipment authorizations, advanced shipment notices, and invoices, using standardized document formats.

electronic document—The electronic representation of a document that can be printed.

electronic form—An electronic version of a paper form. These forms eliminate the cost of printing, storing, and distributing paper forms.

electronic funds transfer (EFT)—A computerized system that processes financial transactions and information about these transactions or performs the exchange of value between two parties.

electronic invoice presentment and payment (EIPP)—Accepting and sending invoices and payments over the internet.

electronic mail (email)—A technology for handling mail electronically.

electronic market—An internet-based market where most sales occur electronically.

electronic product codes (EPCs)—Codes that are used with RFID tags to carry information on the product that will support warranty programs.

electronic publishing—Representation of text and multimedia documents electronically.

electronic signature—An authentication that validates a transaction by means of an authorization code to identify an individual or group.

email—Acronym for electronic mail.

embezzlement—The fraudulent taking of another's property while acting in a fiduciary capacity.

empathy—A dimension of service quality referring to caring, individualized attention from a service firm.

empirical—Pertaining to a statement or formula based upon experience or observation rather than on deduction or theory.

employee assistance program (EAP)—Employer-provided service aimed at helping employees and their families with personal and work-related problems. Examples include financial counseling and chemical-dependency rehabilitation programs.

employee empowerment—The practice of giving non-managerial employees the responsibility and the power to make decisions regarding their jobs or tasks. It is associated with the practice of transfer of managerial responsibility to the employee. Empowerment allows the employee to take on responsibility for tasks normally associated with staff specialists. Examples include allowing the employee to make scheduling, quality, process design, or purchasing decisions.

employee involvement (EI)—The concept of using the experience, creative energy, and intelligence of all employees by treating them with respect, keeping them informed, and including them and their ideas in decision-making processes appropriate to their areas of expertise. Employee involvement focuses on quality and productivity improvements. Syn: people involvement.

employee stock ownership plan (ESOP)—In the United States, a program that encourages workers to purchase company stock—generally tied into the compensation/benefits package. The intention is to give workers a feeling of participation in the management and direction of the company.

empowerment—A condition whereby employees have the authority to make decisions and take action in their work areas without prior approval. For example, an operator can stop a production process if a problem is detected, or a customer service representative can send out a replacement product if a customer calls with a problem.

encryption—Changing readable words into another form, called a cipher, which hides the text's meaning.

ending inventory—A statement of on-hand quantities or the dollar value of a SKU at the end of a period, often determined by a physical inventory.

end item—A product sold as a completed item or repair part; any item subject to a customer order or sales forecast. Syn: end product, finished good, finished product. See: good.

end-of-life-inventory—Inventory kept on hand to satisfy demand for products that are no longer being manufactured.

end-of-life management—Planning for the phase-out of one product and the phase-in of a new product to avoid both the excessive inventory of and an out-of-stock situation with the old product before the replacement product is available.

endogenous variable—A variable whose value is determined by relationships included within the model.

end product—Syn: end item.

end user—1) The final consumer of a product. 2) The recipient of an output from a computer system.

end-user computing—Use of computer resources by non-information-system personnel to enter, retrieve, manipulate, or print data.

enforced problem solving—The methodology of intentionally restricting a resource (e.g., inventory, storage space, number of workers) to expose a problem that must then be resolved.

engineering change—A revision to a drawing or design released by engineering to modify or correct a part. The request for the change can be from a customer or from production, quality control, another department, or a supplier. Syn: engineering change notice, engineering change order.

engineering change notice—Syn: engineering change.

engineering change order—Syn: engineering change.

engineering characteristics—The technical features designed into a product.

engineering drawings—A visual representation of the dimensional characteristics of a part or assembly at some stage of manufacture.

engineering order—Syn: experimental order.

engineering standard—Design or test guidelines intended to promote the design, production, and test of a part, component, or product in a manner that promotes standardization, ease of maintenance, consistency, adequacy of test procedures, versatility of design, ease of production and field service, and minimization of the number of different tools and special tools required.

engineer-to-order—Products whose customer specifications require unique engineering design, significant customization, or new purchased materials. Each customer order results in a unique set of part numbers, bills of material, and routings. Syn: design-to-order.

en route—A term describing goods in transit.

enterprise—Any undertaking, venture, initiative, or business organization with a defined mission.

enterprise performance management (EPM)—The process of monitoring performance across the enterprise with the goal of improving business performance. An EPM system integrates and analyzes data from many sources, including e-commerce systems, front- and back-office applications, data warehouses, and external data sources. Advanced EPM systems can support many performance methodologies, such as the balanced scorecard.

enterprise resources management—The planning, execution, control, and measurement functions required to effectively operate an enterprise.

enterprise resources planning (ERP)—Framework for organizing, defining, and standardizing the business processes necessary to effectively plan and control an organization so the organization can use its internal knowledge to seek external advantage.

enterprise resources portal—A means for a company to share, exchange, or transact information with an external business partner using internet-based technologies. An enterprise resources portal is often associated with an enterprise resources planning system, which can be configured to share or present such information via an internet portal or hyperlink. An enterprise resources portal can also be one means of implementing a private trading exchange.

entrepreneur—One who organizes resources productively and bears the risk of the venture.

environmentally responsible business—A firm that operates in such a way as to minimize deleterious impacts to society. See: green manufacturing, green supply chain.

environmentally responsible manufacturing—A collection of manufacturing activities that includes design of the product, facility, manufacturing processes, logistics, and supplier relationships that reduce or eliminate environmental waste through innovation and improvements.

environmentally responsible purchasing—Syn: responsible procurement.

environmentally sensitive engineering—Designing with consideration of how a product or its packaging will ultimately be disposed.

Environmental Protection Agency (EPA)—A U.S. agency with regulatory authority over matters affecting the environment, including waste generation and habitat destruction.

environmental scanning—Process used to expose an organization's potential strengths, weaknesses, opportunities, and threats. Many experts emphasize opportunities and threats because the tool is primarily external.

EOQ—Abbreviation for economic order quantity.

EOQ = 1—Reducing setup time and inventory to the point where it is economically sound to produce in batches with a size of one. Often EOQ = 1 is an ideal to strive for, like zero defects.

EOQ tables—Tables listing several ranges of monthly usages in dollars and the appropriate order size in dollars or monthly usage for each usage range.

EPA—Abbreviation for Environmental Protection Agency.

EPC—Abbreviation for electronic product code.

EPM—Abbreviation for enterprise performance management.

equal employment opportunity (EEO)—In the United States, the laws prohibiting discrimination in employment because of race or color, sex, age, handicap status, religion, and national origin.

Equal Employment Opportunity Commission (EEOC)—An administrative agency in the United States that oversees Title VII of the Civil Rights Act, which prohibits employment discrimination based on race, color, religion, sex, or national origin.

equal protection clause—A part of the Fourteenth Amendment to the U.S. Constitution requiring similar treatment of citizens in similar circumstances.

equal runout method—Syn: equal runout quantities.

equal runout quantities—Order quantities for items in a group that result in a supply that covers an equal time for all items. Syn: equal runout method. See: fair-share quantity logic.

equilibrium point—The point in a market where the demand for a product and the supply of that product are exactly equal. If supply were greater, the price would fall. If demand were greater, the price would rise. Free markets tend to move toward their equilibrium point.

equipment class—A means to describe a group of equipment with similar characteristics for purposes of planning and scheduling.

equity—The part of a company's total assets not provided by creditors; owner-invested funds.

equivalent days—The standard hour requirements of a job converted to days for scheduling purposes.

equivalent unit cost—A method of costing that uses the total cost incurred for all like units for a period of time divided by the equivalent units completed during the same time period.

E

equivalent units—A translation of inventories into equivalent finished goods units or of inventories exploded back to raw materials for period end valuation of inventories. An equivalent unit can be the sum of several partially completed units. Two units 50 percent completed are equivalent to one unit 100 percent completed.

ergonomics—Approach to job design that focuses on the interactions between the human operator and such traditional environmental elements as atmospheric contaminants, heat, light, sound, and all tools and equipment.

ERP—Abbreviation for enterprise resources planning.

ES—Abbreviation for early start date.

escalation—An amount or percentage by which a contract price may be adjusted if specified contingencies occur, such as changes in the supplier's raw material or labor costs.

ESI—Abbreviation for early supplier involvement.

ESOP—Acronym for employee stock ownership plan.

estimate at completion (EAC)—Estimated cost of an activity or project when the defined scope of work will be finished. It is the actual cost-to-date plus estimate-to-complete for uncompleted activities.

estimate of error—In statistics, a measure of dispersion. See: standard deviation, standard error, variance.

estimate to complete (ETC)—Expected cost to complete all remaining work for an activity or project.

ETC—Abbreviation for estimate to complete.

ethical standards—A set of guidelines for proper conduct by business professionals. For example, the ISM (formerly NAPM) provides a set of principles and standards for the proper conduct of purchasing activities.

euro—Official currency of the Eurozone, which forms a large part of the European Union.

eurobond—An internationally marketed bond.

eurocurrency—Money that is deposited outside of the country that issued it (outside of the issuing country's control).

eurodollar—A U.S. dollar held in a foreign bank.

European Union (EU)—An economic and political union of European countries, created to strengthen economies and lower trade barriers.

evaporating cloud—In the theory of constraints, a logic-based tool for surfacing assumptions related to a conflict or problem. Once the assumptions are surfaced,

actions to break an assumption and hence solve (evaporate) the problem can be determined.

event—An event is an identifiable point in time among a set of related activities. Graphically, an event can be represented by two approaches: (1) in activity-on-node networks, it is represented by a node; (2) in activity-on-arrow networks, the event is represented by the arrow.

event-based marketing—Promoting goods or services through specific events.

event-on-arrow network—Syn: activity-on-arrow network.

event-on-node network—Syn: activity-on-node network.

everyday low prices (EDLP)—A retail strategy of keeping prices low across all products or services as opposed to having sales at certain times.

exception message—Syn: action message.

exception report—A report that lists or flags only those items that deviate from the plan.

excess capacity—Capacity that is not used to either produce or protect the creation of throughput.

excess inventory—Any inventory in the system that exceeds the minimum amount necessary to achieve the desired throughput rate at the constraint or that exceeds the minimum amount necessary to achieve the desired due date performance. Total inventory = productive inventory + protective inventory + excess inventory.

excess issue—The removal from stock and assignment to a schedule of a quantity higher than the schedule quantity. Syn: overissue.

exchange rate—The rate at which one currency converts to another.

exchange unit—The number of units to be produced before changing the bit, tool, or die. See: process batch.

exclusive use—Carrier vehicles assigned for the exclusive use of a particular shipper.

executing processes—The processes performed to complete a project plan to accomplish the objectives set forth in the project scope.

executive dashboard—A set of cross-functional metrics for measuring company performance that indicates the health of the company. It usually includes the company's key performance indicators. See: dashboard.

executive information system—A software application used by top managers, without assistance, to access information on the current organizational status.

executive sales and operations planning—The portion of sales and operations planning that defines executive decision-making processes to balance supply and demand at the volume level in families, fully integrates financial planning and operational planning, and that provides a forum for establishing and linking high-level strategic plans with day-to-day operations. See: sales and operations planning.

exemplar—A particularly strong practice that should be imitated.

exempt—Generally, a classification of employees/jobs for which compensation is not determined by extending the recorded hours worked by an hourly rate (e.g., pay is specified at an annual or monthly rate). Exempt employees include most professionals, administrative and management personnel, and sales representatives. Specifically, the term refers to and is fully defined by the U.S. Department of Labor Fair Labor Standards Act, which regulates minimum wages and overtime for nonexempt employees. See: exempt positions, nonexempt positions.

exempt carrier—A for-hire carrier that is free from economic regulation.

exempt employee—A person filling an exempt position. See: exempt positions.

exempt positions—Positions that do not require the payment of overtime because they meet the tests of executive, supervisory, or administrative activity, as defined under the Fair Labor Standards Act.

exit interview—An interview given to an employee who is leaving the company. The purpose is to find out why a person is leaving, what was liked and disliked about the job and the company, and what changes would make the department and the company a better place to work.

exogenous variable—A variable whose values are determined by considerations outside the model in question.

expansion—Any increase in the capacity of a plant, facility, or unit, usually by added investment. The scope of this increase extends from the elimination of problem areas to the complete replacement of an existing facility with a larger one.

expected completion quantity—The planned quantity of a manufacturing order after expected scrap.

expected demand—The quantity expected to be consumed during a given time period when usage is at the forecast rate. See: demand during lead time.

expected demand during lead time—Syn: demand during lead time.

expected life—The average length of time a product remains in service or in a serviceable condition.

expected receipt date—Syn: due date.

expected value—The average value that would be observed in taking an action an infinite number of times. The expected value of an action is calculated by multiplying the outcome of the action by the probability of achieving the outcome.

expedite—To rush or chase production or purchase orders that are needed in less than the normal lead time; to take extraordinary action because of an increase in relative priority. Syn: stockchase.

expeditor—A production control person whose primary duty is expediting.

expendables—Syn: consumables.

expense—Expenditures of short-term value, including depreciation, as opposed to land and other fixed capital. See: overhead.

expensed stocks—Syn: floor stocks.

experience curve—Syn: learning curve.

experience curve pricing—The average cost pricing method, but using an estimate of future average costs, based on an experience (learning) curve.

experimental design—A formal plan that details the specifics for conducting an experiment, such as which statistical techniques and responses, factors, levels, blocks, and treatments, are to be used.

experimental order—An order generated by the laboratory, research and development, or engineering group that must be run through regular production facilities with potential future product or market development as a project or team goal. Syn: engineering order, laboratory order, pilot order, R&D order.

experimental research—A form of research (sometimes used in marketing research) where matched sets of people are controlled for certain variables (such as income, age, and so on) while other variables (such as products offered) are varied to test research questions. See: marketing research.

expert system—A type of artificial intelligence computer system that mimics human experts by using rules and heuristics rather than deterministic algorithms.

explode—To perform a bill-of-material explosion.

explode-to-deduct—Syn: backflush.

explosion—Syn: requirements explosion. Ant: implosion.

explosion level—Syn: low-level code.

exponential distribution—A continuous probability distribution where the probability of occurrence either steadily increases or decreases. The steady increase case (positive exponential distribution) is used to model phenomena such as customer service level versus cost. The steady decrease case (negative exponential distribution) is used to model phenomena such as the weight given to any one time period of demand in exponential smoothing.

exponential smoothing forecast—A type of weighted moving average forecasting technique in which past observations are geometrically discounted according to their age. The heaviest weight is assigned to the most recent data. The smoothing is termed exponential because data points are weighted in accordance with an exponential function of their age. The technique makes use of a smoothing constant to apply to the difference between the most recent forecast and the critical sales data, thus avoiding the necessity of carrying historical sales data. The approach can be used for data that exhibit no trend or seasonal patterns. Higher order exponential smoothing models can be used for data with either (or both) trend and seasonality.

export broker—A party that introduces the buyer to the seller and eventually withdraws, getting a fee for services rendered.

export compliance—Cooperating with export rules regarding packaging and documentation.

export license—A document received from a governmental agency authorizing a certain quantity of an export to be sent to a given country.

exports—Products produced in one country and sold in another.

exposures—The number of times per year that the system risks a stockout. The number of exposures is arrived at by dividing the lot size into the annual usage.

express—1) Carrier payment to its customers when ships, rail cars, or trailers are unloaded or loaded in less than the time allowed by contract and returned to the carrier for use. See: demurrage, detention. 2) The use of priority package delivery to achieve overnight or second-day delivery.

express warranty—A positive representation, made by a seller, concerning the nature, character, use, and pur-

pose of goods, that induces the buyer to buy and on which the seller intends the buyer to depend.

extended enterprise—The notion that supply chain partners form a larger entity. See: supply chain community.

extensible markup language (XML)—This language facilitates direct communication among computers on the internet. Unlike the older hypertext markup language (HTML), which provides HTML tags giving instructions to a web browser about how to display information, XML tags give instructions to a web browser about the category of information.

external customer—A person or organization that receives a good, a service, or information but is not part of the organization supplying it. See: customer, internal customer.

external environment—All the factors that exist outside the boundary of the organization that have the possibility of affecting any part of the organization. See: internal environment, organizational environment.

external factory—A situation where suppliers are viewed as an extension of the firm's manufacturing capabilities and capacities. The same practices and concerns that are commonly applied to the management of the firm's manufacturing system should also be applied to the management of the external factory.

external failure costs—The costs related to problems found after the product reaches the customer. This usually includes such costs as warranty and returns.

externality—The costs or benefits of a firm's activities borne or received by others.

external setup time—The time associated with elements of a setup procedure performed while the process or machine is running. Ant: internal setup time.

extranet—A network connection to a partner's network using secure information processing and internet protocols to do business.

extrapolation—Estimation of the future value of some data series based on past observations. Statistical forecasting is a common example. Syn: projection.

extrinsic forecasting method—A forecast method on a correlated leading indicator, such as estimating furniture sales based on housing starts. Extrinsic forecasts tend to be more useful for large aggregations, such as total company sales, than for individual product sales. Ant: intrinsic forecast method. See: quantitative forecasting technique.

F

fabrication—Manufacturing operations for making components, as opposed to assembly operations.

fabrication level—The lowest production level. The only components at this level are parts (as opposed to assemblies or subassemblies). These parts are either procured from outside sources or fabricated within the manufacturing organization.

fabrication order—A manufacturing order to a component-making department authorizing it to produce component parts. See: batch card, manufacturing order.

fabricator—A manufacturer that turns the product of a converter into a larger variety of products. For example, a fabricator may turn steel rods into nuts, bolts, and twist drills, or may turn paper into bags and boxes.

facilitating products—Products that support the operations of a firm but are not sold externally, such as furniture and computers.

facilities—The physical plant, distribution centers, service centers, offices, laboratories, and related equipment.

facility layout—Describes where machines and utilities will be located in a facility, as well as the arrangement of processes.

facility planning—Long range plan of what capacity is needed, when it will be needed, and what facilities will meet these requirements; also, a plan for the layout of these facilities.

factory within a factory—A technique to improve management focus and overall productivity by creating autonomous business units within a larger physical plant. Syn: plant within a plant.

failsafe techniques—Syn: failsafe work methods, poka-yoke.

failsafe work methods—Methods of performing operations so that actions that are incorrect cannot be completed. For example, a part without holes in the proper place cannot be removed from a jig, or a computer system will reject invalid numbers or require double entry of transaction quantities outside the normal range. Called poka-yoke by the Japanese. Syn: failsafe techniques, mistake-proofing, poka-yoke.

failure analysis—The collection, examination, review, and classification of failures to determine trends and to identify poorly performing parts or components.

failure costs—A term used within the cost of poor quality model to include both internal and external failure costs. See: cost of poor quality, external failure costs, internal failure costs.

failure mode analysis (FMA)—A procedure to determine which malfunction symptoms appear immediately before or after a failure of a critical parameter in a system. After all the possible causes are listed for each symptom, the product is designed to eliminate the problems.

failure mode effects analysis (FMEA)—A procedure in which each potential failure mode in every sub-item of an item is analyzed to determine its effect on other sub-items and on the required function of the item.

failure mode effects and criticality analysis (FMECA)—A procedure that is performed after a failure mode effects analysis to classify each potential failure effect according to its severity and probability of occurrence.

Fair Labor Standards Act (FLSA)—Federal law that governs the definitions of management and labor and establishes wage payment and hours worked and other employment practices.

fair return—Within transportation, a profit level accomplishing a rate of return on investment that regulatory agencies deem acceptable given the level of risk.

fair-share quantity logic—The process of equitably allocating available stock among field distribution centers. Fair-share quantity logic is normally used when stock available from a central inventory location is less than the cumulative requirements of the field stocking locations. The use of fair-share quantity logic involves procedures that "push" stock out to the field, instead of allowing the field to "pull" in what is needed. The objective is to maximize customer service from the limited available inventory. See: equal runout quantities.

family—A group of end items whose similarity of design and manufacture facilitates their being planned in aggregate, whose sales performance is monitored together, and, occasionally, whose cost is aggregated at this level.

family contracts—A purchase order that groups families of similar parts together to obtain pricing advantages and a continuous supply of material.

FAQs—Abbreviation for frequently asked questions.

FAS—1) Abbreviation for final assembly schedule. 2) Abbreviation for free alongside ship.

fast-tracking—A project schedule compression technique that overlaps (or performs in parallel) activities that would ordinarily be performed sequentially.

fault isolation—A technique used to identify the cause of a defect.

fault tolerance—The ability of a system to avoid or minimize the disruptive effects of defects by using some form of redundancy or extra design margins.

fault tree analysis—A logical approach to identify the probabilities and frequencies of events in a system that are most critical to uninterrupted and safe operation. This analysis may include failure mode effects analysis (determining the result of component failure interactions toward system safety) and techniques for human error prediction.

feasibility study—An analysis designed to establish the practicality and cost justification of a given project and, if it appears to be advisable to do so, to determine the direction of subsequent project efforts.

feasible economic order quantity—When solving a quantity discount problem, the economic order quantity is feasible if the computed number can be purchased at the cost used in the EOQ problem rather than at some other discount quantity. For example, consider a product that sells for $10 for 1 to 99 units, $9 for 100 to 499 units, and $8 for 500 for more units. If the quantity discount solution calls for purchasing 800 units at the $8 value, the solution is feasible; however if the quantity discount solution calls for purchasing 250 units at this cost the solution is not feasible, because the purchase quantity is not consistent with the purchase price for that quantity.

feature—A distinctive characteristic of a good or service. The characteristic is provided by an option, accessory, or attachment. For example, in ordering a new car, the customer must specify an engine type and size (option), but need not necessarily select an air conditioner (attachment). See: accessory, attachment, option.

feature code—An identifying code assigned to a distinct product feature that may contain one or more specific part number configurations.

Federal Trade Commission (FTC)—The United States governmental agency charged with protecting businesses and consumers from unfair business practices. It also regulates advertising and promotion at the national level.

fee—The charge for the use of the contractor's organization for the period and to the extent specified in the contract.

feedback—The flow of information back into the control system so that actual performance can be compared with planned performance.

feedback loop—The part of a closed-loop system that allows the comparison of response with command.

feeder workstations—An area of manufacture whose products feed a subsequent work area.

feedstock—The primary raw material in a chemical or refining process normally received by pipeline or large-scale bulk shipments. Feedstock availability is frequently the controlling factor in setting the production schedule and rate for a process.

FEFO—Abbreviation for first expiry first out.

FEU—An abbreviation for forty-foot equivalent unit.

fiduciary—One having the duty to act on another's behalf in a trustworthy and confidential fashion.

field—A specified area of a record used for a particular category of data.

field finished goods—Finished goods kept in distribution centers or warehouses.

field service—The functions of installing and maintaining a product for a customer after the sale or during the lease. Field service may also include training and implementation assistance. Syn: after-sale service.

field service parts—Service parts kept in distribution centers or warehouses.

field warehouse—Syn: distribution center.

FIFO—Acronym for first in, first out.

file—An organized collection of records.

file structure—The manner in which records are stored within a file (e.g., sequential, random, index-sequential).

file transfer protocol (FTP)—A protocol used to transfer files over the internet.

fill rate—Syn: customer service ratio.

final assembly—The highest level assembled product, as it is shipped to customers.

final assembly department—The name for the manufacturing department where the product is assembled. See: blending department, pack-out department.

F

final assembly schedule (FAS)—A schedule of end items to finish the product for specific customers' orders in a make-to-order or assemble-to-order environment. It is also referred to as the finishing schedule because it may involve operations other than the final assembly; also, it may not involve assembly (e.g., final mixing, cutting, packaging). The FAS is prepared after receipt of a customer order as constrained by the availability of material and capacity, and it schedules the operations required to complete the product from the level where it is stocked (or master scheduled) to the end-item level.

financial accounting—The use of generally accepted accounting principles to prepare reports to external agencies, such as investors and governmental agencies.

financial benchmarking—Comparing one company's financial results with that of another company. This type of benchmarking need not involve direct contact between the initiator company and the target company, as many financial records are publicly available. See: benchmarking.

financial forecasting—Estimating a firm's future financial statements.

financial leverage management ratios—A set of measurements of the degree to which a firm is financing assets with fixed-charge instruments such as debt or preferred stock.

financial management—The function concerned with ensuring the availability of funds for research and development, operations, and marketing.

finish date—The time of completion of a project or activity. It may be planned, actual, early, late, baseline, or target.

finished good—Syn: end item.

finished goods inventory—Those items on which all manufacturing operations, including final test, have been completed. These products are available for shipment to the customer as either end items or repair parts. Syn: finished products inventory. See: goods.

finished good waivers—Approvals for deviation from normal product specifications.

finished product—Syn: end item.

finished products inventory—Syn: finished goods inventory.

finishing lead time—1) The time that is necessary to finish manufacturing a good after receipt of a customer order. 2) The time allowed for completing the good based on the final assembly schedule.

finish-to-finish—In project management, a network requirement that activity A must be finished before subsequent activity B can finish. See: logical relationship.

finish-to-order—Syn: assemble-to-order.

finish-to-start—In project management, a network requirement that activity A must be finished before activity B can start. See: logical relationship.

finite forward scheduling—An equipment scheduling technique that builds a schedule by proceeding sequentially from the initial period to the final period while observing capacity limits. A Gantt chart may be used with this technique. See: finite loading.

finite loading—Assigning no more work to a work center than the work center can be expected to execute in a given time period. The specific term usually refers to a computer technique that involves calculating shop priority revisions in order to level load operation by operation. Syn: finite scheduling. See: drum-buffer-rope.

finite scheduling—Syn: finite loading.

firewall—A device used to control access to a company's data from the internet or other outside sources.

firm fixed-price contract—A contract in which the seller is paid a set price without regard to costs. Syn: fixed-price contract.

firm master production schedule—A part of the master production schedule in which changes can occur only rarely.

firm offer—A written offer to buy or sell goods that will be held open for a stipulated period.

firm planned order (FPO)—A planned order that can be frozen in quantity and time. The computer is not allowed to change it automatically; this is the responsibility of the planner in charge of the item that is being planned. This technique can aid planners working with MRP systems to respond to material and capacity problems by firming up selected planned orders. In addition, firm planned orders are the normal method of stating the master production schedule. See: planning time fence.

first-article inspection—A quality check on the first component run after a new setup has been completed. Syn: first-piece inspection.

first-come-first-served rule—A dispatching rule under which the jobs are sequenced by their arrival times. See: first-in, first-out.

first expiry first out (FEFO)—A picking methodology assuring that the usage shelf life of items is optimized. Years ago, first in, first out (FIFO) was satisfactory as the shelf-life days for items often didn't vary and FIFO often coincided with the expiry dates. However, re-testing is frequently done to extend shelf-life dates on some lots or batches, while other lots may have typical shelf-life dates shortened because of quality or processes. Thus, FEFO was introduced by software vendors to provide this picking methodology for use with shelf-life controlled items.

first in, first out (FIFO)—A method of inventory valuation for accounting purposes. The accounting assumption is that the oldest inventory (first in) is the first to be used (first out), but there is no necessary relationship with the actual physical movement of specific items. See: first-come-first-served rule, average cost system.

first-mover advantage—The phenomenon of market leadership being gained through market innovation.

first-order smoothing—A single exponential smoothing; a weighted moving average approach that is applied to forecasting problems where the data do not exhibit significant trend or seasonal patterns. Syn: single exponential smoothing, single smoothing.

first pass yield—The ratio of products that conform to specifications without rework or modification to total input.

first-piece inspection—Syn: first-article inspection.

first-tier supplier—One that supplies goods or services directly to a business.

fishbone analysis—A technique to organize the elements of a problem or situation to aid in the determination of the causes of the problem or situation. The analysis relates the effect of the environment to the several possible sources of the problem.

fishbone chart—Syn: cause-and-effect diagram.

fishbone diagram—Syn: cause-and-effect diagram.

fitness for use—A term used to indicate that a good or service fits the customer's defined purpose for that good or service.

five focusing steps—In the theory of constraints, a process to continuously improve organizational profit by evaluating the production system and market mix to determine how to make the most profit using the system constraint. The steps consist of (1) identifying the constraint to the system, (2) deciding how to exploit the constraint to the system, (3) subordinating all nonconstraints to the constraint, (4) elevating the constraint to the system, (5) returning to step 1 if the constraint is broken in any previous step, while not allowing inertia to set in.

five-forces model of competition—A methodology for analyzing competitive pressures in a market and assessing the strength and importance of each of those pressures.

five Ms—The branches of a cause and effect (fishbone) diagram: manpower, methods, materials, machines, and measurements.

five Ss—Five terms beginning with "S" used to create a workplace suitable for lean production. Sort means to separate needed items from unneeded ones and remove the latter. Simplify means to neatly arrange items for use. Scrub means clean up the work area. Standardize means to sort, simplify, and scrub daily. Sustain means to always follow the first four Ss. Sometimes referred to by the Japanese equivalents: seiri, seiton, seiso, seiketsu, and shitsuke.

five whys—The common practice in total quality management is to ask "why" five times when confronted with a problem. By the time the answer to the fifth "why" is found, the ultimate cause of the problem is identified. Syn: five Ws. See: root cause analysis.

five Ws—Syn: five whys.

fixed assets—Assets acquired for use within a company having an estimated useful life of one year or more.

fixed-asset turnover—Sales divided by net fixed assets. Fixed assets reflect asset acquisition price less depreciation.

fixed budget—A budget of expected costs based on a specific level of production or other activity.

fixed cost—An expenditure that does not vary with the production volume; for example, rent, property tax, and salaries of certain personnel.

fixed-cost contribution per unit—An allocation process where total fixed cost for a period is divided by total units produced in that given time period.

fixed-interval order system—Syn: fixed reorder cycle inventory model.

fixed-interval review system—A hybrid inventory system in which the inventory analyst reviews the inventory position at fixed time periods. If the inventory level is found to be above a preset reorder point, no action is taken. If the inventory level is at or below the reorder point, the analyst orders a variable quantity equal to M – x where M is a maximum stock level and x is the current quantity on hand and on order (if any). This hybrid system does not reorder every review interval. It therefore differs from the fixed-interval order system, which automatically places an order whenever inventory is reviewed.

fixed-location storage—A method of storage in which a relatively permanent location is assigned for the storage of each item in a storeroom or warehouse. Although more space is needed to store parts than in a random-location storage system, fixed locations become familiar, and therefore a locator file may not be needed. See: random-location storage.

fixed order period system—A method of inventory planning that measures actual inventory levels at regular intervals of time; either an order is placed every time or a check of inventory levels is made and an order placed if needed. Often the quantity ordered varies from period to period as inventory is restored to a predetermined level. See: fixed order quantity system.

fixed order quantity—A lot-sizing technique in MRP or inventory management that will always cause planned or actual orders to be generated for a predetermined fixed quantity, or multiples thereof, if net requirements for the period exceed the fixed order quantity.

fixed order quantity system—An inventory system, such as economic order quantity, in which the same order quantity is used from order to order. The time between orders (order period) then varies from order to order. Syn: fixed reorder quantity inventory model. See: fixed order period system.

fixed overhead—Traditionally, all manufacturing costs—other than direct labor and direct materials—that continue even if products are not produced. Although fixed overhead is necessary to produce the product, it cannot be directly traced to the final product.

fixed-period quantity—An MRP lot-sizing technique that sets the lot size equal to the net requirements for a given number of periods.

fixed-period requirements—A lot-sizing technique that sets the order quantity to the demand for a given number of periods. See: discrete order quantity.

fixed-position layout—A factory layout that plans for the product to be in a set place; the people, machines, and tools are brought to and from the product.

fixed-position manufacturing—Similar to project manufacturing, this type of manufacturing is mostly used for large, complex projects, where the product remains in one locations for its full assembly period or may move from location to location after considerable work and time are spent on it. Examples of fixed position manufacturing include shipbuilding or aircraft assembly,

where the costs of frequent movement of the product are very high.

fixed-price contract—Syn: firm fixed-price contract.

fixed-price-incentive-fee contract—A contract in which the seller is paid a set price and can earn an additional profit if certain stipulations are met.

fixed property—Property attached to, and not easily removed from, the location.

fixed reorder cycle inventory model—A form of independent demand management model in which an order is placed every n time units. The order quantity is variable and essentially replaces the items consumed during the current time period. Let M be the maximum inventory desired at any time, and let x be the quantity on hand at the time the order is placed. Then, in the simplest model, the order quantity will be M − x. The quantity M must be large enough to cover the maximum expected demand during the lead time plus a review interval. The order quantity model becomes more complicated whenever the replenishment lead time exceeds the review interval, because outstanding orders then have to be factored into the equation. These reorder systems are sometimes called fixed-interval order systems, order level systems, or periodic review systems. Syn: fixed-interval order system, fixed order quantity system, order level system, periodic review system, time-based order system. See: fixed reorder quantity inventory model, hybrid inventory system, independent demand item management models, optional replenishment model.

fixed reorder quantity inventory model—A form of independent demand item management model in expected demand during the replenishment lead time. Fixed reorder quantity models assume the existence of some form of a perpetual inventory record or some form of physical tracking (e.g., a two-bin system that is able to determine when the reorder point is reached). These reorder systems are sometimes called fixed order quantity systems, lot-size systems, or order point-order quantity systems. Syn: fixed order quantity system, lot-size system, order point-order quantity system, quantity-based order system. See: fixed reorder cycle inventory model, hybrid inventory system, independent demand item management models, optional replenishment model, order point, order point system, statistical inventory control, time-phased order point.

fixture—A device to hold and locate a work piece during inspection or production operations. See: jig.

flag of convenience—A ship registered in a nation with low taxes and lax safety regulations. Liberia and Panama are two favorite flags of convenience.

flatbed—A type of truck trailer that has a floor but no enclosure. Sideboards or tie-downs are used to prevent cargo from falling off.

flatcar—A railroad car without sides used for hauling machinery.

flexibility—1) The ability of the manufacturing system to respond quickly, in terms of range and time, to external or internal changes. Six different categories of flexibility can be considered: mix flexibility, design changeover flexibility, modification flexibility, volume flexibility, re-routing flexibility, and material flexibility (see each term for a more detailed discussion). In addition, flexibility involves concerns of product flexibility. Flexibility can be useful in coping with various types of uncertainty (regarding mix, volume, and so on). 2) The ability of a supply chain to mitigate, or neutralize, the risks of demand forecast variability, supply continuity variability, cycle time plus lead-time uncertainty, and transit time plus customs-clearance time uncertainty during periods of increasing or diminishing volume.

flexibility responsiveness—The ability of the firm and its management to change rapidly in response to changes taking place in the marketplace.

flexible automation—Automation that provides short setup times and the ability to switch quickly from one product to another.

flexible benefits/cafeteria plans—Plans designed to give employees a core of minimum basic coverage with the option to choose additional coverage or, sometimes, cash. Employees can customize their benefits packages to suit their personal needs.

flexible budget—A budget showing the costs and revenues expected to be incurred or realized over a period of time at different levels of activity, measured in terms of some activity base such as direct labor hours, direct labor costs, or machine hours. A flexible manufacturing overhead budget gives the product costs of various manufacturing overhead items at different levels of activity. See: step budget.

flexible capability—Machinery's ability to be readily adapted to processing different components on an ongoing basis.

flexible capacity—The ability to operate manufacturing equipment at different production rates by varying staffing levels and operating hours or starting and stopping at will.

flexible machine center (FMC)—An automated system, which usually consists of computer numerical control machines with robots loading and unloading the parts conveyed into, and through, the system. Its purpose is to provide quicker throughput, changeovers, setups, and so forth to enable the manufacturing of multiple products.

flexible manufacturing system (FMS)—A group of numerically controlled machine tools interconnected by a central control system. The various machining cells are interconnected via loading and unloading stations by an automated transport system. Operational flexibility is enhanced by the ability to execute all manufacturing tasks on numerous product designs in small quantities and with faster delivery.

flexible path equipment—Materials handling equipment such as forklifts that do not have to follow fixed paths.

flexible specialization—A strategy based on multi-use equipment, skilled workers, and innovative senior managers to accommodate the continuous change that occurs in the marketplace.

flexible workforce—A workforce whose members are cross-trained and whose work rules permit assignment of individual workers to different tasks.

flextime—An arrangement in which employees are allowed to choose work hours as long as the standard number of work hours is worked.

float—1) The amount of work-in-process inventory between two manufacturing operations, especially in repetitive manufacturing. 2) In supply chains, the time necessary for items such as documents and checks to go from one supply chain partner to another. 3) In the critical path method of project management, the amount of time that an activity's early start or early finish time can be delayed without delaying the completion time of the entire project. There are three types: total float, free float, and independent float. Syn: path float, slack.

floating inventory location system—Syn: random-location storage.

floating order point—An order point that is responsive to changes in demand or to changes in lead time.

floating storage location—Syn: random-location storage.

floor-ready merchandise—Products shipped by a supplier having all needed tags, prices, security devices, and so on already in place.

floor stocks—Stocks of inexpensive production parts held in the factory, from which production workers can draw without requisitions. Syn: bench stocks, expensed stocks.

flowchart—The output of a flowcharting process, a chart that shows the operations, transportation, storages, delays, inspections, and so on related to a process. Flowcharts are drawn to better understand processes. The flowchart is one of the seven tools of quality. Syn: flow diagram. See: block diagram, flow process chart.

flowcharting—A systems analysis tool that graphically presents a procedure. Symbols are used to represent operations, transportations, inspections, storages, delays, and equipment.

flow control—A specific production control system that is based primarily on setting production rates and feeding work into production to meet these planned rates, then monitoring and controlling production. See: shop floor control.

flow diagram—Syn: flowchart.

flow line—Syn: flow shop.

flow manufacturing—Syn: flow shop.

flow order—An order filled, not by moving material through production as an integral lot, but by production made over time and checked by a cumulative count until the flow order quantity is complete.

flow plant—Syn: flow shop.

flow process chart—A graphic, symbolic representation of the work performed, or to be performed, on a product as it passes through some or all of the stages of a process. Typically, the information included in the chart is quantity, distance moved, type of work done (by symbol with explanation), and equipment used. Work times may also be included. The flow process chart symbols (ASME Standard Symbols) generally used are as follows:

O operation: A subdivision of a process that changes or modifies a part, material, or product and is done essentially at one workplace location

→ transportation (move): Change in location of a person, part, material, or product from one workplace to another

■ inspection: Comparison of observed quality or quantity of a product with a quality or quantity standard

▼ storage: Keeping a product, material, or part protected against unauthorized removal

D delay: An event that occurs when an object or person waits for the next planned action

◻ combined activity: Adjustment during testing (e.g., combination of the separate operation and inspection symbols)

Syn: process flowchart, process flow diagram. See: flowchart, process flow.

flow processing—In process systems development, work flows from one workstation to another at a nearly constant rate and with no delays. When producing discrete (geometric) units, the process is called repetitive manufacturing; when producing non-geometric units over time, the process is called continuous manufacturing. A physical-chemical reaction takes place in the continuous flow process.

flow rack—A storage rack using metal shelves equipped with wheels or rollers allowing product to flow from the back to the front of the rack to make the product more accessible for order picking.

flow rate—Running rate; the inverse of cycle time; for example, 360 units per shift (or 0.75 units per minute).

flow shop—A form of manufacturing organization in which machines and operators handle a standard, usually uninterrupted, material flow. The operators generally perform the same operations for each production run. A flow shop is often referred to as a mass production shop or is said to have a continuous manufacturing layout. The plant layout (arrangement of machines, benches, assembly lines, etc.) is designed to facilitate a product "flow." Some process industries (chemicals, oil, paint, etc.) are extreme examples of flow shops. Each product, though variable in material specifications, uses the same flow pattern through the shop. Production is set at a given rate, and the products are generally manufactured in bulk. Syn: flow line, flow manufacturing, flow plant.

flow time—The time between the release of a job to a work center or shop until the job is finished.

flow time efficiency—The ratio of theoretical flow time to the actual flow time through a process.

FLSA—Abbreviation for Fair Labor Standards Act.

fluctuation inventory—Inventory that is carried as a cushion to protect against forecast error. Syn: fluctuation stock. See: inventory buffer.

fluctuation stock—Syn: fluctuation inventory.

FMA—Abbreviation for failure mode analysis.

FMAPE—Abbreviation for forecast mean absolute percentage of error.

FMC—Abbreviation for flexible machine center.

FMEA—Abbreviation for failure mode effects analysis.

FMECA—Abbreviation for failure mode effects and criticality analysis.

FMS—Abbreviation for flexible manufacturing system.

FOB—Abbreviation for free on board.

FOB destination—The supplier pays for transportation to the buyer's location, where the buyer takes possession of the goods.

FOB origination—The buyer takes possession of the goods at the supplier's location, and the buyer must provide transportation.

focused factory—A plant established to focus the entire manufacturing system on a limited, concise, manageable set of products, technologies, volumes, and markets precisely defined by the company's competitive strategy, technology, and economics. See: cellular manufacturing.

focused low-cost strategy—Targeting a market with a low-cost product line in order to lower the cost of sales and increase gross margin.

focus forecasting—A system that allows the user to simulate the effectiveness of numerous forecasting techniques, enabling selection of the most effective one.

focus group—A set of people who are interviewed together for the purpose of collecting marketing data.

focus-group research—A form of research (frequently used in marketing research) where data are gathered by interviewing consumers in groups of 6 to 10 at a time (the focus group). See: marketing research.

focus strategy—Targeting a narrow market with specialized goods or services.

follow-up—Monitoring of job progress to see that operations are performed on schedule or that purchased material or products will be received on schedule.

force field analysis—A technique for analyzing the forces that will aid or hinder an organization in reaching an objective. An arrow pointing to an objective is drawn down the middle of a piece of paper. The factors that will aid the objective's achievement (called the driving forces) are listed on the left side of the arrow; the factors that will hinder its achievement (called the restraining forces) are listed on the right side of the arrow.

forecast—An estimate of future demand. A forecast can be constructed using quantitative methods, qualitative methods, or a combination of methods, and it can be based on extrinsic (external) or intrinsic (internal) factors. Various forecasting techniques attempt to predict one or more of the four components of demand: cyclical, random, seasonal, and trend. Syn: sales forecast. See: Box-Jenkins model, exponential smoothing forecast, extrinsic forecasting method, intrinsic forecasting method, moving average forecast, qualitative forecasting method, quantitative forecasting method.

forecast accuracy—A measurement of forecast usefulness, often defined as the average difference between the forecast value to the actual value. Syn: sales forecast. See: forecast error.

forecast bias—Tendency of a forecast to systematically miss the actual demand (consistently either high or low).

forecast consumption—Syn: consuming the forecast.

forecast error—The difference between actual demand and forecast demand, stated as an absolute value or as a percentage. See: average forecast error, forecast accuracy, mean absolute deviation, tracking signal.

forecast horizon—The period of time into the future for which a forecast is prepared.

forecasting—The business function that attempts to predict sales and use of products so they can be purchased or manufactured in appropriate quantities in advance.

forecast interval—The time unit for which forecasts are prepared, such as week, month, or quarter. Syn: forecast period.

forecast management—The process of making, checking, correcting, and using forecasts. It also includes determination of the forecast horizon.

forecast mean absolute percentage of error (FMAPE)—The absolute error divided by actual demand for "n" periods. Where absolute error is the variation between the actual demand and the forecast for the period expressed as a positive value (without regard for sign).

forecast period—Syn: forecast interval.

foreign freight forwarder—An entity that picks up goods at the production site and coordinates transport to the foreign customer's location.

foreign trade zone (FTZ)—Areas supervised by U.S. Customs and Border Protection that are considered to be outside U.S. territory. Material in the zone is not subject to duty taxes, which are payable when the material is moved outside the zone for consumption. There is no limit on the time material may remain in the zone. Internationally, similar areas are called free trade zones.

forensic procurement—Analyzing root cause-and-effect troubleshooting.

formal culture—The visible segment of the organizational culture, such as policies and procedures, mission statement, and dress codes. See: informal culture.

format—The predetermined arrangement of the characters of data for computer input, storage, or output.

form-fit-function—A term used to describe the process of designing a part or product to meet or exceed the performance requirements expected by customers.

formula—A statement of ingredient requirements. A formula may also include processing instructions and ingredient sequencing directions. Syn: formulation, recipe.

formulation—Syn: formula.

form utility—The value created by changing a good's form through a production process.

forty-foot equivalent unit—A measure of container capacity that is equivalent to two 20-foot equivalency units; that is, a unit equivalent to 40-feet long, 8-feet wide, and approximately 8-feet high.

40/30/30 rule—A rule that identifies the sources of scrap, rework, and waste as 40 percent product design, 30 percent manufacturing processing, and 30 percent from suppliers.

forward buying—The practice of buying materials in a quantity exceeding current requirements but not beyond the point that the long-term need exists.

forward flow scheduling—A procedure for building process train schedules that starts with the first stage and proceeds sequentially through the process structure until the last stage is scheduled.

forward integration—Process of buying or owning elements of the production cycle and the channel of distribution forward toward the final customer. See: vertical integration.

forward pass—In the critical path method of project management, working from the first node to the last node calculating early start times and early finish times as well as the project's duration. See: forward scheduling, backward pass, critical path method.

forward scheduling—A scheduling technique where the scheduler proceeds from a known start date and computes the completion date for an order, usually proceeding from the first operation to the last. Dates generated by this technique are generally the earliest start dates

for operations. See: forward pass. Ant: back scheduling.

Fourier series—A form of analysis useful for forecasting. The model is based on fitting sine waves with increasing frequencies and phase angles to a time series.

4PL—Abbreviation for fourth-party logistics.

four Ps—A set of marketing tools to direct the business offering to the customer. The four Ps are product, price, place, and promotion.

14 Points—W. Edwards Deming's 14 management practices to help companies increase their quality and productivity: (1) create constancy of purpose for improving products and services; (2) adopt the new philosophy; (3) cease dependence on inspection to achieve quality; (4) end the practice of awarding business on price alone; instead, minimize total cost by working with a single supplier; (5) improve constantly and forever every process for planning, production, and service; (6) institute training on the job; (7) adopt and institute leadership; (8) drive out fear; (9) break down barriers between staff areas; (10) eliminate slogans, exhortations, and targets for the workforce; (11) eliminate numerical quotas for the workforce and numerical goals for management; (12) remove barriers that rob people of pride of workmanship and eliminate the annual rating or merit system; (13) institute a vigorous program of education and self-improvement for everyone; and (14) put everybody in the company to work to accomplish the transformation. Syn: Deming's 14 Points.

fourth-party logistics (4PL)—Fourth-party logistics differs from third-party logistics in the following ways: (1) the 4PL organization is often a separate entity formed by a joint venture or other long-term contract between a client and one or more partners; (2) the 4PL organization is an interface between the client and multiple logistics services providers; (3) ideally, all aspects of the client's supply chain are managed by the 4PL organization; and, (4) it is possible for a major 3PL organization to form a 4PL organization within its existing structure. See: third-party logistics.

four-wall inventory—Syn: wall-to-wall inventory.

FPO—Abbreviation for firm planned order.

franchise extension—The placement of a brand name on products outside the company's present sphere of activity.

free alongside ship (FAS)—A term of sale indicating the seller is liable for all changes and risks until the goods sold are delivered to the port on a dock that will be used by the vessel. Title passes to the buyer when the seller has secured a clean dock or ship's receipt of goods.

free float—In the critical path method of project management, the amount of time that a given activity can be delayed without delaying an immediately subsequent activity's early start time. See: float, independent float, total float.

free on board (FOB)—The terms of sale that identify where title passes to the buyer.

free slack—The amount of time by which the completion of an activity in a project network can increase without delaying the start of the next activity.

free trade zone (FTZ)—The international term for what is known in the United States as a foreign trade zone. See: foreign trade zone.

freight bill—A freight carrier's invoice for a shipment.

freight carriers—Companies that move cargo via truck, rail, air, or sea.

freight charge—The rate established for the transportation of freight.

freight collect—The freight and charges to be paid by the consignee.

freight consolidation—The grouping of shipments to obtain reduced costs or improved utilization of the transportation function. Consolidation can occur by market area grouping, grouping according to scheduled deliveries, or using third-party pooling services such as public warehouses and freight forwarders.

freight equalization—The practice by more distant suppliers of absorbing the additional freight charges to match the freight charges of a supplier geographically closer to the customer. This is done to eliminate the competitive advantage of lower freight charges that the nearest supplier has.

freight forwarder—The "middle man" between the carrier and the organization shipping the product. Often combines smaller shipments to take advantage of lower bulk costs.

frequency distribution—A table that indicates the frequency with which data fall into each of any number of subdivisions of the variable. The subdivisions are usually called classes.

frequency of repair—Syn: repair factor.

frequently asked questions (FAQs)—A list of commonly asked questions pertaining to a website (or perhaps software, hardware, and so on) along with the answers to these questions.

fringe benefits—Employer-granted compensations that are not directly tied to salary.

front room—The place where the customer comes into contact with the service operation. Many service operations contain front room and back room operations. See: back room.

frozen master production schedule—The parts of a master production schedule that should not be changed or should be changed rarely.

frozen zone—In forecasting, the periods where no changes can be made to work orders based on changes in demand. This provides stability to the master production schedule.

FRT—Abbreviation for future reality tree.

FTC—Abbreviation for Federal Trade Commission.

FTP—Abbreviation for file transfer protocol.

FTZ—Abbreviation for foreign trade zone.

Full-Baldrige approach—A quality award program modeled after the Malcolm Baldrige National Quality Award and using the same criteria.

full cost pricing—Establishing price at some markup over the full cost (absorption costing). Full costing includes direct manufacturing as well as applied overhead.

full pegging—The ability of a system to automatically trace requirements for a given component all the way up to its ultimate end item, customer, or contract number. Syn: contract pegging.

fully qualified domain name—The complete, registered address (URL) of an internet site.

functional benchmarking—Benchmarking a single function within an organization rather than the entire organization. See: benchmarking.

functionality—The degree to which a product achieves its designed purpose.

functional layout—A facility configuration in which operations of a similar nature or function are grouped together; an organizational structure based on departmental specialty (e.g., saw, lathe, mill, heat treat, press). Syn: job shop layout, process layout.

functional manager—A manager responsible for a specialized department, such as accounting or engineering.

functional organization—A hierarchical organization in which each individual has one clear superior and staff areas are well defined.

functional organizational structure—An organizational structure based on functional specialization, such as sales, engineering, manufacturing, finance, and accounting.

functional requirements—Syn: critical characteristics.

functional silo—A view of an organization where each department is operated independently of the others. Each group is referred to as a silo. See: silo effect.

functional silo syndrome—Suboptimization of an organization's goals due to members of specific functions developing more loyalty to the function's group goals than to the organization's goals.

functional strategy—A strategy that is built from the business strategy for the various business functions, such as finance, marketing, and production. See: strategic planning.

functional systems design—The development and definition of the business functions to be accomplished by a computer system (i.e., preparing a statement of the proposed computer system's data input, data manipulation, and information output in common business terms that can be reviewed, understood, and approved by a user organization). This statement, after approval, provides the basis for the computer system's design.

functional test—Measure of a production component's ability to work as designed to meet a level of performance.

funds flow management—The planning, execution, and control of cash receipts and disbursements with the objective of maintaining the cash balance at a preset positive value. Syn: cash flow management.

funds flow statement—A financial statement showing the flow of cash and its timing into and out of an organization or project. Syn: cash flow statement, statement of cash flows.

funnel experiment—An experiment that demonstrates the effects of tampering. Marbles are dropped through a funnel in an attempt to hit a flat-surfaced target below. The experiment shows that adjusting a stable process to compensate for an undesirable result or an extraordinarily good result will produce output that is worse than if the process had been left alone. See: tampering.

future order—An order entered for shipment at some future date.

future reality tree (FRT)—In the theory of constraints, a logic-based tool for constructing and testing potential solutions before implementation. The objectives are to

(1) develop, expand, and complete the solution and (2) identify and solve or prevent new problems created by implementing the solution.

futures—Contracts for the sale and delivery of commodities at a future time, made with the intention that no commodity be delivered or received immediately.

future value—A present payment's value at some point in the future valued at a given interest rate.

future worth—1) The equivalent monetary value at a designated future date based on the time value of money. 2) The monetary sum, at a given future time, that is equivalent to one or more sums at given earlier times when interest is compounded at a given rate. See: time value of money.

fuzzy logic—A field of logic based on "fuzzy sets," that is, sets in which membership is probabilistic rather than deterministic.

G

GAAP—Acronym for generally accepted accounting principles.

gain sharing—A method of incentive compensation where employees share collectively in savings from productivity improvements. Syn: gain sharing plans.

gain sharing plans—Syn: gain sharing.

GAMP—Acronym for generally accepted manufacturing practices.

G&A—Abbreviation for general and administrative expenses.

Gantt chart—The earliest and best-known type of planning and control chart, especially designed to show graphically the relationship between planned performance and actual performance over time. Named after its originator, Henry L. Gantt, the chart is used for (1) machine loading, in which one horizontal line is used to represent capacity and another to represent load against that capacity; or (2) monitoring job progress, in which one horizontal line represents the production schedule and another parallel line represents the actual progress of the job against the schedule in time. Syn: job progress chart, milestone chart.

gap—When the actual performance level is not equal to the expected performance level.

gap analysis—A tool designed to assess the distance that exists between a service that is offered and customer expectations.

gapped schedule—A schedule in which every piece in a lot is finished at one work center before any piece in the lot can be processed at the succeeding work center; the movement of material in complete lots, causing time gaps between the end of one operation and the beginning of the next. It is a result of using a batched schedule at each operation (work center), where process batch and transfer batch are assumed to be the same or equal. Syn: gap phasing, straight-line schedule. Ant: overlapped schedule.

gap phasing—Syn: gapped schedule.

gatekeeping—A group technique applied by a team leader to effectively manage a situation, discussion, or meeting. For example, in a situation where a dominant spokesperson or person of authority monopolizes a discussion, the gatekeeper will intervene by requesting additional group member's input.

gate review—The formal review process between the major phases of a new product introduction effort. The determination to continue or to stop the project is formally made at each review point or gate.

gateway—The connection that allows data and other information to flow between two networks.

gateway operation—Syn: gateway work center.

gateway work center—A work center that performs the first operation of a particular routing sequence.

GATT—Acronym for general agreement on tariffs and trade.

gauge—An instrument for measuring or testing.

GDSS—Abbreviation for group decision support system.

gemba—A Japanese word meaning shop floor.

genchi genbutsu—A Japanese phrase meaning visit the shop floor to observe what is occurring.

general and administrative expenses (G&A)—The category of expenses on an income statement that includes the costs of general managers, computer systems, research and development, and more.

generally accepted accounting principles (GAAP)—Accounting practices that conform to conventions, rules, and procedures that have general acceptability by the accounting profession.

generally accepted manufacturing practices (GAMP)—A group of practices and principles, independent of any one set of techniques, that define how a manufacturing company should be managed. Included are such elements as the need for data accuracy, frequent commu-nication between marketing and manufacturing, top management control of the production planning process (sales and operations planning process), systems capable of validly translating high-level plans into detailed schedules, and so on. Today GAMP includes such paradigms as just-in-time, theory of constraints, total quality management, business process reengineering, and supply chain management.

general merchandise warehouse—A warehouse for the storage of goods that require no special handling.

general-purpose machinery—Manufacturing resources that can perform several kinds of operations.

general stores—Syn: supplies.

general warehouse—A location where goods usually are stored for long periods of time. The primary purpose is to protect goods until they are needed. The general warehouse is used because the producer or owner either does not have the necessary warehouse space or the cost of storage is better off-site. Usually use of a general warehouse involves minimal handling, movement, and transportation.

general warranty—An assurance that the product is fit for use. See: special warranty, warranty.

generic processing—A means of developing routings or processes for the manufacture of products through a family relationship, usually accomplished by means of tabular data to establish interrelationships. It is especially prevalent in the manufacture of raw material such as steel, aluminum, or chemicals.

GERT—Acronym for graphical evaluation and review technique.

globalization—The interdependence of economies globally that results from the growing volume and variety of international transactions in goods, services, and capital, and also from the spread of new technology.

global marketing—The use of one marketing strategy in all countries in which a company operates, selling a single product worldwide.

global measurements—Measurements used to judge the performance of the system as a whole.

global positioning system (GPS)—A system that uses satellites to locate an object's position.

Global Reporting Initiative (GRI)—A network-based organization that pioneered the world's most widely used sustainability reporting framework.

Global Reporting Initiative (GRI) Reporting Framework—The framework that sets out the principles and performance indicators organizations can use to measure and report their human rights, labor, environment, and anti-corruption practices and outcomes.

global sourcing—Using international sources for supplies.

global strategy—A strategy that focuses on improving worldwide performance through the sales and marketing of common goods and services with minimum product variation by country. Its competitive advantage grows through selecting the best locations for operations in other countries. See: multinational strategy.

global supply chains—Supply chains that include international partners or markets.

glocalization—A combination of "globalization" and "localization." When used in a supply chain context, glocalization is a form of postponement where a product or service is developed for distribution globally but is modified to meet the needs of a local market. The modifications are made to conform with local laws, customs, cultures or preferences.

GNP—Abbreviation for gross national product.

going concern value—The value of the firm as a whole, rather than the sum of the values of the separate parts.

go/no-go—The state of a unit or product. Two parameters are possible: go (conforms to specification) and no-go (does not conform to specification).

good—A tangible product, merchandise, or ware.

goodness of fit—The degree to which a model complies with observed data.

goodwill—An intangible item that is only recorded on a company's books as the result of a purchase. Generally, it is inseparable from the enterprise but makes the company more valuable, for example, a good reputation.

government market—A market in which most or all buyers consist of agencies of federal, state, or local governments. See: consumer market, industrial market, institutional market.

GPS—Abbreviation for global positioning system.

grades—The sublabeling of items to identify their particular makeup and to separate one lot from other production lots of the same item.

grandfather clause—A provision that exempts existing entities from a newly created regulation.

graphical evaluation and review technique (GERT)—A network analysis technique that allows for probability distributions of activity durations and also conditions under which some activities may not be carried out. See: critical path method, network analysis, program evaluation and review technique.

graphical forecasting methods—The use of visual information to predict sales patterns, it typically involves plotting information in a graphical form. It is relatively easy to convert a spreadsheet into a graph that conveys the information visually. Trends and patterns of data are easier to spot, and extrapolation of previous demand can be used to predict future demands.

graphical user interface (GUI)—A connection between the computer and the user employing a mouse and icons so that the user makes selections by pointing at icons and clicking the mouse.

gravity models—An approach used for locating facilities at the "center of gravity." Gravity is determined by the product of the masses of two bodies divided by the square of the distance between them. In gravity models, the population of each neighborhood in the region is used as the mass, and driving time is used as the distance.

gray box design—A situation in which the supplier and client jointly design a product or service. See: black box design.

green belt—A manager or team member who has been trained in six sigma improvement methods and will have full-time responsibilities for process and quality improvement.

green field—The initiation of a new process where no similar initiatives have previously existed.

green logistics—A purchasing firm has the responsibility to properly dispose of packaging supplies received with items ordered.

green manufacturing—A method of producing a good or service that minimizes external cost and pollution. It includes design for reuse, design for disassembly, and design for remanufacture. See: environmentally responsible business.

green marketing—In advertising, promoting products because of their environmental sensitivity.

green reverse logistics—The responsibility of the supplier to dispose of packaging materials or environmentally sensitive materials such as heavy metals.

green supply chain—A supply chain that considers environmental impacts on its operations and takes action

G

along the supply chain to comply with environmental safety regulations and communicate this to customers and partners. See: environmentally responsible business.

GRI—Abbreviation for Global Reporting Initiative.

grid technique—A quantitative model used for locating plants and warehouses by finding the least cost point, given the positions of raw materials and markets.

grievance—A complaint by an employee concerning alleged contract violations handled formally through contractually fixed procedures. If unsettled, a grievance may lead to arbitration.

grievance procedures—Methods identified in a collective bargaining agreement to resolve problems that develop or to determine if a contract has been violated.

gross inventory—The standard cost value of inventory before allowance for excess or obsolete items.

gross margin—The difference between total revenue and the cost of goods sold. Syn: gross profit margin.

gross national product (GNP)—The market value of all goods and services produced in a nation in a given year.

gross profit—Sales minus cost of goods sold.

gross profit margin—Syn: gross margin.

gross profit margin rate—Sales minus cost of goods sold then divided by sales.

gross requirement—The total of independent and dependent demand for a component before the netting of on-hand inventory and scheduled receipts.

gross sales—The total amount charged to all customers during the accounting time period.

gross weight—Vehicle weight including freight or passengers.

group classification code—A part of a material classification technique that provides for designation of characteristics by successively lower order groups of code. Classification may denote function, type of material, size, shape, and so forth.

group decision support system (GDSS)—The software designed to support groups in unstructured decision making by supporting brainstorming, conflict resolution, voting, and other techniques.

grouping—Matching like operations and running them together sequentially, thereby taking advantage of a common setup.

group layout—A layout in which machine groups are arranged to process families of parts with similar characteristics.

group replacement—Replacing an entire set of components, whether failed or not, all at one time (e.g., replacing all the light bulbs in a ceiling fixture).

group technology (GT)—An engineering and manufacturing philosophy that identifies the physical similarity of parts (common routing) and establishes their effective production. It provides for rapid retrieval of existing designs and facilitates a cellular layout.

group technology work cells—A concentrated area for producing parts based on similar operations and/or characteristics to use equipment and labor more efficiently.

groupthink—A situation in which a team seizes on one solution to a problem and does not consider other viable solutions either because members are afraid of confrontation or because they convince themselves that other ideas aren't worth discussing.

growth-share matrix—In marketing, a division of products by relative market share and market growth rate. Products are divided as follows: (1) Cash cows—high market share, low growth rate; (2) Stars—high market share, high growth rate; (3) Dogs—low market share, low growth rate; and (4) Question marks—low market share, high growth rate. Sometimes this same set of terms is used to categorize products by market share and profitability. See: cash cow, dog, question mark, star.

growth trajectory—Syn: ramp rate.

GT—Abbreviation for group technology.

GTS—Grasps the situation.

guarantee—A contractual obligation by one entity to another that a fact regarding a product is true. See: warranty.

GUI—Abbreviation for graphical user interface.

H

handling cost—The cost involved in the movement of material. In some cases, the handling cost depends on the size of the inventory.

hansei—A Japanese word meaning reflection.

hard automation—Use of specialized machines to manufacture and assemble products. Each machine is normally dedicated to one function, such as milling.

hard copy—A printed report, message, or special listing.

hardware—1) In manufacturing, relatively standard items such as nuts, bolts, washers, or clips. 2) In data processing, the computer and its peripherals.

harmonic smoothing—An approach to forecasting based on fitting some set of sine and cosine functions to the historical pattern of a time series. Syn: seasonal harmonics.

harmonized system classification codes—An internationally standardized description of goods that uses a system of numbers to provide increasingly detailed classification and descriptions.

hash total—A control process used to ensure that all documents in a group are present or processed. In practice, the arithmetic sum of data not normally added together is found, the checking (audit) process adds the same data, and a comparison is made. If the sums do not agree, an error exists. Example: the last digit of every part number in an assembly is added, and the last digit of the sum becomes the last digit of the assembly. If the last digit of an assembly is not the same as the sum of the last digit of the components' sum, the assembly must be missing a part or must have the wrong combination of parts.

Hawthorne effect—A study at the Hawthorne Western Electric plant from 1927 to 1932 systematically improved working conditions and productivity improved. Then, when it systematically worsened working conditions, productivity improved. From this study, it was determined that concern by management generally factors into improved productivity.

hazardous waste—Waste, such as chemicals or nuclear material, that is hazardous to humans or animals and requires special handling.

hazmat—Hazardous material defined by environmental laws and legal precedents. A product has been defined as hazardous by regulations that impose stiff fines if the regulations are ignored.

hedge—1) An action taken in an attempt to shield the company from an uncertain event such as a strike, price increase, or currency reevaluation. 2) In master scheduling, a scheduled quantity to protect against uncertainty in demand or supply. The hedge is similar to safety stock, except that a hedge has the dimension of timing as well as amount. A volume hedge or market hedge is carried at the master schedule or production plan level. The master scheduler plans excess quantities over and above the demand quantities in given pe-

riods beyond some time fence such that, if the hedge is not needed, it can be rolled forward before major resources must be committed to produce the hedge and put it in inventory. A product mix hedge is an approach where several interrelated optional items are overplanned. Sometimes, using a planning bill, the sum of the percent mix can exceed 100 percent by a defined amount, thus triggering additional hedge planning. 3) In purchasing, any purchase or sale transaction having as its purpose the elimination of the negative aspects of price fluctuations. See: market hedge, option overplanning, planning bill of material, safety stock, time fence, two-level master.

hedge inventory—A form of inventory buildup to buffer against some event that may not happen. Hedge inventory planning involves speculation related to potential labor strikes, price increases, unsettled governments, and events that could severely impair a company's strategic initiatives. Risk and consequences are unusually high, and top management approval is often required.

hedging—The practice of entering into contracts on a commodity exchange to protect against future fluctuations in the commodity. This practice allows a company to isolate profits to the value-added process rather than to uncontrolled pricing factors. See: speculative buying.

heel—In the process industry, an item used in the manufacture of itself. For example, in the manufacture of plastic, the ingredients will include the parent as well as the components.

heijunka—In just-in-time philosophy, an approach to level production throughout the supply chain to match the planned rate of end product sales.

helper application—Software that assists the browser when audio, video, or large images are requested.

heuristics—A form of problem solving in which the results or rules have been determined by experience or intuition instead of by optimization. Heuristics can be used in such areas as forecasting; lot sizing; or determining production, staff, or inventory levels.

hierarchical database—A method of constructing a database that requires that related record types be linked in tree-like structures, where no child record can have more than one physical parent record.

high-level language (HLL)—Relatively sophisticated computer language that allows users to employ a notation with which they are already familiar. For example: COBOL (business), ALGOL (mathematical and scientific), FORTRAN, BASIC, Java, and Visual Basic.

H

hi-low—A forklift truck with a standing operator.

histogram—A graph of contiguous vertical bars representing a frequency distribution in which the groups or classes of items are marked on the x axis and the number of items in each class is indicated on the y axis. The pictorial nature of the histogram lets people see patterns that are difficult to see in a simple table of numbers. The histogram is one of the seven tools of quality.

historical analogy—A judgmental forecasting technique based on identifying a sales history that is analogous to a present situation, such as the sales history of a similar product, and using that past pattern to predict future sales. See: management estimation.

historical labor standard—Determined by studying actual past labor data for the operation of interest.

HLL—Abbreviation for high-level language.

holding company—In financial management, a firm that controls the voting stock of other firms.

holding costs—Syn: carrying costs.

hold order—A written order directing that certain operations or work be interrupted or terminated pending a change in design or other disposition of the material. Syn: stop work order.

hold points—Stockpoints for semifinished inventory.

holonic network—1) A network of autonomous, distributed human or computer systems with the capability to act in an integrated manner. 2) A network of companies dynamically interacting to act as one system. Each company or holon has a different process and core competency. Virtual enterprises are created by organizing the holons, to take advantage of core competencies.

homogeneous product—A product that is effectively identical from producer to producer.

honeycombing—The practice of removing a pallet of merchandise where the space is not exhausted in an orderly fashion, resulting in a vacant space not usable for storage of other items. This is one of the hidden costs of warehousing.

honeycomb loss—The usable empty storage space in a stack due to storage of only a single stockkeeping unit in the stack to permit better access.

hopper cars—Rail cars that permit bulk commodities to be loaded at the top and removed from the bottom of the car. Some hopper cars have permanent tops that provide protection from bad weather.

HOQ—Abbreviation for house of quality.

horizontal dependency—The relationship between the components at the same level in the bill of material, in which all must be available at the same time and in sufficient quantity to manufacture the parent assembly. See: vertical dependency.

horizontally integrated firm—An organization that seeks to produce or sell a type of product in numerous markets. The horizontal integration exists when an organization produces or sells similar products in various geographical locations. Horizontal integration in marketing occurs more frequently than horizontal integration in production. See: vertically integrated firm.

horizontal marketplace—An online marketplace used by buyers and sellers from multiple industries. This marketplace lowers prices by lowering transaction costs.

horizontal merger—An alliance of two or more competing firms.

hoshin—A Japanese word meaning statement of objectives.

hoshin kanri—See hoshin planning.

hoshin planning—Breakthrough planning. A Japanese strategic planning process in which a company develops up to four vision statements that indicate where the company should be in the next five years. Company goals and work plans are developed based on the vision statements. Periodic audits are then conducted to monitor progress.

host computer—Any computer on a network that is a repository for services available to other computers on the network. It is common to have one host machine provide several services such as the World Wide Web.

housekeeping—The manufacturing activity of identifying and maintaining an orderly environment for preventing errors and contamination in the manufacturing process.

house of quality (HOQ)—A structured process that relates customer-defined attributes to the product's technical features needed to support and generate these attributes. This technique achieves this mapping by means of a six-step process: (1) identification of customer attributes; (2) identification of supporting technical features; (3) correlation of the customer attributes with the supporting technical features; (4) assignment of priorities to the customer requirements and technical features; (5) evaluation of competitive stances and competitive products; and (6) identification of those technical features to be used (deployed) in the final design of the product. HOQ is part of the quality function deployment (QFD) process and forces designers to consider customer needs and the degree to which the proposed designs satisfy these needs. See: customer-defined attributes, quality function deployment.

hub—A large manufacturer or retailer doing business with many trading partners.

hub-and-spoke systems—In warehousing, a system that has a hub (or center point) where sorting or transfers occur, and the spokes are outlets serving the destinations related to the hub.

human factors engineering—A merging of those branches of engineering and the behavioral sciences that concern themselves principally with the human component in the design and operation of human-machine systems. Human factors engineering is based on a fundamental knowledge and study of human physical and mental abilities and emotional characteristics.

human-machine interface—The location where data is transferred from a worker to a computer, or vice-versa.

human relations movement—A movement started in the early 1900s among managers who believed that employees are humans who should be treated with respect in the workplace.

human resources—The portion or department of a company that sets personnel policies and practices.

human resource utilization—Using labor to its fullest potential to maximize product or service output.

hundredweight (cwt)—One hundred pounds.

hurdle rate—The minimum acceptable rate of return on a project.

hybrid EDI—A situation in which only one trading partner is EDI-enabled, while the other continues to use paper and fax. Usually the EDI-enabled partner would have electronic documents converted to fax.

hybrid inventory system—An inventory system combining features of the fixed reorder quantity inventory model and the fixed reorder cycle inventory model. Features of the fixed reorder cycle inventory model and the fixed reorder quantity inventory model can be combined in many different ways. For example, in the order point-periodic review combination system, an order is placed if the inventory level drops below a specified level before the review date; if not, the order quantity is determined at the next review date. Another hybrid inventory system is the optional replenishment model. See: fixed reorder cycle inventory model, fixed reorder quantity

inventory model, optional replenishment model, order point system.

hybrid layout—This layout combines two or more layout types.

hybrid manufacturing process—Syn: hybrid production method.

hybrid organizational structure—An organizational structure that embodies multiple organizational forms (functional, product, or geographical) simultaneously. For example, some functions may be centralized (such as finance and accounting), whereas others may be duplicated geographically (such as sales).

hybrid production method—A production planning method that combines the aspects of both the chase and level production planning methods. Syn: hybrid manufacturing process, hybrid strategy. See: chase production method, level production method, production planning method.

hybrid purchasing organization—A mix of the centralized and decentralized purchasing format—usually decentralized at the corporate level and centralized at the business unit level.

hybrid strategy—Syn: hybrid production method.

hypermedia—An addition to hypertext to include sound, pictures, or music.

hypertext—A system of relating information without using menus or hierarchies.

hypertext links—Links contained within text connecting to other websites or other pages on the current site.

hypertext markup language (HTML)—A language used to create web pages that permits the user to create text, hypertext links, and multimedia elements within the page. HTML is not a programming language, but a way to format text.

hypertext transfer protocol (HTTP)—A protocol that tells computers how to communicate with each other. Most internet addresses begin with http://.

hypothesis testing—Use of statistical models to test conclusions about a population or universe based on sample information.

I

ICC—Abbreviation for Interstate Commerce Commission.

ideal quality—A term used by Genichi Taguchi to refer to the target value of a particular measure. Loss to society increases with the square of the deviation of an actual product from this ideal point.

idle capacity—The available capacity that exists on non-constraint resources beyond the capacity required to support the constraint. Idle capacity has two components: protective capacity and excess capacity.

idle inventory—The inventory generally not needed in a system of linked resources. From a theory of constraints perspective, idle inventory generally consists of protective inventory and excess inventory. See: excess inventory, productive inventory, protective inventory.

idle time—The time when operators or resources (e.g., machines) are not producing product because of setup, maintenance, lack of material, lack of tooling, or lack of scheduling.

IFB—Abbreviation for invitation for bid.

IIE—Abbreviation for Institute of Industrial Engineers.

IMC—Abbreviation for intermodal marketing company.

imperfection—A quality characteristic's departure from its intended level or state without any association to conformance to specification requirements or to the usability of a product or service. See: blemish, defect, nonconformity.

implementation—The act of installing a system into operation. It concludes the system project with the exception of appropriate follow-up or post-installation review.

implied authority—The right of an agent, when directed by a principal to accomplish a task, to do what is reasonably necessary to accomplish it.

implied contract—A binding agreement inferred from the actions of the parties.

implied warranty—A warranty imposed on sellers beyond any express agreement in the contract.

implode—1) Compression of detailed data in a summary-level record or report. 2) Tracing a usage and/or cost impact from the bottom to the top (end product) of a bill of material using where-used logic.

implosion—The process of determining the where-used relationship for a given component. Implosion can be single-level (showing only the parents on the next higher level) or multilevel (showing the ultimate top-level parent). See: where-used list. Ant: explosion.

import broker or sales agent—Purchasing agent who charges a fee for transactions but does not take the title of the goods.

import/export license—Official authorization issued by a government allowing the shipping or delivery of a product across national boundaries.

import merchant—Purchasing agent who buys and takes the title for goods and then resells them.

imports—Products bought in one country and produced in another.

imposed date—A fixed date given to an activity usually "start no earlier than" or "finish no later than."

improve phase—One of the six sigma phases of quality. In this phase, the improvements to products and/or processes are adopted. See: design-measure-analyze-improve-control process.

impulse response—How quickly an estimate or forecast changes when the underlying data of the estimate have changed.

inactive inventory—Stock designated as in excess of consumption within a defined period or stocks of items that have not been used for a defined period.

inbound logistics—The group in charge of moving materials from suppliers or vendors into production processes or storage facilities; or, the actual movement of such material.

inbound stockpoint—A defined location next to the place of use on a production floor. Materials are brought to the stockpoint as needed and taken from it for immediate use. Inbound stockpoints are used with a pull system of material control.

incentive—A reward, financial or otherwise, that compensates a worker for high or continued performance above standard. An incentive is also a motivating influence to induce effort above normal.

incentive arrangements—The incentive contract allows for the sharing of the cost responsibility between the buyer and seller. Incentives are incorporated into the contracts to motivate the supplier to improve its performance in areas such as quality, on-time delivery, and customer satisfaction. There are three elements of an incentive agreement: target cost, target profit, and the sharing agreement.

incentive contract—A contract where the buyer and seller agree to a target cost and maximum price. Cost savings below the target are shared between buyer and seller. If actual cost exceeds the target cost, the cost overrun is shared between buyer and seller up to the maximum price.

incentive pay system—A way to compensate employees based on their job performance.

incentive rate—In transportation, a discounted rate designed to convince a shipper to ship a higher volume in a particular load.

income—Syn: profit.

income statement—A financial statement showing the net income for a business over a given period of time. See: balance sheet, funds flow statement.

incoming business—The number of orders, the dollar value of orders, or the quantity of units that have been received on orders from customers. This volume is particularly important to the forecaster, who must compare incoming business against the forecast rather than against actual shipments when actual shipments do not reflect true customer demand. This situation may exist because of back-ordered items, bottlenecks in the shipping room, and so forth.

in-control process—A process in which the statistical measure being evaluated is in a state of statistical control (i.e., the variations among the observed sampling results can be attributed to a constant system of chance causes). Ant: out-of-control process.

incoterms—Short for International Commercial Terms; created to simplify international transactions.

incremental analysis—A method of economic analysis in which the cost of a single additional unit is compared to its revenue. When the net contribution of an additional unit is zero, total contribution is maximized.

incremental available-to-promise—Syn: discrete available-to-promise.

incremental cost—1) Cost added in the process of finishing an item or assembling a group of items. If the cost of the components of a given assembly equals $5 and the additional cost of assembling the components is $1, the incremental assembly cost is $1, while the total cost of the finished assembly is $6. 2) Additional cost incurred as a result of a decision.

incremental utilization heuristic—Using a worker's full capacity by adding one task at a time (in priority order) up to the maximum capacity, or waiting for the utilization to fall and then adding more tasks.

indented bill of material—A form of multilevel bill of material. It exhibits the highest-level parents closest to the left margin, and all the components going into these parents are shown indented toward the right. All subsequent levels of components are indented farther to the right. If a component is used in more than one parent within a given product structure, it will appear more

than once, under every subassembly in which it is used.

indented tracking—The following of all lot numbers of intermediates and ingredients consumed in the manufacture of a given batch of product down through all levels of the formula.

indented where-used—A listing of every parent item, and the respective quantities required, as well as each of their respective parent items, continuing until the ultimate end item or level-0 item is referenced. Each of these parent items calls for a given component item in a bill-of-material file. The component item is shown closest to the left margin of the listing, with each parent indented to the right, and each of their respective parents indented even further to the right.

independent action—In transportation, the publication of a freight rate that differs from that of the rate bureau to which the publisher is a member. This is a permitted action.

independent demand—The demand for an item that is unrelated to the demand for other items. Demand for finished goods, parts required for destructive testing, and service parts requirements are examples of independent demand. See: dependent demand.

independent demand item management models—Models for the management of items whose demand is not strongly influenced by other items managed by the same company. These models can be characterized as follows: (1) stochastic or deterministic, depending on the variability of demand and other factors; (2) fixed quantity, fixed cycle, or hybrid (optional replenishment). See: fixed reorder cycle inventory model, fixed reorder quantity inventory model, optional replenishment model.

independent float—In project management, the amount of float on an activity that does not affect float on preceding or succeeding activities. See: float, free float, total float.

independent project—A project which, whether or not it is accepted, does not eliminate other projects from eligibility. See: contingent project, mutually exclusive project.

independent trading exchange—A business-to-business marketplace ownership model. These are public sites often used for indirect materials and commodity purchases where the price is the primary factor and where any buyers and sellers for a particular market meet to gain access to a wider market to find the best deals. See: public marketplaces.

index—A value, expressed as a percentage, giving the relationship of a measurement to a base value. A result of 100 would be average while numbers greater than 100 would be above average and those less than 100 would be below average.

indicator—An index of business activities.

indifference point—The point at which two options create the same costs for a specific output level.

indirect costs—Costs that are not directly incurred by a particular job or operation. Certain utility costs, such as plant heating, are often indirect. An indirect cost is typically distributed to the product through the overhead rates.

indirect labor—Work required to support production in general without being related to a specific product (e.g., floor sweeping).

indirect labor cost—The compensation paid to workers whose activities are not related to a specific product.

indirect materials—Syn: supplies.

indirect retail locations—A retailer who sells products to the public but who buys products indirectly through a third-party distributor, rather than directly from the seller.

industrial buyers—Buyers who purchase materials mainly for conversion.

industrial engineering—The engineering discipline concerned with facilities layout, methods measurement and improvement, statistical quality control, job design and evaluation, and the use of management sciences to solve business problems.

industrial facilities management—The installation and maintenance of the physical plant, its surroundings, and the physical assets of an organization.

industrial market—A market where most or all customers are individuals or businesses that buy products to produce other goods and services. Syn: business market, producer market. See: consumer market, government market, institutional market.

industrial revolution—A movement to the use of factories and machines and away from activities done by hand without mechanical assistance.

industrial trucks—Vehicles powered by hand, electricity, or propane for material handling activities in a warehouse. More flexible but slower and less constant than conveyors, they are not in a fixed position. Industrial trucks are the most-common form of materials handling equipment.

industry—A set of companies providing a product or service where each company's offering is a close substitute for its competitors' offerings.

industry analysis—A major study of an industry; its major competitors, customers, and suppliers; and the focus and driving forces within that industry.

industry structure types—Economists have developed models of the types of competition faced by various firms. These types are (1) Pure monopoly—Only one firm provides a particular product or service. The monopoly may be regulated or unregulated; (2) Pure oligopoly—A few companies produce essentially the same product or service and market it within a given area. A company is forced to price its product at the going rate unless it can differentiate its product; (3) Differentiated oligopoly—A few companies produce partially differentiated products or services that are marketed within a given area. Differentiation may be based on quality, features, styling, or services offered along with the product; (4) Monopolistic competition—Many competitors offer partially differentiated products or services. Most competitors focus on market segments where they can meet customers' needs somewhat better than their competitors; and (5) Pure competition—Many competitors offer undifferentiated products or services.

inefficiency risk—The risk of losing customers because another firm has lower unit costs.

infinite loading—Calculation of the capacity required at work centers in the time periods required regardless of the capacity available to perform this work. Syn: infinite scheduling.

infinite scheduling—Syn: infinite loading.

inflation—An ongoing rise in the overall level of prices. Inflation reduces the purchasing power of money.

influence filter—In e-commerce, a device to make stakeholders better satisfied with a website.

informal culture—Organizational characteristics and relationships that are not part of the formal structure but that influence how the organization accomplishes its goals.

information—Data that have been interpreted and that meet the need of one or more managers.

information data warehouse—A repository (typically large) of corporate data that can be accessed using specialized query tools. This technique separates the analysis of data from the recording of data and is often used to combine data from different computing systems to make information access more convenient and coherent. See: data warehouse.

information distribution—Making needed data available to stakeholders in a timely manner.

information flow profile—A graph of the performance of information flow compared to some set of performance criteria.

information system—Interrelated computer hardware and software along with people and processes designed for the collection, processing, and dissemination of information for planning, decision making, and control.

information system architecture—A model of how the organization operates regarding information. The model considers four factors: (1) organizational functions, (2) communication of coordination requirements, (3) data modeling needs, and (4) management and control structures. The architecture of the information system should be aligned with and match the architecture of the organization.

information technology—The technology of computers, telecommunications, and other devices that integrate data, equipment, personnel, and problem-solving methods in planning and controlling business activities. Information technology provides the means for collecting, storing, encoding, processing, analyzing, transmitting, receiving, and printing text, audio, or video information.

information visibility—How extensive information is shared throughout a firm and with other stakeholders.

infrastructural elements—Elements of a strategy including decision rules, policies, personnel guidelines, and organizational structure.

ingredient—In the process industries, the raw material or component of a mixture. See: component.

initial public offering (IPO)—A firm's first sale of common stock.

innovation risk—The risk of losing customers because another firm creates more innovative products.

innovative products—Products that tend to have a high profit margin, be unique, have less competition, and have dynamic demand.

in-process inventory—Syn: work in process.

in-process waiver requests—Requests for waivers on normal production procedures because of deviations in materials, equipment, or quality metrics, where normal product specifications are maintained.

input—Work arriving at a work center or production facility.

input control—Management of the release of work to a work center or production facility.

input/output analysis—Syn: input/output control.

input/output control (I/O)—A technique for capacity control where planned and actual inputs and planned and actual outputs of a work center are monitored. Planned inputs and outputs for each work center are developed by capacity requirements planning and approved by manufacturing management. Actual input is compared to planned input to identify when work center output might vary from the plan because work is not available at the work center. Actual output is also compared to planned output to identify problems within the work center. Syn: input/output analysis. See: capacity control.

input/output devices—Modems, terminals, or various pieces of equipment whose designed purpose relates to manual, mechanical, electronic, visual, or audio entry to and from the computer's processing unit.

input rate capacity—Measurement that takes rates of different inputs and transforms them into a common unit to measure the input. See: capacity utilization.

insourcing—Using the firm's internal resources to provide goods and services. See: make-or-buy decision.

inspection—Measuring, examining, testing, or gauging one or more characteristics of a good or service and comparing the results with specified requirements to determine whether conformity is achieved for each characteristic.

inspection order—An authorization to an inspection department or group to perform an inspection operation.

inspection ticket—Frequently used as a synonym for an inspection order; more properly a reporting of an inspection function performed.

instantaneous receipt—The receipt of an entire lot-size quantity in a very short period of time.

Institute for Supply Management (ISM)—A nonprofit society for purchasing managers and others, formerly the National Association of Purchasing Management (NAPM).

Institute of Industrial Engineers (IIE)—A nonprofit educational organization with members interested in the field of industrial engineering.

institutional market—A market in which most or all customers are one of the following: schools, hospitals, prisons, and other institutions that provide products and services to individuals who are under their care. See: consumer market, government market, industrial market.

instruction sheet—Syn: routing.

intangible—One distinguishing feature of pure services. Pure services cannot be inventoried or carried in stock for long periods of time.

intangible costs—Those costs that are difficult to quantify such as the cost of poor quality or of high employee turnover.

integrated carrier—A company that provides a variety of transportation services including ground, sea, air carriage, and freight forwarding.

integrated change control—In project management, a system under which any changes are coordinated across the entire project.

integrated enterprise—A business or organization made up of individuals who have acquired the knowledge and skills to work with others to make the organization a greater success than the sum of each individual's output. Integration includes increased communication and coordination between individuals and within and across teams, functions, processes, and organizations over time. See: cross-functional integration.

integrated internet marketing (I2M)—The use of internet facilities to sell products, influence stakeholder attitudes, and improve the company's image.

integrated logistics—Syn: service response logistics.

integrated logistics service providers—Organizations that provide one or many logistics services to a customer for a fee.

integrated resource management (IRM)—Syn: resource management.

integrated services digital network (ISDN)—Emerging international standard for using public phone lines to transmit voice and data over the same line.

integrating mechanism—A physical, organizational, or informational entity that allows people and functions to interact freely by transcending boundaries.

intellectual property—Various legal entitlements that attach to certain names, written and recorded media, and inventions.

intelligent agent—A program that regularly gathers information without the owner being present.

interactive—A characteristic of those applications where a user communicates with a computer program via a terminal, entering data and receiving responses from the computer.

interactive computer system—A computer system that supports real-time interaction with a user. The response time to the user is similar to the actual timing of the business or physical process. See: interactive system.

interactive customer care—A generic term for a variety of services provided over the internet. These services include customer service and technical support.

interactive scheduling—Computer scheduling where the process is either automatic or manually interrupted to allow the scheduler the opportunity to review and change the schedule.

interactive system—Refers to those computer applications in which a user communicates with a computer program via a system, entering data and receiving responses from the computer. See: interactive computer system.

interarrival time—Time between the arrival of two sequential customers or events.

interest—1) Financial share in a project or enterprise. 2) Periodic compensation for lending money. 3) In an economy study, synonymous with required return, expected profit, or charge for the use of capital. 4) The cost for the use of capital. Sometimes referred to as the time value of money.

interest rate—The ratio of the interest payment to the principal for a given unit of time. It is usually expressed as a percentage of the principal.

interleaving—Assigning multiple tasks to be performed concurrently, often the assignment of multiple picking orders to a single picker to pick concurrently.

intermediately positioned warehouse—A warehouse located between customers and manufacturing plants to provide increased customer service and reduced distribution cost.

intermediately positioned strategy—To position a warehouse halfway between the supplier and the customer.

intermediate part—Material processed beyond raw material and used in higher level items. See: component.

intermittent production—A form of manufacturing in which the jobs pass through the functional departments in lots, and each lot may have a different routing. See: job shop.

intermodal marketing companies (IMCs)—Organizations that are the intermediary for shippers and intermodal rail carriers.

intermodal transport—1) Shipments moved by different types of equipment combining the best features of each mode. 2) The use of two or more different carrier modes in the through movement of a shipment.

internal controls—The policies and procedures, the documentation, and the plan for an organization that authorize transactions, safeguard assets, and maintain the accuracy of financial records.

internal customer—The recipient (person or department) of another person's or department's output (good, service, or information) within an organization. See: customer, external customer.

internal environment—The chosen domain or scope of activities within which an organization operates, for example, the tasks associated with goods or services to be delivered by the organization. See: external environment, organizational environment.

internal failure costs—The cost of things that go wrong before the product reaches the customer. Internal failure costs usually include rework, scrap, downgrades, reinspection, retest, and process losses.

internal rate of return—The rate of compound interest at which the company's outstanding investment is repaid by proceeds from the project.

internal setup time—The time associated with elements of a setup procedure performed while the process or machine is not running. Ant: external setup time.

internal supply chain—A structure for sharing information within a firm and creating an atmosphere for cooperation between functions to strengthen the firm.

international company—Company that uses production sharing and sells its products in a different country.

international logistics—All functions concerned with the movement of materials and finished goods on a global scale.

International Organization for Standardization (ISO)—Group of cooperating institutes from 155 countries working to develop and publish international standards. It acts as a bridge between public and private sectors.

international procurement office (IPO)—Establishes a global presence for a company by providing localized supply management services in a region that is strategically important. This management approach is a long-term commitment that takes advantage of a region's language and cultural capabilities to use trusted local staff to execute procurement activities that add value to the overall supply chain. Such tasks as local supplier development, contract negotiations, quality audits, and best practice operations provide reduced dependence on third parties and improve overall efficiency and costs.

international standards—Standards established by international standards-setting organizations to promote interoperability among operating environments.

internet—A worldwide network of computers belonging to businesses, governments, and universities that enables users to share information in the form of files and to send electronic messages and have access to a tremendous store of information.

internet operations—Operations performed over the internet encompassing such things as email, telnet, newsgroups, file transfer protocol, and the World Wide Web.

internet service provider (ISP)—A business or organization that sells access to the internet and related services to consumers. For a monthly fee, the service provider offers a software package, username, password, and access to the internet (via various technologies such as dial-up and DSL), which enables users to browse the World Wide Web and USENET and send and receive email. The ISP may also provide a combination of services, including internet transit, domain name registration and hosting, web hosting, and colocation.

interoperation time—The time between the completion of one operation and the start of the next.

interplant demand—One plant's need for a part or product that is produced by another plant or division within the same organization. Although it is not a customer order, it is usually handled by the master production scheduling system in a similar manner. See: interplant transfer.

interplant transfer—The shipment of a part or product by one plant to another plant or division within the corporation. See: interplant demand, transfer pricing.

interpolation—The process of finding a value of a function between two known values. Interpolation may be performed numerically or graphically.

interrelationship digraph—A technique used to define how factors relate to one another. Complex multivariable problems or desired outcomes can be displayed with their interrelated factors. The logical and often causal relationships between the factors can be illustrated.

interrogate—Retrieve information from computer files by use of predefined inquiries or unstructured queries handled by a high-level retrieval language.

interrupt—A break in the normal flow of a computer routine such that the flow can be resumed from that point at a later time. An interrupt is usually caused by a signal from an external source.

interstate commerce—The movement of persons or property across one or more state lines for business purposes.

Interstate Commerce Commission (ICC)—A U.S. regulatory agency charged with enforcing regulations controlling railroads, motor carriers, pipelines, domestic water carriers, domestic surface freight forwarders, and brokers.

intranet—A privately owned network that makes use of internet technology and applications to meet the needs of an enterprise. It resides entirely within a department or company, providing communication and access to information, similar to the internet, with web pages, and so on for internal use only.

in-transit inventory—Material moving between two or more locations, usually separated geographically; for example, finished goods being shipped from a plant to a distribution center.

in-transit lead time—The time between the date of shipment (at the shipping point) and the date of receipt (at the receiver's dock). Orders normally specify the date by which goods should be at the dock. Consequently, this date should be offset by in-transit lead time for establishing a ship date for the supplier.

intrastate commerce—Moving people or materials between points within a single state.

intrinsic forecast method—A forecast based on internal factors, such as an average of past sales. Ant: extrinsic forecast.

inventory—1) Those stocks or items used to support production (raw materials and work-in-process items), supporting activities (maintenance, repair, and operating supplies), and customer service (finished goods and spare parts). Demand for inventory may be dependent or independent. Inventory functions are anticipation, hedge, cycle (lot size), fluctuation (safety, buffer, or reserve), transportation (pipeline), and service parts. 2) All the money currently tied up in the system. As used in theory of constraints, inventory refers to the equipment, fixtures, buildings, and so forth that the system owns—as well as inventory in the forms of raw materials, work-in-process, and finished goods.

inventory accounting—The branch of accounting dealing with valuing inventory. Inventory may be recorded or valued using either a perpetual or a periodic system. A perpetual inventory record is updated frequently or in real time, while a periodic inventory record is counted or measured at fixed time intervals (e.g., every two weeks or monthly). Inventory valuation methods of LIFO, FIFO, or average costs are used with either recording system.

inventory accuracy—When the on-hand quantity is within an allowed tolerance of the recorded balance. This important metric usually is measured as the percent of items with inventory levels that fall within tolerance. Target values usually are 95 percent to 99 percent, depending on the value of the item.

inventory adjustment—A change made to an inventory record to correct the balance, to bring it in line with actual physical inventory balances. The adjustment either increases or decreases the item record on-hand balance.

inventory balance location accuracy—When the inventory count is accurate at specific locations.

inventory buffer—Inventory used to protect the throughput of an operation or the schedule against the negative effects caused by delays in delivery, quality problems, delivery of incorrect quantity, and so on. Syn: inventory cushion. See: fluctuation inventory, safety stock.

inventory control—The activities and techniques of maintaining the desired levels of items, whether raw materials, work in process, or finished products. Syn: material control.

inventory conversion period—The time period needed to produce and sell a product, measured from procurement of raw materials to the sale of the product.

inventory costs—Costs associated with ordering and holding inventory. See: carrying costs, ordering cost.

inventory cushion—Syn: inventory buffer.

inventory cycle—The length of time between two consecutive replenishment shipments.

inventory diversion—The shipment of parts against a project or contract other than the original project or contract for which the items were purchased.

inventory drivers—Those conditions that would lead a company to hold inventory.

inventory effectiveness index—A system to identify non-value-adding inventory and make it visible and provide a process to measure non-value adding inventory and sell or write it off to keep working capital in control.

inventory investment—The dollars that are in all levels of inventory.

inventory issue—1) Items released from an inventory location for use or sale. 2) The inventory record transaction reducing the inventory balance by the amount released.

inventory management—The branch of business management concerned with planning and controlling inventories.

inventory optimization software—A computer application having the capability of finding optimal inventory strategies and policies related to customer service and return on investment over several echelons of a supply chain.

inventory ordering system—Inventory models for the replenishment of inventory. Independent demand inventory ordering models include but are not limited to fixed reorder cycle, fixed reorder quantity, optional replenishment, and hybrid models. Dependent demand inventory ordering models include material requirements planning, kanban, and drum-buffer-rope.

inventory planner—Syn: material planner (first definition).

inventory planning—The activities and techniques of determining the desired levels of items, whether raw materials, work in process, or finished products including order quantities and safety stock levels. Syn: material planning.

inventory policy—A statement of a company's goals and approach to the management of inventories.

inventory pooling—The act of holding inventory in a single location instead of multiple locations.

inventory receipt—An inventory record transaction that records the receipt or arrival of inventory into physical stores by increasing the inventory on-hand balance by the received quantity. Often associated with receipt of a purchase or production order quantity.

inventory record—A history of the inventory transactions of a specific material.

inventory reserve—An accounting deduction from earnings to fairly and reasonably represent the value of inventoried assets on a balance sheet. The inventory reserve is used to make up for the fact that all inventory will not be sold at the cost to the firm.

inventory returns—Items returned to the manufacturer as defective, obsolete, overages, and so forth. An inventory item record transaction records the return or receipt into physical stores of materials from which the item may be scrapped.

inventory shrinkage—Losses of inventory resulting from scrap, deterioration, pilferage, and so forth.

inventory tax—Tax based on the value of inventory on hand at a particular time.

inventory turnover—The number of times that an inventory cycles, or "turns over," during the year. A frequently used method to compute inventory turnover is to divide the average inventory level into the annual cost of sales. For example, an average inventory of $3 million divided into an annual cost of sales of $21 million means that inventory turned over seven times. Syn: inventory turns, turnover. See: inventory velocity.

inventory turns—Syn: inventory turnover.

inventory usage—The value or the number of units of an inventory item consumed over a period of time.

inventory valuation—The value of the inventory at either its cost or its market value. Because inventory value can change with time, some recognition is taken of the age distribution of inventory. Therefore, the cost value of inventory is usually computed on a FIFO basis, LIFO basis, or a standard cost basis to establish the cost of goods sold.

inventory velocity—The speed with which inventory passes through an organization or supply chain at a given point in time as measured by inventory turnover. See: inventory turnover.

inventory visibility—The extent to which inventory information is shared within a firm and with supply chain partners.

inventory write-off—A deduction of inventory dollars from the financial statement because the inventory is of less value. An inventory write-off may be necessary because the value of the physical inventory is less than its book value or because the items in inventory are no longer usable.

invitation for bid (IFB)—Syn: request for proposal.

invoice—A list of goods shipped by the supplier to the buyer stating prices, quantities, and other costs.

involuntary services—Services that are not sought by customers. These include hospitals and prisons.

I/O—Abbreviation for input/output control.

IPO—1) Abbreviation for initial public offering. 2) Abbreviation for international procurement office.

IRM—Abbreviation for integrated resource management.

irregular maintenance—Syn: breakdown maintenance.

ISDN—Abbreviation for integrated services digital network.

Ishikawa diagram—Syn: cause-and-effect diagram.

islands of automation—Stand-alone pockets of automation (e.g., robots, CAD/CAM systems, numerical control machines) that are not connected into a cohesive system.

ISO—Abbreviation for International Organization for Standardization.

ISO certification—In quality management, denotes that a company has obtained an ISO9000 quality standard. Also, it is the process by which a firm achieves such certification.

ISO 14000 Series Standards—A series of generic environmental management standards developed by the International Organization of Standardization, which provide structure and systems for managing environmental compliance with legislative and regulatory requirements and affect every aspect of a company's environmental operations.

isolation—The determination of the location of a failure through the use of accessory support and diagnostic equipment.

ISO 9000—A set of international standards on quality management and quality assurance developed to help companies effectively document the quality system elements to be implemented to maintain an efficient quality system. The standards, initially published in 1987, are not specific to any particular industry, product, or service. The standards were developed by the International Organization for Standardization, known as ISO, a specialized international agency for standardization composed of the national standards bodies of 91 countries. The standards underwent major revision in 2008 and now include ISO 9000:2008 (definitions), ISO 9001:2008 (requirements), and ISO 9004:2008 (continuous improvement). See: ISO/TS 16949, QS 9000.

ISO 9000:2000—A certification process requiring a third-party audit that defines in broad terms what must be done to manage company quality and to document these quality processes. It recently was updated by ISO 9000:2008.

ISO/TS 16949—A standard written by the International Automotive Task Force that applies only to automotive companies. It includes quality management system; management responsibility; resource management; product realization; and measurement, analysis, and improvement. See: QS 9000.

ISO 31000—A standard adopted by the International Standards Organization that outlines principles and a set of guidelines to manage risk in any endeavor. The standard includes guidelines for understanding risk, developing a risk management policy, integrating risk management into organizational processes (including accountability and responsibility), and establishing internal and external risk communication processes. ISO 31000 is not a management system standard and is not intended or appropriate for certification purposes or regulatory or contractual use.

ISO 26000—An international standard adopted by the International Standards Organization to assist organizations in contributing to sustainable development beyond legal compliance through a common understanding of social responsibility. ISO 26000 is not a management system standard and is not intended or appropriate for certification purposes or regulatory or contractual use.

ISP—An abbreviation for internet service provider.

I2M—Abbreviation for integrated internet marketing.

issue—1) The physical movement of items from a stocking location. See: disbursement. 2) Often, the transaction reporting of this activity.

issue cycle time—The time required to generate a requisition for material, pull the material from an inventory location, and move it to its destination.

item—Any unique manufactured or purchased part, material, intermediate, subassembly, or product.

item demand—Demand disaggregated into specific configurations of goods or services. See: item.

item master file—A file containing all item master records for a product, product line, plant, or company. See: master file.

item master record—Syn: item record.

item number—A number that serves to uniquely identify an item. Syn: part number, product number, stock code, stock number.

item record—The "master" record for an item. Typically, it contains identifying and descriptive data and control values (lead times, lot sizes, etc.) and may contain data on inventory status, requirements, planned orders, and costs. Item records are linked by bill of material records (or product structure records), thus defining the bill of material. Syn: item master record, part master record, part record.

J

Java—A general-purpose computer language created by Sun Microsystems.

jidoka—The Japanese term for the practice of stopping the production line when a defect occurs.

jig—A device that holds a piece of work in a desired position and guides the tool or tools that perform the necessary operations. See: fixture.

jishuken—A Japanese word meaning voluntary study groups.

JIT—Acronym for just in time.

JIT master schedule—Syn: level schedule (second definition).

JIT supplier environment—To effectively participate as a supplier under just in time (JIT), a company must supply components and subassemblies in exact quantities, delivery time, and quality. Shipments are made within narrow time windows that are rigidly enforced. Virtually every component must be delivered on time and be within specifications.

job—1) The combination of tasks, duties, and responsibilities assigned to an individual employee and usually considered his or her work assignment. 2) The contents of a work order.

job analysis—A process of gathering (by observation, interview, or recording systems) significant task-oriented activities and requirements about work required of employees.

jobbing—Syn: job shop.

job costing—A cost accounting system in which costs are assigned to specific jobs. This system can be used with either actual or standard costs in the manufacturing of distinguishable units or lots of products. Syn: job order costing.

job description—A formal statement of duties, qualifications, and responsibilities associated with a particular job.

job design—The function of describing a job with respect to its content and the methods to be used. Criteria, such as the degree of job specialization, job enrichment, and job enlargement are useful in designing work content.

job enlargement—An increase in the number of tasks that an employee performs. Job enlargement is associated with the design of jobs, particularly production

jobs, and its purpose is to reduce employee dissatisfaction.

job enrichment—An increase in the number of tasks that an employee performs and an increase in the control over those tasks. It is associated with the design of jobs and especially the production worker's job. Job enrichment is an extension of job enlargement.

job grade—A form of job evaluation that assigns jobs to predetermined job classifications according to the job's relative worth to the organization. Pay scales are usually set for each job grade.

job lot—A specific quantity of a part or product that is produced at one time.

job order—Syn: manufacturing order.

job order costing—Syn: job costing.

job progress chart—Syn: Gantt chart.

job rotation—The practice of an employee periodically changing job responsibilities to provide a broader perspective and a view of the organization as a total system, to enhance motivation, and to provide cross-training.

job sequencing rules—A set of priorities and conditions that specify the order in which jobs are processed because of scarce resources.

job shop—1) An organization in which similar equipment is organized by function. Each job follows a distinct routing through the shop. 2) A type of manufacturing process used to produce items to each customer's specifications. Production operations are designed to handle a wide range of product designs and are performed at fixed plant locations using general-purpose equipment. Syn: jobbing. See: intermittent production, project manufacturing.

job shop layout—Syn: functional layout.

job shop scheduling—The production planning and control techniques used to sequence and prioritize production quantities across operations in a job shop.

job status—A periodic report showing the plan for completing a job (usually the requirements and completion date) and the progress of the job against that plan.

job ticket—Syn: time ticket.

joint order—An order on which several items are combined to obtain volume or transportation discounts.

joint rate—A rate for a route involving two or more carriers to move a shipment.

joint replenishment—Coordinating the lot sizing and order release decision for related items and treating them as a family of items. The objective is to achieve lower costs because of ordering, setup, shipping, and quantity discount economies. This term applies equally to joint ordering (family contracts) and to composite part (group technology) fabrication scheduling. Syn: joint replenishment system.

joint replenishment system—Syn: joint replenishment.

joint venture—An agreement between two or more firms to risk equity capital to attempt a specific business objective.

judgment items—Those inventory items that cannot be effectively controlled by algorithms because of age (new or obsolete product) or management decision (promotional product).

Juran trilogy—Syn: quality trilogy.

jurisdiction—The authority of a governmental agency to undertake its activities.

jury of executive opinion—A forecast given by a group of executives who are knowledgeable about the industry, competition, and the firm.

just in time (JIT)—A philosophy of manufacturing based on planned elimination of all waste and on continuous improvement of productivity. It encompasses the successful execution of all manufacturing activities required to produce a final product, from design engineering to delivery, and includes all stages of conversion from raw material onward. The primary elements of just in time are to have only the required inventory when needed; to improve quality to zero defects; to reduce lead times by reducing setup times, queue lengths, and lot sizes; to incrementally revise the operations themselves; and to accomplish these activities at minimum cost. In the broad sense, it applies to all forms of manufacturing—job shop, process, and repetitive—and to many service industries as well. Syn: short-cycle manufacturing, stockless production, zero inventories.

just-in-time purchasing—This type of purchasing uses few suppliers who have long-term commitments with the organization. Long-term contracts are used, which enable the purchaser to develop and certify the quality process at the supplier.

K

kaizen—The Japanese term for improvement; continuing improvement involving everyone—managers and workers. In manufacturing, kaizen relates to finding and eli-

minating waste in machinery, labor, or production methods. See: continuous process improvement.

kaizen blitz®—A rapid improvement of a limited process area, for example, a production cell. Part of the improvement team consists of workers in that area. The objectives are to use innovative thinking to eliminate non-value-added work and to immediately implement the changes within a week or less. Ownership of the improvement by the area work team and the development of the team's problem-solving skills are additional benefits. See: kaizen event.

kaizen event—A time-boxed set of activities carried out by the cell team during the week of cell implementation. The kaizen event is an implementation arm of a lean manufacturing program. See: kaizen blitz.

kanban—A method of just-in-time production that uses standard containers or lot sizes with a single card attached to each. It is a pull system in which work centers signal with a card that they wish to withdraw parts from feeding operations or suppliers. The Japanese word kanban, loosely translated, means card, billboard, or sign but other signaling devices such as colored golf balls have also been used. The term is often used synonymously for the specific scheduling system developed and used by the Toyota Corporation in Japan. See: move card, production card, synchronized production.

keiretsu—A form of cooperative relationship among companies in Japan where the companies largely remain legally and economically independent, even though they work closely in various ways such as financial backing. A member of a keiretsu generally owns a limited amount of stock in other member companies. A keiretsu generally forms around a bank and a trading company, but "distribution" (supply chain) keiretsu alliances have been formed of companies ranging from raw material suppliers to retailers.

key performance indicator (KPI)—A financial or nonfinancial measure that is used to define and assess progress toward specific organizational goals and typically is tied to an organization's strategy and business stakeholders. A KPI should not be contradictory to other departmental or strategic business unit performance measures.

key success factors—The product attributes, organizational strengths, and accomplishments with the greatest impact on future success in the marketplace.

key supply chain processes—Important steps in producing, marketing, and servicing goods and services.

kit—1) The components of a parent item that have been pulled from stock and readied for movement to a production area. 2) A group of repair parts to be shipped with an order. Syn: kitted material, staged material.

kitted material—Syn: kit.

kitting—The process of constructing and staging kits.

knowledge-based system—A computer program that employs knowledge of the structure of relations and reasoning rules to solve problems by generating new knowledge from the relationships about the subject.

knowledge creation—The propensity for generating knowledge.

knowledge management—Concept of information being used by executives, managers, and employees to more effectively produce product, interface with customers, and navigate through competitive markets.

knowledge management tool—Provides an assortment of information quickly to stakeholders for faster and better decisions.

knowledge worker—A worker whose job is the accumulation, transfer, validation, analysis, and creation of information.

KPI—Abbreviation for key performance indicator.

L

laboratory order—Syn: experimental order.

labor—The people who produce value in a product stream.

labor claim—A factory worker's report that lists the jobs an employee worked on (number of pieces, number of hours, etc.) and often the amount of money to which the employee is entitled. A labor claim is usually made on a labor chit or time ticket. Syn: labor ticket, labor voucher.

labor cost—The dollar amount of labor performed during manufacturing. This amount is added to direct material cost and overhead cost to obtain total manufacturing cost.

labor efficiency—1) Syn: worker efficiency. 2) The average of worker efficiency for all direct workers in a department or facility.

labor efficiency variance—Labor efficiency variance is (actual number of hours worked minus standard number of hours worked) multiplied by standard labor wage

rate. The variance is unfavorable if the actual hours exceed the standard hours. Syn: labor usage variance.

labor grade—A classification of workers whose capability indicates their skill level or craft. See: skill-based compensation, skills inventories.

labor-intensive—When an operation has more expenditures on labor than capital. See: capital-intensive.

labor productivity—A partial productivity measure, the rate of output of a worker or group of workers per unit of time compared to an established standard or rate of output. Labor productivity can be expressed as output per unit of time or output per labor hour. See: machine productivity, productivity.

labor rate variance—Labor rate variance is the sum of the actual wage rate minus the standard wage rate multiplied by the actual number of labor hours. The variance is unfavorable if the actual rate is greater than the standard rate.

labor standard—Under normal conditions, the quantity of worker minutes necessary to finish a product or process.

labor ticket—Syn: labor claim.

labor usage variance—Syn: labor efficiency variance.

labor voucher—Syn: labor claim.

lading—The cargo being transported by a vehicle.

lag capacity strategy—Not adding capacity until the firm is operating at or beyond full capacity. This keeps unit costs minimized by working at full capacity, but does not satisfy total demand.

laid-down cost—The sum of the product and transportation costs. The laid-down cost is useful in comparing the total cost of a product shipped from different supply sources to a customer's point of use.

LAN—Acronym for local area network.

land bridge—Moving goods over water, then land, and then water again to the final point.

landed cost—This cost includes the product cost plus the costs of logistics, such as warehousing, transportation, and handling fees.

lap phasing—Syn: overlapped schedule.

last in, first out (LIFO)—A method of inventory valuation for accounting purposes. The accounting assumption is that the most recently received (last in) is the first to be used or sold (first out) for costing purposes, but there is no necessary relationship with the actual physical movement of specific items. See: average cost systems.

late finish date (LF)—In the critical path method of project management, the last date upon which a given activity can be completed without delaying the completion date of the project.

lateness—Delivery date minus due date. Lateness may be positive or, in the case of early jobs, negative. See: earliness, tardiness.

late order—Syn: past due order.

late start date (LS)—In the critical path method of project management, the last date upon which a given activity can be started without delaying the completion date of the project.

launch phase—In this last phase of product development, either the product is fed into the supply chain or the service is made available to consumers.

law of diminishing marginal returns—A principle that as the quantity of a variable factor applied to a fixed factor is increased, the additional units of the variable factor will result in smaller and smaller increases in output. See: marginal product.

law of variability—The more that variability exists in a process, the less productive that process will be.

layoff—The process by which employees that are not needed for some extended amount of time are given notice that their services are not needed. Benefits may or may not continue in a layoff.

layout—Physical arrangement of resources or centers of economic activity (machines, groups of people, workstations, storage areas, aisles, etc.) within a facility. Layouts include product (linear or line), functional (job shop or process), cellular, and fixed position.

LBO—Abbreviation for leveraged buyout.

LCL—1) Abbreviation for less than carload (lot shipment). 2) Abbreviation for lower control limit.

LDI—Abbreviation for logistics data interchange.

lead capacity strategy—A capacity strategy in which, as demand increases and is expected to increase, capacity is added prior to the realization of demand.

leading indicator—A specific business activity index that indicates future trends. For example, housing starts is a leading indicator for the industry that supplies builders' hardware.

lead logistics providers (LLPs)—Organizations that oversee the third-party logistics operations of their clients.

lead management tool—A tool used by sales personnel that helps them follow a specified sales process to close deals.

lead time—1) A span of time required to perform a process (or series of operations). 2) In a logistics context, the time between recognition of the need for an order and the receipt of goods. Individual components of lead time can include order preparation time, queue time, processing time, move or transportation time, and receiving and inspection time. Syn: total lead time. See: manufacturing lead time, purchasing lead time.

lead-time inventory—Inventory that is carried to cover demand during the lead time.

lead-time offset—A technique used in MRP where a planned order receipt in one time period will require the release of that order in an earlier time period based on the lead time for the item. Syn: component lead-time offset, offsetting.

lead-time scheduling—Development of a schedule of start and completion times of planned operations for a manufacturing order by calculation of the lead time. The calculation includes the duration of all operations, interoperation times, and order administration times. See: back scheduling, central point scheduling, forward scheduling, probable scheduling.

lean—Syn: lean production.

lean enterprise—A group of individuals, functions, and sometimes legally separate but operationally synchronized organizations. The value stream defines the lean enterprise. The objectives of the lean enterprise are to correctly specify value to the ultimate customer, and to analyze and focus the value stream so that it does everything from product development and production to sales and service in a way that actions that do not create value are removed and actions that do create value proceed in a continuous flow as pulled by the customer. Lean enterprise differs from a "virtual corporation" in which the organizational membership and structure keeps changing.

lean manufacturing—Syn: lean production.

lean metric—A metric that permits a balanced evaluation and response—quality without sacrificing quantity objectives. The types of metrics are financial, behavioral, and core-process performance.

lean production—A philosophy of production that emphasizes the minimization of the amount of all the resources (including time) used in the various activities of the enterprise. It involves identifying and eliminating non-value-adding activities in design, production, supply chain management, and dealing with customers. Lean producers employ teams of multiskilled workers at all levels of the organization and use highly flexible, increasingly automated machines to produce volumes of products in potentially enormous variety. It contains a set of principles and practices to reduce cost through the relentless removal of waste and through the simplification of all manufacturing and support processes. Syn: lean, lean manufacturing.

learning curve—A curve reflecting the rate of improvement in time per piece as more units of an item are made. A planning technique, the learning curve is particularly useful in project-oriented industries in which new products are frequently phased in. The basis for the learning curve calculation is that workers will be able to produce the product more quickly after they get used to making it. Syn: experience curve, manufacturing progress curve.

learning management system—A software system for delivering and managing education and training within an organization.

learning organization—1) Group of people who have woven a continuous, enhanced capacity to learn into the corporate culture. 2) An organization in which learning processes are analyzed, monitored, developed, and aligned with competitive goals.

lease—A rental agreement lasting an extended period.

least changeover cost—Determining the lowest cost of making machine changeovers between jobs by sequencing the jobs accordingly.

least-squares method—A method of curve fitting that selects a line of best fit through a plot of data to minimize the sum of squares of the deviations of the given points from the line. See: regression analysis.

least total cost—A dynamic lot-sizing technique that calculates the order quantity by comparing the setup (or ordering) costs and the carrying cost for various lot sizes and selects the lot size where these costs are most nearly equal. See: discrete order quantity, dynamic lot sizing.

least unit cost—A dynamic lot-sizing technique that adds ordering cost and inventory carrying cost for each trial lot size and divides by the number of units in the lot size, picking the lot size with the lowest unit cost. See: discrete order quantity, dynamic lot sizing.

leg—A portion of a complete trip.

legacy systems—A computer application program that is old and interfaces poorly with other applications but is too expensive to replace. It often runs on antiquated hardware.

legal environment—The governmental restrictions placed on an organization regarding the goods and services provided by the business, for example, environmental regulations, export/import restrictions, safety regulations, and mandated deregulations.

lessee—An entity to which a lease is given.

lessor—An entity which gives a lease.

less-than-carload (LCL)—Either a small shipment that does not fill the railcar or a shipment of not enough weight to qualify for a carload quantity rate discount.

less-than-truckload (LTL)—Either a small shipment that does not fill the truck or a shipment of not enough weight to qualify for a truckload quantity (usually set at about 10,000 lbs.) rate discount, offered to a general commodity trucker.

letter of credit—An assurance by a bank that payment will be made as long as the sales terms agreed to by the buyer and seller are met. This method of payment for sales contracts provides a high degree of protection for the seller.

level—Every part or assembly in a product structure is assigned a level code signifying the relative level in which that part or assembly is used within the product structure. Often times the end items are assigned level 0 with the components and subassemblies going into it assigned to level 1 and so on. The MRP explosion process starts from level 0 and proceeds downward one level at a time.

level-demand strategy—A strategy of keeping capacity level and not variable with demand.

leveling—Syn: resource leveling.

level loading—Syn: load leveling.

level of effort—In project management, support activity (e.g., customer liaison) that is not easily measured by discrete accomplishment. It usually has a uniform work rate.

level of service—A measure (usually expressed as a percentage) of satisfying demand through inventory or by the current production schedule in time to satisfy the customers' requested delivery dates and quantities. In a make-to-stock environment, level of service is sometimes calculated as the percentage of orders picked complete from stock upon receipt of the customer order, the percentage of line items picked complete, or the percentage of total dollar demand picked complete. In make-to-order and design-to-order environments, level of service is the percentage of times the customer-requested or acknowledged date was met by shipping complete product quantities. Syn: measure of service, service level. See: cycle service level.

level production method—A production planning method that maintains a stable production rate while varying inventory levels to meet demand. Syn: level strategy, production leveling. See: level schedule.

level production schedule—Syn: level schedule.

level schedule—1) In traditional management, a production schedule or master production schedule that generates material and labor requirements that are as evenly spread over time as possible. Finished goods inventories buffer the production system against seasonal demand. See: level production method. 2) In JIT, a level schedule (usually constructed monthly) in which each day's customer demand is scheduled to be built on the day it will be shipped. A level schedule is the output of the load-leveling process. Syn: JIT master schedule, level production schedule. See: load leveling.

level strategy—Syn: level production method.

leverage-capital structure ratio—An indicator of whether or not a company has the ability to retire its long-term debts.

leveraged buyout (LBO)—A takeover of a company using borrowed funds where assets of the acquired company are used as partial collateral for the loan.

leveraging purchase volume—Buying in large quantities to take advantage of volume price or shipping discounts.

LF—Abbreviation for late finish date.

liabilities—An accounting/financial term (balance sheet classification of accounts) representing debts or obligations owed by a company to creditors. Liabilities may have a short-term time horizon, such as accounts payable, or a longer-term obligation, such as mortgage payable or bonds payable. See: assets, balance sheet, debt, owner's equity.

licensing—Paying a fee for permission to manufacture and sell a product created by another.

life cycle analogy method—A method for forecasting the life cycle of a new product or service, including the introduction, growth, maturity, and decline phases. In addition to time frames, this qualitative technique tries to estimate demand levels.

life cycle assessment (LCA)—Understanding the human and environmental aspects and impacts during the life of a product, process, or service, including energy, ma-

terial, and environmental inputs and outputs. Sometimes called cradle-to-grave analysis, LCA includes raw material extraction through materials processing, manufacture, distribution, use, repair and maintenance, and disposal or recycling.

life cycle analysis—A quantitative forecasting technique based on applying past patterns of demand data covering introduction, growth, maturity, saturation, and decline of similar products to a new product family.

life cycle costing—In evaluating alternatives, the consideration of all costs—including acquisition, operation, and disposition costs—that will be incurred over the entire time of product ownership.

life testing—The simulation of a product's life under controlled real-world conditions to see if it holds up and performs as required.

LIFO—Acronym for last in, first out.

lighter—A short-haul flat-bottomed barge.

lightless plant—Syn: dark factory.

LIMIT—Acronym for lot-size inventory management interpolation technique.

limited access—Securing inventory, usually in a locked environment, to protect it from theft and to help improve inventory count accuracy.

limited liability company—In the United States, a business organization that, as with a corporation, enjoys limited liability yet is not a taxable entity.

limited life material—Material having a finite shelf life.

limited partnership—A partnership having two types of partners: (1) limited partners contribute assets to the company without participating in management and (2) general partners manage the company and are responsible for all debts.

limiting operation—The operation with the least capacity in a series of operations with no alternative routings. The capacity of the total system can be no greater than the limiting operation, and as long as this limiting condition exists, the total system can be effectively scheduled by scheduling the limiting operation and providing this operation with proper buffers. See: protective capacity, protective inventory.

line—1) A specific physical space for the manufacture of a product that in a flow shop layout is represented by a straight line. In actuality, this may be a series of pieces of equipment connected by piping or conveyor systems. 2) A type of manufacturing process used to produce a narrow range of standard items with identical or highly similar designs. Production volumes are high, production and material handling equipment is specialized, and all products typically pass through the same sequence of operations. See: assembly line.

linear decision rules—A modeling technique using simultaneous equations (e.g., the establishment of aggregate workforce levels) based upon minimizing the total cost of hiring, firing, holding inventory, backorders, payroll, overtime, and undertime.

linearity—1) Production at a constant quantity. 2) Use of resources at a level rate, typically measured daily or more frequently.

linear layout—A layout of various machines in one straight line. This type of layout makes it difficult to reallocate operations among workers and machinery.

linear production—Actual production to a level schedule, so that a plotting of actual output versus planned output forms a straight line, even when plotted for a short segment of time.

linear programming—Mathematical models for solving linear optimization problems through minimization or maximization of a linear function subject to linear constraints. For example, in blending gasoline and other petroleum products, many intermediate distillates may be available. Prices and octane ratings as well as upper limits on capacities of input materials that can be used to produce various grades of fuel are given. The problem is to blend the various inputs in such a way that (1) cost will be minimized (profit will be maximized), (2) specified optimum octane ratings will be met, and (3) the need for additional storage capacity will be avoided.

linear regression—A statistical data technique that expresses a variable as a linear function of an independent variable. Linear regression can be used to develop forecasting models.

linear trend forecasting—Using simple linear regression to estimate future trends.

line balancing—1) The balancing of the assignment of the tasks to workstations in a manner that minimizes the number of workstations and minimizes the total amount of idle time at all stations for a given output level. In balancing these tasks, the specified time requirement per unit of product for each task and its sequential relationship with the other tasks must be considered. See: uniform plant loading. 2) A technique for determining the product mix that can be run down an assembly line to provide a fairly consistent flow of

work through that assembly line at the planned line rate.

line efficiency—A measure of actual work content versus cycle time of the limiting operation in a production line. Line efficiency (percentage) is equal to the sum of all station task times divided by the longest task time multiplied by the number of stations. In an assembly line layout, the line efficiency is 100 percent minus the balance delay percentage.

line functions—Areas involved in daily operations. Logistics line functions include inventory control, order processing, warehousing and packaging.

line haul costs—Basic costs of carrier operation to move a container of freight, including driver's wages and usage depreciation. These vary with the cost per mile, the distance shipped, and the weight moved.

line item—One item on an order, regardless of quantity.

line loading—The loading of a production line by multiplying the total pieces by the rate per piece for each item to come up with a finished schedule for the line.

line manager—A manager involved in managing a department that is directly involved in making a product.

line manufacturing—Repetitive manufacturing performed by specialized equipment in a fixed sequence.

line scrap—The worth of work in process and raw materials scrapped because of faulty processing as a percentage of the total value of production at standard cost.

line of balance planning—A project planning technique using a lead-time offset chart and a chart of required final assembly completions to graph a third bar chart showing the number of each component that should be completed to date. This bar chart forms a descending line, and aggregate component completions are then plotted against this line of balance. This is a crude form of material planning.

line of credit—A contract that enables a company to borrow funds at any time up to a predetermined limit.

link—The transportation method used in a logistics system to connect the nodes of the system.

liquidity—The ability of a firm to pay debts as they come due.

liquidity ratio—Financial ratios that are indicators of a firm's ability to retire short-term financial obligations.

listserv—Syn: listserver.

list server—Software running on a web-accessed computer that facilitates electronic discussions by emailing submissions from one member to all other members of the discussion group. Syn: listserv.

live load—Syn: available work.

load—The amount of planned work scheduled for and actual work released to a facility, work center, or operation for a specific span of time. Usually expressed in terms of standard hours of work or, when items consume similar resources at the same rate, units of production. Syn: workload.

load center—Syn: work center.

load-distance analysis—In layout analysis, a method of choosing a facility layout based on selecting the layout with the shortest product or material travel per time period.

loading port—The port where cargo is loaded onto an exporting vessel.

load leveling—Spreading orders out in time or rescheduling operations so that the amount of work to be done in sequential time periods tends to be distributed evenly and is achievable. Although both material and labor are ideally level loaded, specific businesses and industries may load to one or the other exclusively (e.g., service industries). Syn: capacity smoothing, level loading. See: level schedule.

load profile—A display of future capacity requirements based on released and/or planned orders over a given span of time. Syn: load projection. See: capacity requirements plan.

load projection—Syn: load profile.

local area network (LAN)—A high-speed data communication system for linking computer terminals, programs, storage, and graphic devices at multiple workstations distributed over a relatively small geographic area such as a building or campus.

local measures—The set of measurements that relates to a resource, operation, process, or part and usually has low correlation to global organization measures. Examples are errors per printed page, departmental efficiency, and volume discounts.

local rate—A rate pertaining to two points served by a single carrier.

locational determinants—Information or factors considered in determining where to put a facility.

location audit—A methodical verification of the location records for an item or group of items in inventory to en-sure that when the record shows an item's location, it is, in fact, in that location.

location grid—A layout of a warehouse used to improve inventory management and cycle counting.

location tag—A bar-coded sign situated at a warehouse location. The location number can be read or scanned.

locator file—A file used in a stockroom (or anywhere) providing information on where each item is located. See: locator system.

locator system—A system for maintaining a record of the storage locations of items in inventory. See: locator file.

logbook—A daily record kept by an interstate driver of driving and duty-related and non-duty-related activities.

logical relationship—In project management, a dependency between two activities or between a milestone and an activity. The four possible relationships are (1) finish-to-start—activity A must be finished before activity B can start; (2) finish-to-finish—activity A must be finished before activity B can finish; (3) start-to-start—activity A must start before activity B can start; and (4) start-to-finish—activity A must start before activity B can finish.

logistics—1) In an industrial context, the art and science of obtaining, producing, and distributing material and product in the proper place and in proper quantities. 2) In a military sense (where it has greater usage), its meaning can also include the movement of personnel.

logistics channel—A set of supply chain partners who participate in storage, transportation, and communications that contribute to the flow of goods.

logistics data interchange (LDI)—The electronic transmission of logistics information via computer systems.

logistics management—The part of supply chain management that oversees the planning and execution of forward and reverse flow of goods and related information between points in the supply chain to meet customer requirements.

logistics strategy—A plan for the logistics elements of a business—including warehousing, information systems, and transportation—that is aligned with the overall business strategy. See: strategic plan.

logistics system—The planning and coordination of the physical movement aspects of a firm's operations such that a flow of raw materials, parts, and finished goods is achieved in a manner that minimizes total costs for the levels of service desired.

log normal distribution—A continuous probability distribution where the logarithms of the variable are normally distributed.

longest-task-time (LTT) heuristic—The method of attaching additional jobs to a workstation based on priority order, with the longest task scheduled first.

long-term planning—Business planning that addresses the strategic needs of the organization. See: business plan, resource planning.

long-term production plan—Syn: aggregate production plan.

long ton—Two thousand two hundred and forty pounds.

loose standard—A standard time greater than that required by a qualified worker with normal skill and effort.

loss leader pricing—Pricing some products below cost to attract customers into the store, in the expectation that they will buy other items as well.

loss to society—According to Genichi Taguchi, a loss to society occurs whenever a dimension of a product differs from its target value. This loss increases with the square of the deviation from the target. According to this concept, a loss to society occurs even though a dimension is within tolerance—as long as the dimension is not exactly on the target. For example, a loss to society might occur because an assembly made of components that are within specification, but not exactly on target, wears out faster than an assembly comprised of components that are all exactly on the target.

lost sale—A potential sale that was not completed, usually due to lack of availability of the item in question.

lost time factor—The complement of utilization, that is one minus the utilization factor. It is the percentage of time lost to machine, tool, and worker unavailability. It can be calculated as the planned hours minus actual hours used, divided by the planned hours. See: balance delay, utilization.

lot—A quantity produced together and sharing the same production costs and specifications. See: batch.

lot control—A set of procedures (e.g., assigning unique batch numbers and tracking each batch) used to maintain lot integrity from raw materials, from the supplier through manufacturing to consumers.

lot cost—In cost accounting, those costs associated with processing a common lot or quantity of parts having the same specifications.

lot-for-lot—A lot-sizing technique that generates planned orders in quantities equal to the net requirements in each period. See: discrete order quantity.

lot number—A unique identification assigned to a homogeneous quantity of material. Syn: batch number, mix number.

lot number control—Assignment of unique numbers to each instance of receipt and carrying forth that number into subsequent manufacturing processes so that, in review of an end item, each lot consumed from raw materials through end item can be identified as having been used for the manufacture of this specific end item lot.

lot number traceability—Tracking parts by lot numbers to a group of items. This tracking can assist in tracing quality problems to their source. A lot number identifies a designated group of related items manufactured in a single run or received from a vendor in a single shipment.

lot operation cycle time—The length of time required from the start of setup to the end of cleanup for a production lot at a given operation, including setup, production, and cleanup.

lot size—The amount of a particular item that is ordered from the plant or a supplier or issued as a standard quantity to the production process. Syn: order quantity.

lot-size code—A code that indicates the lot-sizing technique selected for a given item. Syn: order policy code.

lot-size inventory—Inventory that results whenever quantity price discounts, shipping costs, setup costs, or similar considerations make it more economical to purchase or produce in larger lots than are needed for immediate purposes.

lot-size inventory management interpolation technique (LIMIT)—A technique for looking at the lot sizes for groups of similar products to determine the effect economic lot sizes will have on the total inventory, total setup costs, and machine availability.

lot-size system—Syn: fixed reorder quantity inventory model.

lot sizing—The process of, or techniques used in, determining lot size. See: order policy.

lot splitting—Dividing a lot into two or more sublots and simultaneously processing each sublot on identical (or very similar) facilities as separate lots, usually to compress lead time or to expedite a small quantity. Syn: operation splitting.

lot tolerance percent defective (LTPD)—Expressed in percent defective, the poorest quality in an individual lot that should be accepted. Note: The LTPD is used as a basis for some inspection systems and is commonly associated with a value for a small consumer's risk.

lot traceability—The ability to identify the lot or batch number of product in terms of one or all of the following: its composition, purchased parts, manufacturing date, or shipped items. In certain regulated industries, lot traceability may be a legislative requirement.

low-cost-provider strategy—A strategy of offering the lowest prices in the market to gain share and increase sales volume in industries composed by numerous players offering the same type of products.

lower control limit (LCL)—Control limit for points below the central line in a control chart.

lower specification limit (LSL)—In statistical process control, charting the line that defines the minimum acceptable level of random output. See: tolerance limits.

low-level code—A number that identifies the lowest level in any bill of material at which a particular component appears. Net requirements for a given component are not calculated until all the gross requirements have been calculated down to that level. Low-level codes are normally calculated and maintained automatically by the computer software. Syn: explosion level.

LS—Abbreviation for late start date.

LSL—Abbreviation for lower specification limit.

LTL—Abbreviation for less than truckload.

LTPD—Abbreviation for lot tolerance percent defective.

LTT—Abbreviation for longest-task-time.

lumpy demand—Syn: discontinuous demand.

M

machine attachments—Additional machine parts that decrease the time needed to complete a task and the level of human involvement.

machine center—A production area consisting of one or more machines (and, if appropriate for capacity planning, the necessary support personnel) that can be considered as one unit for capacity requirements planning and detailed scheduling.

machine downtimes—Periods during which a machine is unavailable due to tool breakage, worker unavailability, machine breakdown, maintenance, teardown, setup, and other factors.

machine flexibility—In work-cell design, choosing between general-purpose machinery versus special-purpose machinery, so that the lowest cost and most adaptability is achieved.

machine hours—The amount of time, in hours, that a machine is actually running. Machine hours, rather than labor hours, may be used for planning capacity for scheduling, and for allocating costs.

machine-limited capacity—A production environment where a specific machine limits throughput of the process. See: constraint, throughput.

machine loading—The accumulation by workstation, machine, or machine group of the hours generated from the scheduling of operations for released orders by time period. Machine loading differs from capacity requirements planning in that it does not use the planned orders from MRP but operates solely from released orders. It may be of limited value because of its limited visibility of resources.

machine productivity—A partial productivity measure. The rate of output of a machine per unit of time compared with an established standard or rate of output. Machine productivity can be expressed as output per unit of time or output per machine hour. See: labor productivity, productivity.

machine utilization—A measure of how intensively a machine is being used. Machine utilization compares the actual machine time (setup and run time) to available time.

machining center—A machine capable of performing a variety of metal, wood, or plastic removal operations on a part, usually operated by numerical control.

macro environment—The environment external to a business including technological, economic, natural, and regulatory forces that marketing efforts cannot control.

MAD—Acronym for mean absolute deviation.

mainframe—Large computer system, typically with a separate central processing unit. This high-level computer is designed for the most intensive computational tasks.

maintainability—The characteristic of equipment design and installation that provides the ability for the equipment to be repaired easily and efficiently. See: serviceability.

maintenance, repair, and operating (MRO) supplies— Items used in support of general operations and maintenance such as maintenance supplies, spare parts, and consumables used in the manufacturing process and supporting operations.

maintenance, repair, and overhaul (MRO)—An item for reprocessing in the remanufacturing industry.

major setup—The equipment setup and related activities required to manufacture a group of items in sequence, exclusive of the setup required for each item in the group.

make-or-buy cost analysis—A comparison of all of the costs associated with making an item versus the cost of buying the item.

make-or-buy decision—The act of deciding whether to produce an item internally or buy it from an outside supplier. Factors to consider in the decision include costs, capacity availability, proprietary and/or specialized knowledge, quality considerations, skill requirements, volume, and timing.

make-to-order—A production environment where a good or service can be made after receipt of a customer's order. The final product is usually a combination of standard items and items custom-designed to meet the special needs of the customer. Where options or accessories are stocked before customer orders arrive, the term assemble-to-order is frequently used. Syn: produce-to-order. See: assemble-to-order, make-to-stock.

make-to-stock—A production environment where products can be and usually are finished before receipt of a customer order. Customer orders are typically filled from existing stocks, and production orders are used to replenish those stocks. Syn: produce-to-stock. See: assemble-to-order, make-to-order.

Malcolm Baldrige National Quality Award (MB QA)—An award established by Congress in 1987 to raise awareness of quality management and to recognize U.S. companies that have implemented successful quality management systems. Up to four awards may be given annually in each of three categories: manufacturing company, service company, and small business. The award is named after the late Secretary of Commerce, Malcolm Baldrige, a proponent of quality management. The U.S. Commerce Department's National Institute of Standards and Technology manages the award, and the American Society for Quality (ASQ) administers it. Syn: Baldrige Award.

management—The functions of planning, organizing, and controlling the transformation process and its utility in providing a good or service to customers.

management by objectives (MBO)—A participative goal-setting process that enables the manager or supervisor to construct and communicate the goals of the department to each subordinate. At the same time, the subordinate is able to formulate personal goals and influence the department's goals.

management by walking around (MBWA)—The management technique of managers touring a facility on a regular basis to talk with workers and staff about problems, trends, and potential solutions.

management estimation—A judgmental forecasting technique whereby responsible individuals predict the demand for new products or alter a quantitative forecast for existing products largely on the basis of experience and intuition. Other judgmental forecasting techniques may be used in combination with management estimation to improve the accuracy of the estimate. See: Delphi method, historical analogy, panel consensus, pyramid forecasting.

management information system (MIS)—Integrated approach for providing interpreted and relevant data that can help managers make decisions. This information can reflect the progress or lack of progress made in achieving major objectives.

management science—Syn: operations research.

managerial accounting—A branch of accounting that uses techniques such as break-even analysis, cost-volume-profit analysis, make-buy analysis, and others to provide information used in day-to-day decision making.

man-hour—A unit of measure representing one person working for one hour. The combination of "n" people working for "h" hours produces nh man-hours. Frequent qualifications to the definition include (1) designation of work effort as normal effort; (2) designation of time spent as actual hours.

manifest system—A production control system where the exact sequence of items to be assembled is required.

manual rescheduling—The most common method of rescheduling open orders (scheduled receipts). Under this method, the MRP system provides information on the part numbers and order numbers that need to be rescheduled. Due dates and order quantity changes required are then analyzed and changed by material planners or other authorized persons. Syn: planner intervention. Ant: automatic rescheduling.

manufacturability—A measure of the design of a product or process in terms of its ability to be produced easily, consistently, and with high quality.

manufacturer's agent—Syn: manufacturer's representative.

manufacturer's representative—One who sells goods for several firms but does not take title to them. Syn: manufacturer's agent, manufacturing representative.

manufacturing—A series of interrelated activities and operations involving the design, material selection, planning, production, quality assurance, management, and marketing of discrete consumer and durable goods.

manufacturing authorization—Syn: manufacturing order.

manufacturing automation protocol (MAP)—An application-specific protocol based on the International Standards Organization's open systems interconnection (OSI) standards. It is designed to allow communication between a company's computers and computers from different vendors in the manufacturing shop floor environment.

manufacturing calendar—A calendar used in inventory and production planning functions that consecutively numbers only the working days so that the component and work order scheduling may be done based on the actual number of workdays available. Syn: M-day calendar, planning calendar, production calendar, shop calendar. See: resource calendar.

manufacturing capital asset value—The depreciated value of manufacturing fixed assets.

manufacturing cycle—Syn: manufacturing lead time.

manufacturing cycle efficiency—The ratio of value-added time to manufacturing lead time or cycle time. Manufacturing cycle time can be improved by the reduction of manufacturing lead time by eliminating non-value-added activities such as inspecting, moving, and queuing.

manufacturing data sheet—Syn: routing.

manufacturing engineering—The engineering discipline concerned with designing and improving production processes. See: process engineering.

manufacturing environment—The framework in which manufacturing strategy is developed and implemented. Elements of the manufacturing environment include

external environmental forces; corporate strategy; business unit strategy; other functional strategies (marketing, engineering, finance, etc.); product selection; product/process design; product/process technology; and management competencies. Often refers to whether a company, plant, product, or service is make-to-stock, make-to-order, or assemble-to-order. Syn: production environment.

manufacturing execution systems (MES)—Programs and systems that participate in shop floor control, including programmed logic controllers and process control computers for direct and supervisory control of manufacturing equipment; process information systems that gather historical performance information, then generate reports; graphical displays; and alarms that inform operations personnel what is going on in the plant currently and a very short history into the past. Quality control information is also gathered and a laboratory information management system may be part of this configuration to tie process conditions to the quality data that are generated. Thereby, cause-and-effect relationships can be determined. The quality data at times affect the control parameters that are used to meet product specifications either dynamically or off line.

manufacturing instruction—A set of detailed instructions for carrying out a manufacturing process. It is usually referenced by the routing and thus can simplify the content of the routing.

manufacturing layout strategies—An element of manufacturing strategy. It is the analysis of physical capacity, geography, functional needs, corporate philosophy, and product-market/process focus to systematically respond to required facility changes driven by organizational, strategic, and environmental considerations.

manufacturing lead time—The total time required to manufacture an item, exclusive of lower level purchasing lead time. For make-to-order products, it is the length of time between the release of an order to the production process and shipment to the final customer. For make-to-stock products, it is the length of time between the release of an order to the production process and receipt into inventory. Included here are order preparation time, queue time, setup time, run time, move time, inspection time, and put-away time. Syn: manufacturing cycle, production cycle, production lead time. See: lead time.

manufacturing order—A document, group of documents, or schedule conveying authority for the manufacture of specified parts or products in specified quantities. Syn:

job order, manufacturing authorization, production order, production release, run order, shop order, work order. See: assembly parts list, batch card, blend order, fabrication order, mix ticket, work order.

manufacturing order reporting—Syn: production reporting and status control.

manufacturing philosophy—The set of guiding principles, driving forces, and ingrained attitudes that helps communicate goals, plans, and policies to all employees and that is reinforced through conscious and subconscious behavior within the manufacturing organization.

manufacturing planning and control system (MPC)—A closed-loop information system that includes the planning functions of production planning (sales and operations planning), master production scheduling, material requirements planning, and capacity requirements planning. Once the plan has been accepted as realistic, execution begins. The execution functions include input-output control, detailed scheduling, dispatching, anticipated delay reports (department and supplier), and supplier scheduling. A closed-loop MRP system is one example of a manufacturing planning and control system.

manufacturing process—The series of operations performed upon material to convert it from the raw material or a semifinished state to a state of further completion. Manufacturing processes can be arranged in a process layout, product layout, cellular layout, or fixed-position layout. Manufacturing processes can be planned to support make-to-stock, make-to-order, assemble-to-order, and so forth, based on the strategic use and placement of inventories. See: production process, transformation process.

manufacturing process development—The definition and implementation of an execution system for making a part, good, or service that is consistent with the objectives of the firm.

manufacturing progress curve—Syn: learning curve.

manufacturing ramp-up—The final phase of new product and process development, whereby the new product moves from pilot production to full-scale manufacturing.

manufacturing release—The issuance of a manufacturing order into the factory.

manufacturing representative—Syn: manufacturer's representative.

manufacturing resource planning (MRP II)—A method for the effective planning of all resources of a manufacturing company. Ideally, it addresses operational planning in units, financial planning in dollars, and has a simulation capability to answer what-if questions. It is made up of a variety of processes, each linked together: business planning, production planning (sales and operations planning), master production scheduling, material requirements planning, capacity requirements planning, and the execution support systems for capacity and material. Output from these systems is integrated with financial reports such as the business plan, purchase commitment report, shipping budget, and inventory projections in dollars. Manufacturing resource planning is a direct outgrowth and extension of closed-loop MRP.

manufacturing strategy—A collective pattern of decisions that acts upon the formulation and deployment of manufacturing resources. To be most effective, the manufacturing strategy should act in support of the overall strategic direction of the business and provide for competitive advantages (edges).

manufacturing volume strategy—An element of manufacturing strategy that includes a series of assumptions and predictions about long-term market, technology, and competitive behavior in the following areas: (1) the predicted growth and variability of demand, (2) the costs of building and operating different sized plants, (3) the rate and direction of technological improvement, (4) the likely behavior of competitors, and (5) the anticipated impact of international competitors, markets, and sources of supply. It is the sequence of specific volume decisions over time that determines an organization's long-term manufacturing volume strategy.

many-to-many communication—Communication that enables many people to exchange information with many other people.

MAP—Acronym for manufacturing automation protocol.

MAPE—Abbreviation for mean absolute percent error.

MAPI method—1) A procedure for equipment replacement analysis sponsored by the Machinery and Allied Products Institute. 2) A method of capital investment analysis that has been formulated by the Machinery and Allied Products Institute. This method uses a fixed format and provides charts and graphs to facilitate calculations. A prominent feature of this method is that it explicitly includes obsolescence.

mapping—Drawing the organization's processes or relationships that form a business process.

margin—A ratio of an organization's operating profit to revenues, measuring management's ability to control operating expenses.

marginal analysis—A decision rule that optimality occurs where incremental revenue equals incremental cost.

marginal cost—The incremental costs incurred when the level of output of some operation or process is increased by one unit.

marginal cost of capital—The cost of the next dollar, after taxes, that a firm expects to raise for investment.

marginal pricing—Pricing products at a markup over the marginal cost of producing the next item. Marginal costs generally include the variable cost of producing and selling an additional item.

marginal product—In economics, the additional quantity of total output following from a one-unit increase in variable input. See: law of diminishing marginal returns.

marginal revenue—The incremental sales dollars received when the level of output of some operation is increased by one unit.

marginal utility—The additional usefulness and enjoyment received from consuming one more unit of a good or service.

market—A set of buyers and sellers exchanging products. Prices tend to equalize through ongoing exchanges between buyers and sellers. Markets include institutional markets, government markets, industrial markets, and consumer markets. See: consumer market, government market, industrial market, institutional market.

market boundary—The boundary where the laid-down cost for two companies is equal. Laid-down cost is product cost plus unit transportation cost.

market demand—In marketing, the total demand that would exist within a defined customer group in a given geographical area during a particular time period given a known marketing program.

market dominance—When a firm has very little competition.

market driven—Responding to customers' needs.

market hedge—Scheduling or holding an inventory quantity greater than the expected demand because of expected inaccuracy or volatility in the forecasted demand. See: hedge.

marketing—The design, pricing, promotion, and distribution of goods to create transactions with businesses and consumers.

marketing channel—That set of organizations through which a good or service passes in going from a raw state to the final consumer. See: channels of distribution, distribution channel.

marketing cost analysis—The study and evaluation of the relative profitability or costs of different marketing operations in terms of customers, marketing units, commodities, territories, or marketing activities. Cost accounting is typically used.

marketing management—Syn: demand management.

marketing mix—The concept that marketing strategy selects product, price, promotion, and channel targets in selected markets.

marketing research—The systematic gathering, recording, and analyzing of data about problems relating to the marketing of goods and services. Such research may be undertaken by impartial agencies or by business firms or their agents. Marketing research includes several types: (1) market analysis (product potential is a type) is the study of the size, location, nature, and characteristics of markets, (2) sales analysis (or research) is the systematic study and comparison of sales (or consumption) data, (3) consumer research (motivation research is a type) is concerned with the discovery and analysis of consumer attitudes, reactions, and preferences. Syn: market research.

marketing strategy—The basic plan marketing expects to use to achieve its business and marketing objectives in a particular market. This plan includes marketing expenditures, marketing mix, and marketing allocation.

market penetration—The degree to which a product has been accepted by the marketplace. Syn: market reach.

market plan—The output of the market planning process. The market plan includes the current market position, opportunity and issue analysis, marketing objectives and strategies, action plans, programs, projects, budgets, and pro forma profit and loss statement and management controls. Syn: brand plan, product plan.

market planning—The process of developing market plans for products and services. This process is composed of the following phases—identification; research and analysis of market opportunities; selection of target markets; development of marketing strategies; development of the marketing plans, programs, and projects; and management, execution, and control of the market plans, programs, and projects.

market-positioned strategy—A location strategy that focuses on the customer by placing warehouses closer to the customer. See: product-positioned strategy.

market-positioned warehouse—Warehouse positioned to replenish customer inventory assortments and to afford maximum inbound transport consolidation economies from inventory origin points with relatively short-haul local delivery.

market reach—Syn: market penetration.

market research—Syn: marketing research.

market segment—A group of potential customers sharing some measurable characteristics based on demographics, psychographics, lifestyle, geography, benefits, and so forth.

market segmentation—A marketing strategy in which the total market is disaggregated into submarkets, or segments, that share some measurable characteristic based on demographics, psychographics, lifestyle, geography, benefits, and so forth.

market share—The actual portion of current market demand that a company or product achieves.

market strategy—The marketing plan to support the business strategy.

market surveys—Questionnaires designed to get feedback from potential customers about demand for a product or service.

market targeting—The process of developing measurements of the desirability of given market segments and deciding in which market segments to compete.

market value-added—In financial management, the surplus of a firm's equity over the capital that has been invested in the firm.

marks and numbers—Identifying agents placed on products or containers used to identify a shipment or its parts.

marquis partners—Key strategic relationships. By partnering with big players, via equity offerings if necessary, a company creates barriers to entry into supply chain relationships for competitors.

mass customization—The creation of a high-volume product with large variety so that a customer may specify an exact model out of a large volume of possible end items while manufacturing cost is low due to large volume. An example is a personal computer order in which the customer may specify processor speed, memory size, hard disk size and speed, removable storage de-

vice characteristics, and many other options when PCs are assembled on one line and at low cost.

mass marketing—The strategy of sending the same message to all potential customers.

mass production—High-quantity production characterized by specialization of equipment and labor. See: continuous production.

master black belt—In six sigma, quality expert capable of implementing strategic quality efforts including teaching other facilitators (black belts) the quality applications within all levels of the organization.

master budget—The document that consolidates all other budgets of an organization into an overall plan, including the projection of a cash flow statement and an operating statement for the budget period as well as a balance sheet for the end of the budget period. Syn: static budget.

master file—A main reference file of information, such as the item master file or work center file. See: detail file, item master file.

master pack—A large, protective box used to contain smaller boxes. This reduces materials handling activities.

master planning—A group of business processes that includes the following activities: demand management (which includes forecasting and order servicing); production and resource planning; and master scheduling (which includes the master schedule and the rough-cut capacity plan).

master planning of resources—A grouping of business processes that includes the following activities: demand management, which includes the forecasting of sales, the planning of distribution, and the servicing of customer orders; sales and operations planning, which includes sales planning, production planning, inventory planning, backlog planning, and resource planning; master scheduling, which includes the preparation of the master production schedule and the rough-cut capacity plan.

master production schedule (MPS)—The master production schedule is a line on the master schedule grid that reflects the anticipated build schedule for those items assigned to the master scheduler. The master scheduler maintains this schedule, and in turn, it becomes a set of planning numbers that drives material requirements planning. It represents what the company plans to produce expressed in specific configurations, quantities, and dates. The master production schedule is not a sales item forecast that represents a statement of demand. The master production schedule must take into account the forecast, the production plan, and other important considerations such as backlog, availability of material, availability of capacity, and management policies and goals. See: master schedule.

master route sheet—The authoritative route process sheet from which all other format variations and copies are derived.

master schedule—The master schedule is a format that includes time periods (dates), the forecast, customer orders, projected available balance, available-to-promise, and the master production schedule. The master schedule takes into account the forecast; the production plan; and other important considerations such as backlog, availability of material, availability of capacity, and management policies and goals. See: master production schedule.

master schedule item—A part number selected to be planned by the master scheduler. The item is deemed critical in its impact on lower level components or resources such as skilled labor, key machines, or dollars. Therefore, the master scheduler, not the computer, maintains the plan for these items. A master schedule item may be an end item, a component, a pseudo number, or a planning bill of material.

master scheduler—Often the job title of the person charged with the responsibility of managing, establishing, reviewing, and maintaining a master schedule for select items. Ideally, the person should have substantial product, plant, process, and market knowledge because the consequences of this individual's actions often have a great impact on customer service, material, and capacity planning. See: master production schedule.

master scheduling—The process where the master schedule is generated and reviewed and adjustments made to the master production schedule to ensure consistency with the production plan. The master production schedule (the line on the grid) is the primary input to the material requirements plan. The sum of the master production schedules for the items within the product family must equal the production plan for that family.

match capacity strategy—A capacity strategy that strikes a balance between the lead and lag capacity strategies by adding capacity at approximately the rate of actual demand increase.

material analyst—The person assigned responsibility for and identification of the planning requirements for specific items and responsibility for each order.

material class—A means to describe a grouping of materials with similar characteristics for planning and scheduling purposes.

material constraint—Usually a misnomer. Material shortages are rarely the constraint, rather temporary material shortages hinder effective constraint management by inhibiting the ability to fully exploit and/or subordinate to the constraint.

material control—Syn: inventory control.

material definition—A definition of the properties and characteristics of a substance. material-dominated scheduling (MDS)—A technique that schedules materials before processors (equipment or capacity). This technique facilitates the efficient use of materials. MDS can be used to schedule each stage in a process flow scheduling system. MRP systems use material-dominated scheduling logic. See: processor-dominated scheduling.

material-dominated scheduling (MDS)—A technique that schedules materials before processors (equipment or capacity). This technique facilitates the efficient use of materials. MDS can be used to schedule each stage in a process flow scheduling system. MRP systems use material-dominated scheduling logic. See: processor-dominated scheduling.

material flexibility—The ability of the transformation process to handle unexpected variations in material inputs.

material index—The total of raw material weights divided by final product weight.

material list—Syn: picking list.

material lot—A uniquely identifiable amount of a material. This describes the actual quantity or amount of material available, its current state, and its specific property values.

material planner—1) The person normally responsible for managing the inventory levels, schedules, and availability of selected items, either manufactured or purchased. Syn: inventory planner. 2) In an MRP system, the person responsible for reviewing and acting on order release, action, and exception messages from the system. Syn: parts planner, planner.

material planning—Syn: inventory planning.

material receipt inspection—The receiving department compares the incoming material to the purchase order to verify that the correct material and quantity have been received. The material is then inspected for quality and general condition. A material receipt report is prepared and copies are distributed to the appropriate departments such as purchasing and accounting.

material release—The introduction of parts into a production process.

material requirements plan—The result from the process of material requirements planning.

material requirements planning (MRP)—A set of techniques that uses bill of material data, inventory data, and the master production schedule to calculate requirements for materials. It makes recommendations to release replenishment orders for material. Further, because it is time-phased, it makes recommendations to reschedule open orders when due dates and need dates are not in phase. Time-phased MRP begins with the items listed on the MPS and determines (1) the quantity of all components and materials required to fabricate those items and (2) the date that the components and material are required. Time-phased MRP is accomplished by exploding the bill of material, adjusting for inventory quantities on hand or on order, and offsetting the net requirements by the appropriate lead times.

material requisition—This is the first step to placing a replenishment order; initiated by the material user.

material review board (MRB)—An organization within a company, often a standing committee, that determines the resolution or disposition of items that have questionable quality or other attributes.

materials—The components that are processed by an operation.

material safety data sheet (MSDS)—A document that is part of the materials information system and accompanies the product. Prepared by the manufacturer, the MSDS provides information regarding the safety and chemical properties and (if necessary) the long-term storage, handling, and disposal of the product. Among other factors, the MSDS describes the hazardous components of a product; how to treat leaks, spills, and fires; and how to treat improper human contact with the product.

materials efficiency—A concept that addresses the efficiency with which materials are obtained, converted, and shipped in the overall purchasing, production, and distribution process. It can be considered as a companion concept to labor efficiency, and it is potentially more significant as the materials portion of cost of goods sold continues to grow.

materials handling—Movement and storage of goods inside the distribution center. This represents a capital cost and is balanced against the operating costs of the facility.

materials handling system—The system of transportation that receives, moves, and delivers materials during the production or distribution process.

materials handling time—The time necessary to move materials from one work center to the next work center. This time includes waiting for the materials handling equipment and actual movement time.

materials management—The grouping of management functions supporting the complete cycle of material flow, from the purchase and internal control of production materials to the planning and control of work in process to the warehousing, shipping, and distribution of the finished product.

material specification—An explanation of the characteristics of material to be produced or purchased.

materials requisition—1) An authorization that identifies the items and quantities to be withdrawn from inventory. 2) An authorization that identifies the items and quantities to be included in a purchase order. Syn: production materials requisition.

materials system—Connecting material flows contained in a production system.

material sublot—A uniquely identifiable subset of a material lot containing quantity and location. A sublot may be a single item.

material usage variance—The difference between the planned or standard requirements for materials to produce a given item and the actual quantity used for a particular instance of manufacture.

material yield—Syn: yield.

materiel—A term, used more frequently in nonmanufacturing organizations, to refer to the equipment, apparatus, and supplies used by an organization.

mathematical programming—The general problem of optimizing a function of several variables subject to a number of constraints. If the function and constraints are linear in the variables and a subset of the constraints restricts the variables to be nonnegative, a linear programming problem exists.

matrix—A mathematical array having one, two, and sometimes more dimensions, into which collections of data may be stored and processed.

matrix bill of material—A chart made up from the bills of material for a number of products in the same or similar families. It is arranged in a matrix with components in columns and parents in rows (or vice versa) so that requirements for common components can be summarized conveniently.

matrix diagram—A graphical technique used to analyze the relationship between two related groups of ideas.

matrix organizational structure—An organizational structure in which two (or more) channels of command, budget responsibility, and performance measurement exist simultaneously. For example, both product and functional forms of organization could be implemented simultaneously, that is, the product and functional managers have equal authority and employees report to both managers.

maverick spending—A term used when employees or managers purchase from nonqualified suppliers, bypassing established purchasing procedures.

maximum allowable cost—In service organizations, the limit of reimbursement allowed by an agency for the cost of a supply item.

maximum demonstrated capacity—The highest amount of actual output produced in the past when all efforts have been made to optimize the resource; for instance, overtime, additional personnel, extra hours, extra shifts, reassignment of personnel, or use of any related equipment. Maximum demonstrated capacity is the most one could ever expect to produce in a short period of time but represents a rate that cannot be maintained over a long period of time. See: demonstrated capacity.

maximum inventory—The planned maximum allowable inventory for an item based on its planned lot size and target safety stock.

maximum order quantity—An order quantity modifier, applied after the lot size has been calculated, that limits the order quantity to a pre-established maximum.

MBO—Abbreviation for management by objectives.

MBNQA—Abbreviation for the Malcolm Baldrige National Quality Award.

MBWA—Abbreviation for management by walking around.

M-day calendar—Syn: manufacturing calendar.

M-days—Available manufacturing days excluding holidays and weekends.

MDS—Abbreviation for material-dominated scheduling.

mean—The arithmetic average of a group of values. Syn: arithmetic mean.

mean absolute deviation (MAD)—The average of the absolute values of the deviations of observed values from some expected value. MAD can be calculated based on observations and the arithmetic mean of those observations. An alternative is to calculate absolute deviations of actual sales data minus forecast data. These data can be averaged in the usual arithmetic way or with exponential smoothing. See: forecast error, tracking signal.

mean absolute percent error (MAPE)—A measure of statistical variation in a forecast. Computed by dividing each absolute forecast error by the actual demand, multiplying that by 100 to get the absolute percentage error, and computing the average.

mean squared error (MSE)—A measure of statistical variation in a forecast. Computed by squaring the forecast errors and then taking the average of the sum of the squared errors.

mean time between failures (MTBF)—The average time interval between failures for repairable product for a defined unit of measure (e.g., operating hours, cycles, miles). See: reliability.

mean time for failures (MTFF)—Average time for failure of a nonrepairable product (expected life) or average time to first failure of a repairable product. See: reliability.

mean time to repair (MTTR)—The average time that it takes to repair a product.

measurement ton—A measurement equivalent to 40 cubic feet. It is a factor in water transportation rate-setting.

measure of service—Syn: level of service.

measure phase—A phase in the six sigma design-measure-analyze-improve-control process during which current performance is evaluated. See: design-measure-analyze-improve-control process.

measures constraint—A common misnomer. Bad measures are not the constraint. Rather, bad measures hinder effective constraint management by inhibiting the ability to fully exploit and/or subordinate to the constraint.

median—The middle value in a set of measured values when the items are arranged in order of magnitude. If there is no single middle value, the median is the mean of the two middle values.

mediation—The introduction of a neutral third party who attempts to provide alternatives to issues causing conflict that have not been put forth by either party or to change the way the parties perceive the situation. It is often used in collective bargaining to reach an agreement.

mental model—A paradigm of how the world works formed by a person's experiences and assumptions.

merchants—Buyers who purchase for the purpose of reselling.

Mercosur—Southern Common Market.

merge in transit—Combining shipments from several vendors at an intermediate point of shipment and delivering the combined load to the customer.

merger—The acquisition of the assets and liabilities of one company by another.

MES—Abbreviation for manufacturing execution systems.

message distribution—The software component of electronic commerce that enables the sending and receiving of messages.

metered issues—Issues of parts or materials from stores in quantities that correspond to the rate at which materials are used.

methods analysis—That part of methods engineering normally involving an examination and analysis of an operation or a work cycle broken down into its constituent parts to improve the operation, eliminate unnecessary steps, and/or establish and record in detail a proposed method of performance.

methods study—An analysis to improve the efficiency of work by studying the existing method to identify and eliminate wasted motion.

methods-time measurement (MTM)—A system of predetermined motion-time standards, a procedure that analyzes and classifies the movements of any operation into certain human motions and assigns to each motion a predetermined time standard selected by the nature of the motion and the conditions under which it will be made.

metrics—Syn: performance measurement system.

microeconomics—The analysis of the behavior of individual economic decision makers (individuals and firms).

micro-land-bridge traffic—A multimodal transportation solution that moves goods over water and then land, with the final destination inland. See: mini-land-bridge traffic.

middleware—Software that interconnects incompatible applications software and databases from various trading partners into decision-support tools such as ERP.

milestone—In project management, an important event in a project, usually the realization of a significant deliverable.

milestone chart—Syn: Gantt chart.

milestone schedule—In project management, a high-level schedule displaying important deliverables.

military standards—Product standards and specifications for military or defense contractors, units, suppliers, and so forth. These standards sometimes become de facto standards within the civilian community.

milk run—A regular route for pickup of mixed loads from several suppliers. For example, instead of each of five suppliers sending a truckload per week to meet the weekly needs of the customer, one truck visits each of the suppliers on a daily basis before delivering to the customer's plant. Five truckloads per week are still shipped, but each truckload contains the daily requirement from each supplier. See: consolidation.

mini-land-bridge traffic—A multimodal transportation solution that moves goods over water and then land, with the final destination being on the opposite coast. See: micro-land-bridge traffic.

minimum cost order quantity—Syn: economic order quantity.

minimum inventory—The planned lowest amount or level of inventory for an item.

minimum order quantity—An order quantity modifier, applied after the lot size has been calculated, that increases the order quantity to a pre-established minimum.

minimum weight—In transportation, the rate discount volume.

min-max system—A type of order point replenishment system where the minimum (min) is the order point, and the maximum (max) is the "order up to" inventory level. The order quantity is variable and is the result of the max minus available and on-order inventory. An order is recommended when the sum of the available and on-order inventory is at or below the min.

minor setup—The incremental setup activities required when changing from one item to another within a group of items.

MIS—Abbreviation for management information system.

misguided capacity plans—Plans for capacity utilization that are based on erroneous data or assumptions.

mission—The overall goal(s) for an organization set within the parameters of the business scope.

mission statement—The company statement of purpose.

mistake-proofing—Syn: failsafe work methods, poka-yoke.

mix—A breakdown of the total demand or production that identifies different products in an aggregate demand or production run.

mix control—The control of the individual items going through the plant.

mixed-flow scheduling—A procedure used in some process industries for building process train schedules that start at an initial stage and work toward the terminal process stages. This procedure is effective for scheduling where several bottleneck stages may exist. Detailed scheduling is done at each bottleneck stage.

mixed loads—A load having both regulated and exempt items in the same vehicle.

mixed manufacturing—Make-to-stock and make-to-order manufacturing using a single plant and set of equipment.

mixed-model assembly line—An assembly line with more than one type of model passing through it.

mixed-model production—Making several different parts or products in varying lot sizes so that a factory produces close to the same mix of products that will be sold that day. The mixed-model schedule governs the making and the delivery of component parts, including those provided by outside suppliers. The goal is to build every model every day, according to daily demand.

mixed-model scheduling—The process of developing one or more schedules to enable mixed-model production. The goal is to achieve a day's production each day. See: mixed-model production.

mixed production strategy—Syn: hybrid production method. See: chase production method, level production method.

mix flexibility—The ability to handle a wide range of products or variants by using equipment that has short setup times.

mix forecast—Forecast of the proportion of products that will be sold within a given product family, or the proportion of options offered within a product line. Product and option mix as well as aggregate product families must be forecasted. Even though the appropriate level of units is forecasted for a given product line, an inaccurate mix forecast can create material shortages and inventory problems.

mix number—Syn: lot number.

mix ticket—A listing of all the raw materials, ingredients, components, and such that are required to perform a mixing, blending, or similar operation. This listing is often printed on a paper ticket, which also may be used as a turnaround document to report component quantities actually used, final quantity actually produced, etc. This term is often used in batch process or chemical industries. See: assembly parts list, batch card, blend formula, manufacturing order.

modal split—The breakdown of use of transportation modes. Statistics used for the calculation include passenger-miles, ton-miles, and revenue.

mode—The most common or frequent value in a group of values.

model—A representation of a process or system that attempts to relate the most important variables in the system in such a way that analysis of the model leads to insights into the system. Frequently, the model is used to anticipate the result of a particular strategy in the real system.

model number—An item number for a finished good. This number may encompass other parts, such as a user's manual.

modem—A device that converts digital signals to analog signals (and vice versa) so they can be sent over phone lines.

modification flexibility—The capability of the transformation process to quickly implement minor product design changes.

modular architecture—A type of product architecture where the functional pieces correspond to physical pieces. The different physical pieces have their own function, and there is little interaction between them.

modular bill of material—A type of planning bill that is arranged in product modules or options. It is often used in companies where the product has many optional features (e.g., assemble-to-order companies such as automobile manufacturers). See: pseudo bill of material.

modular design strategy—The strategy of planning and designing products so that components or subassemblies can be used in current and future products or assembled to produce multiple configurations of a product. Automobiles and personal computers are examples of modular designs.

modularization—In product development, the use of standardized parts for flexibility and variety. Permits product development cost reductions by using the same item(s) to build a variety of finished goods. This is the first step in developing a planning bill of material process.

modular system—A system architecture design in which related tasks are grouped in self-contained packages. Each package, or module, of tasks performs all of the tasks related to a specific function and advances in functions can be implemented without affecting other packages or modules because of the loose coupling with other modules. One example is a multitiered architecture in which application business rules are separated from the data management rules. Another example is a client-server architecture in which user interface tasks are separated from the application software. See: open system architecture.

module—A self-contained unit of a computer program that communicates with other parts of the program solely through inputs and outputs.

molds—Tools for plastic or chemical production. A mold is the term used for the tools that shape plastic or other soft material parts.

monitoring—The process of comparing actual to planned progress.

monopolistic competition—A market in which many competitors offer partially differentiated products or services within a given geographical area. Most competitors focus on market segments where they can meet customers' needs somewhat better than their competitors. See: industry structure types.

monopoly—Sole control of a market by a company. In the United States, a monopoly is a violation of Article 2 of the Sherman Act.

Monte Carlo simulation—A subset of digital simulation models based on random or stochastic processes.

motion study—A type of methods study focused on therbligs, basic hand and body movements. See: therblig.

move—The physical transportation of inventory from one location to another within a facility. Movements are usually made under the direction and control of the inventory system.

move card—In a just-in-time context, a card or other signal indicating that a specific number of units of a particular item are to be taken from a source (usually an outbound stockpoint) and taken to a point of use (usually an inbound stockpoint). It authorizes the movement of one part number between a single pair of work centers. The card circulates between the outbound stockpoint of the supplying work center and the inbound stockpoint of the using work center. Syn: move signal. See: kanban.

movement inventory—A type of in-process inventory that arises because of the time required to move goods from one place to another.

move order—The authorization to move a particular item from one location to another.

move signal—Syn: move card.

move ticket—A document used in dispatching to authorize or record movement of a job from one work center to another. It may also be used to report other information, such as the actual quantity or the material storage location.

move time—The time that a job spends in transit from one operation to another in the plant.

moving average—An arithmetic average of a certain number (n) of the most recent observations. As each new observation is added, the oldest observation is dropped. The value of n (the number of periods to use for the average) reflects responsiveness versus stability in the same way that the choice of smoothing constant does in exponential smoothing. There are two types of moving average, simple and weighted. See: simple moving average, weighted moving average.

moving average forecast—A forecasting technique that uses a simple moving average or a weighted moving average projected forward as a forecast.

MPC—Abbreviation for manufacturing planning and control.

MPS—Abbreviation for master production schedule.

MRB—Abbreviation for material review board.

MRO—1) Abbreviation for maintenance, repair, and operating. 2) Abbreviation for maintenance, repair, and overhaul.

MRP—Abbreviation for material requirements planning.

MRP nervousness—See: nervousness.

MRP II—Abbreviation for manufacturing resource planning.

MSDS—Abbreviation for material safety data sheet.

MSE—Abbreviation for mean squared error.

M

MTBF—Abbreviation for mean time between failures.

MTFF—Abbreviation for mean time for failures.

MTM—Abbreviation for methods-time measurement.

MTTR—Abbreviation for mean time to repair.

muda (waste)—In lean manufacturing, costs are reduced by reducing waste within a system. There are seven categories of waste: (1) overproduction—excess or too early, (2) waiting—queuing delays, (3) transportation—unneeded movements, (4) processing—poor process design, (5) motion—activities that do not add value, (6) inventory—stock that is sitting is accumulating cost without necessarily providing value, (7) defective units—scrap or rework.

multiactivity chart—Shows how workers interact with each other, or with machines, for different activities.

multicountry strategy—A strategy in which each country market is self-contained. Customers have unique product expectations that are addressed by local production capabilities. Syn: multidomestic strategy.

multicriteria decision models—Models that enable decision makers to evaluate various alternatives across several decision criteria.

multicurrency—Having the capability to handle orders using monies from several countries for billing purposes.

multidomestic strategy—Syn: multicountry strategy.

multifactor productivity—A productivity score that measures output levels relative to more than one input, such as labor or capital.

multilevel bill of material—A display of all the components directly or indirectly used in a parent, together with the quantity required of each component. If a component is a subassembly, blend, intermediate, etc., all its components and all their components also will be exhibited, down to purchased parts and raw materials.

multilevel master schedule—A master scheduling technique that allows any level in an end item's bill of material to be master scheduled. To accomplish this, MPS items must receive requirements from independent and dependent demand sources. See: two-level master schedule.

multilevel where-used—A display for a component listing all the parents in which that component is directly used and the next higher level parents into which each of those parents is used, until ultimately all top-level (level 0) parents are listed.

multilinear regression analysis—Model used for forecasting with more than one independent variable.

multimedia—An interactive combination of two or more of the following: text, graphics, video, audio, and animation all controlled by a personal computer.

multimedia files—Digitized image, video, and audio files that can be retrieved and converted to a form usable by a human.

multimodal solutions—Transportation plans that involve multiple means of transportation and coordinate the physical and information requirements.

multinational corporation—A company with capital investments in more than a single country.

multinational strategy—A strategy that focuses on opportunities to achieve cross-business and cross-country coordination, thereby enabling economies of scope and an improved competitive position with regard to reducing costs, cross-country subsidization, and so on, to outcompete rivals. See: global strategy. multiphase system—Syn: multiple-phase queuing system.

multiple-channel queuing system—A waiting line system that has parallel waiting lines with queues.

multiple-factor productivity—A measure of the productivity of two or more inputs, especially labor, capital costs, energy, and material. See: single-factor productivity.

multiple-item lot-sizing models—Processes or systems used to determine the total replenishment order quantity for a group of related items.

multiple-phase queuing system—Queuing system that performs a service in two or more sequential steps when there are several waiting lines. Syn: multiphase system. See: channel, queuing theory.

multiple regression models—A form of regression analysis where the model involves more than one independent variable, such as developing a forecast of dishwasher sales based upon housing starts, gross national product, and disposable income.

multiple sourcing—Syn: multisourcing. See: dual sourcing.

multiprocessing—The simultaneous use by a computer of two or more central processing units, with each executing its own instruction set and each controlled by a single operating system.

multiskilled—Individuals who are capable of carrying out a variety of tasks.

multisourcing—Procurement of a good or service from more than one independent supplier. Syn: multiple sourcing. Ant: single sourcing. See: dual sourcing.

multivariate control chart—A control chart for evaluating the stability of a process in terms of the levels of two or more variables or characteristics.

mura—A Japanese word meaning unevenness or variability.

muri—A Japanese word meaning strain or overburden.

mutually exclusive project—In capital budgeting, a project that will not be accepted if a competing project is accepted. See: contingent project, independent project.

mystery shoppers—People who pose as customers but who are really studying an organization's service quality to provide feedback to the organization for improvement purposes.

N

n—Sample size (the number of units in a sample).

NAFTA—Acronym for North American Free Trade Agreement.

National Association of Purchasing Management (NAPM)—A nonprofit society for purchasing managers and others, now known as the Institute for Supply Management (ISM).

nationalization—public ownership and operation of a business enterprise.

National Labor Relations Board (NLRB)—In the United States, the federal agency that regulates labor law.

national stock number (NSN)—The individual identification number assigned to an item to permit inventory management in the U.S. supply system.

natural variations—These variations in measurements are caused by environmental elements and cannot be removed. See: common cause variability.

NC—Abbreviation for numerical control.

near-critical activity—In project management, a project activity with a low slack or float value.

need date—The date when an item is required for its intended use. In an MRP system, this date is calculated by a bill-of-material explosion of a schedule and the netting of available inventory against that requirement.

negative float—In project management, the amount of time that must be made up on an activity to get the project back on schedule. See: float.

negligence—The causing of injury to another by failure to use reasonable care.

negotiation—The process by which a buyer and a supplier agree upon the conditions surrounding the purchase of an item or a service.

nemawashi—A Japanese word meaning getting a group to agree on a strategy before beginning to implement it.

nervousness—The characteristic in an MRP system when minor changes in higher level (e.g., level 0 or 1) records or the master production schedule cause significant timing or quantity changes in lower level (e.g., level 5 or 6) schedules and orders. Syn: system nervousness.

nesting—The act of combining several small processes to form one larger process.

net assets—Total assets minus total liabilities.

net change MRP—An approach in which the material requirements plan is continually retained in the computer. Whenever a change is needed in requirements, open order inventory status, or bill of material, a partial explosion and netting is made for only those parts affected by the change. Ant: regeneration MRP.

net income (loss)—The final figure in the income statement.

net inventory—Syn: available inventory.

net operating cash flow—In finance management, the difference between cash inflow and cash outflow for a period. It is found by taking the change in net operating profit after taxes and adding the change in depreciation then subtracting the increase in net working capital requirements.

net operating income—The income before interest and taxes are subtracted. Syn: earnings before interest and taxes.

net operating profit after taxes (NOPAT)—Operating profit less applicable taxes.

net present value—The present (discounted) value of future earnings (operating expenses have been deducted from net operating revenues) for a given number of time periods.

net profit—An absolute measure of financial performance that is calculated as the difference between revenues and expenses. In throughput accounting, net profit is calculated as throughput minus operating expense.

net requirements—In MRP, the net requirements for a part or an assembly are derived as a result of applying gross requirements and allocations against inventory on hand, scheduled receipts, and safety stock. Net requirements, lot-sized and offset for lead time, become planned orders.

net sales—Sales dollars the company receives; gross sales minus returns and allowances.

netting—The process of calculating net requirements.

net weight—The weight of an article exclusive of the weights of all packing materials and containers.

network—1) The interconnection of computers, terminals, and communications channels to facilitate file and peripheral device sharing as well as effective data communication. 2) A graph consisting of nodes connected by arcs.

network analysis—In project management, the calculation of early and late start and finish times for those activities not yet completed. See: critical path method, graphical evaluation and review technique, and program evaluation and review technique (PERT).

network chain—A route through a chain involving multiple network paths, with switching of paths due to resource conflicts.

network diagram—A graphical tool that shows the dependencies between activities in a project, i.e., which activities precede other activities and which can be done in parallel.

networking—Developing relationships with people who may be able to enhance the performance of duties or responsibilities.

net working capital—The current assets of a firm minus its current liabilities. Syn: working capital.

network logic—Activity dependencies that make up a project schedule network diagram.

network loop—A network path that crosses the same activity or node twice. A network loop cannot be analyzed by the critical path method, critical chain, or other traditional network schedule analysis techniques.

network path—Any continuous series of project activities connected by precedence relationships in a project schedule network diagram.

network planning—A generic term for techniques that are used to plan complex projects. Two of the best known network planning techniques are the critical path

method (CPM) and the program evaluation and review technique (PERT).

neural network—A software system loosely based on how the brain works. It tries to simulate the multiple layers of elements called neurons. Each neuron is tied to several neighbors with a value that signifies the strength of the connections. Learning is accomplished by changing the values to cause the network to report appropriate results. Neural networks have been used for market forecasts and other applications.

new product development team—Syn: participative design/engineering.

new product introduction—The development and release of an item that is new to a company's set of offerings.

newsvendor problem—A problem inventory management dealing with determining the single period (e.g., day or week) order quantity which will minimize the cost of sometimes having too much inventory and sometimes having too little.

NLRB—Abbreviation for National Labor Relations Board.

node—In project management, a point connected by arrows in a network.

noise—The unpredictable or random difference between the observed data and the "true process."

nominal capacity—Syn: rated capacity.

nominal group technique—A technique, similar to brainstorming, used by teams to generate ideas on a particular subject. Team members are asked to silently come up with as many ideas as possible, writing them down. Each member is then asked to share one idea, which is recorded. After all the ideas are recorded, they are discussed and prioritized by the group.

nominal interest rate—The noninflation-adjusted interest rate.

nominal trading partner—Any organization external to the firm that provides an essential material or service, but whose financial success is largely independent of the financial success of the supply chain community.

nomogram—A computational aid consisting of two or more scales drawn and arranged so that the results of calculations may be found by the linear connection of points on them. Historically, it was used for calculating economic lot sizes or sample sizes for work measurement observations. Also called an alignment chart.

nonconforming material—Any raw material, part, component, or product with one or more characteristics that depart from the specifications, drawing, or other approved product description.

nonconformity—Failure to fulfill a specified requirement. See: blemish, defect, imperfection.

noncurrent assets—An accounting/financial term (balance sheet classification of accounts) representing the long-term resources owned by a company, including property, plant, and equipment.

nondurable goods—Goods whose serviceability is generally limited to a period of less than three years (such as perishable goods and semidurable goods).

nonevident failure—Failure occurring in either a product or a production process that is not immediately evident. This may be indicative of a faulty design.

nonexempt employee—A person filling a nonexempt position. See: nonexempt positions.

nonexempt positions—Employees not meeting the test of executive, supervisory, or administrative personnel who are paid overtime, as defined by the Fair Labor Standards Act. See: nonexempt employee.

nongovernmental organization (NGO)—A legally constituted organization that operates independently from any government. The term is usually applied only to organizations that pursue some wider social aim with political aspects, but that are not overtly political organizations such as political parties. These types of organizations are called civil society organizations and other names in some jurisdictions.

nonlinear programming—Programming similar to linear programming but incorporating a nonlinear objective function and linear constraints or a linear objective function and nonlinear constraints or both a nonlinear objective function and nonlinear constraints.

nonproduction material—Items (indirect materials and supplies) in the manufacturing process or in the maintenance or operation of a facility that do not generally become part of the final product.

nonrecurring material—Tooling, gauges, and facilities necessary in the manufacturing of the final product and not consumed during manufacturing or shipped with the final product.

nonscheduled hours—Hours when a machine is not generally available to be scheduled for operation; for example, nights, weekends, holidays, lunch breaks, major repair, and rebuilding.

nonsignificant part number—A part number that is assigned to each part but does not convey any information about the part. Nonsignificant part numbers are identifiers, not descriptors. Ant: significant part number.

non-value-added—An activity that does not add value to a product, for example, moving the product from one work center to another inside a facility. One aspect of continuous improvement is the elimination or reduction of non-value-added activities.

non-vessel-operating common carrier (NVOCC)—Carrier that uses ocean liners and works similarly to freight forwarders.

NOPAT—Acronym for net operating profit after taxes.

normal and proper usage—Operation of the equipment with a program of regular maintenance in accordance with generally accepted practices and within the rated capacity and service classification for which it was specified and designed.

normal distribution—A particular statistical distribution where most of the observations fall fairly close to one mean, and a deviation from the mean is as likely to be plus as it is to be minus. When graphed, the normal distribution takes the form of a bell-shaped curve.

normalize—To adjust observed data to a standard base.

normal time—In time study, adjusting the actual time observed by a factor called pace rating. See: pace rating.

North American Free Trade Agreement (NAFTA)—An agreement among the United States, Canada, and Mexico to promote economic prosperity by reducing trade barriers.

no-touch exchange of dies (NTED)—The exchange of dies without human intervention.

np chart—A control chart for evaluating the stability of a process in terms of the total number of units in a sample in which an event of a given classification occurs. Syn: number of affected units chart.

N7—Abbreviation for seven new tools of quality.

NSN—Abbreviation for national stock number.

NTED—Abbreviation for no-touch exchange of dies.

number defective chart—Syn: c chart.

number of affected units chart—Syn: np chart.

numerical control (NC)—A means of operating a machine tool automatically by the use of coded numerical instructions.

NVOCC—Abbreviation for non-vessel-operating common carrier.

O

obeya—A Japanese word meaning "big room," a command center.

objective function—The goal or function that is to be optimized in a model. Most often it is a cost function that should be minimized subject to some restrictions or a profit function that should be maximized subject to some restrictions.

object-oriented programming (OOP)—Within computer programming, the use of coding techniques and tools that reflect the concept of viewing the business environment as a set of elements (or objects) with associated properties (e.g., data, data manipulation/actions, inheritance). The objects encapsulate, through data and functions, the properties of the business that are of interest.

obligated material—Syn: reserved material.

observational research—A form of research (frequently used in marketing research) where data are gathered by direct observation of consumers in the market place. See: marketing research.

obsolescence—1) The condition of being out of date. A loss of value occasioned by new developments that place the older property at a competitive disadvantage. A factor in depreciation. 2) A decrease in the value of an asset brought about by the development of new and more economical methods, processes, or machinery. 3) The loss of usefulness or worth of a product or facility as a result of the appearance of better or more economical products, methods, or facilities.

obsolete inventory—Inventory items that have met the obsolescence criteria established by the organization. For example, inventory that has been superseded by a new model or otherwise made obsolescent. Obsolete inventory will never be used or sold at full value. Disposing of the inventory may reduce a company's profit.

Occupational Safety and Health Act (OSHA)—A U.S. law that applies to all employers in the United States who are engaged in interstate commerce. Its purpose is to ensure safe and healthful working conditions by authorizing enforcement of the standards provided under the act.

occurrence factor—Within the repair/remanufacturing environment, the occurrence factor is associated with how often a repair is required to bring the average part to a serviceable condition (some repair operations do not occur 100 percent of the time). The factor is expressed at the operation level in the routing. See: repair factor, replacement factor.

OC curve—Abbreviation for operating characteristic curve.

OCR—Abbreviation for optical character recognition.

OD—Abbreviation for organizational development.

ODD—Abbreviation for earliest operation due date.

OEE—Abbreviation for overall equipment effectiveness.

OEM—Abbreviation for original equipment manufacturer.

offal material—The by-product or waste of production processes (e.g., chips, shavings, turnings).

offer—A contractual communication that proposes definite terms. A contract is created if the other party accepts those terms.

off-grade—A product whose physical or chemical properties fall outside the acceptable ranges.

offline—Computer work completed either when disconnected from the internet or from an intranet. This term describes anytime when someone cannot be contacted via their computer.

offload—To reschedule or use alternate routings to reduce the workload on a machine, work center, or facility.

offset quantity—Syn: overlap quantity.

offsetting—Syn: lead-time offset.

offshore—Outsourcing a business function to another company in a different country than the original company's country.

offshore factory—A plant that imports or acquires locally all components and then exports the finished product.

OJT—Abbreviation for on-the-job training.

on-demand—Work is completed only when demand occurs. More specifically, it is a process in which a product or service is made only after an order is placed for that product or service.

one-card kanban system—A kanban system where only a move card is employed. Typically, the work centers are adjacent, therefore no production card is required. In many cases, squares located between work centers are used as the kanban system. An empty square signals the supplying work center to produce a standard container of the item. Syn: single-card kanban system. See: two-card kanban system.

100 percent inspection—The act of inspecting or testing every item in an incoming or outgoing lot.

one less at a time—A process of gradually reducing the lot size of the number of items in the manufacturing pipeline to expose, prioritize, and eliminate waste.

one-piece flow—A concept that items are processed directly from one step to the next, one unit at a time. This helps to shorten lead times and lines of communication, thus more quickly identifying problems.

one-to-one marketing—A marketing strategy for sending a particular message to a single customer, often assisted by a marketing database.

one-touch exchange of die (OTED)—The ideal of reducing or eliminating the setup effort required between operations on the same equipment.

on-hand balance—The quantity shown in the inventory records as being physically in stock.

online processing—A method of computer processing in which data are processed immediately on entry into the computer.

online receiving—An unloading process characterized by computers or terminals wherever shipments are received and employees enter delivery data into the system as the shipments are unloaded.

online service—The processing of transaction data as soon as the transaction occurs. It is real-time processing as opposed to batch processing. See: real time.

on order—The number or value of goods or services that have been ordered but not received at a location.

on-order stock—The total of all outstanding replenishment orders. The on-order balance increases when a new order is released, and it decreases when material is received against an order or when an order is canceled.

on-the-job training (OJT)—Learning the skills and necessary related knowledge useful for the job at the place of work or possibly while at work.

on-time delivery—A metric measuring the percent of receipts that were received on time by customers. See: on-time in full.

on-time in full (OTIF)—A delivery scoring system that sets a target goal, usually in percent, and the deliverer tries

to meet that goal of full deliveries and by the delivery date.

on-time schedule performance—A measure (percentage) of meeting the customer's originally negotiated delivery request date. Performance can be expressed as a percentage based on the number of orders, line items, or dollar value shipped on time.

OOP—Abbreviation for object-oriented programming.

open-end purchase order—A purchase agreement similar to a blanket purchase order that provides the added convenience of being able to negotiate additional items and expiration dates.

open master production schedule—The part of the master production schedule that still has available capacity for assigning new orders.

open office—An office, with moveable partitions and furniture, that deemphasizes the compartmentalization of people.

open order—1) A released manufacturing order or purchase order. Syn: released order. See: scheduled receipt. 2) An unfilled customer order.

open period—Accounting time period for which the books will still accept adjusting entries and postings. Ant: closed period.

open system architecture—The capability of software and diverse hardware environments to communicate with each other through the use of standard messaging and protocols respectively. See: modular system.

open-to-buy—A control technique used in aggregate inventory management in which authorizations to purchase are made without being committed to specific suppliers. These authorizations are often reviewed by management using such measures as commodity in dollars and by time period.

open-to-receive—Authorization to receive goods, such as a blanket release, firm purchase order item, or supplier schedule. Open-to-receive represents near-term impact on inventory, and is often monitored as a control technique in aggregate inventory management. The total of open-to-receive, other longer term purchase commitments, and open-to-buy represents the material and services cash exposure of the company.

operating assets—An accounting/financial term representing the resources owned by a company for productive purposes (to generate a profit) including cash, accounts receivable, inventories, equipment, and facilities.

O

operating characteristic curve (OC curve)—A graph used to determine the probability of accepting lots as a function of the quality level of the lots or processes when using various sampling plans. There are three types: Type A curves, which give the probability of acceptance for an individual lot coming from finite production (will not continue in the future); Type B curves, which give the probability of acceptance for lots coming from a continuous process; and Type C curves, which, for a continuous sampling plan, give the long-run percentage of product accepted during the sampling phase.

operating cycle—The three primary activities of a company are purchasing, producing, and selling a product. The operating cycle is calculated by adding the inventory conversion period to the receivables conversion period.

operating decision—Planning operations to meet demand in the short-term or intermediate-term.

operating efficiency—A ratio (represented as a percentage) of the actual output of a piece of equipment, department, or plant as compared to the planned or standard output.

operating environment—The global, domestic, environmental, and stakeholder influences that affect the key competitive factors, customer needs, culture, and philosophy of each individual company. This environment becomes the framework in which business strategy is developed and implemented. Syn: business environment.

operating expense—All the money an organization spends in generating "goal units."

operating exposure—The risk introduced by flexible exchange rates when operating in the global environment, including production, storage, and buying and selling prices.

operating leverage—Comparing an organization's annual sales to its annual costs.

operating profit margin ratio—Earnings before interest and taxes divided by sales.

operating system—A set of software programs that control the execution of the hardware and application programs. The operating system manages the computer and network resources through storage management, disk input/output, communications linkages, program scheduling, and monitoring system usage for performance and cost allocations.

operation—1) A job or task, consisting of one or more work elements, usually done essentially in one location.

2) The performance of any planned work or method associated with an individual, machine, process, department, or inspection. 3) One or more elements that involve one of the following: the intentional changing of an object in any of its physical or chemical characteristics; the assembly or disassembly of parts or objects; the preparation of an object for another operation, transportation, inspection, or storage; planning, calculating, or giving or receiving information.

operational availability—The portion of time a system is available to sustain operations in full.

operational performance measurements—1) In traditional management, performance measurements related to machine, worker, or department efficiency or utilization. These performance measurements are usually poorly correlated with organizational performance. 2) In theory of constraints, performance measurements that link causally to organizational performance measurements. Throughput, inventory, and operating expense are examples. See: global performance measurements, local performance measurements, strategic performance measurements.

operational plan(s)—The set of short-range plans and schedules detailing specific actions. Operational plans are more detailed than strategic and tactical plans and cover a shorter time horizon. See: operational planning, strategic plan, tactical plan.

operational planning—The process of setting goals and targets and establishing measures constrained by and targeted for achieving the strategic and tactical plans. See: operational plan, strategic planning, tactical planning.

operation chart—Syn: routing.

operation costing—A method of costing used in batch manufacturing environments when products produced have common, as well as distinguishing, characteristics; for example, suits. The products are identified and costed by batches or by production runs, based on the variations.

operation description—The details or description of an activity or operation to be performed. The operation description is normally contained in the routing document and could include setup instructions, operating instructions (feeds, speeds, heats, pressure, etc.), and required product specifications or tolerances.

operation due date—1) The date when an operation should be completed so that its order due date can be met. It can be calculated based on scheduled quantities and lead times. 2) A job sequencing algorithm (dispatching rule) giving earlier operation due dates higher priority.

operation duration—The total time that elapses between the start of the setup of an operation and the completion of the operation. Syn: operation time.

operation list—Syn: routing.

operation number—A sequential number, usually two, three, or four digits long, such as 010, 020, 030, that indicates the sequence in which operations are to be performed within an item's routing.

operation overlapping—Syn: overlapped schedule.

operation priority—1) The relative importance an operation is given based on its scheduled due date and/or start date, usually as determined by the back-scheduling process. 2) The relative importance a job is given in a queue of jobs by a priority dispatching heuristic such as shortest processing time first or least slack remaining first.

operation/process yield—The ratio of usable output from a process, process stage, or operation to the input quantity, usually expressed as a percentage.

operation reporting—The recording and reporting of every manufacturing (shop order) operation occurrence on an operation-to-operation basis.

operations—The group that produces the goods and/or services that a company sells.

operation setback chart—A graphical display of the bill of materials and lead-time information provided by the routing for each part. The horizontal axis provides the lead time from raw materials purchase to component manufacture to assembly of the finished product.

operations finite loading—A finite loading technique that aims to minimize possible delays to individual operations and, thus, the potential delay of each scheduled order. Eligible operations from an order or a group of orders are loaded period by period onto a work center or a group of work centers, according to operation-level priority rules. Syn: operations sequencing. See: constraint-oriented finite loading, drum-buffer-rope, order-oriented finite loading.

operation sheet—Syn: routing.

operations management—1) The planning, scheduling, and control of the activities that transform inputs into finished goods and services. 2) A field of study that focuses on the effective planning, scheduling, use, and control of a manufacturing or service organization through the study of concepts from design engineering, industrial engineering, management information sys-

tems, quality management, production management, inventory management, accounting, and other functions as they affect the operation.

operations plan—Syn: production plan.

operations planning—The planning of activities that transform inputs into finished goods and services.

operations process chart—Syn: process chart.

operation splitting—Syn: lot splitting.

operations research—1) The development and application of quantitative techniques to the solution of problems. More specifically, theory and methodology in mathematics, statistics, and computing are adapted and applied to the identification, formulation, solution, validation, implementation, and control of decision-making problems. 2) An academic field of study concerned with the development and application of quantitative analysis to the solution of problems faced by management in public and private organizations. Syn: management science.

operations scheduling—The actual assignment of starting or completion dates to operations or groups of operations to show when these operations must be done if the manufacturing order is to be completed on time. These dates are used in the dispatching function. Syn: detailed scheduling, order scheduling, shop scheduling.

operations sequence—The sequential steps for an item to follow in its flow through the plant. For instance, operation 1: cut bar stock; operation 2: grind bar stock; operation 3: shape; operation 4: polish; operation 5: inspect and send to stock. This information is normally maintained in the routing file.

operations sequence analysis—Method of planning a facility layout by using graphics to determine the placement of departments.

operations sequencing—A technique for short-term planning of actual jobs to be run in each work center based upon capacity (i.e., existing workforce and machine availability) and priorities. The result is a set of projected completion times for the operations and simulated queue levels for facilities.

operation start date—The date when an operation should be started so that its order due date can be met. It can be calculated based on scheduled quantities and lead times or on the work remaining and the time remaining to complete the job.

operations strategy—The total pattern of decisions that shape the long-term capabilities of an operation and their contribution to overall strategy. Operations strategy should be consistent with overall strategy. See: strategic plan.

operation time—The total of setup and run time for a specific task. Syn: operation duration.

operator flexibility—Training machine workers to perform tasks outside their immediate jobs and in problem-solving techniques to improve process flexibility. This is a necessary process in developing a fully cross-trained workforce.

opportunity cost—1) The return on capital that could have resulted had the capital been used for some purpose other than its present use. 2) The rate of return investors must earn to continue to supply capital to a firm.

optical character—A printed character frequently used in utilities billing and credit applications that can be read by a machine without the aid of magnetic ink.

optical character recognition (OCR)—A mechanized method of collecting data involving the reading of hand-printed material or special character fonts. If handwritten, the information must adhere to predefined rules of size, format, and locations on the form.

optical scanning—A technique for machine recognition of characters by their images.

optimal order period—Within a fixed order period inventory system, the time between a status check on the material that balances ordering costs with carrying costs.

optimization—Achieving the best possible solution to a problem in terms of a specified objective function.

optimization models—A class of mathematical models used when the modeler wishes to find the ideal (maximum or minimum) value of some objective function subject to a set of constraints.

option—A choice that must be made by the customer or company when customizing the end product. In many companies, the term option means a mandatory choice from a limited selection. See: feature.

optional replenishment model—A form of independent demand item management model in which a review of inventory on hand plus on order is made at fixed intervals. If the actual quantity is lower than some predetermined threshold, a reorder is placed for a quantity M – x, where M is the maximum allowable inventory and x is the current inventory quantity. The reorder point, R, may be deterministic or stochastic, and in either instance is large enough to cover the maximum expected demand during the review interval plus the replenishment lead time. The optional replenishment model is sometimes called a hybrid system because it combines certain aspects of the fixed reorder cycle inventory model and the fixed reorder quantity inventory model. See: fixed reorder cycle inventory model, fixed reorder quantity inventory model, hybrid inventory system, independent demand item management models.

option overplanning—Typically, scheduling extra quantities of a master schedule option greater than the expected sales for that option to protect against unanticipated demand. This schedule quantity may only be planned in the period where new customer orders are currently being accepted, typically just after the demand time fence. This technique is usually used on the second level of a two-level master scheduling approach to create a situation where more of the individual options are available than of the overall family. The historical average of demand for an item is quantified in a planning bill of material. Option overplanning is accomplished by increasing this percentage to allow for demands greater than forecast. See: demand time fence, hedge, planning bill of material.

order—A general term that may refer to such diverse items as a purchase order, shop order, customer order, planned order, or schedule.

order backlog—Syn: backlog, past due order.

order batching—The process of gathering a group of orders or data before sending them out to the next stage.

order complete manufacture to customer receipt of order—The average time starting when an order is ready for delivery to a customer and when the customer actually receives the delivery.

order consolidation profile—The process of filling an entire order of one customer by bringing all parts of their order together in one place. These items may or may not come from different places or departments.

order control—Control of manufacturing activities by individual manufacturing, job, or shop orders, released by planning personnel and authorizing production personnel to complete a given batch or lot size of a particular manufactured item. Information needed to complete the order (components required, work centers and operations required, tooling required, etc.) may be printed on paper or tickets, often called shop orders or work orders, which are distributed to production personnel. This use of order control sometimes implies an environment where all the components for a given order are picked and issued from a stocking location, all at one time, and then moved as a kit to manufacturing before any activity begins. It is most frequently seen in job shop manufacturing. See: shop floor control.

order cost—A direct labor cost incurred when a purchaser places an order.

order cycle—The progression used by a company starting with receipt of a customer's order and ending with delivery to that customer.

order dating—Syn: order promising.

order entry—The process of accepting and translating what a customer wants into terms used by the manufacturer or distributor. The commitment should be based on the available-to-promise (ATP) line in the master schedule. This can be as simple as creating shipping documents for finished goods in a make-to-stock environment, or it might be a more complicated series of activities, including design efforts for make-to-order products. See: master schedule, order service.

order entry complete to start manufacture—The average time starting when an order is placed by a customer and ending when the manufacturing of that order is completed.

order-fill ratio—Syn: customer service ratio.

order fulfillment lead times—The average amount of time between the customer's order until the customer receives delivery; this includes every manufacturing or processing step in between.

ordering cost—Used in calculating order quantities, the costs that increase as the number of orders placed increases. It includes costs related to the clerical work of preparing, releasing, monitoring, and receiving orders, the physical handling of goods, inspections, and setup costs, as applicable. See: acquisition cost, inventory costs.

order interval—The time period between the placement of orders.

order level system—Syn: fixed reorder cycle inventory model.

order losers—Capabilities of an organization in which poor performance can cause loss of business. Failure to meet customer expectations with delivery of the product is an order loser. See: order qualifiers, order winners.

order management—The planning, directing, monitoring, and controlling of the processes related to customer orders, manufacturing orders, and purchase orders. Regarding customer orders, order management includes order promising, order entry, order pick, pack and ship, billing, and reconciliation of the customer account. Regarding manufacturing orders, order management includes order release, routing, manufacture, monitoring, and receipt into stores or finished goods inventories. Regarding purchasing orders, order management includes order placement, monitoring, receiving, acceptance, and payment of supplier.

order multiples—An order quantity modifier applied after the lot size has been calculated that increases the order quantity to a predetermined multiple.

order-oriented finite loading—A set of finite loading techniques to schedule orders according to order-level priority rules. The techniques aim to either (1) maximize capacity utilization or (2) deliver a high proportion of on-time orders with low work in process. See: constraint-oriented finite loading, drum-buffer-rope.

order penetration point—The key variable in a logistics configuration; the point (in time) at which a product becomes earmarked for a particular customer. Downstream from this point, the system is driven by customer orders; upstream processes are driven by forecasts and plans. Syn: principle of postponement. See: booked orders.

order picking—Selecting or "picking" the required quantity of specific products for movement to a packaging area (usually in response to one or more shipping orders) and documenting that the material was moved from one location to shipping. Syn: order selection. See: batch picking, discrete order picking, zone picking.

order placement—The commitment of a customer to buy a product and the subsequent administrative and data processing steps followed by the supplier.

order point—A set inventory level where, if the total stock on hand plus on order falls to or below that point, action is taken to replenish the stock. The order point is normally calculated as forecasted usage during the replenishment lead time plus safety stock. Syn: reorder point, statistical order point, trigger level. See: fixed reorder quantity inventory model.

order point/order quantity system—Syn: fixed reorder quantity inventory model.

order point system—The inventory method that places an order for a lot whenever the quantity on hand is reduced to a predetermined level known as the order point. Syn: statistical order point system. See: fixed reorder quantity inventory model, hybrid system.

order policy—A set of procedures for determining the lot size and other parameters related to an order. See: lot sizing.

order policy code—Syn: lot-size code.

order preparation—All activities relating to the administration, picking, and packaging of individual customer or work orders.

order preparation lead time—The time needed to analyze requirements and open order status and to create the paperwork necessary to release a purchase order or a production order.

order priority—The scheduled due date to complete all the operations required for a specific order.

order processing—The activity required to administratively process a customer's order and make it ready for shipment or production.

order processing and communication—All activities needed to fill customer orders.

order promising—The process of making a delivery commitment (i.e., answering the question "When can you ship?"). For make-to-order products, this usually involves a check of uncommitted material and availability of capacity, often as represented by the master schedule available-to-promise. Syn: customer order promising, order dating. See: available-to-promise, order service.

order qualifiers—Those competitive characteristics that a firm must exhibit to be a viable competitor in the marketplace. For example, a firm may seek to compete on characteristics other than price, but in order to "qualify" to compete, its costs and the related price must be within a certain range to be considered by its customers. Syn: qualifiers. See: order losers, order winners.

order quantity—Syn: lot size.

order quantity modifiers—Adjustments made to a calculated order quantity. Order quantities are calculated based upon a given lot-sizing rule, but it may be necessary to adjust the calculated lot size because of special considerations (scrap, testing, etc.).

order release—The activity of releasing materials to a production process to support a manufacturing order. See: planned order release.

order reporting—Recording and reporting the start and completion of the manufacturing order (shop order) in its entirety.

order scheduling—Syn: operations scheduling.

order selection—Syn: order picking.

order service—The function that encompasses receiving, entering, and promising orders from customers, distribution centers, and interplant operations. Order service

is also typically responsible for responding to customer inquiries and interacting with the master scheduler on availability of products. In some companies, distribution and interplant requirements are handled separately. See: order entry, order promising.

order shipment—Activity that extends from the time the order is placed upon the vehicle for movement until the order is received, verified, and unloaded at the buyer's destination.

order-to-delivery cycle—The period of time that starts when the customer places an order and ends when the customer receives the order.

order-up-to level—Syn: target inventory level.

order winners—Those competitive characteristics that cause a firm's customers to choose that firm's goods and services over those of its competitors. Order winners can be considered to be competitive advantages for the firm. Order winners usually focus on one (rarely more than two) of the following strategic initiatives: price/cost, quality, delivery speed, delivery reliability, product design, flexibility, after-market service, and image. See: order losers, order qualifiers.

organizational breakdown structure—In project management, a representation of a project's organization relating work packages to organizational units.

organizational change management—The fostering and support of people who champion new technologies, new operating practices, and new products and services that will transform the organization, maintaining its viability and improving its competitive position in step with the change in the business environment in which it functions.

organizational design—The creation of an organizational structure to support the strategic business plans and goals of an enterprise; (e.g., for-profit and not-for-profit companies). Given the mission and business strategy, the organizational structure design provides the framework within which the business operational and management activities will be performed.

organizational development (OD)—The process of building and strengthening core competencies and organizational capabilities that enable the execution of the business strategy and provide a sustainable competitive advantage over time. Organizational development includes staffing the organization, building core competencies and organizational capabilities, and continuous improvement initiatives in response to the changing business environment.

organizational environment—Consists of an external environment (e.g., laws and regulations, technology, economy, competition) and an internal environment (e.g., the domain of products and services to be provided, the processes to be executed, the organizational structure). See: external environment, internal environment.

organization chart—A graphical depiction of relationships between people who work together.

original equipment manufacturer (OEM)—A manufacturer that buys and incorporates another supplier's products into its own products. Also, products supplied to the original equipment manufacturer or sold as part of an assembly. For example, an engine may be sold to an OEM for use as that company's power source for its generator units.

orthogonal arrays—Tools that help maintain independence between different iterations of a product design experiment; introduced to quality analysis by Genichi Taguchi.

OS&D—Abbreviation for over, short, and damaged.

OSHA—Acronym for Occupational Safety and Health Act.

OSI—Abbreviation for open systems interconnection.

OTED—Abbreviation for one-touch exchange of die.

OTIF—Abbreviation for on-time in-full.

outbound consolidation—The gathering of a number of small shipments to a variety of customers into a larger load, which is then shipped to a point near the customers where it is broken down for delivery.

outbound logistics—Every process that is involved in the shipping and holding of products after they are completed until they are received by the customer.

outbound stockpoint—The designated locations near the point of use on a plant floor to which material produced is taken until it is pulled to the next operation.

outlier—A data point that differs significantly from other data for a similar phenomenon. For example, if the average sales for a product were 10 units per month, and one month the product had sales of 500 units, this sales point might be considered an outlier. See: abnormal demand.

out-of-control process—A process in which the statistical measure being evaluated is not in a state of statistical control (i.e., the variations among the observed sampling results can be attributed to a constant system of chance causes). Ant: in-control process.

out-of-pocket costs—Costs that involve direct payments such as labor, freight, or insurance, as opposed to depreciation, which does not.

out of stock—A situation in which there is no inventory at a location available for sale to the customer. See: stockout.

out of spec—A term used to indicate that a unit does not meet a given specification.

outpartnering—The process of involving the supplier in a close partnership with the firm and its operations management system. Outpartnering is characterized by close working relationships between buyers and suppliers, high levels of trust, mutual respect, and emphasis on joint problem solving and cooperation. With outpartnering, the supplier is viewed not as an alternative source of goods and services (as observed under outsourcing) but rather as a source of knowledge, expertise, and complementary core competencies. Outpartnering is typically found during the early stages of the product life cycle when dealing with products that are viewed as critical to the strategic survival of the firm. See: customer-supplier partnership, supplier partner, and customer partner.

output—The product being completed by a process or facility.

output control—A technique for controlling output where actual output is compared to planned output to identify problems at the work center or facility.

output standard—The expected number of units from a process against which actual output will be measured.

outside shop—Suppliers. This term is used to convey the idea that suppliers are an extension of the inside shop or the firm's production facilities.

outsourced cost of goods sold—Costs of goods sold that are not created within the producing company's manufacturing process. Instead, they are outsourced to another company and include the costs of purchasing the service from another company.

outsourcing—The process of having suppliers provide goods and services that were previously provided internally. Outsourcing involves substitution—the replacement of internal capacity and production by that of the supplier. See: subcontracting.

overall equipment effectiveness (OEE)—Measuring the effectiveness of all of the equipment of a company based on usage, performance and production quality.

overall factors—Syn: capacity planning using overall factors.

overhead—The costs incurred in the operation of a business that cannot be directly related to the individual goods or services produced. These costs, such as light, heat, supervision, and maintenance, are grouped in several pools (e.g., department overhead, factory overhead, general overhead) and distributed to units of goods or services by some standard allocation method such as direct labor hours, direct labor dollars, or direct materials dollars. Syn: burden. See: expense.

overhead allocation—In accounting, the process of applying overhead to a product on the basis of a predetermined rate.

overhead base—The denominator used to calculate the predetermined overhead rate used in applying overhead (e.g., estimated direct labor hours, estimated direct labor dollars).

overhead pool—The collection of overhead costs that are to be allocated over a specified group of products.

overissue—Syn: excess issue.

overlapped production—A method of production in which completed pieces of a production lot are processed at one or more succeeding stations while remaining pieces continue to be processed at the original workstation. See: overlapped schedule.

overlapped schedule—A manufacturing schedule that "overlaps" successive operations. Overlapping occurs when the completed portion of an order at one work center is processed at one or more succeeding work centers before the pieces left behind are finished at the preceding work centers. Syn: lap phasing, operation overlapping, telescoping. See: send ahead. Ant: gapped schedule, overlapped production.

overlap quantity—The number of items that need to be run and sent ahead to the following operation before the following "overlap" operation can begin. Syn: offset quantity. See: process batch, transfer batch.

overload—A condition when the total hours of work outstanding at a work center exceed that work center's capacity.

overpack—Reducing total shipping costs by reducing the per-item shipping cost. This is done by including multiple smaller items in one larger box.

overrun—1) The quantity received from manufacturing or a supplier that is in excess of the quantity ordered. 2) The condition resulting when expenditures exceed the budget.

over, short, and damaged (OS&D) report—A report submitted by a freight agent showing discrepancies in billing received and actual merchandise received.

overstated master production schedule—A schedule that includes either past due quantities or quantities that are greater than the ability to produce, given current capacity and material availability. An overstated MPS should be made feasible before MRP is run.

overtime—Work beyond normal established working hours that usually requires that a premium be paid to the workers.

owner's equity—An accounting/financial term (balance sheet classification of accounts) representing the residual claim by the company's owners or shareholders, or both, to the company's assets less its liabilities. See: assets, balance sheet, liabilities.

P

PAC—Acronym for production activity control.

pacemaker—In lean, the resource that is scheduled based on the customer demand rate for that specific value stream. It is that resource which performs an operation or process that governs the flow of materials along the value stream. Its purpose is to maintain a smooth flow through the manufacturing plant; a larger buffer is provided for the pacemaker than other resources so that it can maintain continuous operation. See: constraint.

pace rating—Estimating the level of effort of a subject of methods study, where 100 percent would be the sustainable pace of an average skilled worker.

pacing process—The process in a production line used to signal all other processes in line of the time to produce another unit. It generally is the final process, but it does not have to be.

package to order—A production environment in which a good or service can be packaged after receipt of a customer order. The item is common across many different customers; packaging determines the end product.

packaging—Materials surrounding an item to protect it from damage during transportation. The type of packaging influences the danger of such damage.

packing and marking—The activities of packing for safe shipping and unitizing one or more items of an order, placing them into an appropriate container, and marking and labeling the container with customer shipping destination data, as well as other information that may be required.

packing list—A list showing merchandise packed, a copy of which is sent to the consignee to help verify the shipment.

packing slip—A document that itemizes in detail the contents of a particular package, carton, pallet, or container for shipment to a customer. The detail includes a description of the items, the shipper's or customer's part number, the quantity shipped, and the stockkeeping unit (SKU) of items shipped.

pack-out department—The department that performs the final steps (often including packaging and labeling) before shipment to the customer. See: final assembly department.

page—In information systems, an internet document containing both text and hypertext links to other pages that are stored on the server.

paired-cell overlapping loops of cards (POLCA)—A special material control and replenishment system developed to be used with quick-response manufacturing in cellular manufacturing environments. It is a hybrid push-pull system where the push authority to proceed is generated by high-level manufacturing resources planning. See: quick-response manufacturing.

pallet—A platform designed to be loaded with packages and moved by a forklift. Standard pallet size is 48 inches by 40 inches by 4 inches.

pallet jack—A type of materials handling equipment that combines pallets horizontally but has no lifting capability.

pallet positions—A calculation that determines the space needed for the number of pallets for inventory storage or transportation based on a standard pallet size. Pallet dimensions vary around the globe, but are typically a constant in regional markets. The term is frequently used to quote storage and transportation rates.

pallet rack—A single- or multiple-level structure for storage used to support high stacking of palletized loads.

pallet ticket—A label to track pallet-sized quantities of end items produced to identify the specific sublot with specifications determined by periodic sampling and analysis during production.

panel consensus—A judgmental forecasting technique by which a committee, sales force, or group of experts arrives at a sales estimate. See: Delphi method, management estimation.

paperless purchasing—A purchasing operation that does not employ purchase requisitions or hard-copy purchase orders. In actual practice, a small amount of paperwork usually remains, normally in the form of the supplier schedule.

parallel conversion—A method of system implementation in which the operation of the new system overlaps with the operation of the system being replaced. The old system is discontinued only when the new system is shown to be working properly, thus minimizing the risk and negative consequences of a poor system implementation.

parallel engineering—Syn: participative design/engineering.

parallel implementation strategy—A system implementation technique whereby the current system and the new system are both executed for some period of time. The results of the two systems are compared to ensure that the new system is executing properly. When a level of confidence is built that the new system is executing properly, the old system is turned off and the new system becomes the designated business system.

parallel schedule—The use of two or more machines or job centers to perform identical operations on a lot of material. Duplicate tooling and setup are required.

parameter—A coefficient appearing in a mathematical expression, each value of which determines the specific form of the expression. Parameters define or determine the characteristics or behavior of something, as when the mean and standard deviation are used to describe a set of data.

parameter design—Specifying the product characteristics and production process that will create the expected product performance.

parametric estimating—The use of statistical and historical data to estimate activity parameters such as time or budget.

parent—Syn: parent item.

parent/child relationship—Refers to the logical linkage between higher and lower level items in the bill of material.

parent item—The item produced from one or more components. Syn: parent.

Pareto analysis—Use of the Pareto principle in prioritizing or ranking a range of items to separate the vital few from the trivial many.

Pareto chart—A bar graph that displays the results of a Pareto analysis. It may or may not display the 80-20 variation, but it does show a distinct variation from the few compared to the many.

Pareto diagram—Syn: Pareto chart.

Pareto's law—A concept developed by Vilfredo Pareto, an Italian economist, that states that a small percentage of a group accounts for the largest fraction of the impact, value, and so on. In an ABC classification, for example, 20 percent of the inventory items may constitute 80 percent of the inventory value. See: ABC classification, 80-20.

parking lot—A meeting device whereby off-agenda items are noted for possible inclusion in future agendas. Often a flip chart or whiteboard is used.

par level—In service operations, the maximum supply volume based on established quotas from previous use for a particular supply item, in a particular department, for a specified time period.

part—Generally, a material item that is used as a component and is not an assembly, subassembly, blend, intermediate, etc.

part coding and classification—A method used in group technology to identify the physical similarity of parts.

part family—A collection of parts grouped for some managerial purpose.

partial order—Any shipment received or shipped that is less than the amount ordered.

partial productivity factor—Syn: single-factor productivity.

participative design/engineering—A concept that refers to the simultaneous participation of all the functional areas of the firm in the product design activity. Suppliers and customers are often also included. The intent is to enhance the design with the inputs of all the key stakeholders. Such a process should ensure that the final design meets all the needs of the stakeholders and should ensure a product that can be quickly brought to the marketplace while maximizing quality and minimizing costs. Syn: co-design, concurrent design, concurrent engineering, new product development team, parallel engineering, simultaneous design/engineering, simultaneous engineering, team design/ engineering. See: early manufacturing involvement.

participative management—A system that encompasses various activities of high involvement in which subordinates share a significant degree of decision-making power with their immediate superiors. Participative management draws on the rationale that everyone in an organization is capable of and willing to help guide and direct the organization toward agreed-on goals and objectives.

part master record—Syn: item record.

partnering—The act of one organization committing to a long-term relationship with another organization based on trust and a shared concept of how to satisfy the customer.

partnership—1) A form of business ownership that is not organized as a separate legal entity (i.e., unincorporated business), but entailing ownership by two or more persons. See: corporation, private ownership, public ownership, sole proprietorship. 2) In a supply chain, a relationship based on trust, shared risk, and rewards aimed toward achieving a competitive advantage.

part number—Syn: item number.

part period balancing (PPB)—A dynamic lot-sizing technique that uses the same logic as the least total cost method, but adds a routine called look ahead/look back. When the look ahead/look back feature is used, a lot quantity is calculated, and before it is firmed up, the next or the previous period's demands are evaluated to determine whether it would be economical to include them in the current lot. See: discrete order quantity, dynamic lot sizing.

part record—Syn: item record.

parts bank—1) In the narrow sense, an accumulation of inventory between operations that serves to keep a subsequent operation running although there are interruptions in the preceding operations. See: buffer. 2) In the larger sense, a stockroom or warehouse. The implication is that the contents of these areas should be controlled like the contents of a bank.

parts list—A list of parts, materials, and components required to make an item. See: single level bill of material.

parts planner—Syn: material planner.

parts requisition—An authorization that identifies the item and quantity required to be withdrawn from an inventory. Syn: requisition. See: purchase requisition.

part standardization—A program for planned elimination of superficial, accidental, and deliberate differences between similar parts in the interest of reducing part and supplier proliferation.

part type—A code for a component within a bill of material (e.g., regular, phantom, reference).

passenger-mile—One passenger transported one mile. For example, a bus carrying forty passengers for one hundred miles would accrue 4,000 passenger miles.

passive data gathering—Data gathered when a customer initiates the process by filling out a card or sending an email. The firm develops the feedback form but the customer initiates the use of it.

passive tag—A RFID tag which does not send out data and is not self-powered. See: radio frequency identification (RFID) tag.

past due order—A line item on an open customer order that has an original scheduled ship date that is earlier than the current date. Syn: delinquent order, late order, order backlog. See: backlog.

patent—A legal document giving exclusive rights to the production, use, sale, or other action regarding a product or process.

path—In project management, a set of serially related activities in a network diagram.

path convergence—In project management, the point in a network diagram where one or more parallel paths come together. A delay on any of the parallel paths can conceivably delay network completion.

path divergence—Having parallel network paths exiting from a single node.

path float—Syn: float.

pattern recognition—Classifying raw data based on experience or statistical information.

payback—A method of evaluating an investment opportunity that provides a measure of the time required to recover the initial amount invested in a project.

payback period—The period of time required for a stream of cash flows resulting from a project to equal the project's initial investment.

pay for knowledge—A pay restructuring scheme by which competent employees are rewarded for the knowledge they acquire before or while working for an organization, regardless of whether such knowledge is actually being used at any given time.

pay point—Syn: count point.

P chart—A control chart for evaluating the stability of a process in terms of the percentage of the total number of units in a sample in which an event of a given classification occurs over time. P charts are used where it is difficult or costly to make numerical measurements or where it is desired to combine multiple types of defects into one measurement. Syn: percent chart.

PDCA—Abbreviation for plan-do-check-action.

PDF—Abbreviation for portable document format.

PDM—Abbreviation for product data management.

P:D ratio—A ratio where P is the manufacturing lead time and D is the customer required delivery time. If the P:D ratio exceeds 1.00, either a customer's order will be delayed or production will start as the result of a forecast (make-to-stock) or an anticipated customer order (make-to-order).

peak demand—A specific time when the quantity demanded is greater than all other times.

pegged requirement—A requirement that shows the next-level parent item (or customer order) as the source of the demand.

pegging—In MRP and MPS, the capability to identify for a given item the sources of its gross requirements and/or allocations. Pegging can be thought of as active where-used information. See: requirements traceability.

penetration pricing—Introducing a product below its long-run price to secure entry into a market.

people involvement—Syn: employee involvement.

PE ratio—Abbreviation for price to earnings ratio.

perceived quality—One of the eight dimensions of quality that refers to a subjective assessment of a product's quality based on criteria defined by the observer.

percent chart—Syn: P chart.

percent completed—A comparison of work completed to the current projection of total work.

percent of fill—Syn: customer service ratio.

percent value-added time—The percentage of total cycle time that is spent on activities that provide value to the product or customer.

perfect order—An order in which the "seven Rs" are satisfied: the right product, the right quantity, the right condition, the right place, the right time, the right customer, the right cost.

performance—1) The degree to which an employee or group applies skill and effort to an operation or task as measured against an established standard. 2) One of the eight dimensions of quality that refers to product attributes pertaining to the functioning of a product (e.g., horsepower, signal-to-noise ratio, decibel output).

performance and event management systems—Systems that record and measure the performance of key supply chain processes. With these data, employees can determine when the key processes have changed and why they have changed. These data then are utilized to adjust the existent data.

performance appraisal—Supervisory or peer analysis of work performance. May be made in connection with wage and salary review, promotion, transfer, or employee training.

performance benchmarking—Syn: competitive benchmarking. See: benchmarking, process benchmarking.

performance criterion—The characteristic to be measured (e.g., parts per million defective, business profit). See: performance measure, performance measurement system, performance standard.

performance efficiency—A ratio, usually expressed as a percentage, of the standard processing time for a part divided by its actual processing time. Setups are excluded from this calculation to prevent distortion. A traditional definition includes setup time as part of operation time, but significant distortions can occur as a result of dependent setups.

performance measure—In a performance measurement system, the actual value measured for the criterion. Syn: performance measurement. See: performance criterion, performance measurement system, performance standard.

performance measurement—Syn: performance measure.

performance measurement baseline—An approved plan used to compare against actual execution to identify variances for management control.

performance measurement system—A system for collecting, measuring, and comparing a measure to a standard for a specific criterion for an operation, item, good, service, business, etc. A performance measurement system consists of a criterion, a standard, and a measure. Syn: metrics. See: performance criterion, performance measure, performance standard.

performance measurement units—Time, error rates, accuracy rates, cost, and other measures of system performance.

performance objectives—Measurements that enable the firm to monitor whether or not the firm's strategy is being accomplished. Thus, the measurement should be aligned to strategy. Performance objectives may differ based on the hierarchical level of the firm (e.g., department, business unit, corporation) and should be aligned with the corresponding strategy for that level.

performance rating—Observation of worker performance to rate the productivity of the workers as a percentage in terms of the standard or normal worker performance.

performance standard—In a performance measurement system, the accepted, targeted, or expected value for the criterion. See: performance criterion, performance measure, performance measurement system.

performance variance—The difference between a performance standard and actual performance.

performing organization—The enterprise directly involved in the execution of work.

period capacity—The number of standard hours of work that can be performed at a facility or work center in a given time period.

period costs—All costs related to a period of time rather than a unit of product (e.g., marketing costs, property taxes).

periodic inventory—A physical inventory taken at some recurring interval (e.g., monthly, quarterly, or annual physical inventory). See: physical inventory.

periodic maintenance—Syn: preventive maintenance.

periodic replenishment—A method of aggregating requirements to place deliveries of varying quantities at evenly spaced time intervals, rather than variably spaced deliveries of equal quantities.

periodic review system—Syn: fixed reorder cycle inventory model.

period order quantity—A lot-sizing technique under which the lot size is equal to the net requirements for a given number of periods (e.g., weeks into the future). The number of periods to order is variable, each order size equalizing the holding costs and the ordering costs for the interval. See: discrete order quantity, dynamic lot sizing.

perishability—The fact that an item has a limited shelf life and may be fragile and require special handling.

permission marketing—Syn: relationship marketing.

perpetual inventory—An inventory recordkeeping system where each transaction in and out is recorded and a new balance is computed.

perpetual inventory record—A computer record or manual document on which each inventory transaction is posted so that a current record of the inventory is maintained.

personal discrimination—In transportation, charging different companies with similar deliveries different rates for shipping. This is a policy decision, probably based on importance of the customer.

personal fatigue and unavoidable delay allowance—Factor by which the motion study term "normal time" is increased to allow for personal needs and unavoidable delays.

personnel class—A means to describe a grouping of people with similar characteristics for purposes of scheduling and planning.

PERT—Acronym for program evaluation and review technique.

PFEP—Abbreviation for plan for every part.

phantom bill of material—A bill-of-material coding and structuring technique used primarily for transient (non-stocked) subassemblies. For the transient item, lead time is set to zero and the order quantity to lot-for-lot. A phantom bill of material represents an item that is physically built, but rarely stocked, before being used in the next step or level of manufacturing. This permits MRP logic to drive requirements straight through the phantom item to its components, but the MRP system usually retains its ability to net against any occasional inventories of the item. This technique also facilitates the use of common bills of material for engineering and manufacturing. Syn: blowthrough, transient bill of material. See: pseudo bill of material.

physical distribution—Syn: distribution.

physical inventory—1) The actual inventory itself. 2) The determination of inventory quantity by actual count. Physical inventories can be taken on a continuous, periodic, or annual basis. Syn: annual inventory count, annual physical inventory. See: periodic inventory.

physical supply—The movement and storage of goods from suppliers to manufacturing. The cost of physical supply is ultimately passed on to the customer.

pick and place—Equipment that picks up parts from one station on an assembly line and places them on the next.

pick date—The start date of picking components for a production order. On or before this date, the system produces a list of orders due to be picked, pick lists, tags, and turnaround cards.

picking—The process of withdrawing from stock the components to make assemblies or finished goods. In distribution, the process of withdrawing goods from stock to ship to a distribution warehouse or to a customer.

picking list—A document that lists the material to be picked for manufacturing or shipping orders. Syn: disbursement list, material list, stores issue order, stores requisition.

pick on receipt—Similar to cross-docking, a product is unloaded from an inbound vehicle and loaded directly on an outbound vehicle. Product is received and picked simultaneously, never becoming set in the warehouse.

pick-to-light—A pick system that uses software to light up displays at each pick location and determines how much needs to be picked. The picker uses this as their requirement to pull for that particular order to set of orders.

pick-to-trailer—An order picking system that allows the picker to transfer materials to the trailer from the pick source without any confirmation/checking stages.

pickup and delivery costs—Carrier charges for each shipment pickup and the weight of that shipment. Costs can be reduced if several smaller shipments are consolidated and picked up in one trip.

piece parts—Individual items in inventory at the simplest level in manufacturing (e.g., bolts and washers).

piece rate—The amount of money paid for a unit of production. It serves as the basis for determining the total pay for an employee working in a piecework system.

piece rate pay system—A compensation system based upon volume of output of an individual worker.

piecework—Work done on a piece rate.

piggyback—Syn: trailer on a flatcar.

pilot—Syn: pilot test.

pilot lot—A relatively small preliminary order for a product. The purpose of this small lot is to correlate the product design with the development of an efficient manufacturing process.

pilot order—Syn: experimental order.

pilot plant—A small-scale production facility used to develop production processes and to manufacture small quantities of new products for field testing and so forth. Syn: semiworks.

pilot test—1) In computer systems, a test before final acceptance of a new business system using a subset of data with engineered cases and documented results. 2) Generally, production of a quantity to verify manufacturability, customer acceptance, or other management requirements before implementation of ongoing production. Syn: pilot, walkthrough.

pipeline inventory—Syn: pipeline stock.

pipeline stock—Inventory in the transportation network and the distribution system, including the flow through intermediate stocking points. The flow time through the pipeline has a major effect on the amount of inventory required in the pipeline. Time factors involve order transmission, order processing, scheduling, shipping, transportation, receiving, stocking, review time, and so forth. Syn: pipeline inventory. See: distribution system, transportation inventory.

place—One of the four Ps (product, price, place, and promotion) that constitute the set of tools used to direct the business offering to the customer. Place is the distribution tactic used to provide the product to the customer. Distribution answers the questions of where, when, and how the product is made available. See: four Ps.

place utility—Usefulness to the customer created by having the product delivered to a desired location.

plan—A predetermined course of action over a specified period of time that represents a projected response to an anticipated environment to accomplish a specific set of adaptive objectives.

plan deliver—Establishing plans for action over time that project appropriation of supply resources to meet delivery requirements.

plan-do-check-act cycle—Syn: plan-do-check-action.

plan-do-check-action (PDCA)—A four-step process for quality improvement. In the first step (plan), a plan to effect improvement is developed. In the second step (do), the plan is carried out, preferably on a small scale. In the third step (check), the effects of the plan are observed. In the last step (action), the results are studied to determine what was learned and what can be predicted. The plan-do-check-¬action cycle is sometimes referred to as the Shewhart cycle (because Walter A. Shewhart discussed the concept in his book Statistical Method from the Viewpoint of Quality Control) and as the Deming circle (because W. Edwards Deming introduced the concept in Japan; the Japanese subsequently called it the Deming circle). Syn: plan-do-check-act cycle, Shewhart circle of quality, Shewhart cycle. See: Deming circle.

plan for every part (PFEP)—Consolidated information stored in a single record that contains everything needed to know about a part to plan it effectively. It includes usage, container information, storage location, item description, and supplier or procurement information.

plan make—Establishing plans for action over time that project appropriation of production resources to meet production requirements.

planned finish date—Syn: scheduled finish date.

planned issue—A disbursement of an item predicted by MRP through the creation of a gross requirement or allocation. Syn: controlled issue.

planned issue receipt—A transaction that updates the on-hand balance and the related allocation or open order.

planned load—The standard hours of work required by the planned production orders.

planned order—A suggested order quantity, release date, and due date created by the planning system's logic when it encounters net requirements in processing MRP. In some cases, it can also be created by a master scheduling module. Planned orders are created by the computer, exist only within the computer, and may be changed or deleted by the computer during subsequent processing if conditions change. Planned orders at one level will be exploded into gross requirements for components at the next level. Planned orders, along with released orders, serve as input to capacity requirements planning to show the total capacity requirements by work center in future time periods. See: planning time fence.

planned order receipt—The quantity planned to be received at a future date as a result of a planned order release. Planned order receipts differ from scheduled receipts in that they have not been released. Syn: planned receipt.

planned order release—A row on an MRP table that is derived from planned order receipts by taking the planned receipt quantity and offsetting to the left by the appropriate lead time. See: order release.

planned receipt—1) An anticipated receipt against an open purchase order or open production order. 2) Syn: planned order receipt.

planned start date—Syn: scheduled start date.

planned value—In project management, the total value (including overhead) of approved estimates for planned activities.

planner—Syn: material planner.

planner/buyer—Syn: supplier scheduler.

planner intervention—Syn: manual rescheduling.

planning—The process of setting goals for the organization and choosing various ways to use the organization's resources to achieve the goals.

planning and control process—A process consisting of the following steps: plan, execute, measure, and control.

planning bill—Syn: planning bill of material.

planning bill of material—An artificial grouping of items or events in bill-of-material format used to facilitate master scheduling and material planning. It may include the historical average of demand expressed as a percentage of total demand for all options within a feature or for a specific end item within a product family and is used as the quantity per in the planning bill of material. Syn: planning bill. See: hedge, option overplanning, production forecast, pseudo bill of material.

planning board—Syn: control board.

planning calendar—Syn: manufacturing calendar.

planning fence—Syn: planning time fence.

planning horizon—The amount of time a plan extends into the future. For a master schedule, this is normally set to cover a minimum of cumulative lead time plus time for lot sizing low-level components and for capacity changes of primary work centers or of key suppliers. For longer term plans the planning horizon must be long enough to permit any needed additions to capacity. See: cumulative lead time, planning time fence.

planning time fence—A point in time denoted in the planning horizon of the master scheduling process that marks a boundary inside of which changes to the schedule may adversely affect component schedules, capacity plans, customer deliveries, and cost. Outside the planning time fence, customer orders may be booked and changes to the master schedule can be made within the constraints of the production plan. Changes inside the planning time fence must be made manually by the master scheduler. Syn: planning fence. See: cumulative lead time, demand time fence, firm planned order, planned order, planning horizon, time fence.

planning values—Values that decision makers use to translate the sales forecast into resource requirements to determine the feasibility and costs of alternative approaches.

planogram—A graph or map of allotted shelf space based on an analysis of sales date indicating the best arrangement of products on a store shelf.

plan source—Establishing plans for action over time that project appropriation of material resources to meet supply chain requirements.

plan stability—The percent difference between the production that was planned and the production that was actually completed. The numerator is the difference between actual and planned production, divided by the planned production. This information then is used to adjust production standards.

plant finished goods—Finished goods inventory held in plant rather than being shipped to a customer.

plant layout—Configuration of the plant site with lines, buildings, major facilities, work areas, aisles, and other pertinent data, such as department boundaries.

plant rate—The total value added by a plant divided by the total direct labor hours in particular time period. This percentage allows the scheduling at the rough cut and capacity requirements level of the plan.

plant within a plant—Syn: factory within a factory.

platform products—A grouping of products to share common parts, components, and characteristics (a common platform), so that design and production resources can be used to reduce cost and time to market.

PLC—Abbreviation for programmable logic controller.

pledging of accounts receivable—The act of securing a loan by pledging a company's accounts receivable.

PLM—Abbreviation for product life cycle management.

PMBOK®—Abbreviation for project management body of knowledge. A registered trademark of the Project Management Institute, Inc.

point-of-purchase (POP) display—A sales promotion tool located at a checkout counter.

point of sale (POS)—The relief of inventory and computation of sales data at the time and place of sale, generally through the use of bar coding or magnetic media and equipment.

point-of-sale information—Information about customers collected at the time of sale.

point-of-use delivery—Direct delivery of material to a specified location on a plant floor near the operation where it is to be used.

point-of-use inventory—Inventory placed in the production process near where it is used. See: dock-to-stock inventory.

point-of-use storage—Keeping inventory in specified locations on a plant floor near the operation where it is to be used.

point reporting—The recording and reporting of milestone manufacturing order occurrences, typically done at checkpoint locations rather than operations and easily controlled from a reporting standpoint.

Poisson distribution—A type of statistical distribution frequently used to model the arrival of customers or entities into a queuing system.

poka-yoke (mistake-proof)—Mistake-proofing techniques, such as manufacturing or setup activity designed in a way to prevent an error from resulting in a product defect. For example, in an assembly operation, if each correct part is not used, a sensing device detects that a part was unused and shuts down the operation, thereby preventing the assembler from moving the incomplete part to the next station or beginning another operation. Sometimes spelled poke-yoke. Syn: failsafe techniques, failsafe work methods, mistake-proofing.

policies—Definitive statements of what should be done in the business.

policy constraint—A common misnomer. Bad policies are not the constraint, rather they hinder effective constraint management by inhibiting the ability to fully exploit and/or subordinate to the constraint.

political environment—External factors related to the political process, including laws and regulations, taxation codes, and others, at the local, state, federal, and international levels of government.

pooling—1) In transportation, shipments from multiple companies are placed together in the same shipment in order to reduce the costs of each shipment. 2) In production, that action that combines in parallel previously independent processes to reduce the total variance compared to the variances that would occur when the processes were independent.

POP—Acronym for point of purchase.

population—The entire set of items from which a sample is drawn.

portal—A multiservice website that provides access to data that may be secured by each user's role. Users can aggregate data and perform basic analysis. Portal ownership can be independent, private, or consortium-based. Yahoo! is an example of a consumer portal. Business portals are often connected with a customer relationship management or supplier relationship management system. Portals can include structured data, such as ERP information, pictures, and documents. Unlike exchanges or marketplaces, portals generally can display and aggregate data without integration between application software.

portfolio—In project management, a collection of projects that are grouped to facilitate management. They are not necessarily interdependent.

POS—Abbreviation for point of sale.

positioning strategy—Within manufacturing, a plan for inventory, product design, and production process.

possession utility—Product desirability created by marketing efforts.

post deduct—In a JIT system, work in process materials used to build finished goods are relieved from inventory by multiplying the number of units completed by the number of parts in the bill of material. Effective only if the bill of material is accurate and manufacturing lead times are short. See: backflushing.

post-deduct inventory transaction processing—Syn: backflush.

postponement—A product design strategy that shifts product differentiation closer to the consumer by postponing identity changes, such as assembly or packaging, to the last possible supply chain location.

post-release—The period after the product design has been released to manufacturing when the product has ongoing support and product enhancement.

post-transaction elements—Customer services that are provided after a product or service is sold, including warranties, returns, and complaint resolution.

potency—The measurement of active material in a specific lot, normally expressed in terms of an active unit. Typically used for such materials as solutions.

PPAP—Abbreviation for production part approval process.

PPB—Abbreviation for part period balancing.

PPP—Abbreviation for public-private partnering.

precedence relationship—In the critical path method of project management, a logical relationship that one node has to the succeeding node. The terms precedence relationship, logical relationship, and dependency are used somewhat interchangeably.

predatory pricing—Lowering prices below cost to drive out competition and then raising prices again. In the United States, this is a violation of Article 2 of the Sherman Act.

predecessor activity—1) In project management, in an activity-on-arrow network, the activity that enters a node. 2) In project management, in an activity-on-node network, the node at the tail of the arrow.

pre-deduct inventory transaction processing—A method of inventory bookkeeping where the book (computer) inventory of components is reduced before issue, at the time a scheduled receipt for their parents or assemblies is created via a bill-of-material explosion. This approach has the disadvantage of a built-in differential between the book record and what is physically in stock. See: backflush.

predetermined motion time—An organized body of information, procedures, techniques, and motion times employed in the study and evaluation of manual work elements. It is useful in categorizing and analyzing all motions into elements whose unit times are computed according to such factors as length, degree of muscle control, and precision. The element times provide the basis for calculating a time standard for the operations. Syn: synthetic time standard.

predetermined time standards—A table of times of basic motions used to prepare artificial standards (i.e., without direct observation of a worker). See: therbligs.

predictable maintenance—Syn: predictive maintenance.

prediction—An intuitive estimate of demand taking into account changes and new factors influencing the market, as opposed to a forecast, which is an objective projection of the past into the future.

predictive maintenance—A type of preventive maintenance based on nondestructive testing and statistical analysis, used to predict when required maintenance should be scheduled. Syn: predictable maintenance.

pre-expediting—The function of following up on open orders before the scheduled delivery date, to ensure the timely delivery of materials in the specified quantity.

preferred stock—A type of stock entitling the owner to dividends before common stockholders are entitled to them.

preferred supplier—The supplier of choice.

prepaid—A term denoting that transportation charges have been or are to be paid at the point of shipment by the sender.

pre-receiving—Paying for materials before receipt to prepare for incoming products and goods.

prerelease—The period of product specification, design, and design review.

prerequisite tree (PRT)—A necessity-based logic diagram that facilitates answering the third question in the change sequence: How do we effect the change? A PRT shows the relationship between the injections, desirable effects or ambitious target, and the obstacles that block the implementation of the injections. A PRT includes the intermediate objectives required to overcome the obstacles and shows the sequence in which they must be achieved for successful implementation.

present value—The value today of future cash flows. For example, the promise of $10 a year from now is worth something less than $10 in hand today.

pre-transaction elements—Customer service elements that pertain to the period before a product or service is sold, including flexibility, customer policies, and mission statement.

prevention costs—The costs caused by improvement activities that focus on the reduction of failure and appraisal costs. Typical costs include education, quality training, and supplier certification. Prevention costs are one of four categories of quality costs.

prevention vs. detection—A term used to contrast two types of quality activities. Prevention refers to those activities designed to prevent nonconformances in goods and services. Detection refers to those activities designed to detect nonconformances already in goods and services. Syn: designing in quality vs. inspecting in quality.

preventive maintenance—The activities, including adjustments, replacements, and basic cleanliness, that forestall machine breakdowns. The purpose is to ensure that production quality is maintained and that delivery schedules are met. In addition, a machine that is well cared for will last longer and cause fewer problems. Syn: periodic maintenance.

price—One of the four Ps (product, price, place, and promotion) that constitute the set of tools used to direct the business offering to the customer. Price is the amount charged for the product offering. The price set must take into account competition, substitute products, and internal business costs to return a desirable product margin. See: four Ps.

price analysis—The examination of a seller's price proposal or bid by comparison with price benchmarks, without examination and evaluation of all of the separate elements of the cost and profit making up the price in the bid.

price break—A discount given for paying early, buying in quantity, and so forth. See: discount.

price-break model—Syn: quantity discount model.

price discrimination—Selling the same products to different buyers at different prices.

price elasticity—The degree of change in buyer demand in response to changes in product price. It is calculated by dividing the percentage of change in quantity bought by the percentage of change of price. Prices are considered elastic if demand varies with changes in price. If demand changes only slightly when the price changes, demand is said to be inelastic. For example, demand for most medical services is relatively inelastic, but demand for automobiles is generally elastic.

price erosion—Increased competition and efficiencies in production over time cause the price to gradually reduce.

price point—The relative price position at which the product will enter the market compared to direct and indirect competitors' prices. It is considered within the context of the price-range options available: high, medium, or low.

price prevailing at date of shipment—An agreement between a purchaser and a supplier that the price of the goods ordered is subject to change at the supplier's discretion between the date the order is placed and the date the supplier makes shipment and that the then-established price is the contract price.

price protection—An agreement by a supplier with a purchaser to grant the purchaser any reduction in price that the supplier may establish on its goods before shipment of the purchaser's order or to grant the purchaser the lower price should the price increase before shipment. Price protection is sometimes extended for an additional period beyond the date of shipment.

price schedule—The list of prices applying to varying quantities or kinds of goods.

price skimming—Introducing a product above its long-run price to maximize product margin before others can enter the market.

price to earnings (PE) ratio—The current price of a stock relative to its earnings per share.

prima facie—Latin for at first sight or on the face of it. Something is presumed to be true.

primary demand—The demand for a category of products rather than for a specific brand.

primary location—The designation of a certain storage location as the standard, preferred location for an item.

primary operation—A manufacturing step normally performed as part of a manufacturing part's routing. Ant: alternate operation.

primary process—A process that performs the main value-added activities of an organization.

primary work center—The work center where an operation on a manufactured part is normally scheduled to be performed. Ant: alternate work center.

prime costs—Direct costs of material and labor. Prime costs do not include general, sales, and administrative costs.

prime operations—Critical or most significant operations whose production rates must be closely planned.

prime rate—The interest rate charged by banks to their most preferred customers.

principal—The party authorizing an agent to act on his or her behalf.

principle of postponement—Syn: order penetration point.

prioritization matrix—A special type of matrix chart used to show the priorities of items by applying criteria and weighting factors to each item.

priority—In a general sense, the relative importance of jobs (i.e., the sequence in which jobs should be worked on). It is a separate concept from capacity.

priority control—The process of communicating start and completion dates to manufacturing departments in order to execute a plan. The dispatch list is the tool normally used to provide these dates and priorities based on the current plan and status of all open orders.

priority planning—The function of determining what material is needed and when. Master production scheduling and material requirements planning are the elements used for the planning and replanning process to maintain proper due dates on required materials. priority report—Syn: dispatch list. private brand—A brand applied by a distributor rather than a manufacturer.

priority report—Syn: dispatch list.

priority rules—Simple heuristics used to select the order in which jobs will be processed.

private carrier—A group that provides transportation exclusively within an organization. Ant: common carrier.

private key—In information systems, an encryption key that is known only by the sender and receiver of the message. See: public key.

private label—Also known as store or dealer brands, these are products that are designed and produced by one company, but carry the name of the store that sells them. Oftentimes called generic to the purchaser.

private ownership—A form of business ownership in which the business is either owned by a single person (i.e., proprietorship) or organized under law as a separate legal entity but in which the company stock is not publicly traded. See: partnership, public ownership.

private trading exchange (PTX)—A trade exchange hosted by a single company to facilitate collaborative e-commerce with its trading partners. As opposed to public e-marketplaces, a private exchange provides the host company with control over many factors, including who may participate (and in what manner), how participants may be connected, and what contents should be presented (and to whom). The ultimate goal might be to improve supply chain efficiencies and responsiveness through improved process visibility and collaboration, advanced integration platforms, and customization capabilities.

private warehouse—A company-owned warehouse.

proactive—A strategy of anticipating issues and presenting beneficial solutions to the customer.

probabilistic demand models—Statistical procedures that represent the uncertainty of demand by a set of possible outcomes (i.e., a probability distribution) and that suggest inventory management strategies under probabilistic demands.

probability—Mathematically, a number between 0 and 1 that estimates the fraction of experiments (if the same experiment were being repeated many times) in which a particular result would occur. This number can be either subjective or based upon the empirical results of experimentation. It can also be derived for a process to give the probable outcome of experimentation.

probability and impact matrix—A matrix combining two dimensions of risk: (1) likelihood of occurrence and (2) impact if it happens.

probability distribution—A table of numbers or a mathematical expression that indicates the frequency with which each of all possible results of an experiment should occur.

probability tree—A graphic display of all possible outcomes of an event based on the possible occurrences and their associated probabilities.

probable scheduling—A variant of scheduling that considers slack time to increase or decrease the calculated lead time of an order. Interoperation and administrative lead time components are expanded or compressed by a uniform "stretching factor" until no difference exists between the schedule of operations obtained by forward and backward scheduling. See: lead time scheduling.

problem-solving storyboard—A technique based on the plan/do/check/action problem-solving process. The steps being taken and the progress toward the resolution of a problem are continuously planned and updated.

procedure manual—A formal organization and indexing of a firm's procedures. Manuals are usually printed and distributed to the appropriate functional areas.

process—1) A planned series of actions or operations (e.g., mechanical, electrical, chemical, inspection, test) that advances a material or procedure from one stage of completion to another. 2) A planned and controlled treatment that subjects materials or procedures to the influence of one or more types of energy (e.g., human, mechanical, electrical, chemical, thermal) for the time required to bring about the desired reactions or results.

process average—Expected value of the percentage defective of a given manufacturing process.

process batch—The quantity or volume of output that is to be completed at a workstation before switching to a different type of work or changing an equipment setup.

process benchmarking—Benchmarking focused on the target firm's business processes, including process flows, operating systems, and process technologies. See: benchmarking.

process capability—Refers to the ability of the process to produce parts that conform to (engineering) specifications. Process capability relates to the inherent variability of a process that is in a state of statistical control. See: Cp, Cpk, process capability analysis.

process capability analysis—A procedure to estimate the parameters defining a process. The mean and standard deviation of the process are estimated and compared to the specifications, if known. This comparison is the basis for calculating capability indexes. In addition, the form of the relative frequency distribution of the characteristic of interest may be estimated. Syn: capability study. See: process capability.

process capability index—The value of the tolerance specified for the characteristic divided by the process capability. There are several types of process capability indices, including the widely used Cpk and Cp.

P

process chart—A chart that represents the sequence of work or the nature of events in process. It serves as a basis for examining and possibly improving the way the work is carried out. Syn: operations process chart. See: flow process chart, process flow.

process control—1) The function of maintaining a process within a given range of capability by feedback, correction, and so forth. 2) The monitoring of instrumentation attached to equipment (valves, meters, mixers, liquid, temperature, time, etc.) from a control room to ensure that a high-quality product is being produced to specification.

process control chart—Syn: control chart.

process controllers—Computers designed to monitor the manufacturing cycle during production, often with the capability to modify conditions, to bring the production back to within prescribed ranges.

process costing—A cost accounting system in which the costs are collected by time period and averaged over all the units produced during the period. This system can be used with either actual or standard costs in the manufacture of a large number of identical units.

process decision program chart—A technique used to show alternate paths to achieving given goals. Applications include preparing contingency plans and maintaining project schedules.

process design—The design of the manufacturing method.

process engineering—The discipline of designing and improving the manufacturing equipment and production process to support the manufacture of a product line. See: manufacturing engineering.

process flexibility—The design of the manufacturing system, including operators and machinery, that allows quick changeovers to respond to near-term changes in product volume and mix. A necessary tool in lean and just in time.

process flow—The sequence of activities that when followed results in a product or service deliverable. See: flow process chart, process chart.

process flow analysis—A procedure to evaluate the effectiveness of a sequence of business activities. The analysis determines which elements of the flow are value-added and eliminates those that are not, determines which parts of the process can be automated, evaluates activities as to whether they contribute to the core competencies of the business or are candidates for outsourcing, and designs a structure for the activities of the process that remain to improve productivity.

process flowchart—Syn: flow process chart.

process flow diagram—A graphical and progressive representation of the various steps, events, and tasks that make up an operations process. This diagram provides the viewer with a picture of what actually occurs when a product is manufactured or a service is performed.

process flow production—A production approach with minimal interruptions in the actual processing in any one production run or between production runs of similar products. Queue time is virtually eliminated by integrating the movement of the product into the actual operation of the resource performing the work.

process flow scheduling—A generalized method for planning equipment usage and material requirements that uses the process structure to guide scheduling calculations. It is used in flow environments common in process industries.

process focused—A type of manufacturing organization in which both plant and staff management responsibilities are delineated by production process. A highly centralized staff coordinates plant activities and intracompany material movements. This type of organization is best suited to companies whose dominant orientation is to a technology or a material and whose manufacturing processes tend to be complex and capital intensive. See: product focused, process-focused organization.

process-focused organization—An organization that is oriented toward executing linked activities that constitute a given end-to-end business process with a given set of resources. Responsibilities of the members of the organization are oriented toward the performance of the process that creates the product or service and not toward a product or functional silo. See process focused, product focused.

process-focused production—This type of factory operation requires frequent machine changeover and produces small batches of unique products that flow along different paths.

process hours—The time required at any specific operation or task to process the product.

process improvement—The activities designed to identify and eliminate causes of poor quality, process variation, and non-value-added activities.

process industries—The group of manufacturers that produce products by mixing, separating, forming, and/or performing chemical reactions. Paint manufacturers, refineries, and breweries are examples of process industries.

process integration—Coordinating operations and consolidating data to simplify processes and increase efficiency.

process layout—Syn: functional layout.

process list—A list of operations and procedures in the manufacture of a product. It may also include a statement of material requirements.

process manufacturing—Production that adds value by mixing, separating, forming, and/or performing chemical reactions. It may be done in either batch or continuous mode. See: project manufacturing.

process map—A diagram of the flow of a production process or service process through the production system. Standardized symbols are used to designate processing, flow directions, branching decisions, input/output, and other aspects of the process.

processor-dominated scheduling—A technique that schedules equipment (processor) before materials. This technique facilitates scheduling equipment in economic run lengths and the use of low-cost production sequences. This scheduling method is used in some process industries. See: material-dominated scheduling.

process organization structure—An organizational structure in which people are removed from their functional departments and placed into a group that works as a single unit to perform the entire linked process. This is in contrast to a functional organization in which the activities that make up the process are performed by people in multiple functionally oriented departments.

process oriented—A characteristic in which the focus is on the interrelated processes in a business environment. It includes the activities to transform inputs into outputs that have value.

process planning—Determining the technological steps and sequence required to produce a product or service at the required quality level and cost.

process selection—An economic analysis used to decide which process should be used when operations can be performed by more than one process.

process sheet—Detailed manufacturing instructions issued to the plant. The instructions may include specifications on speeds, feed, temperatures, tools, fixtures, and machines and sketches of setups and semifinished dimensions.

process steps—The operations or stages within the manufacturing cycle required to transform components into intermediates or finished goods. From a larger perspective, the operations or stages within any business required to turn inputs into outputs.

process stocks—Raw ingredients or intermediates available for further processing into marketable products.

process time—The time during which the material is being changed, whether it is a machining operation or an assembly. Syn: residence time.

process train—A representation of the flow of materials through a process industry manufacturing system that shows equipment and inventories. Equipment that performs a basic manufacturing step, such as mixing or packaging, is called a process unit. Process units are combined into stages, and stages are combined into process trains. Inventories decouple the scheduling of sequential stages within a process train.

process yield—See: yield.

procurement—The business functions of procurement planning, purchasing, inventory control, traffic, receiving, incoming inspection, and salvage operations.

procurement credit card—Credit cards with a predetermined credit limit issued to buyers. Syn: corporate purchasing cards.

procurement cycle—Syn: procurement lead time.

procurement lead time—The time required to design a product, modify or design equipment, conduct market research, and obtain all necessary materials. Lead time begins when a decision has been made to accept an order to produce a new product and ends when production commences. Syn: procurement cycle, total procurement lead time. See: time-to-market.

procurement services provider—A company that has product, sourcing, and supply management knowledge and acts as an outsourced process by other companies and provides procurement help. They are most often used by companies where procurement is a significant part of business, but the company lacks the expertise to effectively manage the process. This is a third-party process.

producer—One who creates a good or service.

producer market—Syn: industrial market.

producer's risk (α)—For a given sampling plan, the probability of not accepting a lot, the quality of which

P

has a designated numerical value representing a level that is generally desired to accept. Usually the designated value will be the acceptable quality level (AQL). See: type I error.

produce-to-order—Syn: make-to-order.

produce-to-stock—Syn: make-to-stock.

producibility—The characteristics of a design that enable the item to be produced and inspected in the quantity required at least cost and minimum time.

product—1) Any good or service produced for sale, barter, or internal use. 2) One of the four Ps (product, price, place, and promotion) that constitute the set of tools for directing the business offering to the customer. The product can be promoted as a distinctive item. See: four Ps.

product and market focus—Developing products based on dimensions like service to similar customers, volume, or customization.

product audit—The reinspection of any product to verify the adequacy of acceptance or rejection decisions made by inspection and testing personnel.

product-based layout—A type of layout where resources are arranged sequentially according to the steps required to make a particular complex product.

product benchmarking—This benchmarking is used for new product design or for a product upgrade. This often includes reverse engineering (dismantling) competing products to determine their strengths and weaknesses. See: benchmarking.

product configuration catalog—A listing of all upper level configurations contained in an end-item product family. Its application is most useful when there are multiple end-item configurations in the same product family. It is used to provide a transition linkage between the end-item level and a two-level master production schedule. It also provides a correlation between the various units of upper level product definition.

product configurator—A system, generally rule-based, to be used in design-to-order, engineer-to-order, or make-to-order environments where numerous product variations exist. Product configurators perform intelligent modeling of the part or product attributes and often create solid models, drawings, bills of material, and cost estimates that can be integrated into CAD/CAM and MRP II systems as well as sales order entry systems.

product cost—Cost allocated by some method to the products being produced. Initially recorded in asset (in-ventory) accounts, product costs become an expense (cost of sales) when the product is sold.

product data management (PDM)—A system that tracks the configurations of parts and bills of material and also the revisions and history of product designs. It facilities the design release, distributes the design data to multiple manufacturing sites, and manages changes to the design in a closed-loop fashion. It provides the infrastructure that controls the design cycle and manages change.

product differentiation—A strategy of making a product distinct from the competition on a nonprice basis such as availability, durability, quality, or reliability.

product diversification—A marketing strategy that seeks to develop new products to supply current markets.

product engineering—The discipline of designing a product or product line to take advantage of process technology and improve quality, reliability, and so forth.

product family—A group of products with similar characteristics, often used in production planning (or sales and operations planning). Syn: product line.

product flexibility—The ease with which current designs can be modified in response to changing market demands.

product focused—A type of manufacturing organization in which both plant and staff responsibilities are delineated by product, product line, or market segment. Management authority is highly decentralized, which tends to make the company more responsive to market needs and more flexible when introducing new products. This type of organization is best suited to companies whose dominant orientation is to a market or consumer group and where flexibility and innovation are more important than coordinated planning and tight control. See: process focused, process-focused organization.

product-focused production—A type of operation designed to process only a few different products, which are usually produced for inventory; production rates tend to be greater than the demand rate.

product genealogy—A record, usually on a computer file, of the history of a product from its introduction into the production process through its termination. The record includes lot or batch sizes used, operations performed, inspection history, options, and where-used information.

product grade—The categorization of goods based upon the range of specifications met during the manufacturing process.

product group—Syn: product line.

product group forecast—A forecast for a number of similar products. See: aggregate forecast, product group.

product layout—Another name for flow process layout. The system is set up for a limited range of similar products. Focused-factory production would also be considered in this category. See: flow processing, focused factory.

product life cycle management (PLM)—The process of facilitating the development, use, and support of products that customers want and need. PLM helps professionals envision the creation and preservation of product information, both to the customer and along the reverse-logistics portion of the supply chain.

product velocity—Units sold per period.

production—The conversion of inputs into finished products.

production activity control (PAC)—The function of routing and dispatching the work to be accomplished through the production facility and of performing supplier control. PAC encompasses the principles, approaches, and techniques needed to schedule, control, measure, and evaluate the effectiveness of production operations. See: shop floor control.

production and inventory management—General term referring to the body of knowledge and activities concerned with planning and controlling rates of purchasing, production, distribution, and related capacity resources to achieve target levels of customer service, backlogs, operating costs, inventory investment, manufacturing efficiency, and ultimately, profit and return on investment.

production and operations management (POM)—Managing an organization's production of goods or services; managing the process of taking inputs and creating outputs.

production calendar—Syn: manufacturing calendar.

production capability—1) The highest sustainable output rate that could be achieved for a given product mix, raw materials, worker effort, plant, and equipment. 2) The collection of personnel, equipment, material, and process segment capabilities. 3) The total of the current committed, available, and unattainable capability of the production facility. The capability includes the capacity of the resource.

production card—In a just-in-time context, a card or other signal for indicating that items should be made for use or to replace some items removed from pipeline stock. See: kanban.

production control—The function of directing or regulating the movement of goods through the entire manufacturing cycle from the requisitioning of raw material to the delivery of the finished products.

production cycle—Syn: manufacturing lead time.

production cycle elements—Elements of manufacturing strategy that define the span of an operation by addressing the following areas: (1) the established boundaries for the firm's activities, (2) the construction of relationships outside the firm's boundaries (i.e., suppliers, distributors, and customers), (3) circumstances under which changes in established boundaries or relationships are necessary, (4) the effect of such boundary or relationship changes on the firm's competitive position. The production cycle elements must explicitly address the strategic implications of vertical integration in regard to (a) the direction of such expansion, (b) the extent of the process span desired, and (c) the balance among the resulting vertically linked activities.

production environment—Syn: manufacturing environment.

production forecast—A projected level of customer demand for a feature (option, accessory, etc.) of a make-to-order or an assemble-to-order product. Used in two-level master scheduling, it is calculated by netting customer backlog against an overall family or product line master production schedule and then factoring this product's available-to-promise by the option percentage in a planning bill of material. See: assemble-to-order, planning bill of material, two-level master schedule.

production kanban—A signal, usually a card, used to trigger the production of a part.

production lead time—Syn: manufacturing lead time.

production level—Syn: production rate.

production leveling—Syn: level production method.

production line—A series of pieces of equipment dedicated to the manufacture of a specific number of products or families.

production lot—A group of material that is processed in one stage of production and put in inventory for further production (or for shipment to customers).

production management—1) The planning, scheduling, execution, and control of the process of converting in-

P

puts into finished goods. 2) A field of study that focuses on the effective planning, scheduling, use, and control of a manufacturing organization through the study of concepts from design engineering, industrial engineering, management information systems, quality management, inventory management, accounting, and other functions as they affect the transformation process.

production material—Any material used in the manufacturing process.

production materials requisition—Syn: materials requisition.

production network—The complete set of all work centers, processes, and inventory points, from raw materials sequentially to finished products and product families. It represents the logical system that provides the framework to attain the strategic objectives of the firm based on its resources and the products' volumes and processes. It provides the general sequential flow and capacity requirement relationships among raw materials, parts, resources, and product families.

production order—Syn: manufacturing order.

production part approval process (PPAP)—A Big Three automotive process outlining requirements for approval of production parts. Its purpose is to measure whether a supplier can, with regularity, fulfill these requirements.

production plan—The agreed-upon plan that comes from the production planning (sales and operations planning) process, specifically the overall level of manufacturing output planned to be produced, usually stated as a monthly rate for each product family (group of products, items, options, features, and so on). Various units of measurement can be used to express the plan: units, tonnage, standard hours, number of workers, and so on. The production plan is management's authorization for the master scheduler to convert it into a more detailed plan, that is, the master production schedule. See: sales and operations planning, sales plan.

production planning—A process to develop tactical plans based on setting the overall level of manufacturing output (production plan) and other activities to best satisfy the current planned levels of sales (sales plan or forecasts), while meeting general business objectives of profitability, productivity, competitive customer lead times, and so on, as expressed in the overall business plan. The sales and production capabilities are compared, and a business strategy that includes a sales plan, a production plan, budgets, pro forma financial statements, and supporting plans for materials and workforce requirements, and so on, is developed. One

of its primary purposes is to establish production rates that will achieve management's objective of satisfying customer demand by maintaining, raising, or lowering inventories or backlogs, while usually attempting to keep the workforce relatively stable. Because this plan affects many company functions, it is normally prepared with information from marketing and coordinated with the functions of manufacturing, sales, engineering, finance, materials, and so on. See: aggregate planning, production plan, sales and operations planning, sales plan.

production planning and control strategies—An element of manufacturing strategy that includes the design and development of manufacturing planning and control systems in relation to the following considerations: (1) market-related criteria—the required level of delivery speed and reliability in a given market segment, (2) process requirement criteria—consistency between process type (job shop, repetitive, continuous, etc.) and the production planning and control system, (3) organization control levels—systems capable of providing long-term planning and short-term control capabilities for strategic and operational considerations by management. Production planning and control strategies help firms develop systems that enable them to exploit market opportunities while satisfying manufacturing process requirements.

production planning methods—The approach taken in setting the overall manufacturing output to meet customer demand by setting production levels, inventory levels, and backlog. Companies can use a chase, level, or hybrid production planning method. See: chase production method, hybrid production method, level production method.

production process—The activities involved in converting inputs into finished goods. See: manufacturing process, transformation process.

production rate—The rate of production usually expressed in units, cases, or some other broad measure, expressed by a period of time (e.g., per hour, shift, day, or week). Syn: production level.

production release—Syn: manufacturing order.

production report—A statement of the output of a production facility for a specified period. The information normally includes the type and quantity of output; workers' efficiencies; departmental efficiencies; costs of direct labor, direct material, and the like; overtime worked; and machine downtime.

production reporting and status control—A vehicle to provide feedback to the production schedule and allow for corrective action and maintenance of valid on-hand and on-order balances. Production reporting and status control normally include manufacturing order authorization, release, acceptance, operation start, delay reporting, move reporting, scrap and rework reporting, order close-out, and payroll interface. Syn: manufacturing order reporting, shop order reporting.

production schedule—A plan that authorizes the factory to manufacture a certain quantity of a specific item. It is usually initiated by the production planning department.

production scheduling—The process of developing the production schedule.

production sharing—A network of companies that participates in product design, production, marketing, distribution, and service.

production standard—A time standard to produce piece parts and assemblies.

production system—A system that accepts inputs and converts them to the desired outputs.

production time—Setup time plus total processing time, where total processing time is processing time per piece multiplied by the number of pieces.

production validation—Demonstrating that a production process will consistently lead to the expected results.

productive capacity—In the theory of constraints: The maximum of the output capabilities of a resource (or series of resources) or the market demand for that output for a given time period. See: excess capacity, idle capacity, protective capacity.

productive inventory—In the theory of constraints: The inventory required to meet production requirements without allowance for unplanned delays. See: idle inventory, protective inventory.

productivity—1) An overall measure of the ability to produce a good or a service. It is the actual output of production compared to the actual input of resources. Productivity is a relative measure across time or against common entities (labor, capital, etc.). In the production literature, attempts have been made to define total productivity where the effects of labor and capital are combined and divided into the output. One example is a ratio that is calculated by adding the dollar value of labor, capital equipment, energy, and material, and so forth and dividing it into the dollar value of output in a given time period. This is one measure of total factor productivity. See: efficiency, labor productivity, machine productivity, utilization. 2) In economics, the ratio of output in terms of dollars of sales to an input such as direct labor in terms of the total wages. This is called single factor productivity or partial factor productivity.

product layout—Layout of resources arranged sequentially based on the product's routing.

product liability—The responsibility a producer bears when someone is injured during the use of his or her product.

product life cycle—1) The stages a new product goes through from beginning to end (i.e., the stages that a product passes through from introduction through growth, maturity, and decline). 2) The time from initial research and development to the time at which sales and support of the product to customers are withdrawn. 3) The period of time during which a product can be produced and marketed profitably.

product line—A group of products whose similarity in manufacturing procedures, marketing characteristics, or specifications enables them to be aggregated for planning; marketing; or, occasionally, costing. Syn: product family, product group.

product load profile—A listing of the required capacity and key resources needed to manufacture one unit of a selected item or family. The resource requirements are further defined by a lead-time offset to predict the impact of the product on the load of the key resources by specific time period. The product load profile can be used for rough-cut capacity planning to calculate the approximate capacity requirements of the master production schedule. See: bill of resources, resource profile, rough-cut capacity planning.

product manager—Syn: brand manager.

product manager concept—A marketing method in which a manager is given complete responsibility for managing the introduction, stocking policy, marketing, and sales of a specific product.

product-market-focused organization—A firm in which individual plants are dedicated to manufacturing a specific product or product group.

product mix—The proportion of individual products that make up the total production or sales volume. Changes in the product mix can mean drastic changes in the manufacturing requirements for certain types of labor and material.

P

product-mix flexibility—The ability to change over quickly to other products produced in a facility, as required by demand shifts in mix.

product number—Syn: item number.

product or service liability—The obligation of a company to make restitution for loss related to personal injury, property damage, or other harm caused by its goods or services.

product plan—Syn: market plan.

product-positioned strategy—Locating operations close to the sources of supply. See: market-positioned strategy.

product-positioned warehouse—The warehouse located close to the manufacturing plants that acts as a consolidation point for products.

product positioning—The marketing effort involved in placing a product in a market to serve a particular niche or function. Syn: service positioning.

product profiling—1) A graphical device used to ascertain the level of fit between a manufacturing process and the order-winning criteria of its products. Product profiling can be used at the process or company level to compare the manufacturing capabilities with the market requirements to determine areas of mismatch and identify steps needed for realignment. 2) Removing material around a predetermined boundary by means of numerically controlled machining. The numerically controlled tool path is automatically generated on the system.

product quality—Attribute that reflects the capability of a product to satisfy customers' needs.

product segments—The shared information between a plan-of-resources and a production rule for a specific product. It is a logical grouping of personnel resources, equipment resources, and material specifications required to carry out the production step.

product/service hierarchy—In sales and operations planning, a general approach to dividing products or services into families, brands, and subfamilies for various planning levels. This ensures that a correct top-down or bottom-up approach is taken to grouping (or aggregating) demand at each subsequent level. Forecasts are more accurate the higher up the product hierarchy they are developed; consequently, forecasts should usually be driven down from the top.

product specification—A statement of acceptable physical, electrical, and/or chemical properties or an acceptable range of properties that distinguish one product or grade from another.

product structure—The sequence of operations that components follow during their manufacture into a product. A typical product structure would show raw material converted into fabricated components, components put together to make subassemblies, subassemblies going into assemblies, and so forth.

product structure record—A computer record defining the relationship of one component to its immediate parent and containing fields for quantity required, engineering effectivity, scrap factor, application selection switches, and so forth.

product tree—A graphical (or tree) representation of the bill of material such as is shown below:

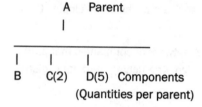

profit—1) Gross profit—earnings from an ongoing business after direct costs of goods sold have been deducted from sales revenue for a given period. 2) Operating profit—earnings or income after all expenses (selling, administrative, depreciation) have been deducted from gross profit. 3) Net profit—earnings or income after adjusting for miscellaneous income and expenses (patent royalties, interest, capital gains) and tax from operating profit. Syn: income.

profitability—A measure of the excess income over expenditure during a given period of time.

profitability analysis—In activity-based cost accounting, the examination of profit received from cost objects to attempt to optimize profitability. A variety of views may be examined including customer, distribution channel, product, and regions.

profitability index—In financial management, the net present value of a projected stream of income from a project (potential investment) divided by the investment in the project. It is used to select among competing potential investments.

profitability ratio—An indicator of whether or not a company is generating profits at an acceptable rate. It includes such measurements as return on total assets, return on equity, and profit margin.

profit center—An assigned responsibility center that has authority to affect both the revenues earned and the costs incurred by and allocated to the center. Operational effectiveness is evaluated in terms of the amount of profit generated.

profit margin—1) The difference between the sales and cost of goods sold for an organization, sometimes expressed as a percentage of sales. 2) In traditional accounting, the product profit margin is the product selling price minus the direct material, direct labor, and allocated overhead for the product, sometimes expressed as a percentage of selling price.

profit ratio—Profit divided by sales.

profit sharing—A plan by which employees receive compensation, above their normal wages, based on company profitability. The purpose is to motivate employees and recognize their efforts.

pro forma financial statements—Financial statements that are based on an assumed scenario rather than an actual experience.

profound knowledge—A quality-related concept created by W. Edwards Deming. The four aspects of profound knowledge are appreciation of a system, knowledge about variation, theory of knowledge, and psychology.

program—In project management, a coordinated set of related projects usually including ongoing work.

program directive—A report by the program manager to inform supporting departments concerning an active or planned program or project.

program evaluation and review technique (PERT)—In project management, a network analysis technique in which each activity is assigned a pessimistic, most likely, and optimistic estimate of its duration. The critical path method is then applied using a weighted average of these times for each node. PERT computes a standard deviation of the estimate of project duration. See: critical path method, graphical evaluation and review technique, and network analysis.

programmable logic controller (PLC)—An electronic device that is programmed to test the state of input process data and to set output lines in accordance with the input state, thus providing control instructions or branching to another set of tests. Programmable controllers provide factory floor operations with the ability to monitor and rapidly control hundreds of parameters, such as temperature and pressure.

program management—The activities involved in the realization of a product or service offered to customers. The responsibilities include planning, directing, and controlling one or more projects of a new or continuing nature; initiating any acquisition processes necessary to get the project work under way; and monitoring performance. See: program manager.

program manager—A person assigned program management responsibilities for the implementation activities associated with a new or ongoing product or service offering to customers. See: program management.

progressive operations—Passing work from station to station.

progress payments—Payments arranged in connection with purchase transactions requiring periodic payments in advance of delivery for certain amounts or for certain percentages of the purchase price.

project—An endeavor with a specific objective to be met within predetermined time and dollar limitations and that has been assigned for definition or execution. See: project manufacturing, project management.

project-based layout—A type of layout where the good or product is stationary and the workers come to the site to work on it.

project calendar—A calendar of working days and nonworking days that shows when scheduled activities are idle. Typically, it includes holidays and weekends. See: resource calendar.

project costing—An accounting method of assigning valuations that is generally used in industries where services are performed on a project basis. Each assignment is unique and costed without regard to other assignments. Examples are shipbuilding, construction projects, and public accounting firms. Project costing is opposed to process costing, where products to be valued are homogeneous.

project duration—The elapsed duration from project start date through project finish date.

projected available balance—An inventory balance projected into the future. It is the running sum of on-hand inventory minus requirements plus scheduled receipts and planned orders. Syn: projected available inventory.

projected available inventory—Syn: projected available balance.

projected finish date—The current estimate of the date when an activity will be completed.

projected on hand—Projected available balance, excluding planned orders.

projected start date—The current estimate of the date when an activity will begin.

projection—Syn: extrapolation.

project life cycle—In project management, a set of project phases (objectives definition, requirements de-

P

finition, external and internal design, construction, system test, and implementation and maintenance), whose definition is determined by the needs of those controlling the project.

project management—The use of skills and knowledge in coordinating the organizing, planning, scheduling, directing, controlling, monitoring, and evaluating of prescribed activities to ensure that the stated objectives of a project, manufactured good, or service are achieved. See: project.

Project Management Body of Knowledge (PMBOK®)—All the knowledge within the project management profession; this includes all published and unpublished material, knowledge that rests with practitioners and academics, and practices that range from traditional to innovative.

project management team—In project management, the personnel assigned to a project who are directly involved in management activities.

project manufacturing—A type of manufacturing process used for large, often unique, items or structures that require a custom design capability (engineer-to-order). This type of process is highly flexible and can cope with a broad range of product designs and design changes. Product manufacturing usually uses a fixed-position type layout. See: batch (fourth definition), continuous production, job shop (second definition), process manufacturing, project, repetitive manufacturing.

project model—A time-phased project planning and control tool that itemizes major milestones and points of user approval.

project network—A diagram showing the technological relationships among activities in a project.

project phase—In project management, a set of related project activities that usually go together to define a project deliverable.

project plan—In project management, a document that has been approved by upper management that is to be used in executing and controlling a project. It documents assumptions, facilitates communication, and documents the approved budget and schedule. It may exist at a summary or a detailed level.

project production—Production in which each unit or small group of units is managed by a project team created especially for that purpose.

project risk management—In project management, a systematic process of controlling project risk. It includes maximizing the likelihood and effect of positive events

and minimizing the likelihood and effect of negative events.

project schedule—In project management, a list of activities and their planned completion dates that collectively achieve project milestones.

project scope—In project management, the work required to create a product with given features and options.

project summary work breakdown structure—A work breakdown structure that is developed down to the subproject level of detail. See: work breakdown structure.

project team—An inclusive term incorporating the workers assigned to the project, the project managers, and sometimes the project sponsor.

project team directory—A list of team member names, roles, and communication information.

promissory note—An agreement to pay a stipulated amount during an agreed time period.

promotion—One of the four Ps (product, price, place, and promotion) that constitute the set of tools used to direct the business offering to the customer. Promotion is the mechanism whereby information about the product offering is communicated to the customer and includes public relations, advertising, sales promotions, and other tools used to persuade customers to purchase the product offering. See: four Ps.

promotional product—A product that is subject to wide fluctuations in sales because it is usually sold at a reduced price or with some other sales incentive.

proof of delivery—Carrier's records indicating the person signing for delivery with the date, time, and other related information.

proportional rate—A lower rate given to specific parts of a shipment, instead of the entire rate being charged for only one part of the shipment.

proprietary assembly—An assembly designed by a manufacturer that may be serviced only with component parts supplied by the manufacturer and whose design is owned or licensed by its manufacturer.

proprietary data—Any financial, technical, or other information developed at the expense of the person or other entity submitting it, deemed to be of strategic or tactical importance to the company. It may be offered to customers on a restricted-use basis.

protection time—Syn: safety lead time.

protective capacity—The resource capacity needed to protect system throughput—ensuring that some capacity above the capacity required to exploit the constraint is available to catch up when disruptions inevitably occur. Nonconstraint resources need protective capacity to rebuild the bank in front of the constraint or capacity-constrained resource (CCR) and/or on the shipping dock before throughput is lost and to empty the space buffer when it fills.

protective inventory—In the theory of constraints, the amount of inventory required relative to the protective capacity in the system to achieve a specific throughput rate at the constraint. See: limiting operation.

protective packaging—Wrapping or covering of material that provides containment, protection, and identification of inventory in a warehouse. The material must be contained in such a way that will support movement and storage and will fit into the dimension of storage space and transportation vehicles.

protocol—In information systems, a set of rules for defining the format and relationships for sharing information between devices. These rules govern the transmission of data across a network and serve as the grammar of data communication languages.

prototype—1) A product model constructed for testing and evaluation to see how the product performs before releasing the product to manufacture. 2) Model consisting of all files and programs needed for a business application.

prototyping—1) A specialized product design and development process for developing a working model of a product. 2) A specialized system development process for performing a determination where user needs are extracted, presented, and developed by building a working model of the system. Generally, these tools make it possible to create all files and processing programs needed for a business application in a matter of days or hours for evaluation purposes.

provisioning—The process of identifying and purchasing the support items and determining the quantity of each support item necessary to operate and maintain a system.

proxy—1) A written document authorizing an agent to vote a shareholder's stock at a shareholder meeting. 2) The agent designated in 1).

PRT—Abbreviation for prerequisite tree.

pseudo bill of material—An artificial grouping of items that facilitates planning. See: modular bill of material, phantom bill of material, planning bill of material, super bill of material.

psychographics—The grouping of consumers according to their behavior patterns and lifestyles.

public key—In information systems, a system where one person holds a private key (an encryption code defining access rights) but shares another key with a set of people with whom that person will communicate. See: private key.

publicly traded corporation—A corporation whose stock is available on a national exchange.

public ownership—A business formed under law as a separate legal entity and where stock is publicly traded. See: partnership, private ownership.

public-private partnering—Cooperation between a government entity and one or more private enterprises to perform work or utilize facilities.

public relations—The function that oversees a program to earn public understanding and acceptance.

public warehouse—The warehouse space that is rented or leased by an independent business providing a variety of services for a fee or on a contract basis.

pull signal—Any signal that indicates when to produce or transport items in a pull replenishment system. For example, in just-in-time production control systems, a kanban card is used as the pull signal to replenish parts to the using operation. See: pull system.

pull system—1) In production, the production of items only as demanded for use or to replace those taken for use. See: pull signal. 2) In material control, the withdrawal of inventory as demanded by the using operations. Material is not issued until a signal comes from the user. 3) In distribution, a system for replenishing field warehouse inventories where replenishment decisions are made at the field warehouse itself, not at the central warehouse or plant.

pull-through distributions—Supply chain activities that are started by the consumer. Instead of the manufacturer "pushing" products to stores, in a pull-through distribution consumers purchase items, which signals the manufacturer to produce more of that product. This is effectively the consumer "pulling" products to the store.

punitive damages—The money awarded a plaintiff, not as payment for the plaintiff's losses, but as punishment for the defendant's conduct.

pup—A 28-foot trailer, usually used in trucking enterprises.

P

purchase consolidation—The pooling of purchasing requirements by multiple areas in a company, or even across companies.

purchased part—An item sourced from a supplier.

purchase order—The purchaser's authorization used to formalize a purchase transaction with a supplier. A purchase order, when given to a supplier, should contain statements of the name, part number, quantity, description, and price of the goods or services ordered; agreed-to terms as to payment, discounts, date of performance, and transportation; and all other agreements pertinent to the purchase and its execution by the supplier.

purchase price discount—A pricing strategy in which a seller offers a customer a cheaper price in exchange for purchasing more goods.

purchase price variance—The difference in price between the amount paid to the supplier and the planned or standard cost of that item.

purchase requisition—An authorization to the purchasing department to purchase specified materials in specified quantities within a specified time. See: parts requisition.

purchasing—The term used in industry and management to denote the function of and the responsibility for procuring materials, supplies, and services.

purchasing agent—A person authorized by the company to purchase goods and services for the company.

purchasing capacity—The act of buying capacity or machine time from a supplier. A company can then schedule and use the capacity of the machine or a part of the capacity of the machine as if it were in its own plant.

purchasing lead time—The total lead time required to obtain a purchased item. Included here are order preparation and release time; supplier lead time; transportation time; and receiving, inspection, and put-away time. See: lead time, supplier lead time, time-to-product.

purchasing performance measurement—Syn: supplier measurement.

purchasing unit of measure—Syn: unit of measure (purchasing).

pure competition—A market in which many competitors offer undifferentiated products or services within a given geographical area. Competitors are forced to accept the market price for their product. See: industry structure types.

pure monopoly—A market in which only one firm provides a particular product or service within a given area. The monopoly may be regulated or unregulated. See: industry structure types.

pure oligopoly—A market in which a few companies produce essentially the same product or service and market it within a given area. A company is forced to price its product at the going rate unless it can differentiate its product. See: industry structure types.

pure services—Services that result in few or no tangible products to the customer (e.g., education).

push-back rack—Palletized materials are stored on a wheeled rack structure and pushed up a slightly sloping ramp from which they can eventually slide down to an aisle.

push system—1) In production, the production of items at times required by a given schedule planned in advance. 2) In material control, the issuing of material according to a given schedule or issuing material to a job order at its start time. 3) In distribution, a system for replenishing field warehouse inventories where replenishment decision making is centralized, usually at the manufacturing site or central supply facility. See: pull system.

push technology—The automatic updates in selected services, such as news or weather, that occur periodically as information is sent via the internet. The source of the information "pushes" it upon the customer. Syn: webcasting.

put-away—Removing the material from the dock (or other location of receipt), transporting the material to a storage area, placing that material in a staging area and then moving it to a specific location, and recording the movement and identification of the location where the material has been placed.

put-away time—The lead time between when a raw material or component arrives and when the items are available in the store. Syn: dock-to-stock time.

put-to-light—A process that uses lights to ensure materials are placed in the correct locations. Also, it is used to ensure that picked items are placed correctly.

pyramid forecasting—A forecasting technique that enables management to review and adjust forecasts made at an aggregate level and to keep lower level forecasts in balance. The procedure begins with the roll up (aggregation) of item forecasts into forecasts by product group. The management team establishes a (new) forecast for the product group. The value is then forced down (disaggregation) to individual item forecasts so that they are consistent with the aggregate plan. The approach combines the stability of aggregate forecasts and the application of management judgment with the need to forecast many end items within the constraints of an aggregate forecast or sales plan. See: management estimation, planning bill of material, product group forecast.

Q

QCD—Abbreviation for quality, cost, delivery.

Q chart—A control chart for evaluating the stability of a process in terms of a quality score. The quality score is the weighted sum of the count of events of various classifications, where each classification is assigned a weight. Syn: quality chart, quality score chart.

QFD—Abbreviation for quality function deployment.

QRM—Abbreviation for quick-response manufacturing.

QRP—Abbreviation for quick-response program.

QS 9000—A variation of ISO 9000 certification with additional requirements tailored for the automobile industry, including suppliers. QS 9000 is being superseded by ISO/ TS 16949, which incorporates many European standards. See: ISO 9000, ISO/TS 16949.

qualifiers—Syn: order qualifiers. See: order losers, order winners.

qualitative forecasting techniques—An approach to forecasting that is based on intuitive or judgmental evaluation. It is used generally when data are scarce, not available, or no longer relevant. Common types of qualitative techniques include: personal insight, sales force estimates, panel consensus, market research, visionary forecasting, and the Delphi method. Examples include developing long-range projections and new product introduction.

quality—Conformance to requirements or fitness for use. Quality can be defined through five principal approaches: (1) Transcendent quality is an ideal, a condition of excellence. (2) Product-based quality is based on a product attribute. (3) User-based quality is fitness for use. (4) Manufacturing-based quality is conformance to requirements. (5) Value-based quality is the degree of excellence at an acceptable price. Also, quality has two major components: (1) quality of conformance—quality is defined by the absence of defects, and (2) quality of design—quality is measured by the degree of customer satisfaction with a product's characteristics and features.

quality assurance/control—Two terms that have many interpretations because of the multiple definitions for the words "assurance" and "control." For example, "assurance" can mean the act of giving confidence, the state of being certain, or the act of making certain; "control" can mean an evaluation to indicate needed corrective responses, the act of guiding, or the state of a process in which the variability is attributable to a constant system of chance causes. One definition of quality assurance is all the planned and systematic activities implemented within the quality system that can be demonstrated to provide confidence that a good or service will fulfill requirements for quality. One definition for quality control is the operational techniques and activities used to fulfill requirements for quality. Often, however, quality assurance and quality control are used interchangeably, referring to the actions performed to ensure the quality of a good, service, or process. See: quality control.

quality at the source—A producer's responsibility to provide 100 percent acceptable quality material to the consumer of the material. The objective is to reduce or eliminate shipping or receiving quality inspections and line stoppages as a result of supplier defects.

quality audit—A systematic, independent examination and review to determine whether quality activities and related results comply with planned arrangements and whether these arrangements are implemented effectively and are suitable to achieve the objectives.

quality characteristic—A property of a product or service that is important enough to count or measure. See: performance measurement system.

quality chart—Syn: Q chart.

quality circle—A small group of people who normally work as a unit and meet frequently to uncover and solve problems concerning the quality of items produced, process capability, or process control. Syn: quality control circle. See: small group improvement activity.

quality control—The process of measuring quality conformance by comparing the actual with a standard for the characteristic and acting on the difference. See: quality assurance/control.

quality control circle—Syn: quality circle.

quality, cost, delivery (QCD)—Key measurements of customer satisfaction. Kaizen activity strives to improve these measurements.

Q

quality costs—The overall costs associated with prevention activities and the improvement of quality throughout the firm before, during, and after production of a product. These costs fall into four recognized categories: internal failure costs, external failure costs, appraisal costs, and prevention costs. Internal failure costs relate to problems before the product reaches the customer. These usually include rework, scrap, downgrades, reinspection, retest, and process losses. External failure costs relate to problems found after the product reaches the customer. These usually include such costs as warranty and returns. Appraisal costs are associated with the formal evaluation and audit of quality in the firm. Typical costs include inspection, quality audits, testing, calibration, and checking time. Prevention costs are those caused by improvement activities that focus on reducing failure and appraisal costs. Typical costs include education, quality training, and supplier certification.

quality engineering—The engineering discipline concerned with improving the quality of products and processes.

quality function deployment (QFD)—A methodology designed to ensure that all the major requirements of the customer are identified and subsequently met or exceeded through the resulting product design process and the design and operation of the supporting production management system. QFD can be viewed as a set of communication and translation tools. QFD tries to eliminate the gap between what the customer wants in a new product and what the product is capable of delivering. QFD often leads to a clear identification of the major requirements of the customers. These expectations are referred to as the voice of the customer (VOC). See: house of quality.

quality loss function—A parabolic approximation of the quality loss that occurs when a quality characteristic deviates from its target value. The quality loss function is expressed in monetary units: The cost of deviating from the target increases quadratically as the quality characteristic moves farther from the target. The formula used to compute the quality loss function depends on the type of quality characteristic being used. The quality loss function was first introduced in this form by Genichi Taguchi.

quality policy—A top-management statement of the overall quality direction of an organization as required by ISO 9001.

quality score chart—Syn: Q chart.

quality tree—An analytical tool that visualizes that quality is composed of four layers of achievement: (1) inspection, (2) process measurement and improvement, (3) process control, and (4) design for quality.

quality trilogy—A three-pronged approach to managing quality proposed by Joseph Juran. The three legs are quality planning (developing the products and processes required to meet customer needs), quality control (meeting product and process goals), and quality improvement (achieving unprecedented levels of performance). Syn: Juran trilogy.

quantitative forecasting techniques—An approach to forecasting where historical demand data are used to project future demand. Extrinsic and intrinsic techniques are typically used. See: extrinsic forecasting method, intrinsic forecasting method.

quantity-based order system—Syn: fixed reorder quantity inventory model.

quantity discount—A price reduction allowance determined by the quantity or value of a purchase.

quantity discount model—A variation of the economic order quantity model in which the assumption of a single price is relaxed and there is a schedule of prices based on specific volumes. Syn: price-break model.

quantity per—The quantity of a component to be used in the production of its parent. This value is stored in the bill of material and is used to calculate the gross requirements for components during the explosion process of MRP.

quarantine—The setting aside of items from availability for use or sale until all required quality tests have been performed and conformance certified.

quasi manufacturing—A type of service operation that closely resembles a manufacturing process; focus is on production process, technology, costs, and quality.

question mark—In marketing, a slang term for a low market share but high growth rate product. See: growth-share matrix.

queue—A waiting line. In manufacturing, the jobs at a given work center waiting to be processed. As queues increase, so do average queue time and work-in-process inventory.

queue discipline—A parameter in queuing theory that determines the order in which customers are to be served.

queue length—The quantity of items in a queue that are awaiting service.

queue management—Tactics to deal with an excess number of items, such as products or customers, waiting in line for service.

queue ratio—The ratio of the hours of slack within the job to the queue originally scheduled.

queue time—The amount of time a job waits at a work center before setup or work is performed on the job. Queue time is one element of total manufacturing lead time. Increases in queue time result in direct increases to manufacturing lead time and work-in-process inventories.

queuing analysis—The study of waiting lines. See: queuing theory.

queuing theory—The collection of models dealing with waiting line problems; for example, problems for which customers or units arrive at some service facility at which waiting lines or queues may build. Syn: waiting line theory. See: queuing analysis.

quick asset ratio—A measure of a firm's financial stability. It is defined as (current assets – inventory)/current liabilities. A value greater than one is desirable. Syn: quick ratio, acid test, acid test ratio.

quick changeover—The ability to shorten machine setups between different machine operation requirements to increase process flexibility. Most concentration is on reducing external setup time first, then on internal setup issues. This reduces economic order quantity, queue and manufacturing lead times, and work in process inventory; it improves quality, process, and material flows.

quick ratio—Syn: quick asset ratio.

quick-response manufacturing (QRM)—A manufacturing technique based on time-based competition to drive continuous improvement. With its roots in the strategies adopted by the Japanese in the 1980s and developed further by the University of Wisconsin, quick-response manufacturing focuses on the relentless pursuit of lead time reduction. Using manufacturing resources planning for higher-level planning, it often uses a replenishment technique called paired-cell overlapping loops of cards, which combines the best of push and pull strategies. See: paired-cell overlapping loops of cards.

quick-response program (QRP)—A system of linking final retail sales with production and shipping schedules back through the chain of supply; employs point-of-sale scanning and electronic data interchange, and may use direct shipment from a factory to a retailer.

quotation—A statement of price, terms of sale, and description of goods or services offered by a supplier to a prospective purchaser; a bid. When given in response to an inquiry, it is usually considered an offer to sell. See: bid.

quotation expiration date—The date on which a quoted price is no longer valid.

R

rack—A storage device for handling material in pallets. A rack usually provides storage for pallets arranged in vertical sections with one or more pallets to a tier. Some racks accommodate more than one-pallet-deep storage.

racking—A function performed by a rack-jobber, a full-function intermediary who performs all regular warehousing functions and some retail functions, typically stocking a display rack.

radio frequency identification (RFID)—A system using electronic tags to store data about items. Accessing these data is accomplished through a specific radio frequency and does not require close proximity or line-of-sight access for data retrieval. See: active tag, passive tag, semi-passive tag.

RAM—Abbreviation for responsibility assignment matrix.

ramp rate—The speed at which a company expands or grows. Syn: growth trajectory.

R&D—Abbreviation for research and development.

R&D order—Syn: experimental order.

random access—A manner of storing records in a computer file so that an individual record may be accessed without reading other records.

random cause—Syn: common causes.

random component—A component of demand usually describing the impact of uncontrollable variation on demand. See: decomposition, time series analysis.

random events—1) occurrences that have no discernable pattern. 2) In statistics, unexplained movements occurring in historical (time series) data. See: random variation.

random-location storage—A storage technique in which parts are placed in any space that is empty when they arrive at the storeroom. Although this random method requires the use of a locator file to identify part locations, it often requires less storage space than a fixed-

R

location storage method. Syn: floating inventory location system, floating storage location. See: fixed-location storage.

random numbers—A sequence of integers or group of numbers (often in the form of a table) that show absolutely no relationship to each other anywhere in the sequence. At any point, all values have an equal chance of occurring, and they occur in an unpredictable fashion.

random sample—A selection of observations taken from all the observations of a phenomenon in such a way that each chosen observation has the same possibility of selection.

random variation—A fluctuation in data that is caused by uncertain or random occurrences. See: random events.

range—In statistics, the spread in a series of observations. For example, the anticipated demand for a particular product might vary from a low of 10 to a high of 500 per week. The range would therefore be 500 – 10, or 490.

range chart—Syn: R chart.

rapid prototyping—1) The transformation of product designs into physical prototypes. Rapid prototyping relies on techniques such as cross-functional teams, data sharing, and advanced computer and communication technology (e.g., CAD, CAM, stereolithography, data links). Rapid prototyping involves producing the prototype on production equipment as often as possible. It improves product development times and allows for cheaper and faster product testing, assessment of the ease of assembly and costs, and validation before actual production tooling. 2) The transformation of system designs into computer system prototypes with which the users can experiment to determine the adequacy of the design to address their needs. See: 3D printing.

rapid replenishment—A replenishment strategy in which the supplier prepares shipments at predetermined intervals and varies the quantity based on recent sales data. Sales data may be supplied via a point-of-sale system. See: continuous replenishment.

rate-based scheduling—A method for scheduling and producing based on a periodic rate (e.g., daily, weekly, monthly). This method has traditionally been applied to high-volume and process industries. The concept has also been applied within job shops using cellular layouts and mixed-model level schedules where the production rate is matched to the selling rate.

rate basis point—The center of shipping in a specific area; used to determine shipping rates.

rated capacity—The expected output capability of a resource or system. Capacity is traditionally calculated from such data as planned hours, efficiency, and utilization. The rated capacity is equal to hours available × efficiency × utilization. Syn: calculated capacity, effective capacity, nominal capacity, standing capacity.

rate of return on investment—The efficiency ratio relating profit or cash flow incomes to investments. Several different measures of this ratio are in common use.

rate variance—The difference between the actual output rate of product and the planned or standard output rate.

ratification—The situation wherein a principal, failing to repudiate an agent's unauthorized conduct, is bound by the conduct.

rationalization exercise—A process of reducing the population of figures such as stockkeeping unit counts or supplier lists.

rationing—The allocation of product among consumers. When price is used to allocate product, it is allocated to those willing to pay the most.

raw material—Purchased items or extracted materials that are converted via the manufacturing process into components and products.

raw materials inventory—Inventory of material that has not undergone processing at a facility.

RCCP—Abbreviation for rough-cut capacity planning.

R chart—A control chart in which the subgroup range, R, is used to evaluate the stability of the variability within a process. Syn: range chart.

reach—The percentage of target customers who receive an advertising message.

reactive maintenance—Syn: breakdown maintenance.

reactor—A special vessel to contain a chemical reaction.

real property—Land and associated rights improvements, utility systems, buildings, and other structures.

real time—The technique of coordinating data processing with external related physical events as they occur, thereby permitting prompt reporting of conditions. See: online service.

reasonable rate—A pricing strategy that allows a company to profit, but not to achieve monopolistic profits. Normally determined by industry pricing analysis.

receipt—1) The physical acceptance of an item into a stocking location. 2) Often, the transaction reporting of this activity.

receivables conversion period—The length of time required to collect sales receipts. Syn: average collection period.

receiving—The function encompassing the physical receipt of material, the inspection of the shipment for conformance with the purchase order (quantity and damage), the identification and delivery to destination, and the preparation of receiving reports.

receiving point—The location to which material is being shipped. Ant: shipping point.

receiving report—A document used by the receiving function of a company to inform others of the receipt of goods purchased.

recency, frequency, monetary (RFM)—Giving customers the highest rating who have bought recently, bought many times, and bought in large amounts.

reconciling inventory—Comparing the physical inventory figures with the perpetual inventory record and making any necessary corrections.

reconsignment—Permission by a carrier to alter the destination and/or consignee after the shipment has reached its original destination.

record—1) A collection of data fields arranged in a predefined format. 2) A set of related data that a computer program treats as a unit.

record accuracy—A measure of the conformity of recorded values in a bookkeeping system to the actual values; for example, the on-hand balance of an item maintained in a computer record relative to the actual on-hand balance of the items in the stockroom.

recovery time—In periods of insufficient capacity, jobs back up indefinitely. This leads to increased lead times and missed due dates. Recovery time is a period of time when capacity exceeds demand to allow the system to empty out. If there is not enough recovery time before the next episode of insufficient capacity, in-process inventory and lead times continue to grow.

recycle—1) The reintroduction of partially processed product or carrier solvents from one operation or task into a previous operation. 2) A recirculation process.

red bead experiment—An experiment developed by W. Edwards Deming to illustrate the impossibility of putting employees in rank order of performance. The experiment shows that it would be a waste of management's time to try to find out why one worker produced more

errors than another; management should instead improve the system, making it possible for everyone to achieve higher quality.

redundancy—1) A backup capability, coming either from extra machines or from extra components within a machine, to reduce the effects of breakdowns. 2) The use of one or more extra or duplicating components in a system or equipment (often to increase reliability).

redundant component—A backup part of a machine or product.

reference capacity model—A simulation model with accurate operational details and demand forecasts that can provide practical capacity utilization predictions. Various alternatives for system operation can be evaluated effectively.

refurbished goods—Syn: remanufactured parts.

refurbished parts—Syn: remanufactured parts.

regen—Slang abbreviation for regeneration MRP. Pronounced "ree-jen."

regeneration MRP—An MRP processing approach where the master production schedule is totally reexploded down through all bills of material, to maintain valid priorities. New requirements and planned orders are completely recalculated or "regenerated" at that time. Ant: net change MRP.

registration to standards—A process in which an accredited, independent third-party organization conducts an on-site audit of a company's operations against the requirements of the standard to which the company wants to be registered. Upon successful completion of the audit, the company receives a certificate indicating that it has met the standard requirements.

regression analysis—A statistical technique for determining the best mathematical expression describing the functional relationship between one response and one or more independent variables. See: least-squares method.

regularized schedule—A schedule having certain items produced at regular intervals.

rejected inventory—Inventory that does not meet quality requirements but has not yet been sent to rework, scrapped, or returned to a supplier.

rejection—The act of identifying an item as not meeting quality specifications.

relational database—A software program that allows users to obtain information drawn from two or more data-

R

bases that are made up of two-dimensional arrays of data.

relationship map—A graphic map of the relationship between the business functions. It shows the inputs and outputs flow across functions. It is useful to show how processes are currently performed, disconnections in processes, and proposed processes. Relationship maps show the products and services of a given unit, how work flows through organizational boundaries, and the relationships between functions represented by boxes in the map.

relationship marketing—A form of target marketing in which the type and time of communications are determined by the customer. Syn: permission marketing.

release—The authorization to produce or ship material that has already been ordered.

released order—Syn: open order.

release-to-start manufacturing—The time it takes from when an order is released until the beginning of the manufacturing process. This delay occurs because of the movement of materials and the changing of lines. It is non-productive time that increases lead time.

relevant costs—Those costs incurred because of a decision. The costs would not have resulted unless the decision was made and implemented. They are relevant to the decision.

relevant range—The range of activity planned for a firm.

reliability—The probability that a product will perform its specified function under prescribed conditions without failure for a specified period of time. It is a design parameter that can be made part of a requirements statement. See: mean time between failures, mean time for failures.

reliability engineering—The function responsible for the determination and application of appropriate reliability tasks and criteria during the design, development, manufacture, test, and support of a product that will result in achieving of the specified product reliability.

remanufactured parts—Components or assemblies that are refurbished or rebuilt to perform the original function. Syn: refurbished goods, refurbished parts.

remanufacturing—1) An industrial process in which worn-out products are restored to like-new condition. In contrast, a repaired product normally retains its identity, and only those parts that have failed or are badly worn are replaced or serviced. 2) The manufacturing environment where worn-out products are restored to like-new condition.

remanufacturing resource planning—A manufacturing resource planning system designed for remanufacturing facilities.

remedial maintenance—Unscheduled maintenance performed to return a product or process to a specified performance level after a failure or malfunction.

remote diagnostics—The capability of determining the cause of a problem from an off-site location.

reneging—A queuing theory term for leaving a line after entering it but before receiving service. See: balking.

reorder cycle—Syn: replenishment lead time.

reorder point—Syn: order point.

reorder quantity—1) In a fixed-reorder quantity system of inventory control, the fixed quantity that should be ordered each time the available stock (on-hand plus on-order) falls to or below the reorder point. 2) In a variable reorder quantity system, the amount ordered from time period to time period will vary. Syn: replenishment order quantity.

repairables—Items that are technically feasible to repair economically.

repair bill of material—In remanufacturing, the bill of material defining the actual work required to return a product to service. This bill is constructed based on inspection and determination of actual requirements. See: disassembly bill of material.

repair factor—The percentage of time on average that an item must be repaired for return to a serviceable condition. The repair factor is also expressed as a percentage applied to the quantity per assembly on the bill of material. It is useful for forecasting materials and capacity requirements for planning purposes. Syn: frequency of repair. See: occurrence factor, replacement factor.

repair order—Syn: rework order.

repair parts—Syn: service parts.

repair parts demand—Syn: service parts demand.

repeatability of measurement—The variation in measurements obtained when one measurement instrument is used several times by an appraiser while measuring the identical characteristic on the same part.

repetitive industries—The group of manufacturers that produce high-volume, low-variety products such as spark plugs, lawn mowers, and paper clips. See: repetitive manufacturing.

repetitive manufacturing—The repeated production of the same discrete products or families of products. Repetitive methodology minimizes setups, inventory, and manufacturing lead times by using production lines, assembly lines, or cells. Work orders are no longer necessary; production scheduling and control are based on production rates. Products may be standard or assembled from modules. Repetitive is not a function of speed or volume. Syn: repetitive process, repetitive production. See: project manufacturing.

repetitive process—Syn: repetitive manufacturing.

repetitive production—Syn: repetitive manufacturing.

replacement cost—A method of setting the value of inventories based upon the cost of the next purchase.

replacement cost systems—A method of inventory valuation that assigns an item cost based on the next item price incurred.

replacement factor—The percentage of time on average that an item will require replacement. The replacement factor is also expressed as a percentage applied to the quantity per assembly on the bill of material. It is useful for forecasting materials and capacity requirements for planning purposes. See: occurrence factor, repair factor.

replacement order—An order for the replacement of material that has been scrapped.

replacement parts—Parts that can be used as substitutes that differ from completely interchangeable service parts in that they require some physical modification (e.g., boring, cutting, drilling) before they can replace the original part.

replan cycle—The time it takes to implement a new production plan into the plant's actual production plan. Done after completion of the last cycle and is a rolling document.

replanning frequency—In an MRP system, the amount of time between successive runs of the MRP model. If the planner does not run MRP frequently enough, the material plan becomes inaccurate as material requirements and inventory status change with the passage of time.

replenishment—Relocating material from a bulk storage area to an order pick storage area, and documenting this relocation.

replenishment interval—Syn: replenishment period.

replenishment lead time—The total period of time that elapses from the moment it is determined that a product should be reordered until the product is back on the shelf available for use. Syn: reorder cycle.

replenishment order quantity—Syn: reorder quantity.

replenishment period—The time between successive replenishment orders. Syn: replenishment interval. See: review period.

reprocessed material—Goods that have gone through selective rework or recycle.

reproducibility—A production program's ability to regularly produce products of the correct quantity and quality.

request for information (RFI)—An inquiry to a potential supplier about that supplier's product or service for potential use in the business. The inquiry can provide certain business requirements or be of a more general exploratory nature. See: request for proposal (RFP).

request for proposal (RFP)—A document used to solicit vendor responses when the functional requirements and features are known but no specific product is in mind. Syn: invitation for bid (IFB). See: request for information (RFI).

request for quote (RFQ)—A document used to solicit vendor responses when a product has been selected and price quotations are needed from several vendors.

required capacity—Syn: capacity required.

requirements definitions—Specifying the inputs, files, processing, and outputs for a new system, but without expressing computer alternatives and technical details.

requirements explosion—The process of calculating the demand for the components of a parent item by multiplying the parent item requirements by the component usage quantity specified in the bill of material. Syn: explosion.

requirements traceability—The capability to determine the source of demand requirements through record linkages. It is used in analyzing requirements to make adjustments to plans for material or capacity. See: pegging.

requisition—Syn: parts requisition.

rerouting flexibility—Accommodating unavailability of equipment by quickly and easily using alternate machines in the processing sequence.

rescheduling—The process of changing order or operation due dates, usually as a result of their being out of phase with when they are needed.

rescheduling assumption—A fundamental assumption of MRP logic that existing open orders can be rescheduled in nearer time periods far more easily than new orders can be released and received. As a result, planned order receipts are not created until all scheduled receipts have been applied to cover gross requirements.

rescheduling notice—A message from planning system software to change the planned start and/or finish date of an order. This often is the result of a change in plans of a parent item. See: nervousness.

research and development (R&D)—A function that performs basic and applied research and develops potential new products.

resellers—Organizations intermediate in the manufacturing and distribution process, such as wholesalers and retailers.

reservation—The process of designating stock for a specific order or schedule. See: allocation.

reserve—Contingency funds set aside to mitigate risk.

reserved material—Material on hand or on order that is assigned to specific future production or customer orders. Syn: allocated material, assigned material, obligated material.

reserve stock—Syn: safety stock.

residence time—Syn: process time.

residual income—The net operating income that an investment center earns above the minimum required return on its operating assets.

residual inventory—Inventory created by the canceling or rescheduling of an order or left over because of lot sizing.

resiliency—Resiliency in the supply chain is the ability to return to a position of equilibrium after experiencing an event that causes operational results to deviate from expectations. Resiliency is increased by strategically increasing the number of response options and/or decreasing the time to execute those options. Resiliency is improved by risk monitoring and control.

resource—Anything that adds value to a good or service in its creation, production, or delivery.

resource breakdown structure—A hierarchical structure that breaks resources into categories and types; can be useful for plan resource schedules, including human resources.

resource calendar—A calendar of working days and nonworking days that shows when resources are idle. Typically, the calendar includes holidays and weekends. See: manufacturing calendar.

resource-constrained schedule—Syn: resource-limited schedule. See: drum-buffer-rope.

resource contention—Simultaneous need for a common resource. Syn: concurrency.

resource driver—The objects that are linked to an activity that consumes resources at a specified rate. For example, a resource driver is a purchase order (the object) that when placed (the activity) consumes hours (the rate) of purchasing (the resource).

resource leveling—The process of scheduling (and rescheduling) the start and finish dates of operations (or activities) to achieve a consistent rate of resource usage so that resource requirements do not exceed resource availability for a given time period. Syn: leveling.

resource limited schedule—Project schedule with no early or late start or finish dates. The activity, and scheduled start and finish dates, show the expected availability of resources. Syn: resource-constrained schedule.

resource-limited scheduling—The scheduling of activities so that predetermined resource availability pools are not exceeded. Activities are started as soon as resources are available (with respect to logical constraints), as required by the activity. When not enough of a resource exists to do all tasks on a given day, a priority decision is made. Project finish may be delayed, if necessary, to alter schedules constrained by resource usage.

resource management—1) The planning and validation of all organizational resources. 2) The effective identification, planning, scheduling, execution, and control of all organizational resources to produce a good or service that provides customer satisfaction and supports the organization's competitive edge and, ultimately, organizational goals. 3) An emerging field of study emphasizing the systems perspective, encompassing both the product and process life cycles, and focusing on the integration of organizational resources toward the effective realization of organizational goals. Resources include materials; maintenance, repair, and operating supplies; production and supporting equipment; facilities; direct and indirect employees; staff; administrative and professional employees; information; knowledge; and capital. Syn: integrated resource management.

resource planning—Capacity planning conducted at the business plan level. The process of establishing, measuring, and adjusting limits or levels of long-range capacity. Resource planning is normally based on the production plan but may be driven by higher level plans beyond the time horizon for the production plan (e.g., the business plan). It addresses those resources that take long periods of time to acquire. Resource planning decisions always require top management approval. Syn: resource requirements planning. See: capacity planning, long-term planning.

resource profile—The standard hours of load placed on a resource by time period. Production lead-time data are taken into account to provide time-phased projections of the capacity requirements for individual production facilities. See: bill of resources, capacity planning using overall factors, product load profile, rough-cut capacity planning.

resource requirements planning—Syn: resource planning.

response time—The elapse of time or average delay between the initiation of a transaction and the results of the transaction.

responsibility assignment matrix (RAM)—A tool to ensure that each component of work in a project is assigned to a responsible person.

responsible landfill—Landfill operations designed to turn waste into recoverable resources, minimize the amount of space consumed, and maximize the operational life of the landfill.

responsible procurement—Assuring the use of ethical sources of goods and services to bring about a positive impact and minimize the negative impact on societies and environments, including reduce, reuse, and recycle of materials, where a firm does business. It includes processes for identifying, assessing, and managing the environmental, social, and ethical risk in the supply chain. Syn: environmentally responsible purchasing.

responsiveness—A dimension of service quality referring to the promptness and helpfulness in providing a service.

retailer—A business that takes title to products and re-sells them to final consumers.

retail method—A method of inventory valuation in which the value is determined by applying a predetermined

percentage based on retail markup to the retail price, to determine its inventory value based on cost.

retainage—A percentage of a contract value that is withheld pending project completion and approval.

retention efficiency—In marketing, a measurement of how well a company creates repeat customers.

retirement of debt—The termination of a debt obligation by appropriate settlement with the lender. Understood to be in full amount unless partial settlement is specified.

retrofit—An item that replaces components originally installed on equipment; a modification to in-service equipment.

return disposal costs—The costs that occur from discarding or recycling products that are returned because they have reached the end of their useful life or are obsolete. Commonplace in consumer goods industry.

return goods handling—The work a company puts into accepting returned goods from their customers.

return material authorization (RMA)—1) A form that must be completed that describes the product returned and why it was returned. 2) A number given to authorize the acceptance of returned items. 3) Should require signatory authorization to return the goods.

return merchandise authorization—Syn: return material authorization.

return on assets (ROA)—Net income for the previous 12 months divided by total assets. See: return on owner's equity (ROE).

return on investment (ROI)—A relative measure of financial performance that provides a means for comparing various investments by calculating the profits returned during a specified time period. In the theory of constraints, ROI is calculated as throughput minus operating expense divided by investment.

return on net assets—Profit divided by assets excluding depreciation.

return on owner's equity (ROE)—A financial measurement of how successful a company is in creating income for the owners of the organization. A comparison of the ROE with the ROA indicates the effectiveness of financial leverage employed by the firm. The measurement is calculated by dividing the net income by average owner's equity. See: return on assets (ROA).

returns inventory costs—All of the costs associated with handling returned inventory.

R

returns management process—A process of handling returns that includes environmentally sound disposal or recycling, composing repair instructions, warranty repairs, and collecting return data.

returns processing cost—All of the costs associated with dealing with returned items after they have been received. These costs occur when returned items are repaired, discarded, or replaced.

return to supplier—Material that has been rejected by the buyer's inspection department and is awaiting shipment back to the supplier for repair or replacement.

revenue—The income received by a company from sales or other sources, such as stock owned in other companies.

reverse auction—An internet auction in which suppliers attempt to underbid their competitors. Company identities are known only by the buyer.

reverse engineering—The process of disassembling, evaluating, and redesigning a competitor's product for the purpose of manufacturing a product with similar characteristics without violating any of the competitor's proprietary manufacturing technologies.

reverse flow scheduling—A scheduling procedure used in some process industries for building process train schedules that starts with the last stage and proceeds backward (countercurrent to the process flow) through the process structure.

reverse logistics—A complete supply chain dedicated to the reverse flow of products and materials for the purpose of returns, repair, remanufacture, and/or recycling.

reverse logistics service—A service that arranges for the disposal of returned products.

reverse supply chain—The planning and controlling of the processes of moving goods from the point of consumption back to the point of origin for repair, reclamation, recycling, or disposal. See: reverse logistics.

review period—The time between successive evaluations of inventory status to determine whether to reorder. See: replenishment period.

revision level—A number or letter representing the number of times a part drawing or specification has been changed.

rework—Reprocessing to salvage a defective item or part.

rework lead time—The time required to rework material in-house or at a supplier's location.

rework order—A manufacturing order to rework and salvage defective parts or products. Syn: repair order, spoiled work order.

RFID—Abbreviation for radio frequency identification.

RFM—Abbreviation for recency, frequency, monetary.

RFP—Abbreviation for request for proposal.

RFQ—Abbreviation for request for quote.

right the first time—A term used to convey the concept that it is beneficial and more cost-effective to take the necessary steps the first time to ensure that a good or service meets its requirements than to provide a good or service that will need rework or not meet customers' needs. In other words, an organization should engage in defect prevention rather than defect detection.

right-to-work state—A state that allows workers to choose whether or not to join a union.

risk acceptance—A decision to take no action to deal with a risk or an inability to format a plan to deal with the risk.

risk adjusted discount rate—A discount rate that is higher for more risky projects and lower for less risky projects.

risk analysis—A review of the uncertainty associated with the research, development, and production of a product, service, or project.

risk avoidance—Changing a plan to eliminate a risk or to protect plan objectives from its impact.

risk breakdown structure—A tool that helps identify potential project risks, organized by risk categories and subcategories.

risk category—A cluster of risk causes with a label such as external, environmental, technical, or organizational.

risk management planning—The process of defining how to identify and minimize risk factors for a project.

risk mitigation—Reducing the exposure to risk, either by its likelihood or its impact.

risk pooling—A method often associated with the management of inventory risk. Manufacturers and retailers that experience high variability in demand for their products can pool together common inventory components associated with a broad family of products to buffer the overall burden of having to deploy inventory for each discrete product.

risk register—A report that has summary information on qualitative risk analysis, quantitative risk analysis, and risk response planning. This register contains all identified risks and associated details.

risk response plan—A document defining known risks including description, cause, likelihood, costs, and proposed responses. It also identifies current status on each risk.

risk response planning—The process of developing a plan to avoid risks and to mitigate the effect of those that cannot be avoided.

RMA—Abbreviation for return material authorization.

ROA—Abbreviation for return on assets.

robotics—Replacing activities previously performed by humans with mechanical devices or robots that can be either operated by humans or run by computer. Difficult-to-do, dangerous, or monotonous tasks are likely candidates for robots to perform.

robust design—Type of design for a product or service that plans for intended performance even in the face of a harsh environment.

robustness—The condition of a product or process design that remains relatively stable with a minimum of variation even though factors that influence operations or usage, such as environment and wear, are constantly changing.

ROE—Abbreviation for return on owner's equity.

ROI—Abbreviation for return on investment.

rolling forecast—Moving the forecast horizon forward to new periods by adding recent data (and perhaps dropping the oldest data).

rolling wave planning—A form of planning where the work to be performed in the near term is planned in detail and longer term work is planned at a lesser level of detail.

roll-on/roll-off container ship—A ship that allows trailers to be driven on and off without the use of cranes.

root cause analysis—Analytical methods to determine the core problem(s) of an organization, process, product, market, and so forth. See: current reality tree, five whys, stratification analysis.

rope—One of the three devices required for proper management of operations. (The other two are drum and buffer.) The rope is the information flow from the drum to the front of the line (material release), which chokes the release of materials to match the flow through the constraint.

RORO—Acronym for roll-on/roll-off container ship.

rough-cut capacity planning (RCCP)—The process of converting the master production schedule into requirements for key resources, often including labor; machinery; warehouse space; suppliers' capabilities; and, in some cases, money. Comparison to available or demonstrated capacity is usually done for each key resource. This comparison assists the master scheduler in establishing a feasible master production schedule. Three approaches to performing RCCP are the bill of labor (resources, capacity) approach, the capacity planning using overall factors approach, and the resource profile approach. See: bill of resources, capacity planning, capacity planning using overall factors, product load profile, resource profile.

route sheet—Syn: routing.

routing—1) Information detailing the method of manufacture of a particular item. It includes the operations to be performed, their sequence, the various work centers involved, and the standards for setup and run. In some companies, the routing also includes information on tooling, operator skill levels, inspection operations and testing requirements, and so on. Syn: bill of operations, instruction sheet, manufacturing data sheet, operation chart, operation list, operation sheet, route sheet, routing sheet. See: bill of labor, bill of resources. 2) In information systems, the process of defining the path a message will take from one computer to another computer.

routing sheet—Syn: routing.

run—A quantity of production being processed.

run chart—A graphical technique that illustrates how a process is performing over time. By statistically analyzing a run chart, a process can be determined to be under or out of control. The most common types of data used to construct the charts are ranges, averages, percentages/counts, and individual process attributes (e.g., temperature). Syn. run diagram. See: C chart, P chart, R chart, U chart, X-bar chart.

run diagram—Syn: run chart.

running sum of forecast errors—The arithmetic sum of the differences between actual and forecasted demand for the periods being evaluated.

run order—Syn: manufacturing order.

run-out list—1) A list of items to be scheduled into production in sequence by the dates at which the present available stock is expected to be exhausted. 2) A statement of ingredients required to use up an available resource (e.g., how much "a" resource is required to consume 300 pounds of "x").

run-out method—A method of assigning available production or storage capacity to products based on the product's demand and inventory level.

run sheet—A log-type document used in continuous processes to record raw materials used, quantity produced, in-process testing results, and so on. It may serve as an input document for inventory records.

run size—Syn: standard batch quantity.

run standards—Syn: run time.

run time—The time required to process a piece or lot at a specific operation. Run time does not include setup time. Syn: run standards.

rush order—An order that for some reason must be fulfilled in less than normal lead time.

S

safety capacity—In the theory of constraints: The planned amount by which the available capacity exceeds current productive capacity. This capacity provides protection from planned activities, such as resource contention, and preventive maintenance and unplanned activities, such as resource breakdown, poor quality, rework, or lateness. Safety capacity plus productive capacity plus excess capacity is equal to 100 percent of capacity. Syn: capacity cushion. See: protective capacity.

safety factor—1) The ratio of average strength to the worst stress expected. It is essential that the variation, in addition to the average value, be considered in design. 2) The numerical value used in the service function (based on the standard deviation or mean absolute deviation of the forecast) to provide a given level of customer service. For example, if the item MAD is 100 and a .95 customer service level (safety factor of 2.06) is desired, then a safety stock of 206 units should be carried. This safety stock must be adjusted if the forecast interval and item lead times differ. Syn: service factor. See: service function.

safety lead time—An element of time added to normal lead time to protect against fluctuations in lead time so that an order can be completed before its real need date. When used, the MRP system, in offsetting for lead time, will plan both order release and order completion for earlier dates than it would otherwise. Syn: protection time, safety time.

safety stock—1) In general, a quantity of stock planned to be in inventory to protect against fluctuations in demand or supply. 2) In the context of master production scheduling, the additional inventory and capacity planned as protection against forecast errors and short-term changes in the backlog. Overplanning can be used to create safety stock. Syn: buffer stock, reserve stock. See: hedge, inventory buffer.

safety time—Syn: safety lead time.

salable goods—A part or assembly authorized for sale to final customers through the marketing function.

sale-and-leaseback—An agreement by which a firm first sells its assets to a financial institution and then leases these same assets from the financial institution.

sales and operations planning (S&OP)—A process to develop tactical plans that provide management the ability to strategically direct its businesses to achieve competitive advantage on a continuous basis by integrating customer-focused marketing plans for new and existing products with the management of the supply chain. The process brings together all the plans for the business (sales, marketing, development, manufacturing, sourcing, and financial) into one integrated set of plans. It is performed at least once a month and is reviewed by management at an aggregate (product family) level. The process must reconcile all supply, demand, and new-product plans at both the detail and aggregate levels and tie to the business plan. It is the definitive statement of the company's plans for the near to intermediate term, covering a horizon sufficient to plan for resources and to support the annual business planning process. Executed properly, the sales and operation planning process links the strategic plans for the business with its execution and reviews performance measurements for continuous improvement. See: aggregate planning, executive sales and operations planning, production plan, production planning, sales plan, tactical planning.

sales cycle time—Time from a product entering a floor until it is completely sold out.

sales forecast—Syn: forecast accuracy, forecast.

sales mix—The proportion of individual product-type sales volumes that make up the total sales volume.

sales order configuration—Syn: customer order servicing system.

sales order number—A unique control number assigned to each new customer order, usually during order entry. It is often used by order promising, master scheduling, cost accounting, invoicing, and so forth. For some make-to-order products, it can also take the place of an end item part number by becoming the control number that is scheduled through the finishing operations.

sales plan—A time-phased statement of expected customer orders anticipated to be received (incoming sales, not outgoing shipments) for each major product family or item. It represents sales and marketing management's commitment to take all reasonable steps necessary to achieve this level of actual customer orders. The sales plan is a necessary input to the production planning process (or sales and operations planning process). It is expressed in units identical to those used for the production plan (as well as in sales dollars). See: aggregate planning, production plan, production planning, sales and operations planning.

sales planning—The process of determining the overall sales plan to best support customer needs and operations capabilities while meeting general business objectives of profitability, productivity, competitive customer lead times, and so on, as expressed in the overall business plan. See: production planning, sales and operations planning.

sales promotion—1) Sales activities that supplement both personal selling and marketing, coordinate the two, and help to make them effective (e.g., displays). 2) More loosely, the combination of personal selling, advertising, and all supplementary selling activities. 3) Promotion activities—other than advertising, publicity, and personal selling—that stimulate interest, trial, or purchase by final customers or others in the marketing channel.

sales quota—The level of sales that an individual or group is expected to meet.

sales representative—An employee authorized to accept a customer's order for a product. Sales representatives usually go to the customer's location when industrial products are being marketed.

salvage—Property that, because of its worn, damaged, deteriorated, or incomplete condition or specialized nature has no reasonable prospect of sale or use as serviceable property without major repairs or alterations, but that has some value in excess of its scrap value.

salvage value—1) The cost recovered or that could be recovered from used property when removed, sold, or scrapped. A factor in appraisal of property value and in computing depreciation. 2) The market value of a machine or facility at any point in time. Normally, an estimate of an asset's net value at the end of its estimated life.

sample—A portion of a universe of data chosen to estimate some characteristics about the whole universe. The universe of data could consist of sizes of customer orders, number of units of inventory, number of lines on a purchase order, and so forth.

sample average—A key measure that represents the central tendency of a sample.

sample range—The largest value in a sample minus the smallest value in the sample.

sample size—The number of elements selected for analysis from the population.

sample standard deviation—A key measure that represents the spread or dispersion of a sample.

sampling—1) A statistical process where generalizations regarding an entire body of phenomena are drawn from a relatively small number of observations. 2) In marketing, the delivery of free trial goods to consumers.

sampling distribution—The distribution of values of a statistic calculated from samples of a given size.

sampling plan—Within acceptance sampling, the determination of the sample size and the number of defectives that will trigger rejection of a lot.

sawtooth diagram—A quantity-versus-time graphic representation of the order point/order quantity inventory system showing inventory being received and then used up and reordered.

SBQ—Abbreviation for standard batch quantity.

SBT—Abbreviation for scan-based trading.

SBU—Abbreviation for strategic business unit.

scalability—1) How effectively a company can grow its business in order to meet demand. 2) How effectively the solution to a problem can be scaled up as the problem's size increases.

scan-based trading (SBT)—As an item is sold, scanned information is sent to the manufacturer and creates a replacement order of that item. Used often in large retail store chains as well as large volume product producers.

Scanlon plan—A system of group incentives on a company-wide or plant-wide basis that sets up one measure that reflects the results of all efforts. The universal standard is the ratio of labor costs to sales value added by production. If there is an increase in production sales value with no change in labor costs, productivity has increased while unit cost has decreased.

scanner—An electronic device that optically converts coded information into electrical control signals for data collection or system transaction input.

scarcity—A concept central to economics that means less of a good is freely available than consumers would like.

scatter chart—A graphical technique to analyze the relationship between two variables. Two sets of data are plotted on a graph, with the y axis used for the variable to be predicted and the x axis used for the variable to make the prediction. The graph will show possible relationships (although two variables might appear to be related, they might not be—those who know most about the variables must make that evaluation). The scatter chart is one of the seven tools of quality. Syn: cross plot, scatter diagram, scatterplot.

scatter diagram—Syn: scatter chart.

scatterplot—Syn: scatter chart.

SCEM—Abbreviation for supply chain event management.

scenario forecasts—Plans for how an organization will respond to anticipated future situations.

scenario planning—A planning process that identifies critical events before they occur and use this knowledge to determine effective alternatives.

schedule—A timetable for planned occurrences (e.g., shipping schedule, master production schedule, maintenance schedule, supplier schedule). Some schedules include the starting and ending time for activities (e.g., project schedule).

schedule activity—During a project, a specific piece of work performed that has estimated costs, duration, and resource requirements.

schedule board—Syn: control board.

schedule chart—Usually a large piece of graph paper used in the same manner as a control board. Where the control board often uses strings and markers to represent plans and progress, the schedule chart is typically filled in with pencil. See: control board.

schedule control—Control of a plant floor by schedules rather than by job orders (called order control). Schedules are derived by taking requirements over a period of time and dividing by the number of workdays allowed to run the parts or assemblies. Production completed is compared with the schedule to provide control. This type of control is most frequently used in repetitive and process manufacturing.

scheduled downtime—Planned shutdown of equipment or plant to perform maintenance or to adjust to softening demand.

scheduled finish date—In project management, an activity's planned finish time, normally between the early finish time and the late finish time. It may reflect resource limitations. Syn: planned finish date.

scheduled load—The standard hours of work required by scheduled receipts (i.e., open production orders).

scheduled receipt—An open order that has an assigned due date. See: open order.

scheduled start date—In project management, an activity's planned start time, normally between the early start time and the late start time. It may reflect resource limitations. Syn: planned start date.

schedule harmony—In supply chains, the arrival of goods at a transfer point with a small buffer time in front of their departure via a different transportation mode.

schedule performance index (SPI)—Earned value (EV) divided by planned value (PV), which measures a project's schedule efficiency.

scheduler—A general term that can refer to a material planner, dispatcher, or a combined function.

schedule variance (SV)—Earned value (EV) minus planned value (PV), which measures a project's schedule performance.

scheduling—The act of creating a schedule, such as a shipping schedule, master production schedule, maintenance schedule, or supplier schedule.

scheduling algorithm—Syn: scheduling rules.

scheduling rules—Basic rules that can be used consistently in a scheduling system. Scheduling rules usually specify the amount of time to allow for a move, queue, load calculation, and so forth. Syn: scheduling algorithm.

scientific inventory control—Syn: statistical inventory control.

scientific management—Managing a production system using scientific principles. Usually refers to the principles established by Frederick Taylor.

scope—In project management, the totality of products to be created by a project.

scope change—In project management, a change to a project's scope, usually requiring an adjustment to the project's budget and schedule.

scope definition—In project management, subdividing a project into smaller components to facilitate management.

SCOR®—An acronym for Supply Chain Operations Reference-model.

scorecard—This is a performance measurement tool used by a company that summarizes its key performance indicators. Another use of scorecard is to measure the supply chain members and ensure that their performance is meeting company standards.

scrap—Material outside of specifications and possessing characteristics that make rework impractical.

scrap factor—A factor that expresses the quantity of a particular component that is expected to be scrapped upon receipt from a vendor, completion of production, or while that component is being built into a given assembly. It is usually expressed as a decimal value. For a given operation or process, the scrap factor plus the yield factor is equal to one. If the scrap factor is 30 percent (or .3), then the yield is 70 percent (or .7). In manufacturing planning and control systems, the scrap factor is usually related to a specific item in the item master, but may be related to a specific component in the product structure. For example, if 50 units of a product are required by a customer and a scrap factor of 30 percent (a yield of 70 percent) is expected, then 72 units (computed as 50 units divided by .7) should be started in the manufacturing process. Syn: scrap rate. See: yield, yield factor.

scrap rate—Syn: scrap factor.

s-curve—In project management, graphic display of cumulative project attributes such as costs, labor hours, or percentage of work. The name derives from the typical shape of the curve.

SDS—Abbreviation for single-digit setup.

search engines—Web software that enables a user to find a page or website devoted to a particular topic.

search models—Operations research models that attempt to find optimal solutions with adaptive searching approaches.

seasonal adjustment—Syn: seasonal index.

seasonal component—A component of demand, usually describing the impact of variations that occur because of the time of year (quarter, month, week) on demand. See: decomposition, time series analysis.

seasonal harmonics—Syn: harmonic smoothing.

seasonal index—A number used to adjust data to seasonal demand. Syn: seasonal adjustment. See: base series.

seasonal inventory—Inventory built up to smooth production in anticipation of a peak seasonal demand. Syn: seasonal stock.

seasonality—A repetitive pattern of demand from year to year (or other repeating time interval) with some periods considerably higher than others. Syn: seasonal variation. See: base series.

seasonal stock—Syn: seasonal inventory.

seasonal variation—See: seasonality.

SEC—Abbreviation for the Securities and Exchange Commission (U.S.).

secondary highways—Highways that are predominantly rural in nature.

second-order smoothing—A method of exponential smoothing for trend situations that employs two previously computed averages, the singly and doubly smoothed values, to extrapolate into the future. Syn: double smoothing.

second-tier suppliers (or customers)—A supplier's suppliers (or customer's customers).

secular trend—The general direction of the long-run change in the value of a particular time series.

secure electronic transaction (SET)—In e-commerce, a system for guaranteeing the security of financial transactions conducted over the internet.

secure server—In e-commerce, a web server that protects users' messages from interception while being transmitted over the internet.

Securities and Exchange Commission (SEC)—A U.S. government agency that has primary responsibility for enforcing the federal securities laws and regulating the securities industry. The SEC was created by the Securities Exchange Act of 1934 with a mission to protect investors; maintain fair, orderly, and efficient markets; and facilitate capital formation.

segment customers—Grouping customers by common characteristics to facilitate sales.

seiketsu—A term that refers to standardization (e.g., standard locations for tools and equipment). See: five Ss.

seiri—A term that refers to organizing or throwing away things that are not needed. See: five Ss.

S

seiso—A term that states that a productive workplace is found through cleanliness. See: five Ss.

seiton—A term that refers to neatness in the workplace that is achieved by straightening offices and work areas. See: five Ss.

self-directed work team—Generally, a small, independent, self-organized, and self-controlling group in which members flexibly plan, organize, determine, and manage their duties and actions, as well as perform many other supportive functions. It may work without immediate supervision and can often have authority to select, hire, promote, or discharge its members.

seller's market—A market condition in which goods cannot easily be secured (purchased) and when the economic forces of business tend to cause goods to be priced at the supplier's estimate of value.

selling and administrative cost—Those costs that are associated with the marketing, sales, and administrative functions for a plant or company. This is a function of overhead costing and is an important number in the COGS (costs of goods sold) calculation.

selling expense—An expense or class of expense incurred in selling or marketing (e.g., salespersons' salaries and commissions, advertising, samples, shipping costs).

selling, general, and administrative (SG&A) expenses—The fixed costs associated with a company. Examples are salaries, marketing costs, customer service, occupancy expenses, and other overhead. In retail this is called the "cost of selling."

semifinished goods—Products that have been stored uncompleted awaiting final operations that adapt them to different uses or customer specifications.

semipassive tag—An RFID tag that sends out data, is self-powered, and widens its range by harnessing power from the reader. See: radio frequency identification (RFID).

semiprocess flow—A manufacturing configuration in which most jobs go through the same sequence of operations even though production is in job lots.

semivariable costs—Costs that change in increments. They remain fixed over a given range, and outside that range, the cost changes to a new level.

semiworks—Syn: pilot plant.

send ahead—The movement of a portion of a lot of material to a subsequent operation before completion of the current operation for all units of the lot. The purpose of sending material ahead is to reduce the manufacturing lead time. See: overlapped schedule.

sensei—A Japanese word meaning teacher or one with experience.

sensitivity analysis—A technique for determining how much an expected outcome or result will change in response to a given change in an input variable. For example, given a projected level of resources, what would be the effect on net income if variable costs of production increased 20 percent?

sensors—Devices that can monitor differences in conditions to control equipment on a dynamic basis.

separable cost—A cost that is assignable to a given portion of a business.

sequencing—Determining the order in which a manufacturing facility is to process a number of different jobs in order to achieve certain objectives.

sequential—In numeric sequence, normally in ascending order.

sequential development process—A process in which the product or services idea must clear specific hurdles before it can go on the next development phase.

sequential-sampling plan—Controlling quality by repeatedly sampling units and each time making a decision to accept or reject a batch or to continue sampling.

serial number—A unique number assigned for identification to a single piece that will never be repeated for similar pieces. Serial numbers are usually applied by the manufacturer but can be applied at other points, including by the distributor or wholesaler.

serial shipping container code—An 18-character designation identifying boxes or pallets that are part of a shipment covered by an automated shipment notice.

serpentine picking—A picking technique aimed at reducing travel time by 50 percent and improving the flow of pickers down each aisle. This technique involves picking from both sides of each aisle as the picker goes down it. This is in contrast to picking from one side of the aisle and then crossing to the other side.

server—A computer, or software package, that provides a specific kind of service to client software running on other computers. The term can refer to a particular piece of software, for example a web server, or to the machine on which the software is running. A single server machine could have several different server software packages running on it, thus providing many different servers to clients on the network.

server address—The internet address of a server.

server factory—A facility making minor improvements to products; set up primarily to avoid the host country's barriers to trade.

service—Sometimes used to describe those activities that support the production or distribution functions in any organization, such as customer service and field service.

serviceability—1) Design characteristic that facilitates the easy and efficient performance of service activities. Service activities include those activities required to keep equipment in operating condition, such as lubrication, fueling, oiling, and cleaning. 2) A measurement of the degree to which servicing of an item will be accomplished within a given time under specified conditions. See: maintainability. 3) The competitive advantage gained when an organization focuses on aspects such as the speed and courtesy in which customer complaints and questions are answered, following up with customers after the sale to ensure satisfaction, and offering on-site service for product repairs. 4) Measure of repairs and maintenance based on cost, speed, and convenience.

service blueprint—A service analysis method that allows service designers to identify processes involved in the service delivery system, isolate potential failure points in the system, establish time frames for the service delivery, and set standards for each step that can be quantified for measurement.

service bureau model—A business strategy in which a company outsources certain products and services from another company. The company prefers to concentrate on its core business rather than expending resources on the outsourced item.

service capacity—The number of daily customers a firm is designed to serve; actual throughput may be larger or smaller.

service factor—Syn: safety factor.

service function—A mathematical relationship of the safety factor to service level (i.e., the fraction of demand routinely met from stock).

service industry—1) In its narrowest sense, an organization that provides an intangible product (e.g., medical or legal advice). 2) In its broadest sense, all organizations except farming, mining, and manufacturing. This definition of service industry includes retail trade; wholesale trade; transportation and utilities; finance, insurance, and real estate; construction; professional, personal, and social services; and local, state, and federal governments.

service level—Syn: level of service.

service level agreement (SLA)—A document that represents the terms of performance for organic support.

service-oriented architecture (SOA)—A style of information technology (IT) design that guides all aspects of creating and using business services throughout their life cycles, as well as defining and provisioning the IT infrastructure that enables different computer applications to exchange data and participate in business processes, regardless of the operating systems or programming languages underlying those applications.

service parts—Those modules, components, and elements that are planned to be used without modification to replace an original part. Syn: repair parts, spare parts.

service parts demand—The need or requirement for a component to be sold by itself, as opposed to being used in production to make a higher level product. Syn: repair parts demand, spare parts demand.

service parts revenue—The value of sales of replacement parts to external and internal customers, net of discounts and coupons.

service phases—The number of phases necessary to service a new arrival in the system.

service positioning—Syn: product positioning.

service rate—In queuing theory, the rate at which arrivals are processed through the production or service system, in arrivals per unit of time. See: queuing theory.

service reliability—A dimension of service quality referring to the capability of a service provider to perform dependably and accurately.

service response logistics—Obtaining, producing, and distributing material for wholesaling and retailing; supply chain management is focused on location, service, and capacity issues. Syn: integrated logistics.

service time—The time taken to serve a customer (e.g., the time required to fill a sales order or the time required to fill a request at a tool crib).

service vs. investment chart—A curve showing the amount of inventory that will be required to give various levels of customer service.

servo system—A control mechanism linking a system's input and output, designed to feed back data on system output to regulate the operation of the system.

S

SET—Acronym for secure electronic transaction.

setup—1) The work required to change a specific machine, resource, work center, or line from making the last good piece of item A to making the first good piece of item B. 2) The refitting of equipment to neutralize the effects of the last lot produced (e.g., teardown of the just-completed production, preparation of the equipment for production of the next scheduled item). Syn: changeover, turnaround, turnaround time.

setup costs—Costs such as scrap costs, calibration costs, downtime costs, and lost sales associated with preparing the resource for the next product. Syn: changeover costs, turnaround costs.

setup flexibility—The ability for a change to a different product to be made with little delay.

setup lead time—Syn: setup time.

setup time—The time required for a specific machine, resource, work center, process, or line to convert from the production of the last good piece of item A to the first good piece of item B. Syn: setup lead time.

seven new tools (N7)—A set of quality improvement tools developed by the Japanese Society for QC Technique Development. The N7 are affinity diagram, interrelationship digraph, matrix diagram, tree diagram, prioritization matrix, process decision program chart, and activity network diagram. See: basic seven tools of quality.

seven tools of quality—Syn: basic seven tools of quality.

seven zeros—The seven zeros are an essential part of the Toyota Production System. They are zero defects, zero excess lot size, zero setups, zero breakdowns, zero excess handling, zero lead time, and zero surging.

SG&A—Abbreviation for selling, general and administrative.

shape—An element of variability results that measures the output of a process. If a process results in product dimensions falling within a bell-shaped curve, then the process is running normally.

shared services—Consolidation of support processes to form a separate unit to provide services to the parent company and external customers. This lowers costs and may improve support because the shared-services unit is more focused.

shareholder wealth—The present value of all anticipated payments to the shareholders of a firm.

shelf life—The amount of time an item may be held in inventory before it becomes unusable.

shelf life control—A technique of physical first-in, first-out usage aimed at minimizing stock obsolescence.

Shewhart circle of quality—Syn: plan-do-check-action.

Shewhart cycle—Syn: plan-do-check-action.

Shingo's seven wastes—Shigeo Shingo, a pioneer in the Japanese just-in-time philosophy, identified seven barriers to improving manufacturing. They are the waste of overproduction, waste of waiting, waste of transportation, waste of stocks, waste of motion, waste of making defects, and waste of the processing itself.

ship-age limit—The date after which a product cannot be shipped to a customer.

shipper-carriers—Companies that ship goods in their own vehicles. Many large retailers are shipper-carriers as they own their own fleets.

shipping—The function that performs tasks for the outgoing shipment of parts, components, and products. It includes packaging, marking, weighing, and loading for shipment.

shipping lane—A specific route that ocean liners take between ports to help traffic flow and to avoid the most dangerous areas of the ocean.

shipping lead time—The number of working days normally required for goods to move between a shipping and receiving point, plus acceptance time in days at the receiving point.

shipping manifest—A document that lists the pieces in a shipment. A manifest usually covers an entire load regardless of whether the load is to be delivered to a single destination or too many destinations. Manifests usually list the items, piece count, total weight, and the destination name and address for each destination in the load.

shipping order debit memo—The document used to authorize the shipment of rejected material back to the supplier and create a debit entry in accounts payable.

shipping point—The location from which material is sent. Ant: receiving point.

shipping tolerance—An allowable deviation that the supplier can ship over or under the contract quantity.

shitsuke—The effort and discipline required to continually enforce changes made in an organization. See: five Ss.

shojinka—Continually balancing the number of workers in a work center to meet demand with a minimum number of workers. It requires a line design, such as U-shaped, that supports varying the number of workers.

shop calendar—Syn: manufacturing calendar.

shop committee—That committee that represents the union in its relations and negotiations with a company or plant. This is the first stage for the unionized employees to vet complaints.

shop floor control—A system for using data from the shop floor to maintain and communicate status information on shop orders (manufacturing orders) and on work centers. Shop floor control can use order control or flow control to monitor material movement through the facility. The major subfunctions of shop floor control are (1) assigning priority of each shop order; (2) maintaining working-process quantity information; (3) conveying shop order status information to the office; (4) providing actual output data for capacity control purposes; (5) providing quantity by location by shop order for work-in-process inventory and accounting purposes; and (6) providing measurement of efficiency, utilization, and productivity of the workforce and machines. The major subfunctions for flow control are based primarily on production rates and feeding work into production to meet these planned rates, then monitoring and controlling production. See: flow control, order control, production activity control.

shop order—Syn: manufacturing order.

shop order close-out station—A stocking point on the shop floor where completed production of components is transacted (received) into and subsequently transacted (issued) to assembly or other downstream operations. This technique is used to reduce material handling by avoiding the need to move items into and out of stockrooms, while simultaneously enabling a high degree of inventory record accuracy.

shop order reporting—Syn: production reporting and status control.

shop packet—A package of documents used to plan and control the shop floor movement of an order. The packet may include a manufacturing order, operations sheets, engineering blueprints, picking lists, move tickets, inspection tickets, and time tickets.

shop planning—The function of coordinating the availability of material handling, material, resources, setup, and tooling so that an operation or job can be done on a particular machine. Shop planning is often part of the dispatching function. The term shop planning is sometimes used interchangeably with dispatching, although dispatching does not necessarily include shop planning. For example, the selection of jobs might be handled by the centralized dispatching function, while the actual shop planning might be done by the foreman or a representative.

shop scheduling—Syn: operations scheduling.

shop traveler—Syn: traveler.

shortage cost—The marginal profit that is lost when a customer orders an item that is not immediately available in stock.

shortage gaming—When suppliers ration or apportion supplies, and buyers, in response, inflate their orders in an attempt to receive what they actually need.

short-cycle manufacturing—Syn: just in time.

shortest processing time (SPT) rule—A dispatching rule that directs the sequencing of jobs in ascending order by processing time. If this rule is followed, the most jobs at a work center per time period will be processed. As a result, the average lateness of jobs at that work center is minimized, but some jobs will be very late. Syn: smallest processing time rule.

short-haul discrimination—A pricing strategy in which more is charged for a shorter haul than for a longer haul, when the route and the delivery are the same. Used to push the long-haul process.

short-range planning horizon—A planning/forecasting time frame encompassing a few days to at most a few weeks.

short shipment—A situation in which a piece of freight designated by the shipping document is missing from delivery.

short-term planning—The function of adjusting limits or levels of capacity within relatively short periods of time, such as parts of a day, a day, or a week.

shrinkage—Reductions of actual quantities of items in stock, in process, or in transit. The loss may be caused by scrap, theft, deterioration, evaporation, and so forth.

shrinkage factor—A percentage factor used to compensate for the expected loss during the manufacturing cycle of an item. This factor differs from the scrap factor in that it affects all components of the item, where the scrap factor relates to only one component's usage. Syn: shrinkage rate.

shrinkage rate—Syn: shrinkage factor.

SIC—Abbreviation for standard industrial classification.

S

sigma—A Greek letter (Σ) commonly used to designate the standard deviation of a population.

signed message—In information systems, a message for which the sender can be authenticated.

significant part number—A part number that is intended to convey certain information, such as the source of the part, the material in the part, or the shape of the part. Using numbers to represent this information usually makes these part numbers longer than corresponding nonsignificant part numbers. Ant: nonsignificant part number.

significant variances—Those differences between planned and actual performance that exceed established thresholds and that require further review, analysis, and action.

silo effect—A departmental organization with poor communication between departments.

simple interest—1) Interest that is not compounded (i.e., interest not added to the income-producing investment or loan). 2) The interest charged under the condition that interest in any time period is only charged on the principal.

simple moving average—A moving average where the oldest data point is dropped and the newest data point is included in the calculation. All data points are assigned equal weights. See: moving average, weighted moving average.

simple regression—Regression analysis involving only one independent variable.

simplex algorithm—A procedure for solving a general linear programming problem.

simplex method—An approach to solving linear programming models.

simplification—Improving quality and cutting costs by removing complexity from a product or service.

simulation—1) The technique of using representative or artificial data to reproduce in a model various conditions that are likely to occur in the actual performance of a system. It is frequently used to test the behavior of a system under different operating policies. 2) Within MRP II, using the operational data to perform what-if evaluations of alternative plans to answer the question, "Can we do it?" If yes, the simulation can then be run in the financial mode to help answer the question, "Do we really want to?" See: what-if analysis.

simultaneous design/engineering—Syn: participative design/engineering.

simultaneous engineering—Syn: participative design/engineering.

single-card kanban system—Syn: one-card kanban system.

single-channel, single-phase system—A queuing system that has only one channel for arrivals to enter and only one phase to completely service the arrival.

single-digit setup (SDS)—The idea of performing setups in less than 10 minutes. See: single-minute exchange of die.

single exponential smoothing—Syn: first-order smoothing.

single-factor productivity—The average amount of a given product (output) attributed to a unit of a given resource (input). Factors include labor and capital. Syn: partial productivity factor. See: multiple-factor productivity.

single integrator solution—An enterprise resources planning implementation chosen entirely from one vendor.

single-level backflush—A form of backflush that reduces inventory of only the parts used in the next level down in an assembly or subassembly.

single-level bill of material—A display of components that are directly used in a parent item. It shows only the relationships one level down.

single-level where-used—Single-level where-used for a component lists each parent in which that component is directly used and in what quantity. This information is usually made available through the technique known as implosion.

single-minute exchange of die (SMED)—The concept of setup times of less than 10 minutes, developed by Shigeo Shingo in 1970 at Toyota. See: single-digit setup.

single-period inventory models—Inventory models used to define economical or profit maximizing lot-size quantities when an item is ordered or produced only once (e.g., newspapers, calendars, tax guides, greeting cards, or periodicals) while facing uncertain demands. Syn: static inventory models.

single-sampling plan—A quality control method of taking only one sample and then making a decision to accept or reject a batch of items.

single smoothing—Syn: first-order smoothing.

single-source supplier—A company that is selected to have 100 percent of the business for a part although

S

alternate suppliers are available. See: sole-source supplier.

single sourcing—A method whereby a purchased part is supplied by only one supplier. Traditional manufacturers usually have at least two suppliers for each component part they purchase to ensure continuity of supply and (more so) to foster price competition between the suppliers. A JIT manufacturer will frequently have only one supplier for a purchased part so that close relationships can be established with a smaller number of suppliers. These close relationships (and mutual interdependence) foster high quality, reliability, short lead times, and cooperative action. Ant: multisourcing. See: sole source.

SIPOC—An acronym for supplier, input, process, output, customer (pronounced "sye-pahk").

six sigma—A methodology that furnishes tools for the improvement of business processes. The intent is to decrease process variation and improve product quality.

six sigma quality—The six sigma approach is a set of concepts and practices that key on reducing variability in processes and reducing deficiencies in the product. Important elements are (1) Producing only 3.4 defects for every one million opportunities or operations; (2) Process improvement initiatives striving for six sigma-level performance. Six sigma is a business process that permits organizations to improve bottom-line performance, creating and monitoring business activities to reduce waste and resource requirements while increasing customer satisfaction.

skew—The degree of nonsymmetry shown by a frequency or probability distribution.

skill-based compensation—A method of employee compensation that bases the employee's wage rate on the number of skills the employee is qualified to perform. People who are qualified to do a wider variety of skills are paid more. See: labor grade.

skills inventories—An organized file of information on each employee's skills, abilities, knowledge, and experience, usually maintained by a personnel office. See: labor grade.

skills matrix—A visual tool to show the skills/skill levels of employees. This is mostly used when forming a team so the leader knows what skills are necessary to accomplish the team's goals. This also is used when using a full-cross training process to ensure that all workers are cross trained to the same levels.

SKU—Abbreviation for stockkeeping unit. Pronounced as "skew."

SLA—Abbreviation for service level agreement.

slack—Syn: float, slack time.

slack time—In project management, the amount of time that an activity may be delayed from its early start without delaying the project finish date. Syn: slack.

slack time rule—A dispatching rule that directs the sequencing of jobs based on slack time. Slack time is equal to (days left until due date × hrs/day) minus standard hours of work left on this specific job; for example, $(5 \times 8) - 12 = 28$ hours of slack. The lower the amount of slack time, the higher the priority in sequencing of jobs.

slot based production—A term used in lean manufacturing that describes a production schedule that is held level, but leaves some openings to meet unexpectedly high levels of demand. This is a part of the "extra capacity" planning process.

slow-moving items—Those inventory items with a low turnover; items in inventory that have a relatively low rate of usage compared to the normal amount of inventory carried.

smallest processing time rule—Syn: shortest processing time rule.

small group improvement activity—An organizational technique for involving employees in continuous improvement activities. See: quality circle.

SMART—Abbreviation for simple, measurable, achievable, reasonable, and trackable.

smart label—A label with an embedded radio frequency identification tag.

SMED—Abbreviation for single-minute exchange of die.

smoothing—The process of averaging data by a mathematical process or by curve fitting, such as the least-squares method or exponential smoothing.

smoothing constant—In exponential smoothing, the weighting factor that is applied to the most recent demand, observation, or error. In this case, the error is defined as the difference between actual demand and the forecast for the most recent period. The weighting factor is represented by the symbol α. Theoretically, the range of α is 0.0 to 1. Syn: alpha factor, smoothing factor.

smoothing inventories—Inventories used when upstream production levels are less than downstream demand.

S

smoothing factor—Syn: smoothing constant.

SOA—Abbreviation for service-oriented architecture.

social responsibility—Commitment by top management to behave ethically and to contribute to community development. This may also entail improving the workforce's quality of life.

software—The programs and documentation necessary to make use of a computer.

smoothing models—Another name for forecasting models that utilize moving averages. The forecast is "smoothed" in the sense that averages have less variability than individual periods.

software as a service—Computer services are provided by a third party that keeps all of the software and hardware in its place of business and the company using the services accesses them via the internet. A very common technique used to outsource technological state-of-the-art costs that can be avoided.

sole proprietorship—A form of business in which one person has ownership and control. See: corporation, partnership.

sole source—The situation where the supply of a product is available from only one organization. Usually technical barriers such as patents preclude other suppliers from offering the product. See: single sourcing.

sole-source supplier—The only supplier capable of meeting (usually technical) requirements for an item. See: single-source supplier.

sorting—The function of physically separating a homogeneous subgroup from a heterogeneous population of items.

source document—An original written or printed record of some type that is to be converted into machine-readable form.

source inspection—Inspection at the source of supply or production (e.g., the supplier or the work center) as opposed to inspection following receipt from the supplier or following transfer of the items from one work center to another.

sourcing—The process of identifying a company that provides a needed good or service.

sourcing decisions—High-level decisions regarding which products or services will be produced within a company and which will be purchased from external supply chain partners. These decisions normally are based on supplier cost and capability by comparison to producing the product in house.

Southern Common Market (Mercosur)—A market/customs alliance between Argentina, Brazil, Paraguay, and Uruguay created by the Treaty of Ascuncion (1991).

space buffer—Physical space immediately after the constraint that can accommodate output from the constraint when there is a stoppage downstream that would otherwise force the constraint to stop too.

spare parts—Syn: service parts.

spare parts demand—Syn: service parts demand.

SPC—Abbreviation for statistical process control.

special cause—Syn: assignable cause.

specialization—Producing a limited product line in order to focus on a product or a process. Specialization is often intended to improve productivity and reduce costs.

special-purpose machinery—Machines that are designed to perform a small number of activities. They are not as flexible as general purpose machinery but they may be faster and more accurate.

special warranty—An assurance that the product is fit for the specific purpose for which the product will be used. See: general warranty, warranty.

specification—A clear, complete, and accurate statement of the technical requirements of a material, an item, or a service, and of the procedure to determine if the requirements are met.

specification limits—Syn: tolerance limits.

specific identification—This method keeps track of the units of the beginning inventory and the units purchased—that is, specific identification of the purchase cost of each item. This may be done through a coding method or serial number identification.

specific performance—A contract remedy requiring defendants to do what they have contracted to do.

speculative buying—Purchasing an item not immediately needed in anticipation of future price increase. See: buying down, hedge, hedging.

speed of design process—The time frame that a product or service is designed to satisfy customer needs and regulations and be field-tested before entering a market.

spend analysis—A purchasing activity in which a firm explores its spending patterns to identify opportunities to reduce costs or improve quality. This process is a part of value analysis as well as cost-benefit analysis.

spend management—Managing the outflow of funds in order to buy goods and services. The term is intended to

S

encompass such processes as outsourcing, procurement, e-procurement, and supply chain management.

SPI—Abbreviation for schedule performance index.

split-case order picking—A process for filling less-than-full-case orders. This requires items to be picked from a case or other container.

split delivery—A method by which a larger quantity is ordered on a purchase order to secure a lower price, but delivery is divided into smaller quantities and spread out over several dates to control inventory investment, save storage space, and so forth.

split lot—A manufacturing order quantity that has been divided into two or more smaller quantities, usually after the order has been released. The quantities of a split lot may be worked on in parallel, or a portion of the original quantity may be sent ahead to a subsequent operation to be worked on while work on the remainder of the quantity is being completed at the current operation. The purpose of splitting a lot is to reduce the lead time of the order.

spoiled work order—Syn: rework order.

sponsor—A person who provides financial support, in cash or in kind.

spot buy—A purchase made for standard off-the-shelf material or equipment, on a one-time basis.

spot demand—Demand, having a short lead time, that is difficult to estimate. Usually supply for this demand is provided at a premium price.

spot stock warehousing—Positioning seasonal items in proximity to the market. When the season ends, these items are either disposed or relocated to a more centralized location.

spread—Variability of an action. Often measured by the range or standard deviation of a particular dimension.

SPT—Abbreviation for shortest processing time rule.

SQC—Abbreviation for statistical quality control.

SQL—Abbreviation for structured query language.

SRM—Abbreviation for supplier relationship management.

stabilization stock—An inventory that is carried on hand above the base inventory level to provide protection against incurring overtime or downtime.

stable demand—Products that keep a similar demand pattern no matter what the season or time. Staple products fall into this category.

stacked lead time—Syn: cumulative lead time.

staged material—Syn: kit.

staging—Pulling material for an order from inventory before the material is required. This action is often taken to identify shortages, but it can lead to increased problems in availability and inventory accuracy.

staging and consolidation—Physically moving material from the packing area to a staging area, based on a prescribed set of instructions related to a particular outbound vehicle or delivery route, often for shipment consolidation purposes.

stakeholders—People with a vested interest in a company, including managers, employees, stockholders, customers, suppliers, and others.

standard—1) An established norm against which measurements are compared. 2) An established norm of productivity defined in terms of units of output per set time (units/hour) or in standard time (minutes per unit). 3) The time allowed to perform a specific job including quantity of work to be produced. See: standard time.

standard allowance—The established or accepted amount by which the normal time for an operation is increased within an area, plant, or industry to compensate for the usual amount of personal, fatigue, and unavoidable delay times.

standard batch quantity (SBQ)—The quantity of a parent that is used as the basis for specifying the material requirements for production. The quantity per is expressed as the quantity to make the SBQ, not to make only one of the parent. Often used by manufacturers that use some components in standard quantities or by process-related manufacturers. Syn: run size.

standard components—Components of a finished product that are easy to manufacture and are made by many suppliers, making them more of commodity to buy at low cost.

standard containers—Predetermined, specifically sized containers used for storing and moving components. These containers protect the components from damage and simplify the task of counting components.

standard cost accounting system—A cost accounting system that uses cost units determined before production for estimating the cost of an order or product. For management control purposes, the standards are compared to actual costs, and variances are computed.

standard costs—The target costs of an operation, process, or product including direct material, direct labor, and overhead charges.

S

standard deviation—A measurement of dispersion of data or of a variable. The standard deviation is computed by finding the differences between the average and actual observations, squaring each difference, adding the squared differences, dividing by n – 1 (for a sample), and taking the square root of the result. See: estimate of error.

standard error—A measurement of the variability of statistics such as the sample mean. See: estimate of error.

standard hours—Syn: standard time.

standard industrial classification (SIC)—Classification codes that are used to categorize companies into industry groupings.

standardization—1) The process of designing and altering products, parts, processes, and procedures to establish and use standard specifications for them and their components. 2) Reduction of the total numbers of parts and materials used and products, models, or grades produced. 3) The function of bringing a raw ingredient into standard (acceptable) range per the specification before introduction to the main process.

standardized ingredient—A raw ingredient that has been preprocessed to bring all its specifications within standard ranges before it is introduced to the main process. This preprocessing minimizes variability in the production process.

standardized product—A product that can be made in large quantities, or continuously, because of very few product designs.

standard output—An estimate of what should be produced, given a certain level of resources. Can be stated in units per hour or units per period (day, shift, etc.).

standard ratio—A relationship based on a sample distribution by value for a particular company. When the standard ratio for a particular company is known, certain aggregate inventory predictions can be made (e.g., the amount of inventory increase that would be required to provide a particular increase in customer service).

standard service—Service that is the same for most customers.

standard time—The length of time that should be required to (1) set up a given machine or operation and (2) run one batch or one or more parts, assemblies, or end products through that operation. This time is used in determining machine requirements and labor requirements. Standard time assumes an average worker following prescribed methods and allows time for per-

sonal rest to overcome fatigue and unavoidable delays. It is also frequently used as a basis for incentive pay systems and as a basis of allocating overhead in cost accounting systems. Syn: standard hours. See: standard.

standing capacity—Syn: rated capacity.

standing order—Syn: blanket purchase order.

star—A slang term used to refer to a high-growth, high-profit-margin product. See: growth-share matrix.

start date—In project management, the time an activity begins; this may be defined as an actual start date or a planned start date.

start manufacture to order complete manufacture—The time from when the manufacturing of an order starts until an order is ready to be shipped to the customer.

start-to-finish—In project management, a network requirement that activity A must start before subsequent activity B can finish. See: logical relationship.

start-to-start—In project management, a network requirement that activity A must start before subsequent activity B can start. See: logical relationship.

startup—That period starting with the date of initial operation during which the unit is brought up to acceptable production capacity and quality within estimated production costs. Startup is the activity that commences on the date of initial activity and has significant duration on most projects, but is often confused (used interchangeably) with date of initial operation.

startup audit—The technique of having an implementation team tour or visit the implementation site on a frequent basis and use the "management by walking around" technique to identify problems and solutions.

startup costs—The extra operating costs to bring the plant or product on-stream incurred between the completion of construction and the start of normal operations. In addition to the difference between actual operating costs during that period and normal costs, they include employee training, equipment tests, process adjustments, salaries and travel expense of temporary labor staff and consultants, report writing, post-startup monitoring, and associated overhead. Additional capital required to correct plant problems may be included. Startup costs are sometimes capitalized.

statement of cash flows—Syn: funds flow statement.

statement of work—1) A description of products to be supplied under a contract. 2) In projection management, the first project planning document that should be prepared. It describes the purpose, history, deliverables, and measurable success indicators for a project. It captures the support required from the customer and identifies contingency plans for events that could throw the project off course. Because the project must be sold to management, staff, and review groups, the statement of work should be a persuasive document.

static budget—Syn: master budget.

static inventory models—Syn: single-period inventory models.

statistical control—The situation where variations among the observed samples can be attributed to a constant system of chance causes.

statistical control charts—Data are collected from physical measurements, or customer surveys, and plotted on a chart so that conformance to specifications or customer satisfaction can be tracked and improved.

statistical inventory control—The use of statistical methods to model the demands and lead times experienced by an inventory item or group of items. Demand during lead time and between reviews can be modeled, and reorder points, safety stocks, and maximum inventory levels can be defined to strive for desired customer service levels, inventory investments, manufacturing and distribution efficiency, and targeted returns on investments. Syn: scientific inventory control. See: fixed reorder quantity inventory model.

statistical order point—Syn: order point.

statistical order point system—Syn: order point system.

statistical process control (SPC)—The application of statistical techniques to monitor and adjust an operation. Often the term statistical process control is used interchangeably with statistical quality control.

statistical quality control (SQC)—The application of statistical techniques to control quality. Often the term statistical process control is used interchangeably with statistical quality control, although statistical quality control includes acceptance sampling as well as statistical process control.

statistical safety stock calculations—The mathematical determination of safety stock quantities considering forecast errors, lot sizes, desired customer service levels, and the ratio of lead time to the length of the forecast period. Safety stock is frequently the product of the appropriate safety factor and the standard deviation or mean absolute deviation of the distribution of demand forecast errors.

statistical thinking—The ability to draw conclusions based on data.

statute of limitations—A statute restricting the length of time in which a lawsuit may be filed.

steady state—Waiting lines are subject to wide fluctuations when they first are created in a simulation model. A less variable (steady) state emerges after the line has existed for some time. Usually data are not collected from the simulation until after steady state is reached. See: transient state.

step budget—A budget that establishes anticipated targets at which an operation will perform for each step or level of production. A step budget can be likened to several different fixed budgets. This method of budgeting is useful because most of the manufacturing overhead expenditures vary in steps, not as a straight line. See: flexible budget.

step-function scheduling—Scheduling logic that recognizes run length to be a multiple of the number of batches to be run rather than simply a linear relationship of run time to total production quantity.

stickering—Placing manufacturer-or customer-requested stickers on the boxes of the product being sent to them. These are typically done so that the customer, typically a retailer, can more effectively track its inventory. Bar coding is commonly a part of the stickering process.

stochastic models—Models where uncertainty is explicitly considered in the analysis.

stock—1) Items in inventory. 2) Stored products or service parts ready for sale, as distinguished from stores, which are usually components or raw materials.

stockchase—Syn: expedite.

stock code—Syn: item number.

stock dividend—A dividend paid to shareholders in stock rather than cash.

stockkeeping unit (SKU)—1) An inventory item. For example, a shirt in six colors and five sizes would represent 30 different SKUs. 2) In a distribution system, an item at a particular geographic location. For example, one product stocked at the plant and at six different distribution centers would represent seven SKUs.

stockless production—Syn: just in time.

stockless purchasing—Buying material, parts, supplies, and so on, for direct use by the departments involved, as opposed to receiving them into stores and subsequently issuing them to the departments. The intent is to reduce inventory investment, increase cash flow, re-

S

duce material handling and storage, and provide better service. See: dock-to-stock inventory.

stock number—Syn: item number.

stock order—An order to replenish stock, as opposed to a production order to make a particular product for a specific customer.

stockout—A lack of materials, components, or finished goods that are needed. See: backorder.

stockout costs—The costs associated with a stockout. Those costs may include lost sales, backorder costs, expediting, and additional manufacturing and purchasing costs.

stockout percentage—A measure of the effectiveness with which a company responds to actual demand or requirements. The stockout percentage can be a measurement of total orders containing a stockout to total orders, or of line items incurring stockouts to total line items ordered during a period. One formula is: stockout percentage = (1 − customer service ratio) × 100 percent. Ant: customer service ratio.

stockout probability—Syn: cycle service level.

stockpoint—A designated location in an active area of operation into which material is placed and from which it is taken. Not necessarily a stockroom isolated from activity, it is a way of tracking and controlling active material.

stock record card—A ledger card that contains inventory status for a given item.

stock split—The issuance of new shares to stockholders without requiring additional equity.

stock status—A report showing the inventory on hand and usually showing the inventory on order and some sales or usage history for the products that are covered in the stock status report.

stop sequence—A loading procedure in which the first stop is loaded last.

stop work order—Syn: hold order.

storage—The retention of parts or products for future use or shipment.

storage costs—A subset of inventory carrying costs, including the cost of warehouse utilities, material handling personnel, equipment maintenance, building maintenance, and security personnel.

store—A storage point located upstream of a work station intended to make it easier to see customer requirements.

stores—1) Stored materials used in making a product. 2) The room where stored components, parts, assemblies, tools, fixtures, and so forth are kept.

stores issue order—Syn: picking list.

stores ledger card—A card on which records of the items on hand and on order are maintained.

stores requisition—Syn: picking list.

straight-line depreciation—A method of depreciation whereby the amount to be recovered (written off as an expense) is spread uniformly over the estimated life of the asset in terms of time periods. See: depreciation.

straight-line schedule—Syn: gapped schedule.

strategic alliance—A relationship formed by two or more organizations that share information (proprietary), participate in joint investments, and develop linked and common processes to increase the performance of both companies. Many organizations form strategic alliances to increase the performance of their common supply chain.

strategic benchmarking—Benchmarking how others compete. It often involves benchmarking across industries. See: benchmarking.

strategic business unit (SBU)—An approach to strategic planning that develops a plan based on products. A company's products are typically grouped into strategic business units (SBUs) with each SBU evaluated in terms of strengths and weaknesses vis-à-vis similar business units made and marketed by competitors. The units are evaluated in terms of their competitive strengths, their relative advantages, life cycles, and cash flow patterns.

strategic deployment—See hoshin planning.

strategic drivers—Factors that influence business unit and manufacturing strategies.

strategic mission—A statement of the future business scope of an enterprise. The statement incorporates what is being satisfied (customer needs), who is being satisfied (customer groups), and how the company creates value for the customer (processes, technologies, and core competencies).

strategic partnerships—Alliances with top supplier and buyer performers to enhance a firm's performance.

strategic performance measurements—Measurements that relate to the long-term goals of a business. Examples include profitability, market share, growth, and productivity. See: global performance measurements, operational performance measurements.

S

strategic plan—The plan for how to marshal and determine actions to support the mission, goals, and objectives of an organization. Generally includes an organization's explicit mission, goals, and objectives and the specific actions needed to achieve those goals and objectives. See: business plan, operational plan, strategic planning, strategy, tactical plan.

strategic planning—The process of developing a strategic plan. See: operational planning, strategic plan, tactical planning.

strategic quality planning—Weaving quality considerations into strategic business plans.

strategic sourcing—A comprehensive approach for locating and sourcing key material suppliers, which often includes the business process of analyzing total-spend-for-material spend categories. There is a focus on the development of long-term relationships with trading partners who can help the purchaser meet profitability and customer satisfaction goals. From an information technology applications perspective, strategic sourcing includes automation of request for quote (RFQ), request for proposal (RFP), electronic auctioning (e-auction or reverse auction), and contract management processes.

strategic variables—The most important variables that effect the business environment and business strategy. These are typically the economic situation, population demographics, changes in technology, and government policies.

strategy—The strategy of an enterprise identifies how a company will function in its environment. The strategy specifies how to satisfy customers, how to grow the business, how to compete in its environment, how to manage the organization and develop capabilities within the business, and how to achieve financial objectives. See: strategic plan.

stratification analysis—A statistical tool for determining root causes in which observed historical data are separated by particular characteristics to determine the effect of each characteristic upon the observed results. See: root cause analysis.

strict liability—A tort doctrine requiring those engaging in very hazardous activities or those manufacturing very hazardous items be held to a high standard of conduct.

strict performance—The performance of a contract good enough for the contractor to be paid full price less the other party's losses.

structured problem solving—a defined process applied to determine, evaluate and resolve an identified problem. The methodology includes (1) the collection of factual data, (2) defining why the situation is a problem, (3) defining a concise definition of what the problem is, (4) generation of possible solutions, without discussing solutions at this time, and (5) evaluation of the pros and cons of each option within the organization's objectives and feasibility, (6) implementation of the solution selected.

subassembly—An assembly that is used at the next level of the bill of material to build another assembly.

subcontracting—Sending production work outside to another manufacturer. See: outsourcing.

subcontractor and supplier networks—Creating long-term contracts between a manufacturer and several suppliers of parts and components.

suboptimization—A solution to a problem that is best from a narrow point of view but not from a higher or overall company point of view. For example, a department manager who would not have employees work overtime to minimize the department's operating expense may cause lost sales and a reduction in overall company profitability.

subplant—An organizational structure within a factory, consisting of a compact entrepreneurial unit, either process-oriented or product-oriented and structured to achieve maximum productivity.

substitutability—When a buyer can purchase similar products from different suppliers. This increases the buyer's power as the buyer doesn't have to rely on just one supplier.

substitution—The use of a nonprimary product or component, normally when the primary item is not available.

sub-tier supplier—A supplier who delivers a product to a direct supplier to the customer.

successor activity—1) In project management, in an activity-on-arrow network, the activity (arrow) that departs a node. 2) In project management, in an activity-on-node network, the activity at the tip of the arrow.

summarized bill of material—A form of multilevel bill of material that lists all the parts and their quantities required in a given product structure. Unlike the indented bill of material, it does not list the levels of manufacture and lists a component only once for the total quantity used.

S

summarized where-used—A form of an indented where-used bill of material that shows all parents in which a given component is used, the required quantities, and all the next-level parents until the end item is reached. Unlike the indented where-used, it does not list the levels of manufacture.

summary judgment—A judicial ruling that no essential facts are in dispute and that one party to the suit merits judgment as a matter of law.

sum of deviations—Syn: cumulative sum.

sunk cost—1) The unrecovered balance of an investment. It is a cost, already paid, that is not relevant to the decision concerning the future that is being made. Capital already invested that for some reason cannot be retrieved. 2) A past cost that has no relevance with respect to future receipts and disbursements of a facility undergoing an economic study. This concept implies that since a past outlay is the same regardless of the alternative selected, it should not influence the choice between alternatives.

super bill of material—A type of planning bill, located at the top level in the structure, that ties together various modular bills (and possibly a common parts bill) to define an entire product or product family. The quantity per relationship of the super bill to its modules represents the forecasted percentage of demand of each module. The master-scheduled quantities of the super bill explode to create requirements for the modules that also are master scheduled. See: pseudo bill of material.

superflush—A technique to relieve all components down to the lowest level using the complete bill of material, based on the count of finished units produced or transferred to finished goods inventory.

supermarket approach—A way of managing inventory and improving picking by making all parts easy to take off of a shelf, much like the shelves of a supermarket. Inventory is then restocked in such a way that employees always have easy access.

supervisor estimate—An estimate, made by a knowledgeable manager, of the labor required for an operation.

supplier—1) Provider of goods or services. See: vendor. 2) Seller with whom the buyer does business, as opposed to vendor, which is a generic term referring to all sellers in the marketplace.

supplier alternate—A seller other than the primary one. The supplier alternate may or may not supply the items purchased, but is usually approved to supply those items.

supplier audit—Auditing supplier processes as part of a supplier development system.

supplier base—The group of suppliers from which a firm acquires goods and services. Syn: supply base.

supplier certification—Certification procedures verifying that a supplier operates, maintains, improves, and documents effective procedures that relate to the customer's requirements. Such requirements can include cost, quality, delivery, flexibility, maintenance, safety, and ISO quality and environmental standards.

supplier clustering—Deliberately sole sourcing remote suppliers within a small geographical area to facilitate joint shipments of what would otherwise be less-than-truckload quantities.

supplier development—Technical and financial assistance given to existing and potential suppliers to improve quality and/or due date/performance.

supplier footprint—Describes the supply base for a particular material, component, or service. When stratified properly for leverage, cost impact, risk, and performance can lead to a supplier footprint transition plan for consolidated leverage, supply-base reduction, and focused effort.

supplier-input-process-output-customer (SIPOC) diagram—A high-level process map that shows substantial subprocesses in an organization's process together with the structure of the process represented by the suppliers, inputs, outputs, and customers. A SIPOC diagram defines the critical aspects of a process without losing the overall perspective.

supplier lead time—The amount of time that normally elapses between the time an order is received by a supplier and the time the order is shipped. Syn: vendor lead time. See: purchasing lead time.

supplier-managed inventory—A relationship where the buyer maintains inventory usually at its facility and provides the supplier information about the amount of stock on hand. It is the responsibility of the supplier to monitor this information and send replacement items when the inventory reaches a particular level.

supplier measurement—The act of measuring the supplier's performance to a contract. Measurements usually cover delivery reliability, lead time, and price. Syn: purchasing performance measurement. See: vendor measurement.

S

supplier number—A numerical code used to distinguish one supplier from another.

supplier-owned inventory—A system in which the supplier not only controls the inventory, but owns it and keeps in close to the consumer until it is purchased by the consumer. Falls within the supplier managed inventory umbrella.

supplier partner—A supplier organization with which a company has formed a customer-supplier partnership. See: outpartnering.

supplier partnership—The establishment of a working relationship with a supplier organization whereby two organizations act as one. Syn: collaborative supply relationship.

supplier performance evaluation—Monitoring and evaluating key suppliers on cost, quality, engineering, purchasing, and so on, based on an agreed set of measurements.

supplier quality assurance—The confidence that a supplier's goods or services will fulfill its customers' needs. This confidence is achieved by creating a relationship between the customer and supplier that ensures that the product will be fit for use with minimal corrective action and inspection. According to J.M. Juran, nine primary activities are needed: (1) define product and program quality requirements, (2) evaluate alternative suppliers, (3) select suppliers, (4) conduct joint quality planning, (5) cooperate with the supplier during the execution of the contract, (6) obtain proof of conformance to requirements, (7) certify qualified suppliers, (8) conduct quality improvement programs as required, and (9) create and use supplier quality ratings.

supplier relationship management (SRM)—A comprehensive approach to managing an enterprise's interactions with the organizations that supply the goods and services the enterprise uses. The goal of SRM is to streamline and make more effective the processes between an enterprise and its suppliers. SRM is often associated with automating procure-to-pay business processes, evaluating supplier performance, and exchanging information with suppliers. An e-procurement system often comes under the umbrella of a supplier relationship management family of applications.

supplier scheduler—A person whose main job is working with suppliers regarding what is needed and when. Supplier schedulers are in direct contact with both MRP and the suppliers. They do the material planning for the items under their control, communicate the resultant schedules to their assigned suppliers, do follow-up, resolve problems, and advise other planners and the master scheduler when purchased items will not arrive on time to support the schedule. The supplier schedulers are normally organized by commodity, as are the buyers. By using the supplier scheduler approach, the buyers are freed from day-to-day order placement and expediting, and therefore have the time to do cost reduction, negotiation, supplier selection, alternate sourcing, and so forth. Syn: planner/buyer, vendor scheduler.

supplier scheduling—A purchasing approach that provides suppliers with schedules rather than with individual hard-copy purchase orders. Normally, a supplier scheduling system will include a business agreement (contract) for each supplier, a weekly (or more frequent) schedule for each supplier extending for some time into the future, and individuals called supplier schedulers. Also required is a formal priority planning system that works well, because it is essential in this arrangement to provide the supplier with valid due dates. Syn: vendor scheduling.

supplies—Materials used in manufacturing that are not normally charged to finished production, such as cutting and lubricating oils, machine repair parts, glue, or tape. Syn: general stores, indirect materials.

supply—1) The quantity of goods available for use. 2) The actual or planned replenishment of a product or component. The replenishment quantities are created in response to a demand for the product or component or in anticipation of such a demand.

supply base—Syn: supplier base.

supply chain—The global network used to deliver products and services from raw materials to end customers through an engineered flow of information, physical distribution, and cash.

supply chain community—The set of trading partners and nominal trading partners that define a complete supply chain.

supply chain design—The determination of how to structure a supply chain. Design decisions include the selection of partners, the location and capacity of warehouse and production facilities, the products, the modes of transportation, and supporting information systems.

supply chain event management (SCEM)—A term associated with supply chain management software applications, where users have the ability to flag the occurrence of certain supply chain events to trigger some form of alert or action within another supply chain application. SCEM can be deployed to monitor supply

S

chain business processes such as planning, transportation, logistics, or procurement. SCEM can also be applied to supply chain business intelligence applications to alert users to any unplanned or unexpected event.

supply chain execution—Execution-oriented software applications for effective procurement and supply of goods and services across a supply chain. It includes manufacturing, warehouse, and transportation execution systems, and systems providing visibility across the supply chain.

supply chain integration—When supply chain partners interact at all levels to maximize mutual benefit.

supply chain inventory visibility—Software applications that permit monitoring events across a supply chain. These systems track and trace inventory globally on a line-item level and notify the user of significant deviations from plans. Companies are provided with realistic estimates of when material will arrive.

supply chain management—The design, planning, execution, control, and monitoring of supply chain activities with the objective of creating net value, building a competitive infrastructure, leveraging worldwide logistics, synchronizing supply with demand, and measuring performance globally.

supply chain mastery—A firm's ability to achieve superior results through exceptional management of revenue generation, segmented supplier and customer management, collaboration and information sharing, risk management, data analysis, and appropriate use of technology.

supply chain network design systems—Systems created among all members of the supply chain in order to get all members on the same page and with the same goals in order to promote efficiency.

Supply Chain Operations Reference (SCOR®) model—A process reference model developed and endorsed by the Supply Chain Council as the cross-industry, standard diagnostic tool for supply chain management. The SCOR model describes the business activities associated with satisfying a customer's demand, which include plan, source, make, deliver, and return. Use of the model includes analyzing the current state of a company's processes and goals, quantifying operational performance, and comparing company performance to benchmark data. SCOR has developed a set of metrics for supply chain performance, and Supply Chain Council members have formed industry groups to collect best practices information that companies can use to evaluate their supply chain performance.

supply chain planning—The determination of a set of policies and procedures that govern the operation of a supply chain. Planning includes the determination of marketing channels, promotions, respective quantities and timing, inventory and replenishment policies, and production policies. Planning establishes the parameters within which the supply chain will operate.

supply chain resilience—The ability of a supply chain to anticipate, create plans to avoid or mitigate, and/or to recover from disruptions to supply chain functionality.

supply chain risk—The variety of possible events and their outcomes that could have a negative effect on the flow of goods, services, funds, or information resulting in some level of quantitative or qualitative loss for the supply chain.

supply chain visibility—The ability of supply chain partners to access demand and production information from trading partners.

supply rate—Production rate, or quantity of units per unit of time, sent to inventory.

supply uncertainty—The risk of interruptions in the flow of components from upstream suppliers.

support costs—In activity-based cost accounting, activity costs not directly related with producing a product, such as the cost of the information system.

support functions—Activities such as accounting and information systems that do not directly participate in production but that are nevertheless essential.

surge capacity—The ability to meet sudden, unexpected increases in demand by expanding production with existing personnel and equipment.

surge tank—A container to hold output from one process and feed it to a subsequent process. It is used when line balancing is not possible or practical or only on a contingency basis when downstream equipment is non-operational.

surplus—A situation in which an oversupply exists.

surrogate driver—In activity-based cost accounting, a substitute for the best possible driver that is useful because it is less costly and almost as accurate.

survey research—A form of research (frequently used in marketing research) where data are collected by mailing questionnaires to a group of people within a target audience. See: marketing research.

sustainability—Activities that provide present benefit without compromising the needs of future generations.

S

sustaining activity—In activity-based cost accounting, an activity that is not directly beneficial to any specific cost object but does benefit the organization as a whole.

sweepstakes—A marketing promotion in which prizes are awarded, usually by chance.

SWOT—Abbreviation for strengths, weaknesses, opportunities, and threats.

SWOT analysis—An analysis of the strengths, weaknesses, opportunities, and threats of and to an organization. SWOT analysis is useful in developing strategy.

synchronized production—A manufacturing management philosophy that includes a consistent set of principles, procedures, and techniques where every action is evaluated in terms of the global goal of the system. Both kanban, which is a part of the JIT philosophy, and drum-buffer-rope, which is a part of the theory of constraints philosophy, represent synchronized production control approaches. Syn: synchronous manufacturing. See: drum-buffer-rope, kanban, synchronous scheduling.

synchronous control—A pull-type production control system that is based on setting production rates and feeding work into production to meet the planned rates, then monitoring and controlling production.

synchronous manufacturing—Syn: synchronized production.

synchronous scheduling—Scheduling processes (kanban in just in time and drum-buffer-rope in theory of constraints environments) that focus on synchronizing all operations to the constraint of the system. See: synchronized production.

synthetic time standard—Syn: predetermined motion time.

system—A regularly interacting or interdependent group of items forming a unified whole toward the achievement of a goal.

system constraint—In supply chain management, the supply chain is viewed as the complete system. The system constraint is the resource at any one of the trading partners that is most limiting the end-to-end throughput of the supply chain.

system layout planning (SLP)—A facility layout methodology that develops the layout of a facility by considering the importance of proximity of each department to the other departments.

system nervousness—See: nervousness.

systems analysis—1) The analyzing in detail of the information needed for an organization, the characteristics and components of the current information system, and the requirements of any proposed changes to the information system. 2) A method of problem solving that encompasses the identification, study, and evaluation of interdependent parts and their attributes that function in an ongoing process and that constitute an organic whole.

systems audit—The audit of any activity that can affect final product quality.

systems concept—An attempt to create the most efficient complete system as opposed to the most efficient individual parts. A "whole process" or "whole company" operating system that is driven by cause and effect.

systems network—A group of interconnected nodes. This implies redundancy in connections and some means (e.g., machines) for implementing the connection.

systems rollup—Integrating computer systems; this enables faster data retrieval and better information system responsiveness.

systems thinking—A school of thought that focuses on recognizing the interconnections between the parts of a system and synthesizing them into a unified view of the whole.

systems view—A holistic approach to management that considers how actions impact the production process. Included within the system are suppliers, product design, process design, the production process, distribution, and customers.

T

tactical buying—The purchasing process focused on transactions and nonstrategic material buying. It is closely aligned with the "ordering" portion of executing the purchasing transaction process. The characteristics for tactical buying include stable, limited fluctuations, defined standard specifications, noncritical to production, no delivery issues, and high reliability concerning quality-standard material with very little concern for rejects. See: strategic sourcing.

tactical plan(s)—The set of functional plans (e.g., production plan, sales plan, marketing plan) synchronizing activities across functions that specify production levels, capacity levels, staffing levels, funding levels, and so on, for achieving the intermediate goals and objectives to support the organization's strategic plan. See: aggregate planning, operational plan, production planning, sales and operations planning, strategic plan, tactical planning.

tactical planning—The process of developing a set of tactical plans (e.g., production plan, sales plan, marketing plan). Two approaches to tactical planning exist for linking tactical plans to strategic plans—production planning and sales and operations planning. See: operational planning, strategic planning, tactical plan.

tact time—Syn: takt time.

Taguchi methodology—A concept of off-line quality control methods conducted at the product and process design stages in the product development cycle. This concept, expressed by Genichi Taguchi, encompasses three phases of product design: system design, parameter design, and tolerance design. The goal is to reduce quality loss by reducing the variability of the product's characteristics during the parameter phase of product development. Syn: Taguchi methods.

Taguchi methods—Syn: Taguchi methodology.

takt time—Sets the pace of production to match the rate of customer demand and becomes the heartbeat of any lean production system. It is computed as the available production time divided by the rate of customer demand. For example, assume demand is 10,000 units per month, or 500 units per day, and planned available capacity is 420 minutes per day. The takt time = 420 minutes per day/ 500 units per day = 0.84 minutes per unit. This takt time means that a unit should be planned to exit the production system on average every 0.84 minutes. Syn: tact time.

tampering—Action taken to compensate for variation within the control limits of a stable system. Tampering increases rather than decreases variation, as evidenced in the funnel experiment. See: funnel experiment.

T&M—Abbreviation for time and materials.

tangibles—Things that can be quantitatively measured or valued, such as the costs of physical assets. A dimension of service quality referring to the physical appearance of the service facility, including the personnel and equipment.

tank inventory—Goods stored in tanks. These goods may be raw materials, intermediates, or finished goods. The description of inventory as tank inventory indicates the necessity of calculating the quantity on hand from the levels within the tanks.

tapering rate—A rate structure in which a shipping rate increases as the distance shipped increases, but the increases are not directly correlated to the increase in the distance shipped.

tardiness—For jobs that are late, the delivery date minus the due date. See: earliness, lateness.

tare weight—The weight of a substance, obtained by deducting the weight of the empty container from the gross weight of the full container.

target costing—The process of designing a product to meet a specific cost objective. Target costing involves setting the planned selling price, subtracting the desired profit as well as marketing and distribution costs, thus leaving the required manufacturing or target cost.

target inventory level—In a min-max inventory system, the equivalent of the maximum. The target inventory is equal to the order point plus a variable order quantity. It is often called an order-up-to inventory level and is used in a periodic review system. Syn: order-up-to level.

target market—1) A fairly homogeneous group of customers to whom a company wishes to appeal. 2) A definable group of buyers to which a marketer has decided to market.

target marketing—The process of focusing marketing activities specifically on those people who are most likely to buy a company's products and services. Data gathered on people who use the internet are enabling companies to identify and focus on more likely candidates.

tariff—An official schedule of taxes and fees imposed by a country on imports or exports.

task—1) In project management, the lowest level to which work can be subdivided on a project. 2) In activity-based cost accounting, a task, a subdivision of an activity, is the least amount of work. Tasks are used to describe activities.

task interleaving—An attempt at reducing/eliminating "deadheading," or driving an empty material handling vehicle. A warehouse management system directs a material carrying vehicle to put away materials as it goes to pick up other materials.

TBC—Abbreviation for time-based competition.

TBL—Abbreviation for triple bottom line.

TCO—Abbreviation for total cost of ownership.

TCP/IP—Abbreviation for transmission control protocol/internet protocol.

team design/engineering—Syn: participative design/engineering.

teardown—All work items required between the end of one operation or job and the start of setup for the next operation or job, both jobs requiring the same machinery or facilities. See: teardown time.

teardown bill of material—Syn: disassembly bill of material.

teardown time—The time needed to remove a setup from a machine or facility. Teardown is an element of manufacturing lead time, but it is often allowed for in setup or run time rather than separately. See: teardown.

technical components—Parts that are difficult to make, have long lead times, and require expert knowledge to produce. They are parts that are produced by only a few suppliers because of these characteristics. Tooling to produce these products usually is owned by the customer to avoid proprietary or patent issues.

technical/office protocol (TOP)—An application-specific protocol based on open systems interconnection (OSI) standards. It is designed to allow communication between computers from different suppliers in the technical development and office environments.

technologies—The terms, concepts, philosophies, hardware, software, and other attributes used in a field, industrial sector, or business function.

technology transfer—The transmission of technology (e.g., knowledge, skills, software, hardware) from one country, organization, business, or entity to another country, organization, business, or entity.

TEI—Abbreviation for total employee involvement.

telecommunications—Transmission of voice and image data at a distance by electronic means.

telescoping—Syn: overlapped schedule.

telnet (TN)—Software that enables a user to log on to remote computers.

tender offer—An offer by an organization to buy a block of shares directly from shareholders of another organization.

terminal delivery allowance—A discount provided if freight is delivered to or picked up from the carrier's terminal.

terminal-handling costs—Carrier charges dependent on the number of times a shipment must be loaded, handled and unloaded. Cost can be reduced by consolidating shipments into fewer parcels or by shipping in truckload quantities.

terminal value—The value of an operation or entity at the end of the period considered.

terminals—In transportation, locations where carriers load and unload goods to and from vehicles. Also used to make connections between local pickup and delivery service and line-haul service. Functions performed in terminals include weighing connections with other routes and carriers, vehicle routing, dispatching, maintenance, paperwork, and administration. Terminals may be owned and operated by the carrier or the public.

terms and conditions—All the provisions and agreements of a contract.

TEU—Abbreviation for twenty-foot equivalent unit.

theoretical capacity—The maximum output capability, allowing no adjustments for preventive maintenance, unplanned downtime, shutdown, and so forth.

theoretical cycle time—The amount of time, eliminating all stops, waiting, and additional time due to error, that is needed for one item to go through an entire process.

theory of constraints (TOC)—A holistic management philosophy developed by Dr. Eliyahu M. Goldratt that is based on the principle that complex systems exhibit inherent simplicity. Even a very complex system comprising thousands of people and pieces of equipment can have, at any given time, only a very, very small number of variables—perhaps only one, known as a constraint—that actually limit the ability to generate more of the system's goal.

theory of constraints accounting—A cost and managerial accounting system that accumulates costs and revenues into three areas—throughput, inventory, and operating expense. It does not create incentives (through allocation of overhead) to build up inventory. The system is considered to provide a truer reflection of actual revenues and costs than traditional cost accounting. It is closer to a cash flow concept of income than is traditional accounting. The theory of constraints (TOC) accounting provides a simplified and more accurate form of direct costing that subtracts true variable costs (those costs that vary with throughput quantity). Unlike traditional cost accounting systems in which the focus is generally placed on reducing costs in all the various accounts, the primary focus of TOC accounting is on aggressively exploiting the constraint(s) to make more money for the firm. Syn: constraint accounting, throughput accounting.

therbligs—The 17 basic movements identified by Frank and Lillian Gilbreth. (The name of the term is essentially Gilbreth spelled backwards.) Examples of movements

T

include grasp, move, release, select, and position. See: predetermined time standards.

third-order smoothing—Syn: triple smoothing.

third-party logistics (3PL)—A buyer and supplier team with a third party that provides product delivery services. This third party may provide added supply chain expertise.

third-party logistics company—A company that manages all or part of another company's product delivery operations.

third-party registration system—Using an outside party (rather than the buyer) to determine the adequacy of a seller's product quality. If several buyers use the same third party system, such as ISO9000, the seller avoids having multiple audits.

third-party transportation services—Outside firms providing transportation of goods.

third-party warehousing—The outsourcing of the warehousing function by the seller of the goods.

Thomas Register—A privately produced reference set that includes a listing of part suppliers by product type and geographic area.

three-bin kanban—Simple kanban structure that focuses on cycling three bins of material continually and provides a visible method to align replenishment with consumption. One bin is ready to ship from the supplier at all times, while two are back to back in manufacturing/production at or near point of use. As the front bin empties, a signal is sent to the supplier to send a full bin and the back bin is issued forward into production. See: kanban.

3D printing—The process of layering materials to make products and components using computer data. Syn: additive manufacturing. See: rapid prototyping.

3PL—Abbreviation for third-party logistics.

three-point estimate—A project management technique that uses three cost or duration estimates to stand for the optimistic (O), most likely (M), and pessimistic (P) situation. The mean value (MV) is often found using $MV=(O+4M+P)/6$. This technique can improve the accuracy of cost or duration estimates when underlying assumptions are uncertain.

threshold costs—A company's variable costs, which must be covered for a company to continue to stay in business.

throughput—The rate at which the system generates "goal units." Because throughput is a rate, it is always expressed for a given time period—such as, per month, week, day, or even minute. If the goal units are money, throughput will be an amount of money per time period. In that case, throughput is calculated as revenues received minus totally variable costs divided for the chosen time period.

throughput accounting—A management accounting method that is based on the belief that because every system has a constraint that limits global performance, the most effective way to evaluate the impact that any proposed action will have on the system as a whole is to look at the expected changes in the global measures of throughput, inventory, and operating expense.

throughput time—Syn: cycle time (second definition).

tiered workforce—A strategy used to vary workforce levels, where additional full-time or part-time employees are hired during peak demand periods, while a smaller, permanent staff is maintained year-round. This technique is used heavily in perishable seasonal goods industries (e.g. chocolate production, nursery plants, etc.).

tier one—The group of suppliers that are directly responsible for not only product supply but product development.

tiger teams—Teams that attempt to achieve a specific goal within a short time period.

time and attendance—A collection of data relating to an employee's record of absences and hours worked.

time and materials (T&M) contract—A type of contract that is a hybrid between cost-reimbursable and fixed-time contracts.

time-based competition (TBC)—A corporate strategy that emphasizes time as the vehicle for achieving and maintaining a sustainable competitive edge. Its characteristics are (1) it deals only with those lead times that are important to the customers; (2) the lead-time reductions must involve decreases in both the mean and the variance; and (3) the lead-time reductions must be achieved through system/process analysis (the processes must be changed to reduce lead times). TBC is a broad-based strategy. Reductions in lead times are achieved by changing the processes and the decision structures used to design, produce, and deliver products to the customers. TBC involves design, manufacturing, and logistical processes.

time-based order system—Syn: fixed reorder cycle inventory model.

time bucket—A number of days of data summarized into a columnar or row-wise display. A weekly time bucket would contain all of the relevant data for an entire week. Weekly time buckets are considered to be the largest possible (at least in the near and medium term) to permit effective MRP.

time buffer—Protection against uncertainty that takes the form of time.

time card—A document recording attendance time, often used for indicating the number of hours for which wages are to be paid. Syn: clock card.

time-definite services—Delivery of goods and services where an agreement has been reached on the day and time of the delivery.

time fence—A policy or guideline established to note where various restrictions or changes in operating procedures take place. For example, changes to the master production schedule can be accomplished easily beyond the cumulative lead time, while changes inside the cumulative lead time become increasingly more difficult to a point where changes should be resisted. Time fences can be used to define these points. See: demand time fence, hedge, planning time fence.

time-now date—Syn: data date.

time period safety stock—A safety stock that is based on usage over a designated time frame. The period can be set as days, weeks, or months. Safety stock varies directly with the demand. This differs from statistical-based safety stocks in that the amount is not based on deviation from demand.

time-phased order point (TPOP)—MRP-like time planning logic for independent demand items, where gross requirements come from a forecast, not via explosion. This technique can be used to plan distribution center inventories as well as to plan for service (repair) parts, because MRP logic can readily handle items with dependent demand, independent demand, or a combination of both. Time-phased order point is an approach that uses time periods, thus allowing for lumpy withdrawals instead of average demand. When used in distribution environments, the planned order releases are input to the master schedule dependent demands. See: fixed reorder quantity inventory model.

time phasing—The technique of expressing future demand, supply, and inventories by time period. Time phasing is one of the key elements of material requirements planning.

time series—A set of data that is distributed over time, such as demand data in monthly time periods. Various patterns of demand must be considered in time series analysis: seasonal, trend, cyclical, and random.

time series analysis—Analysis of any variable classified by time in which the values of the variable are functions of the time periods. Time series analysis is used in forecasting. A time series consists of seasonal, cyclical, trend, and random components. See: cyclical component, random component, seasonal component, trend component.

time series forecasting—A forecasting method that projects historical data patterns into the future. It involves the assumption that the near-term future will be like the recent past.

times interest earned—Ratio of profits before payment of interest and income taxes (EBIT) to interest on debt.

time stamping—Tracking with each transaction the time of occurrence. It is used in period closings and to tie end items to samples for certification of item properties.

time standard—The predetermined times allowed for the performance of a specific job. The standard will often consist of two parts, that for machine setup and that for actual running. The standard can be developed through observation of the actual work (time study), summation of standard micromotion times (predetermined or synthetic time standards), or approximation (historical job times).

time study—Timing employees as they accomplish jobs for the purpose of setting time standards.

timetables—Schedules that are organized by starting location/destination and show the times for departures and arrivals.

time ticket—An operator-entered labor claim. Syn: job ticket.

time-to-market—The total time required to design, build, and deliver a product (timed from concept to delivery). See: procurement lead time.

time-to-product—The total time required to receive, fill, and deliver an order for an existing product to a customer, timed from the moment that the customer places the order until the customer receives the product. See: purchasing lead time.

time to reliably replenish (TRR)—The time in which a part can reliably be obtained if necessary.

time utility—When a delivery gets to a customer at exactly the right time (not early, not late).

T

time value of money—1) The cumulative effect of elapsed time on the money value of an event, based on the earning power of equivalent invested funds. See: future worth, present value. 2) The interest rate that capital is expected to earn.

tipping point—The moment when something unique becomes common. The term often refers to the popular acceptance of new technologies. The concept has been applied to any process in which beyond a certain point, the rate at which the process (chemical, sociological, environmental, etc.) proceeds increase dramatically.

TMS—Abbreviation for transportation management system.

TN—Abbreviation for telnet.

TOC—Abbreviation for theory of constraints.

TOC performance measures—In the theory of constraints, throughput, inventory, and operating expense are considered performance measures that link operational decisions to organizational profit.

TOFC—Abbreviation for trailer on a flatcar.

tolerance—Allowable departure from a nominal value established by design engineers that is deemed acceptable for the functioning of the good or service over its life cycle.

tolerance limits—1) The upper and lower extreme values permitted by the tolerance. 2) In work measurement, the limits between which a specified operation time value or other work unit will be expected to vary. See: lower specification limit, upper specification limit. Syn: specification limits.

tolerance stack up—When two or more components, all within tolerance limits but some distance from the specification itself, are assembled together the assembly may be subject to early failure because of the interaction between the components.

ton-mile—A way to measure the transportation of freight. It is the multiplication of weight being transported (in tons) by the distance it is being transported (in miles). Heavily used in rail and ship transportation mode.

tool—Any instrument, such as a saw blade, that is the working part of a machine.

tool calibration frequency—The recommended length of time between tool calibrations. It is normally expressed in days.

tool issue order—Syn: tool order.

tool number—The identification number assigned to reference and control a specific tool.

tool order—A document authorizing issue of specific tools from the tool crib or other storage. Syn: tool issue order.

TOP—Acronym for technical/office protocol.

top management commitment (quality)—In the total quality management philosophy, participation of the highest-level official in the organization's quality improvement efforts. Participation includes establishing and serving on a quality committee, establishing quality policies and goals, deploying those goals to lower levels of the organization, providing the resources and training that the lower levels need to achieve the goals, participating in quality improvement teams, reviewing organization-wide progress, recognizing those who have performed well, and revising the current reward system to reflect the importance of achieving the quality goals.

total annual material receipts—The amount (in dollars) of all direct materials that were received in a calendar year. This number should fall very close to the direct material dollars that were used in a calendar year in a lean environment.

total cost analysis—In purchasing, a process by which a firm seeks to identify and quantify all of the major costs associated with various sourcing options.

total cost concept—In logistics, the idea that all logistical decisions that provide equal service levels should favor the option that minimizes the total of all logistical costs and not be used on cost reductions in one area alone, such as lower transportation charges.

total cost consideration—Considering all cost impacts, rather than just one cost impact, on customer service improvement.

total cost curve—1) In cost-volume-profit (breakeven) analysis, the total cost curve is composed of total fixed and variable costs per unit multiplied by the number of units provided. Breakeven quantity occurs where the total cost curve and total sales revenue curve intersect. See: break-even chart, break-even point. 2) In inventory theory, the total cost curve for an inventory item is the sum of the costs of acquiring and carrying the item. See: economic order quantity.

total cost of ownership (TCO)—In supply chain management, the total cost of ownership of the supply delivery system is the sum of all the costs associated with every activity of the supply stream. The main insight that TCO offers to the supply chain manager is the understanding that the acquisition cost is often a very small portion of the total cost of ownership.

total cost of quality—A sum that includes costs associated with rework, scrap, warranty costs, and other costs associated with preventing or resolving quality problems.

total cost of quality curve—A curve that suggests there is some optimal quality level, Q*. The curve is calculated by adding costs of internal and external failures, prevention costs, and appraisal costs. The optimal quality level occurs where this curve reaches a minimum point. It is a single turning point curve that always has a minimum.

total costs—Considering all cost impacts, rather than just one cost impact, on customer service improvement.

total cumulative manufacturing cycle time—Average time between a part entering a manufacturing system and completion of final packaging.

total employee involvement (TEI)—An empowerment program in which employees are invited to participate in actions and decision making that were traditionally reserved for management.

total factor productivity—A measure of productivity (of a department, plant, strategic business unit, firm, etc.) that combines the individual productivities of all its resources, including labor, capital, energy, material, and equipment. These individual factor productivities are often combined by weighting each according to its monetary value and then adding them. For example, if material accounts for 40 percent of the total cost of sales and labor 10 percent of the total cost of sales, etc., total factor productivity = .4 (material productivity) + .1 (labor productivity) + etc.

total fixed costs—Costs that remain constant in total regardless of changes in activity.

total float—In project management, the length of time an activity can be late without delaying succeeding activities. See: float, free float, independent float.

total lead time—Syn: lead time.

total line-haul cost—Basic costs of carrier operation to move a container of freight, including driver's wages and usage depreciation, which vary with the distance shipped and the cost per mile.

total make cycle time—Average cumulative processing time between a part entering a manufacturing system and completion of manufacturing activities (not including packaging).

total preventive maintenance—Syn: total productive maintenance.

total procurement lead time—Syn: procurement lead time.

total productive maintenance (TPM)—Preventive maintenance plus continuing efforts to adapt, modify, and refine equipment to increase flexibility, reduce material handling, and promote continuous flows. It is operator-oriented maintenance with the involvement of all qualified employees in all maintenance activities. Syn: total preventive maintenance.

total quality control (TQC)—The process of creating and producing the total composite good and service characteristics (by marketing, engineering, manufacturing, purchasing, etc.) through which the good and service will meet the expectations of customers.

total quality engineering (TQE)—The discipline of designing quality into the product and manufacturing processes by understanding the needs of the customer and performance capabilities of the equipment. See: design for quality.

total quality management (TQM)—A term coined to describe Japanese-style management approaches to quality improvement. Since then, total quality management (TQM) has taken on many meanings. Simply put, TQM is a management approach to long-term success through customer satisfaction. TQM is based on the participation of all members of an organization in improving processes, goods, services, and the culture in which they work. The methods for implementing this approach are found in teachings of such quality leaders as Philip B. Crosby, W. Edwards Deming, Armand V. Feigenbaum, Kaoru Ishikawa, J.M. Juran, and Genichi Taguchi.

total value analysis—A method of economic analysis in which a model expresses the dependent variable of interest as a function of independent variables, some of which are controllable.

total variable costs—Costs that vary in total in proportion to changes in activity.

total waste management (TWM)—A methodology that enables finding solutions to waste issues while keeping in mind financial elements and the business case.

touches—A statistic that is used to determine efficiency for costing/pricing functions. A touch is anytime that a labor activity is utilized during the manufacturing or service creation process. This brought about the term "touch labor" for direct labor personnel.

touch labor—Syn: direct labor.

T

Toyota Production System (TPS)—A manufacturing methodology developed at Toyota that has evolved into the concepts of just in time and lean manufacturing.

TPM—Abbreviation for total productive maintenance.

TPOP—Abbreviation for time-phased order point.

TPS—Abbreviation for Toyota Production System.

TQC—Abbreviation for total quality control.

TQE—Abbreviation for total quality engineering.

TQM—Abbreviation for total quality management.

traceability—1) The attribute allowing the ongoing location of a shipment to be determined. 2) The registering and tracking of parts, processes, and materials used in production, by lot or serial number.

tracer—A request to a transportation line to trace a shipment to expedite its movement or to verify delivery.

tracing—In activity-based cost accounting, connecting resources to activities to cost objects using underlying causal drivers to understand how costs occur during normal business activities.

tracking capacity strategy—Adding capacity in small amounts to attempt to respond to changing demand in real time in the marketplace. This approach may satisfy total demand and help minimize unit costs, but it can be difficult in some situations to add incremental amounts of capacity, especially if the facility has no more space available.

tracking signal—The ratio of the cumulative algebraic sum of the deviations between the forecasts and the actual values to the mean absolute deviation. Used to signal when the validity of the forecasting model might be in doubt. See: forecast error, mean absolute deviation.

trade bloc—An agreement between countries intended to reduce or remove barriers to trade within member countries. Frequently, but not always, those countries are geographically close. Examples of trade blocs are the European Economic Community and the North American Free Trade Agreement (NAFTA). Syn: trading bloc.

trade secret—Knowledge of a manufacturing process that gives the owner an advantage over competitors who do not have it. Trade secrets are legally protectable.

trading bloc—Syn: trade bloc.

trading company—A company that introduces foreign buyers and sellers and arranges all product export/import details, documentation, and transportation.

trading partner—Any organization external to the firm that plays an integral role within the supply chain community and whose business fortune depends on the success of the supply chain community.

trading partner agreement—A contract between trading partners that describes all facets of their business together. This is a legal and binding agreement suitable for legal purposes as well as standard working agreements.

traffic—A department or function charged with the responsibility for arranging the most economic classification and method of shipment for both incoming and outgoing materials and products.

traffic department—The area of an organization that plans and executes shipping requirements.

traffic management—Control of transportation carriers, modes, and services.

trailer on a flatcar (TOFC)—A specialized form of containerization in which motor and rail transport coordinate. Syn: piggyback.

training aid—An item to enhance training, usually minor in nature. Training aids may include charts, graphs, slides, and schematics.

transaction channel—A distribution network that deals with change of ownership of goods and services including the activities of negotiation, selling, and contracting.

transactions—Individual events reported to the system (e.g., issues, receipts, transfers, adjustments).

transfer batch—The quantity of an item moved between sequential work centers during production. See: batch, overlap quantity.

transfer price—Price that one segment (subunit, department, division, etc.) of an organization charges for a good or service supplied to another segment of the same organization.

transfer pricing—The pricing of goods or services transferred from one segment of a business to another. See: interplant transfer.

transformation process—The process of converting inputs into finished goods or services. In a service firm, the input may be a customer. Syn: transformation system. See: manufacturing process, production process.

transformation system—Syn: transformation process.

transient bill of material—Syn: phantom bill of material.

transient state—In waiting line models, early behavior of a characteristic of the model, such as line length, is more erratic than eventual performance of the line. Data are usually not collected from the model until less erratic behavior emerges. See: steady state.

transit inventory—Inventory in transit between manufacturing and stocking locations. See: transportation inventory.

transition tree (TRT)—In the theory of constraints, a logic-based tool for identifying and sequencing actions in accomplishing an objective. The transitions represent the states or stages in moving from the present situation to the desired objective.

transit privilege—A service provided by a shipper that allows the purchasing company to stop a shipment midroute to allow changes to the delivery, but pay the nonstop rate.

transit time—A standard allowance that is assumed on any given order for the movement of items from one operation to the next. Syn: travel time.

translation software—Software that converts business data into an electronic data interchange standard format and vice versa.

transmission acknowledgement—The receiver of a transmission notifies the sender that the transmission was received error free.

transmission control protocol/internet protocol (TCP/IP)—The communication protocol used by the internet.

transparency—A company allows outsiders, typically customers, to see some internal information, typically regarding an order, without giving any more than the outsider requires.

transportation—The function of planning, scheduling, and controlling activities related to mode, vendor, and movement of inventories into and out of an organization.

transportation brokers—Firms that find shipments for carriers for a fee.

transportation cycle time—A logistics performance measure of the lead time required for a product to reach its final destination; the time between leaving a warehouse and arriving at the destination.

transportation inventory—Inventory that is in transit between locations. See: pipeline stock, transit inventory.

transportation legal classifications—Legal regulatory classification of transportation by product, shipping size, rates, carriers, and types of services.

transportation management system (TMS)—A computer application system designed to manage transportation operations. These systems typically offer modules focused on specific functions, such as intermodal transportation, import/export management, fleet service management, and load planning and optimization.

transportation method—A linear programming model concerned with minimizing the costs involved in supplying requirements to several locations from several sources with different costs related to the various combinations of source and requirement locations.

transportation mode—The way an item is transported.

transportation requirements planning (TRP)—Using existing MRP, DRP, or ERP databases to plan transportation requirements based on actual demand.

transport stocks—A carrier material to move solids in solution or slurry or to dilute ingredients to safe levels for reaction.

traveler—A copy of the manufacturing order that actually moves with the work through the shop. Syn: shop traveler.

traveling purchase requisition—A purchase requisition designed for repetitive use. After a purchase order has been prepared for the goods requisitioned, the form is returned to the originator, who holds it until a repurchase of the goods is required. The name is derived from the repetitive travel between the originating and purchasing departments. Syn: traveling requisition.

traveling requisition—Syn: traveling purchase requisition.

travel time—Syn: transit time.

treasury stock—Common stock that has been repurchased by the issuing company.

tree diagram—1) A management technique used to analyze a situation in increasing detail. The full range of tasks to be accomplished to achieve a primary goal and supporting subgoal may be illustrated. 2) In the theory of constraints, a diagram relating effects to underlying causes. See: current reality tree, future reality tree.

trend—General upward or downward movement of a variable over time (e.g., demand, process attribute).

trend adjusted exponential smoothing forecasting—A form of exponential smoothing forecasting that includes

T

a factor for increasing or decreasing tendencies in the data due to things such as population growth or income changes.

trend analysis—An analysis to determine whether trend (general upward or downward change) exists in data. See: trend forecasting models.

trend component—A component of demand, usually describing the impact of increasing or decreasing growth on demand. See: time series analysis.

trend control chart—A control chart in which the deviation of the subgroup average, X-bar, from an expected trend in the process level is used to evaluate the stability of a process.

trend forecasting models—Methods for forecasting sales data when a definite upward or downward pattern exists. Models include double exponential smoothing, regression, and triple smoothing. See: trend analysis.

trigger level—Syn: order point.

triple bottom line (TBL)—An approach that measures the economic, social, and environmental impact of an organization's activities with the intent of bringing value for both its shareholders and society.

triple smoothing—A method of exponential smoothing that accounts for accelerating or decelerating trends, such as would be experienced in a fad cycle. Syn: third-order smoothing.

TRP—Abbreviation for transportation requirements planning.

TRR—Abbreviation for time to reliably replenish.

TRT—Abbreviation for transition tree.

truckload carriers—Carriers that deliver/charge only for full truckload shipments.

truckload lot—A truck shipment that qualifies for a lower freight rate because it meets a minimum weight and/or volume.

trust—A fiduciary relationship in which the trustee holds ownership for the benefit of another party (benefactor).

TS 16949—Syn: ISO/TS 16949.

turnaround—Syn: setup.

turnaround costs—Syn: setup costs.

turnaround time—Syn: setup.

turnkey system—1) Computer packages that are already prepared by a hardware manufacturer or software house and are ready to run. 2) Any system of machines that is ready for immediate use.

turnover—1) Syn: inventory turnover. 2) In the United Kingdom and certain other countries, annual sales volume.

turnover ratio—An indicator of whether or not a company is using its assets efficiently. It is measured by dividing sales by average assets during a particular period.

turns—Syn: inventory turnover.

twenty-foot equivalent unit (TEU)—A measure of cargo capacity equivalent to a standard container (i.e., 20-feet long, 8-feet wide, and approximately 8-feet high).

TWM—Abbreviation for total waste management.

two-bin inventory system—A type of fixed-order system in which inventory is carried in two bins. A replenishment quantity is ordered when the first bin (working) is empty. During the replenishment lead time, material is used from the second bin. When the material is received, the second bin (which contains a quantity to cover demand during lead time plus some safety stock) is refilled and the excess is put into the working bin. At this time, stock is drawn from the first bin until it is again exhausted. This term is also used loosely to describe any fixed-order system even when physical "bins" do not exist. Syn: bin reserve system. See: visual review system.

two-card kanban system—A kanban system where a move card and production card are employed. The move card authorizes the movement of a specific number of parts from a source to a point of use. The move card is attached to the standard container of parts during movement to the point of use of the parts. The production card authorizes the production of a given number of parts for use or replenishment. Syn: dual-card kanban system. See: one-card kanban system.

two-level master schedule—A master scheduling approach in which a planning bill of material is used to master schedule an end product or family, along with selected key features (options and accessories). See: hedge, multilevel master schedule, production forecast.

type I error—An incorrect decision to reject something (such as a statistical hypothesis or a lot of products) when it is acceptable. See: producer's risk.

type II error—An incorrect decision to accept something when it is unacceptable. See: consumer's risk.

U

ubiquity—In inventory control, a raw material that is found at all locations.

U chart—A control chart for evaluating the stability of a process in terms of the average count of events of a given classification per unit occurring in a sample. Syn: count-per-unit chart.

UCL—Abbreviation for upper control limit.

UDE—Abbreviation for undesirable effect. Pronounced "oodee."

U-lines—Production lines shaped like the letter "U." The shape allows workers to easily perform several nonsequential tasks without much walk time. The number of workstations in a U-line is usually determined by line balancing. U-lines promote communication.

unattainable capability—The portion of the production capability that cannot be attained. This is typically caused by factors such as equipment unavailability, suboptimal scheduling, or resource limitations.

uncertainty—Unknown future events that cannot be predicted quantitatively within useful limits; for example, an accident that destroys facilities, a major strike, or an innovation that makes existing products obsolete.

uncontrollable factors—In the environment of a production system, those factors that cannot be changed (e.g., temperature, natural causes, weather, vibration).

under-capacity scheduling—Allowing more time than should be necessary to complete a day's work. As a result, a daily quota is met more often and workers have time to cross-train or perform maintenance on their tools and machines.

undertime—A condition occurring when more personnel are on the payroll than are required to produce the planned output.

undesirable effects (UDE)—In theory of constraints: Those negative aspects of an environment that are noted so that a current reality tree may be constructed.

unfair labor practice—Activities by management or labor that violate the National Labor Relations Act. Failure to bargain in good faith is an example.

UN Global Compact Management Model—A framework for guiding companies through the process of formally committing to, assessing, defining, implementing, mea-

suring, and communicating the United Nations Global Compact and its principles.

uniform-delivered pricing—A type of geographic pricing policy in which all customers pay the same delivered price regardless of their location. A company allocates the total transportation cost among all customers.

uniform plant loading—In lean, the distribution of work between work stations so that the time required for each station to complete all tasks is as close to equal as possible. See: line balancing.

uniform product code—A retail product numbering and bar coding system that identifies the item and the manufacturer.

uniform resource locator (URL)—A means of locating web pages regardless of where they are on the internet.

uniform warehouse receipts act—An act that regulates public warehousing; it sets up the legal responsibilities of warehouse managers and determines the receipts that can be issued.

union contract—A formal contract, usually covering two-to-six years, between a union representing employees and their company that covers all aspects of pay, working conditions, and strike options.

union free—A designation that indicates that a company or operation does not have a union contract.

union shop—A facility in which all hourly employees are unionized, or more formally a clause in a collective bargaining agreement under which membership in the union is required as a condition of employment. Union shops are illegal in some regions.

unit cost—Total labor, material, and overhead cost for one unit of production (e.g., one part, one gallon, one pound).

United Nations Global Compact—A voluntary initiative whereby companies embrace, support, and enact, within their sphere of influence, a set of core values in the areas of human rights, labor standards, the environment, and anticorruption.

unitization—In warehousing, the consolidation of several units into larger units for fewer handlings.

unit load—A shipping unit made up of a number of items, or bulky material, arranged or constrained so the mass can be picked up or moved as a single unit. Reduces material handling costs. Often shrink-packed on a pallet before shipment.

unit load concept—Waiting for a container or pallet to be filled before the material is moved.

unit of driver measure—The common unit of measure used to group similar processes, so that comparisons can be made easily.

unit of issue—The standard issue quantity of an item from stores (e.g., pounds, each, box of 12, package of 20, case of 144).

unit of measure—The unit in which the quantity of an item is managed (e.g., pounds, each, box of 12, package of 20, case of 144).

unit-of-measure conversion—A standard conversion ratio that a company or its computer system uses to quickly enter in the amount delivered based on a known quantity within each unit of measure (e.g., a case of soda contains 24 cans).

unit of measure (purchasing)—The unit used to purchase an item. This may or may not be the same unit of measure used in the internal systems. For example, purchasing buys steel by the ton, but it may be issued and used in square inches. Syn: purchasing unit of measure.

unit-size—To combine a number of packages into one unit by attaching them together.

units-of-production depreciation—A method of depreciation whereby the amount to be recovered (written off as a period expense) is calculated based on estimated life of the equipment in units to be produced over the life and the number of units produced in a given time period. See: depreciation.

universality—The strategy of designing a product initially intended for one market in such a way that it can also be sold in other markets. It is a form of standardization.

universe—The population, or large set of data, from which samples are drawn. Usually assumed to be infinitely large or at least very large relative to the sample.

unplanned issue—An issue transaction that updates the quantity on hand but for which no allocation exists.

unplanned order—After a forecast has been developed, an unplanned order is any order outside of this forecast.

unplanned receipt—A receipt transaction that updates the quantity on hand but for which no order exists.

unplanned repair—Repair and replacement requirements that are unknown until remanufacturing teardown and inspection.

upcharges—Additional charges that are added to a delivered bill that are not included in the original contract. These occur because of unforeseen increases to the deliverer's cost base.

upgrade—Improvement in operating characteristics.

upper control limit (UCL)—Control limit for points above the central line in a control chart.

upper specification limit (USL)—In statistical process control, the line that defines the maximum acceptable level of random output. See: tolerance limits.

upside flexibility—The ability of a facility to increase their output and ability to deliver, for the foreseeable future, because of a non-forecasted increase in demand. The main drivers of this flexibility are the availability of direct labor and/ or direct materials and the actual production capacity of the facility.

upstream—Used as a relative reference within a firm or supply chain to indicate moving in the direction of the raw material supplier.

URL—Abbreviation for uniform resource locator.

usage—The number of units or dollars of an inventory item consumed over a period of time.

usage variance—Deviation of the actual consumption of materials as compared to the standard.

usage rate—Demand per product per unit of time.

use as is—Classification for material that has been declared to be unacceptable per the specifications, yet can be used.

user-friendly—Characteristic of computer software or hardware that makes it easy for the user or operator to use the programs or equipment with a minimum of specialized knowledge or recourse to operating manuals.

user interface—The portion of a computer system through which the end user interacts with the system. It may include the keyboard, mouse, touch-screen, and other devices.

USL—Abbreviation for upper specification limit.

utilization—1) A measure (usually expressed as a percentage) of how intensively a resource is being used to produce a good or service. Utilization compares actual time used to available time. Traditionally, utilization is the ratio of direct time charged (run time plus setup time) to the clock time available. Utilization is a percentage between 0 percent and 100 percent that is equal to 100 percent minus the percentage of time lost due to the unavailability of machines, tools, workers, and so forth. See: efficiency, lost time factor, productivity. 2) In the theory of constraints, activation of a resource that productively contributes to reaching the goal. Over-activation of a resource does not productively utilize a resource. See: available time.

V

valid schedule—A detailed, feasible calendar of specific items flowing into and through a factory.

valuation—The technique of determining worth, typically of inventory. Valuation of inventories may be expressed in standard dollars, replacement dollars, current average dollars, or last-purchase-price dollars.

value—The worth of an item, good, or service.

value added—1) In accounting, the addition of direct labor, direct material, and allocated overhead assigned at an operation. It is the cost roll-up as a part goes through a manufacturing process to finished inventory. 2) In current manufacturing terms, the actual increase of utility from the viewpoint of the customer as a part is transformed from raw material to finished inventory. It is the contribution made by an operation or a plant to the final usefulness and value of a product, as seen by the customer. The objective is to eliminate all non-value-added activities in producing and providing a good or service.

value-added network (VAN)—A network, often supporting EDI, providing services additional to those provided by common carriers.

value-added productivity per employee—A measure that is determined by three things: total output of a company, materials purchased, and total employment. To come up with this number, one must subtract materials purchased from total output and then divide that number by total employment. It allows a company to understand easily how much production the typical employee is producing.

value-adding/non-value-adding—The assessment of each of the company's activities to determine if that activity adds value to the organization or its customers. If an activity is considered non-value-adding it should be eliminated to increase an organization's efficiency.

value analysis—The systematic use of techniques that identify a required function, establish a value for that function, and finally provide that function at the lowest overall cost. This approach focuses on the functions of an item rather than the methods of producing the present product design.

value-based management (VBM)—The concept of satisfying customers to create shareholder wealth.

value chain—The functions within a company that add value to the goods or services that the organization sells to customers and for which it receives payment.

value chain analysis—An examination of all links a company uses to produce and deliver its products and services starting from the origination point and continuing through delivery to the final customer.

value chain initiative—This initiative combines software, hardware, and supply chain companies to develop an integrated system to support software sharing among diverse applications.

value-driven enterprise—An organization that is designed and managed to add utility from the viewpoint of the customer in the transformation of raw materials into a finished good or service.

value engineering and/or analysis—A disciplined approach to the elimination of waste from products or processes through an investigative process that focuses on the functions to be performed and whether such functions add value to the good or service.

value index—A measure that uses the performance and importance scores for various dimensions of performance for an item or service to calculate a score that indicates the overall value of an item or service to a customer.

value-of-service pricing—Allowing the market to determine the price.

value of transfers—The amount transferred, in a fiscal year, from one stage of the manufacturing process to another. For example, it is the amount of raw materials that are transformed into work in process.

value perspective—A quality perspective that holds that quality must be judged, in part, by how well the characteristics of a particular product or service align with the needs of a specific user.

value stream—The processes of creating, producing, and delivering a good or service to the market. For a good, the value stream encompasses the raw material supplier, the manufacture and assembly of the good, and the distribution network. For a service, the value stream consists of suppliers, support personnel and technology, the service "producer," and the distribution channel. The value stream may be controlled by a single business or a network of several businesses.

value stream map—A graph displaying the sequence of operations needed to produce and deliver a product or service.

value stream mapping—A lean production tool to visually understand the flow of materials from supplier to customer that includes the current process and flow as well as the value-added and non-value-added time of all the process steps. Used to lead to reduction of waste, decrease flow time, and make the process flow more efficient and effective.

valve inventory—In a just-in-time context, inventory at a stockpoint that is too large to be located next to the point of use of the material, and from which material is drawn by a pull system. The valve inventory is often located at a stockpoint in the plant's receiving area.

VAN—Acronym for value-added network.

variable—A quantity that can assume any of a given set of values. Ant: constant.

variable cost—An operating cost that varies directly with a change of one unit in the production volume (e.g., direct materials consumed, sales commissions).

variable costing—An inventory valuation method in which only variable production costs are applied to the product; fixed factory overhead is not assigned to the product. Traditionally, variable production costs are direct labor, direct material, and variable overhead costs. Variable costing can be helpful for internal management analysis but is not widely accepted for external financial reporting. For inventory order quantity purposes, however, the unit costs must include both the variable and allocated fixed costs to be compatible with the other terms in the order quantity formula. For make-or-buy decisions, variable costing should be used rather than full absorption costing. Syn: direct costing.

variable overhead—All manufacturing costs, other than direct labor and direct materials, that vary directly with production volume. Variable overhead is necessary to produce the product, but cannot be directly assigned to a specific product.

variables data—Measurement information. Control charts based on variables data include average (X-bar) charts, range (R) charts, and sample standard deviations charts.

variable yield—The condition that occurs when the output of a process is not consistently repeatable either in quantity, quality, or combinations of these.

variance—1) The difference between the expected (budgeted or planned) value and the actual. 2) In statistics, a measurement of dispersion of data. See: estimate of error.

variation—A change in data, a characteristic, or a function that is caused by one of four factors: special causes, common causes, tampering, or structural variation.

VATI Analysis—In the theory of constraints, a procedure for determining the general flow of parts and products from raw materials to finished products (logical product structure). A V logical structure starts with one or a few raw materials, and the product expands into a number of different products as it flows through divergent points in its routings. The shape of an A logical structure is dominated by converging points. Many raw materials are fabricated and assembled into a few finished products. A T logical structure consists of numerous similar finished products assembled from common assemblies, subassemblies, and parts. An I logical structure is the simplest of production flows, where resources are shared between different products and the flow is in a straight line sequence, such as an assembly line. Once the general parts flow is determined, the system control points (gating operations, convergent points, divergent points, constraints, and shipping points) can be identified and managed.

VBM—Abbreviation for value-based management.

vehicle—Carrying and power unit to move goods over ways. Includes all forms of transportation means except pipeline. The carrier generally owns or leases the vehicles, but a shipper also may own or lease.

velocity—1) The rate of change of an item with respect to time. See: inventory turnover, lead time. 2) In supply chain management, a term used to indicate the relative speed of all transactions, collectively, within a supply chain community. A maximum velocity is most desirable because it indicates higher asset turnover for stockholders and faster order-to-delivery response for customers.

vendor—Any seller of an item in the marketplace. See: supplier.

vendor lead time—Syn: supplier lead time.

vendor-managed inventory (VMI)—A means of optimizing supply chain performance in which the supplier has access to the customer's inventory data and is responsible for maintaining the inventory level required by the customer. This activity is accomplished by a process in which resupply is done by the vendor through regularly scheduled reviews of the on-site inventory. The on-site inventory is counted, damaged or outdated goods are removed, and the inventory is restocked to predefined levels. The vendor obtains a receipt for the restocked inventory and accordingly invoices the customer. See: continuous replenishment.

vendor measurement—The act of measuring the vendor's performance to a contract. Measurements usually cover delivery reliability, lead time, quality, and price. See: supplier measurement.

vendor-owned inventory (VOI)—Syn: consigned stocks.

vendor scheduler—Syn: supplier scheduler.

vendor scheduling—Syn: supplier scheduling.

venture team—A set of individuals assigned outside normal channels to develop ideas for new products.

vertical dependency—The relationship between a parent item and a component in its bill of material that defines the need for the component based on producing the parent, without regard to the availability of other components at the same level in the bill of material. See: horizontal dependency.

vertical display—A method of displaying or printing output from an MRP system where requirements, scheduled receipts, projected balance, and so forth are displayed vertically. Vertical displays are often used in conjunction with bucketless systems. Ant: horizontal display.

vertical integration—The degree to which a firm has decided to directly produce multiple value-adding stages from raw material to the sale of the product to the ultimate consumer. The more steps in the sequence, the greater the vertical integration. A manufacturer that decides to begin producing parts, components, and materials that it normally purchases is said to be backward integrated. Likewise, a manufacturer that decides to take over distribution and perhaps sale to the ultimate consumer is said to be forward integrated. See: backward integration, forward integration.

vertically integrated firm—An organization with functions that were previously performed by suppliers but are now done internally. See: horizontally integrated firm.

vertical marketing—A coordinated product marketing system, with activities undertaken by one company, for a supply chain.

vertical marketing system—A marketing system that focuses on the means to reduce the traditional independence of indirect channels. The system strategically seeks to increase the integration and interdependence of channels by uniting them with common objectives and team management (e.g., franchising, cooperatives, vertical integration).

vertical marketplace—An online marketplace connecting buyers and sellers within the same industry. It enables lower prices by lowering transaction costs.

vertical merger—An alliance of two firms where one firm is a supplier to the other.

vestibule training—A variant of job rotation in which a separate work area is set up for a trainee so that the actual work situation does not pressure the trainee. Examples are cockpit simulators and other machine simulators.

viral marketing—An advertisement that is embedded into web-based technology, e.g., email or pop-up ads, that can easily move through the internet and get in front of the target audience who may never have seen it otherwise.

virtual cell—A logical rather than physical grouping of manufacturing resources. Resources in virtual cells can be dispersed throughout a facility. Product mix changes may change the layout of a virtual cell. This technique is used when it is not practical to move the equipment.

virtual corporation—The logical extension of outpartnering. With the virtual corporation, the capabilities and systems of the firm are merged with those of the suppliers, resulting in a new type of corporation where the boundaries between the suppliers' systems and those of the firm seem to disappear. The virtual corporation is dynamic in that the relationships and structures formed change according to the changing needs of the customer.

virtual factory—A changed transformation process most frequently found under the virtual corporation. It is a transformation process that involves merging the capabilities and capacities of the firm with those of its suppliers. Typically, the components provided by the suppliers are those that are not related to a core competency of the firm, while the components managed by the firm are related to core competencies. One ability found in the virtual factory is that it can be restructured quickly in response to changing customer demands and needs.

virtual inventory systems—A virtual system that enables supply chain partners to share data in a central database.

virtual organization—Short-term alliances between independent organizations in a potentially long-term relationship to design, produce, and distribute a product. Organizations cooperate based on mutual values and act as a single entity to third parties.

virtual reality—Hardware and software that create an apparently real environment.

virtual supply chain—A collection of firms that typically exists for only a short period. Virtual supply chains are more flexible than traditional supply chains, but less efficient.

virtual trading exchange—An online trading exchange that enables both information integration and collaboration between multiple trading partners.

visibility—The ability to view important information throughout a facility or supply chain no matter where in the facility or supply chain the information is located.

vision—The shared perception of the organization's future—what the organization will achieve and a supporting philosophy. This shared vision must be supported by strategic objectives, strategies, and action plans to move it in the desired direction. See: vision statement.

vision statement—An organization's statement of its vision. See: vision.

visits—In e-commerce, the set of requests made by one user at one website. If there is no activity within a given time frame (usually 30 minutes), the visit is considered closed.

visual control—The control of authorized levels of activities and inventories in a way that is instantly and visibly obvious. This type of activity and inventory control is used in a workplace organization where everything has an assigned place and is in its place.

visual inspection—Inspection performed without test instruments.

visual review system—A simple inventory control system where the inventory reordering is based on actually looking at the amount of inventory on hand. Usually used for low-value items, such as nuts and bolts. See: two-bin inventory system.

vital few, useful many—A term used by J.M. Juran to describe his use of the Pareto principle in quality management, which he first described in 1950. (The principle was used much earlier in economics and inventory control methodologies.) The principle suggests that most effects come from relatively few causes; that is, 80 percent of the effects come from 20 percent of the possible causes. The 20 percent of the possible causes are referred to as the "vital few"; the remaining causes are referred to as the "useful many." When Juran first defined this principle, he referred to the remaining causes as the "trivial many," but since no prob-

lems are trivial in quality assurance, he changed it to "useful many."

VMI—Abbreviation for vendor-managed inventory.

VOC—Abbreviation for voice of the customer.

VOI—Abbreviation for vendor-owned inventory.

voice of the customer (VOC)—Actual customer descriptions in words for the functions and features customers desire for goods and services. In the strict definition, as relates to quality function deployment (QFD), the term customer indicates the external customer of the supplying entity.

volume flexibility—The ability of the transformation process to quickly accommodate large variations in production levels.

voluntary layoff—Layoffs where the employees are given the option of taking a non-paid leave from their work for a short, specified period of time.

voucher—A written document that bears witness to, or "vouches" for, something. A voucher generally is an instrument showing services performed or goods purchased and authorizing payment to the supplier.

W

Wagner-Whitin algorithm—A mathematically complex, dynamic lot-sizing technique that evaluates all possible ways of ordering to cover net requirements in each period of the planning horizon to arrive at the theoretically optimum ordering strategy for the entire net requirements schedule. See: discrete order quantity, dynamic lot sizing.

waiting line theory—Syn: queuing theory.

wait time—The time a job remains at a work center after an operation is completed until it is moved to the next operation. It is often expressed as a part of move time.

waiver—Authorization to accept an item that, during production or upon inspection, is found to depart from specified requirements, but nevertheless is considered suitable for use as is or after rework.

walkthrough—Syn: pilot test.

wall-to-wall inventory—An inventory management technique in which material enters a plant and is processed through the plant into finished goods without ever having entered a formal stock area. Syn: four-wall inventory.

WAN—Acronym for wide area network.

wand—A device connected to a bar-code reader to identify a bar code.

wandering bottleneck—An undesirable effect in which the bottleneck moves relatively frequently from one resource to another.

warehouse—A place to receive, store, and ship materials.

warehouse demand—The need for an item to replenish stock at a branch warehouse. Syn: branch warehouse demand.

warehouse management and transportation execution systems—Logistics information systems that initiate and control the movement of materials between supply chain partners.

warehouse management system (WMS)—A computer application system designed to manage and optimize workflows and the storage of goods within a warehouse. These systems often interface with automated data capture and enterprise resources planning systems.

warehouses (distribution centers)—Facilities used to store inventory. Decisions driving warehouse management include site selection, number of facilities in the system, layout, and methods of receiving, storing, and retrieving goods.

warehousing—The activities related to receiving, storing, and shipping materials to and from production or distribution locations.

warrant of merchantability—An implied warranty that goods are fit for the use to which they are generally applied.

warranty—A commitment, either expressed or implied, that a certain fact regarding the subject matter of a contract is presently true or will be true. The word should be distinguished from guarantee, which means a contract or promise by an entity to answer for the performance of a product or person. See: general warranty, guarantee, special warranty.

warranty costs—All of the costs associated with a warranty; these include shipping, receiving, repairing, replacement, and the materials needed for repair or replacement.

waste—1) Any activity that does not add value to the good or service in the eyes of the consumer. 2) A byproduct of a process or task with unique characteristics requiring special management control. Waste production can usually be planned and somewhat controlled.

Scrap is typically not planned and may result from the same production run as waste. See: hazardous waste.

waterspider—An expert worker who makes the rounds of workstations and provides assistance, as needed. The waterspider knows all processes well enough to take over if needed. At Toyota, this position is a prerequisite to supervision and management positions.

wave picking—A method of selecting and sequencing picking lists to minimize the waiting time of the delivered material. Shipping orders may be picked in waves combined by common carrier or destination, and manufacturing orders in waves related to work centers.

waybill—A document containing a list of goods with shipping instructions related to a shipment.

ways—Paths over which a carrier operates, including right-of-way, roadbed, tracks, and other physical facilities. May be owned by the government or privately held by the carrier or provided by nature.

webcasting—Syn: push technology.

web directory—A list of web pages that is structured hierarchically.

webpage—A document containing hypertext links to certain other documents including multimedia documents.

web services—A common internet or intranet framework that enables the movement of data from one application to another, without the requirement for a direct connection between two supply chain applications and without regard to the underlying operating system for those applications.

weight confirmation—The process of confirming a shipment arrival only by confirming the correct weight has been delivered.

weighted-factor rating model—A method to analyze the advantages of various locations along several qualitative and quantitative dimensions.

weighted moving average—An averaging technique in which the data to be averaged are not uniformly weighted but are given values according to their importance. See: moving average, simple moving average.

weighted-point plan—A supplier selection and rating approach that uses the input gathered in the categorical plan approach and assigns weights to each evaluation category. A weighted sum for each supplier is obtained and a comparison made. The weights used should sum to 100 percent for all categories. See: categorical plan.

what-if analysis—The process of evaluating alternate strategies by answering the consequences of changes to forecasts, manufacturing plans, inventory levels, and so forth. See: simulation.

what-if simulation—An approach to conducting a what-if analysis usually found in MRP II and ERP systems.

what you see is what you get (WYSIWYG)—Computer speak that means what the file appears to the editor appears the exact same way to the end user.

where-used list—A listing of every parent item that calls for a given component, and the respective quantity required, from a bill-of-material file. See: implosion.

wholesaler—Syn: distributor.

wide area network (WAN)—A public or private data communication system for linking computers distributed over a large geographic area.

will call—A service process that allows customers to walk up to the seller's facility and pick up the parts they have previously ordered.

WIP—Acronym for work in process.

withdrawal—1) Removal of material from stores. 2) A transaction issuing material to a specific location, run, or schedule.

withdrawal kanban—An indicator that a container can be transported between work areas.

WMS—Abbreviation for warehouse management system.

workaround—A project management technique that provides a response to a negative risk that has happened. A workaround is different from a contingency plan because a workaround is not planned before the risk event occurs.

work breakdown structure—In project management, a hierarchical description of a project in which each lower level is more detailed. See: project summary work breakdown structure.

work cell—Dissimilar machines grouped together into a production unit to produce a family of parts having similar routings.

work center—A specific production area, consisting of one or more people and/or machines with similar capabilities, that can be considered as one unit for purposes of capacity requirements planning and detailed scheduling. Syn: load center.

work center schedule—Syn: dispatch list.

work center where-used—A listing (constructed from a routing file) of every manufactured item that is routed (primary or secondary) to a given work center.

worker efficiency—A measure (usually computed as a percentage) of worker performance that compares the standard time allowed to complete a task to the actual worker time to complete it. Syn: labor efficiency.

worker productivity—The value of total goods and services produced by an employee divided by the labor hours required to produce those goods and services.

workers' compensation—The replacement of an employee's loss of earnings capacity caused by an occupational injury or disease. Formerly known as workmen's compensation.

working capital—Syn: net working capital.

working stock—Stock located in a facility which is used to fulfill demand.

work in process (WIP)—A good or goods in various stages of completion throughout the plant, including all material from raw material that has been released for initial processing up to completely processed material awaiting final inspection and acceptance as finished goods inventory. Many accounting systems also include the value of semifinished stock and components in this category. Syn: in-process inventory.

workload—Syn: load.

workman's compensation—This is a state-administered program whereby employees are guaranteed medical coverage in case they are injured on the job and companies are limited as to their liability for such job-related injuries.

work measurement—Estimating how long it takes for an employee to produce one unit of output.

work order—1) An order to the machine shop for tool manufacture or equipment maintenance; not to be confused with a manufacturing order. Syn: manufacturing order, work ticket. 2) An authorization to start work on an activity (e.g., maintenance) or product.

work package—In project management, a deliverable at the bottom of a work breakdown structure. This may be treated as a subproject to be assigned to a project manager to plan and execute, in which case this manager will define new activities.

workplace organization—The arrangement of tools, equipment, materials, and supplies according to their frequency of use. Those items that are never used are removed from the workplace, and those items that are used frequently are located for fast, easy access and

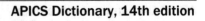